Targeted Sanctions

International sanctions have become the instrument of choice for policy-makers dealing with a variety of different challenges to international peace and security. This is the first comprehensive and systematic analysis of all the targeted sanctions regimes imposed by the United Nations since the end of the Cold War. Drawing on the collaboration of more than fifty scholars and policy practitioners from across the globe (the Targeted Sanctions Consortium), the book analyses two new data-bases, one qualitative and one quantitative, to assess the different purposes of UN targeted sanctions, the Security Council dynamics behind their design, the relationship of sanctions with other policy instruments, implementation challenges, diverse impacts, unintended consequences, policy effectiveness, and institutional learning within the UN. The book is organized around comparisons across cases, rather than country case studies, and introduces two analytical innovations: case episodes within country sanctions regimes and systematic differentiation among different purposes of sanctions.

THOMAS J. BIERSTEKER is Gasteyger Professor of International Security and Conflict Studies and Director of the Programme for the Study of International Governance at The Graduate Institute, Geneva.

SUE E. ECKERT is Senior Fellow at the Watson Institute for International and Public Affairs at Brown University.

MARCOS TOURINHO is Visiting Professor and Research Fellow at the Center for International Relations of Fundação Getulio Vargas in São Paulo, Brazil.

Targeted Sanctions

The Impacts and Effectiveness of United Nations Action

Edited by

Thomas J. Biersteker
The Graduate Institute, Geneva

Sue E. Eckert
Brown University

Marcos Tourinho
*Fundação Getulio Vargas,
São Paulo, Brazil*

CAMBRIDGE
UNIVERSITY PRESS

University Printing House, Cambridge CB2 8BS, United Kingdom

Cambridge University Press is part of the University of Cambridge.

It furthers the University's mission by disseminating knowledge in the pursuit of education, learning and research at the highest international levels of excellence.

www.cambridge.org
Information on this title:www.cambridge.org/9781107593091

© Cambridge University Press 2016

First published 2016

Printed in the United Kingdom by Clays, St Ives plc

Library of Congress Cataloguing in Publication data
Biersteker, Thomas J., editor. | Eckert, Sue E., editor. | Tourinho, Marcos, editor.
Targeted sanctions : the impacts and effectiveness of United Nations action / edited by Thomas J. Biersteker, Sue E. Eckert, Marcos Tourinho.
New York : Cambridge University Press, 2016. |
Includes bibliographical references and index.
LCCN 2016000276 | ISBN 9781107593091 (paperback)
LCSH: Sanctions (International law) | United Nations – Sanctions.
LCC KZ6373 .T37 2016 | DDC 341.5/82–dc23
LC record available at http://lccn.loc.gov/2016000276

ISBN 978-1-107-13421-8 Hardback
ISBN 978-1-107-59309-1 Paperback

Contents

Figures

Tables

Contributors

PAUL BENTALL, Senior Principal Research Analyst, Multilateral Research Group, at the UK Government's Foreign and Commonwealth Office, United Kingdom.

THOMAS J. BIERSTEKER, Gasteyger Professor of International Security and Director of the Programme for the Study of International Governance at The Graduate Institute of International and Development Studies, Geneva, Switzerland.

ALIX BOUCHER, independent consultant in Washington, DC, United States.

MICHAEL BRZOSKA, Professor and Director of the Institute for Peace Research and Security Policy at the University of Hamburg (IFSH), Germany.

ENRICO CARISCH served the United Nations from 2002 to 2009 as an investigator on Security Council-mandated panels of sanctions monitors and is now engaged in sanctions training and capacity enhancements for Member States and the private sector with Compliance and Capacity International, LLC, in New York City, United States.

ANDREA CHARRON, Assistant Professor of Political Studies and Deputy-Director of the Centre for Defence and Security Studies at the University of Manitoba, Canada.

CATY CLEMENT, Senior Programme Advisor and Senior Fellow in the Leadership, Crisis and Conflict Management Programme at the Geneva Centre for Security Policy (GCSP), Switzerland.

SUE E. ECKERT, Senior Fellow at the Watson Institute for International and Public Affairs at Brown University, United States.

KIMBERLY ANN ELLIOTT, Senior Fellow at the Center for Global Development, Washington, DC, United States.

MIKAEL ERIKSSON, Deputy Research Director at the Swedish Defence Research Agency, Stockholm, Sweden.

FRANCESCO GIUMELLI, Assistant Professor in the Department of International Relations and International Organization at the University of Groningen, The Netherlands.

GEORGE A. LOPEZ, The Rev. Theodore M. Hesburgh, CSC Professor of Peace Studies, Emeritus Kroc Institute for International Peace Studies University of Notre Dame, United States.

CLARA PORTELA, Assistant Professor of Political Science at Singapore Management University, Singapore.

LORAINE RICKARD-MARTIN is a partner in Compliance and Capacity Skills International, and former sanctions committee secretary in the Security Council Affairs Division, United Nations Department of Political Affairs, New York City, United States.

MARCOS TOURINHO, Research Fellow and Visiting Professor at the Center for International Relations, School of Social Sciences at the Fundação Getulio Vargas, São Paulo, Brazil.

PETER WALLENSTEEN, Senior Professor in the Department of Peace and Conflict Research, Uppsala University, Research Professor at the Kroc Institute, University of Notre Dame, United States, and Director of the Uppsala Conflict Data Program and leader of the Special Program on Targeted Sanctions, at Uppsala University, Sweden.

Abbreviations

ACP	African, Caribbean and Pacific Group of States
AG	Australia Group
AMISOM	African Union Military Observer Mission in Somalia
AQ	Al-Qaida
AQT	Al-Qaida/Taliban
ASEAN	Association of Southeast Asian Nations
AU	African Union
AU/PSC	African Union Peace and Security Council
CAR	Central African Republic
CFSP	Common Foreign and Security Policy
CIT–MAP	Countering Illicit Trafficking – Mechanism Assessment Project
CNDP	National Congress for the Defence of the People (DRC rebel group)
CPLP	Community of Portuguese Speaking Countries
CT	Counter-terrorism
CTC	Counter-Terrorism Committee
CTED	Counter-Terrorism Committee Executive Directorate
CTITF	Counter-Terrorism Implementation Task Force
DDR	Disarmament, Demobilisation, and Reintegration
DPA	Department of Political Affairs (United Nations)
DPKO	Department of Peacekeeping Operations (United Nations)
DPRK	Democratic People's Republic of Korea
DRC	Democratic Republic of the Congo
E-10	Ten elected members of the United Nations Security Council
E3 plus 3	France, Germany, United Kingdom, China, Russia, and the United States

ECJ	European Court of Justice
ECOWAS	Economic Community of West African States
EITI	Extractive Industries Transparency Initiative
EP	Sanction regime case episode
EU	European Union
FARC	Revolutionary Armed Forces of Colombia
FATF	Financial Action Task Force (on money laundering and terrorism financing)
FRY	Former Yugoslavia
FRY I	Sanctions regime imposed on the Former Yugoslavia in the 1990s
FRY II or Kosovo	Sanctions regime imposed on the Former Yugoslavia over Kosovo
GNI	Gross national income
HCHR	High Commissioner for Human Rights (United Nations)
HRC	Human Rights Council (United Nations)
IAEA	International Atomic Energy Agency
IBRD	International Bank for Reconstruction and Development
ICAO	International Civil Aviation Organization
ICC	International Criminal Court
ICJ	International Court of Justice
ICTR	International Criminal Tribunal for Rwanda
ICTY	International Criminal Tribunal for the former Yugoslavia
IFI	International financial institutions
IMF	International Monetary Fund
INTERPOL	International Police (International Criminal Police Organization)
IO	International organization
ISAC	International Sanctions Administrations Capacity
ISAF	International Security Assistance Force (Afghanistan)
ISIL	Islamic State of Iraq and the Levant
KPCS	Kimberley Process Certification Scheme
LAS	League of Arab States
Libya I	Sanctions regime imposed on Libya in the 1990s
Libya II	Sanctions regime imposed on Libya in 2011
M23	March 23 Movement also known as Congolese Revolutionary Army (DRC rebel group)

MINURCAT	United Nations Mission in the Central African Republic and Chad
MINUSMA	United Nations Multidimensional Integrated Stabilization Mission (Mali)
MINUSTAH	United Nations Stabilization Mission in Haiti
MNF	Multinational Force in Haiti
MONUC	United Nations Organization Mission in the Democratic Republic of the Congo
MONUSCO	United Nations Organization Stabilization Mission in the Democratic Republic of the Congo
MS	Member State
MTCR	Missile Technology Control Regime
NATO	North Atlantic Treaty Organization
NGO	Non-governmental organization
NIAC	National Iranian American Council
NSG	Nuclear Suppliers Group
OAS	Organization of American States
OAU	Organization of African Unity
OCHA	Office for the Coordination of Humanitarian Affairs (United Nations)
ODA	Office for Disarmament Affairs (United Nations)
OECD	Organisation for Economic Co-operation and Development
OPCW	Organization for the Prohibition of Chemical Weapons
OSCE	Organization for Security and Co-operation in Europe
P5	Permanent Five (United Nations Security Council)
PK	Peacekeeping
PoC	Protection of civilians
PoE	Panel of Experts
R2P	Responsibility to Protect
RUF	Revolutionary United Front (Sierra Leone)
SADC	Southern African Development Community
SAMCOMM	Sanctions Assistance Missions Communication Centre
SAMs	Sanctions Assistance Missions
SCAD	Security Council Affairs Division (United Nations Department of Political Affairs)
SCR	Security Council Resolution
SCSL	Special Court for Sierra Leone

SGBV	Sexual and gender-based violence
SIPRI	Stockholm International Peace Research Institute
SRSG	Special Representative of the Secretary-General
SSR	Security sector reform
STL	Special Tribunal for Lebanon
Sudan I	Sanctions regime imposed on Sudan in the 1990s
Sudan II	Sanctions regime imposed on Sudan over Darfur
TFG	Transitional Federal Government (Somalia)
TIES	Threat and imposition of economic sanctions
TSC	Targeted Sanctions Consortium
UAE	United Arab Emirates
UIC	United Islamic Courts (Somalia)
UK	United Kingdom of Great Britain and Northern Ireland
UN	United Nations
UNAMA	United Nations Assistance Mission in Afghanistan
UNAMID	African Union/United Nations Hybrid Operation in Darfur
UNHCR	Office of the United Nations High Commissioner for Refugees also known as the United Nations Refugee Agency
UNICEF	United Nations Children's Fund
UNIIIC	United Nations International Independent Investigation Commission (Lebanon)
UNITA	National Union for the Total Independence of Angola
UNITAF	Unified Task Force (Somalia)
UNMIL	United Nations Mission in Liberia
UNMIS	United Nations Mission in the Sudan
UNOCI	United Nations Operation in Côte d'Ivoire
UNODC	United Nations Office on Drugs and Crime
UNOGBIS	United Nations Peacebuilding Support Office in Guinea-Bissau
UNSC	United Nations Security Council
UNSCOM	United Nations Special Commission (Iraq)
UNSMIL	United Nations Support Mission in Libya
US	United States of America
USD	United States dollar
UTA	Union de Transports Aériens
WFP	World Food Programme
WMD	Weapon of mass destruction

Introduction

Sue E. Eckert, Thomas J. Biersteker, and Marcos Tourinho

The use of targeted sanctions as a central instrument to address challenges to international peace and security has been a defining feature of UN Security Council practice since the end of the Cold War. The comprehensive sanctions imposed on Iraq following its invasion of Kuwait in 1990 exacted a heavy toll on the Iraqi economy, as well as its citizens. Reports concerning the death of 500,000 Iraqi children – a figure originating in a UNICEF report on infant mortality in sanctions-era Iraq – raised alarm among human rights groups and some Member States, and were used by Iraqi president Saddam Hussein to campaign against the sanctions. One effort to mitigate humanitarian consequences of the embargo, notably the Oil-for-Food Programme, was slow to be put into effect and did not always reach its intended beneficiaries. While arguments persist as to whether the severe consequences were Saddam Hussein's doing or a product of the sanctions alone, recognition of the significant humanitarian costs of the blunt instrument of comprehensive sanctions was nearly universal. The terrible price of the Iraqi sanctions created an enduring awareness of the negative effects sanctions can have on innocent civilians.[1]

In view of the consequences and controversy over the Iraq sanctions, the UN Security Council decisively moved away from comprehensive sanctions. In fact, no new sanctions imposed by the United Nations since 1994 have included comprehensive economic measures. Rather, the Security Council adjusted the instrument to focus on individuals and entities responsible for the actions or behaviour posing threats to international peace and security or on economic sectors that support their proscribed activities. Commonly referred to as 'smart'[2] or targeted

---

[1] T. G. Weiss, D. Cortright, G. A. Lopez, and L. Minear, *Political Gain and Civilian Pain: Humanitarian Impacts of Economic Sanctions* (Lanham, MD: Rowman & Littlefield Publishers, 1997); J. Gordon, *Invisible War: The United States and the Iraq Sanctions* (Cambridge, MA: Harvard University Press, 2010).

[2] The editors use the term 'targeted' rather than 'smart' sanctions because it describes the measures in a less value-laden manner. Characterizing UN sanctions as 'smart', in

sanctions, the Security Council has utilized this modified form of sanctions to limit the humanitarian impact with growing frequency – most often to address armed conflict and terrorism, but also to consolidate peace agreements, support peacebuilding, address unconstitutional changes of government, limit the proliferation of nuclear weapons, and most recently to protect civilians under the Responsibility to Protect. Targeted sanctions are directed at leaders, decision-makers, their principal supporters, or individual sectors of an economy or geographic regions, rather than indiscriminately at an entire population.[3]

Despite this turn to targeted measures and the move away from comprehensive sanctions, however, there has been only limited recognition of these developments in popular discourse, in most policy discussions, and in the scholarly community. The widespread perception remains that sanctions are harmful and invariably result in significant humanitarian costs. Most public treatments of the sanctions topic conflate the two types of sanctions, failing to distinguish between targeted and comprehensive measures, notwithstanding the passage of two decades since the United Nations last imposed comprehensive sanctions. To the extent that discussions within policy circles or deliberations among academic specialists address targeted sanctions, there appears to be a general assumption that targeted sanctions are normatively 'better' than comprehensive sanctions, simply because they must have less of a humanitarian impact, but not that they are necessarily more effective in achieving their purposes.

The continued lack of information surrounding UN targeted sanctions, the negligible appreciation for the change in the nature of the sanctions instrument over time, as well as an intuition that targeted sanctions are preferable in terms of policy outcomes in comparison to other alternatives are the principal reasons that the Targeted Sanctions Consortium (TSC) was formed. Notwithstanding more than twenty years of United Nations' experience with targeted sanctions, until recently, there had been no systematic, comprehensive, comparative assessment of the instrument of UN targeted sanctions.

---

contrast to the previous practice of comprehensive sanctions as 'stupid', is overly simplistic and fails to elucidate understanding of the policy instrument in scholarly analysis. Although targeted sanctions can vary in their degree of discrimination (and may not in practice reach their targets), they necessarily select a limited portion of the population or economy as targets of the measures.

[3] As Chapters 1 and 9 indicate, however, this does not mean that targeted sanctions do not produce any unintended consequences or humanitarian costs to the broader population. Depending on their specific design, they can do both.

Background to the Targeted Sanctions Consortium

Due to the critiques of comprehensive sanctions against Iraq, and noting the increasing use of targeted sanctions, the Swiss government convened in 1998 and 1999 workshops of experts interested in refining UN targeted financial sanctions. The Interlaken Process, as it was called, proposed elements for effective financial sanctions, including recommendations for the design and implementation of targeted sanctions at the UN and national levels. The contributions of the Interlaken Process were consolidated in a manual developed by the Watson Institute for International Studies at Brown University in 2001, providing draft language for resolutions and identifying best practices for more effective targeted financial sanctions implementation. Following the Interlaken model, the German government led an effort to examine travel bans, aviation sanctions, and arms embargoes by the United Nations in 1999–2000, resulting in the Bonn-Berlin Manual. The Stockholm Process, sponsored by Sweden in 2001–2002, provided recommendations and a manual focused on the implementation of targeted sanctions.[4] In each of these initiatives, important assessments of Security Council sanctions occurred, resulting in recommendations to ensure the improvement and continued viability of the targeted sanctions instrument. The principal authors of all three process manuals are involved in the Targeted Sanctions Consortium and have contributed chapters to this volume.

In spite of the gradual refinements and increased use of targeted sanctions by the UN Security Council, public and scholarly debates remained dominated by an assumption that 'sanctions don't work'. There was little systematic empirical information at the time upon which assessments of the impacts and effectiveness of UN targeted sanctions could be based. Important work had been conducted by Hufbauer, Schott, and Elliott,[5] but their analysis included a mix of unilateral and multilateral measures, and the database they assembled contained both comprehensive and

---

[4] The Interlaken Process resulted in the publication by T. Biersteker, S. Eckert, A. Halegua, N. Reid, and P. Romaniuk of *Targeted Financial Sanctions: A Manual for Design and Implementation* (Providence: Watson Institute for International Studies, Brown University, 2001). Available at: www.seco.admin.ch/themen/00513/00620/00639/00641/index.html?lang=en. The Bonn-Berlin Process manual was edited by M. Brzoska, *Design and Implementation of Arms Embargoes and Travel and Aviation and Related Sanctions: Results of the Bonn-Berlin Process* (Bonn: Bonn International Center for Conversion, 2001). The Stockholm Process manual was edited by P. Wallensteen, C. Staibano, and M. Eriksson, *Making Targeted Sanctions Effective: Guidelines for the Implementation of UN Policy Options* (Stockholm: Elanders Gotab, 2003).

[5] G. C. Hufbauer, J. J. Schott, and K. A. Elliott, *Economic Sanctions Reconsidered*, 2nd edn (Washington, DC: Peterson Institute for International Economics, 1990); G. C. Hufbauer et al., *Economic Sanctions Reconsidered*, 3rd ed (Washington, DC: Peterson Institute for International Economics, 2007).

targeted sanctions. While their research was considered definitive as to when sanctions in general might be expected to work, it did not specifically address targeted sanctions imposed by the UN Security Council. Without empirical information, it was impossible to draw conclusions about the impacts and effectiveness of those tools, as well as to ascertain whether and how targeted sanctions do indeed work. Lacking a systematic assessment, it was not possible to make policy recommendations to enhance the effectiveness of sanctions implementation. It was from this perspective regarding the importance of both informing the public debate and engaging with policy communities internationally that the TSC was formed.

Targeted Sanctions Consortium

From its inception, the purpose of the TSC was to conduct a comprehensive, systematic, and comparative assessment of the impacts and effectiveness of UN targeted sanctions, the first such initiative. Co-directed by Thomas J. Biersteker (The Graduate Institute, Geneva) and Sue Eckert (Watson Institute for International Studies, Brown University), and later joined by Marcos Tourinho (Fundação Getulio Vargas, São Paulo), who contributed in the research, database development, and the writing and editing of this volume, the TSC drew upon the expertise of more than fifty scholars and policy practitioners from around the world in an effort to investigate different aspects of targeted sanctions design, practice, implementation, and effectiveness.

Formally commenced with a workshop at the Graduate Institute in Geneva in October 2009, the TSC had three unique organizational features that characterized its formation and work. First, it was open to a broad range of international scholars addressing sanctions – a collective enterprise engaging formal theorists, constructivists, game theorists, quantitative analysts, and policy specialists. In an effort to draw on the interest and expertise of a growing number of scholars worldwide researching targeted sanctions, particularly younger scholars, the project directors reached out to academics working on related topics to invite their participation. In particular, efforts were made to include scholars across geographic regions. Eventually, participants from around the world comprised the TSC – from Africa, Asia, Europe, and North and South America. A list of participants in the Targeted Sanctions Consortium, from which all of the authors included in this book were drawn, is included in Appendix 4.[6]

---

[6] Not all individuals listed in Appendix 4 continue as active TSC participants, as a number of practitioners in particular have rotated to other policy assignments. The results of the

Second, in order to ensure that the research addressed policy-relevant questions and resulted in findings valuable for both academic and policy communities, the TSC engaged policy practitioners from the beginning in the design of the project and conduct of the research. In particular, UN officials (former or current at the time) and representatives of Member States involved in the implementation of sanctions participated, and constitute nearly half of the TSC membership. Most academic research endeavours, even those with policy aspirations, tend to produce a one-way 'dialogue' of policy prescriptions addressed to practitioners in a concluding chapter of a completed study, rather than engaging practitioners at the outset in the design of the research.

Third, the TSC research was organized not around individual country case studies which typified previous sanctions analysis, but by a conceptual approach focusing on cross-cutting themes – including political will, purposes, international norms, the interaction of sanctions with other policy instruments, implementation, and enforcement – facilitating comparison across cases. This thematic approach has been continued from the initial research design to the organizational structure of this book. The general method utilized by the TSC began with detailed narrative case studies of individual country sanctions regimes (some of which were authored by former policy practitioners), but the eventual research outputs transcended those case studies. The case studies were structured on a template common to all and were used as the basis for the construction of two new and original databases – one qualitative and one quantitative, as discussed below.

The first phase of the TSC project focused on defining the parameters of the project, its scope, and analytical approach. Based on the participation of both scholarly and policy participants, the group developed and refined the project design. Since the research involved a broad range of individuals throughout the world, a common framework of analysis was necessary. For these purposes, an international workshop on methods of evaluation was convened.[7] Following a review of the state of the art of knowledge about the impacts and effectiveness of multilateral targeted sanctions, the workshop resulted in agreement on a general research framework. This included the use of sanctions episodes as a unit of analysis, broadening the purposes of sanctions beyond coercion or the change of behaviour also to include constraint and signalling, and

---

research and the analyses contained in this volume are, of course, independent of the official positions of the governments represented by the practitioners included in the TSC.

[7] We are grateful for the support of the Swiss government for this workshop.

determining elements to be addressed in each case.[8] The TSC co-directors developed these conclusions into Terms of Reference (ToR) that established research methods, priorities, concepts, and elements to be addressed in each case.[9] An electronic template based upon the ToR was also provided to facilitate the gathering of common information on each case of UN targeted sanctions.

TSC participants then engaged in original research on major UN targeted sanctions country regimes.[10] During this phase, sixteen different teams comprised of both scholars and practitioners were commissioned to conduct research on the impacts and effectiveness of targeted sanctions in the most important country sanctions regimes. These were later expanded to include *all* UN targeted sanctions' country sanctions regimes in place while this book was being written: Al-Qaida, Angola, Central African Republic, Côte d'Ivoire, Democratic People's Republic of Korea (DPRK), Democratic Republic of the Congo (DRC), Ethiopia-Eritrea, Former Yugoslavia (1991–1996), Former Yugoslavia (over Kosovo), Guinea-Bissau, Haiti, Iran, Iraq, Lebanon, Liberia, Libya in the 1990s, Libya after 2011, Rwanda, Sierra Leone, Somalia, Sudan (1996–2001), Sudan (since 2004), and the Taliban. The common framework for analysis provided by the ToR helped to ensure consistency across cases and was refined over time.[11]

Most researchers involved in writing the initial case studies met at a June 2011 workshop hosted by the Foreign Office in London for a preliminary comparative discussion of their research. The meeting, supported by the Foreign Office and the Federal Department of Foreign Affairs of Switzerland, discussed preliminary research findings on a

---

[8] The concepts of sanctions episodes and multiple purposes of targeted sanctions are largely based on the analytical frameworks developed by Mikael Eriksson and Francesco Giumelli, respectively, as discussed in Chapters 1 and 2.

[9] These elements included background context; determination of the beginning of episodes; identification of the principal purpose or purposes, different audiences signalled, and decision-making process; assessment of political will; relationship between UN sanctions and other international initiatives/actors; identification of principal episodes; assessment of implementation; identification of direct and indirect impacts, and principal unintended consequences; assessments of effectiveness; and identification and/or selection of paired counterfactual case(s).

[10] We originally intended to conduct interviews with targets, but in practice this proved not to be feasible in most cases. The editors continue to view this particular aspect of inquiry important for future research, however, as discussed in Chapter 12.

[11] UN sanctions continually evolve – in three months from the end of 2013 through March 2014, two new sanctions regimes (CAR and Yemen) and an additional episode to the ongoing sanctions due to the situation in Libya were added. To ensure the TSC databases and assessments remain current, the project managers have committed to annual assessments and recoding. The research phase was conducted with the generous financial support from the governments of Canada, the United Kingdom, and Switzerland.

thematic basis, thereby facilitating the comparative analysis of the sanctions cases. General categories of purposes, impacts, coordination challenges, interactions with other sanctions regimes, relationships to other policy instruments, design and implementation challenges, evasion, unintended consequences, and importantly, the effectiveness of UN targeted sanctions were examined across the range of cases. An attempt was also made to evaluate changes in effectiveness of targeted sanctions over time, to determine the degree of learning on the part of targets, states, and the UN.

Following a revision of each country case study, the editors began development of the TSC databases in August 2011 to synthesize and summarize the assessments of the impacts and effectiveness of UN targeted sanctions. They expanded, consolidated, and harmonized the rich case material received from research teams to construct comparable, qualitative, and quantitative data sets out of the research. Distinct episodes within each country sanctions regime constitute the core unit of analysis, and the database constructed includes a total of sixty-three case episodes for comparative analysis, with 296 variables for each case episode. Qualitative executive summaries of each country case were prepared by the editors and are available in *SanctionsApp* and in a forthcoming volume. They provide valuable précises regarding the background to each case of UN targeted sanctions, the rationale for the determination of episodes, a catalogue of the measures adopted, purpose(s) of the sanctions, unintended consequences, as well as a short-hand explanations of how effectiveness was assessed, and the contribution of the UN sanctions to the policy outcome.[12] The quantitative database will be accessible publically for use by scholarly and policy communities upon the publication of this book.

With the objective of disseminating the initial results of the research to policy communities, the editors produced *The Impacts and Effectiveness of UN Targeted Sanctions: A Guide for Policymakers on the Design and Implementation of Targeted Sanctions*, focused on practical lessons from the empirical research for the design and implementation of future United Nations targeted sanctions.[13] With support from the Swiss government, the editors developed *SanctionsApp*, a smartphone application designed

[12] Because the qualitative data set provides such significant information in a readily assessable format, it will be published as a separate volume to this edited book.
[13] The report was supported by the Government of Canada and released at a meeting hosted by the Mission of Canada to the United Nations on 27 April 2012. The material was updated to include six additional cases and improved evaluations of effectiveness in November 2013, published under the title *The Effectiveness of United Nations Targeted Sanctions*, available at: http://graduateinstitute.ch/internationalgovernance/UN_Targeted_Sanctions.html.

to democratize access to critical information about UN targeted sanctions to Member States, the scholarly community, and to the general public. Created out of the TSC research, the app is updated regularly at the Graduate Institute, Geneva to ensure that the assessments remain current. *SanctionsApp* facilitates efficient access in real time to information based on the TSC data sets. The texts of hundreds of operational and other relevant paragraphs of UN targeted sanctions resolutions are accessible, and interactive filtering features based on the TSC's quantitative database are employed.[14]

The work of the Targeted Sanctions Consortium culminates with the publication of this volume, which provides state-of-the-art, empirically driven, information about a range of themes relevant to the study of UN targeted sanctions, with broader implications for the analysis of international sanctions in general. To produce the volume, individual chapter authors were invited to utilize the TSC qualitative and quantitative data sets to provide a comprehensive and comparative analysis of the entire universe of UN targeted sanctions regimes.

Acknowledgements and disclaimer

The editors wish to thank the participants of the Targeted Sanctions Consortium for their intellectual commitment to and enthusiasm for the challenges represented by UN sanctions. Some are self-professed 'sanctions-geeks', and all of them gave generously of their time to a project that has been years in the making.

In particular, special appreciation is reserved for those TSC research team members who authored chapters in this volume: Paul Bentall, Alix Boucher, Michael Brzoska, Rico Carisch, Andrea Charron, Caty Clement, Kimberly Elliott, Mikael Eriksson, Francesco Giumelli, George Lopez, Clara Portela, Loraine Rickard-Martin, and Peter Wallensteen. Most received only token honoraria, if that; and every one of them worked tirelessly to conform to high standards and expectations. While the process was demanding, we hope you are pleased with the outcome of our collective journey.

The editors also gratefully acknowledge the Governments of Switzerland, Canada, and the United Kingdom for their financial contributions in support of the research of the TSC. The effort would not have been possible without their assistance. It should be noted, of course,

---

[14] Officially launched at the Swiss Mission to the United Nations in New York in June 2013, *SanctionsApp* is updated automatically for those downloading it. A Web-based version with regular Internet access was made available in October 2015.

that the commentary and analysis contained in this book represent the views of the editors (or the chapter authors), and are not necessarily endorsed by any of the governments that have supported the TSC project. Two anonymous reviewers for Cambridge University Press provided unusually extensive and constructive comments that spurred us to strengthen the final manuscript, and we are grateful to John Haslam for his encouragement and support.

We also extend our sincere gratitude to the research and other assistants who spent countless hours searching for information, rechecking our coding, ensuring smooth and productive workshops, and generally doing whatever they could, above and beyond what was asked of them, to ensure the quality and rigour of the TSC project and related products. We appreciate the many efforts of Cecilia Cannon, Georg von Kalckreuth, Amber Khalid, Daniel Norfolk, Dominika Ornatowska, and Sandra Reimann in Geneva over the course of the past five years. In São Paulo, Camila Amaral and Thiago Kunis provided valuable support whenever needed. Harsh Bedi in Geneva saw to it that the manuscript was edited with consistency, accuracy, and care. Special recognition, however, goes to Zuzana Hudáková, who mastered the subject matter in record time, routinely challenged our thinking and assessments, and provided the highest quality research and analysis, painstakingly updating all of the data incorporated in the final manuscript. We thank her for her significant support and many intellectual contributions to this collaborative endeavour.

Mark Sawoski and Nancy Biersteker were exceedingly generous with their hospitality and company in the multiple coding meetings that took place over the course of three years between Little Compton, in the United States, and the village of Prayon in Switzerland.

Finally, it is important that we offer some caveats. While this volume is based on substantial analysis of both the qualitative and quantitative databases, it is important to acknowledge from the outset the inherent limitations of research on sanctions, including the TSC research and approach.

In the simplest of terms, each UN sanctions case is unique with incomparably complex dynamics. No two sanctions regimes are the same, and by definition, each episode is inimitable. The distinctive complexity of each, combined with the relatively small sample size for some categories, makes generalizations and causal inferences difficult. Thus, there are risks in overgeneralizing from such distinctive and unique cases. Moreover, UN sanctions are always combined with other measures and never applied in isolation (in all sixty-three TSC episodes). Isolating the contribution of UN sanctions to policy outcomes is the most difficult analytical aspect of the exercise. While we have attempted to be methodologically consistent and rigorous in our approach, ultimately databases represent thousands of semi-subjective judgements made by researchers.

The findings and recommendations contained in this book, while by no means the final word, hopefully contribute to a better understanding and assessment of the functioning and effectiveness of United Nations targeted sanctions, a critical instrument to maintain international peace and security.

1   Thinking about United Nations targeted sanctions

Thomas J. Biersteker, Marcos Tourinho, and Sue E. Eckert

The use of targeted sanctions by the UN Security Council (UNSC) has gone through significant transformation over the past twenty-five years. Following the devastating humanitarian consequences of the comprehensive trade embargo imposed on Iraq in 1990, a substantial review of the design and implementation of sanctions took place. Albeit with some delay, as a response to that policy debacle, the UN Security Council decidedly shifted towards the imposition of targeted, not comprehensive sanctions. In only two instances (the former Yugoslavia in 1992 and Haiti in 1994), the Security Council imposed new comprehensive measures for a period (following targeted ones), but the last time a comprehensive trade embargo was imposed by the UN was in 1994. Today, most international and *all* UN sanctions are targeted sanctions.

Despite this transformation in the use of sanctions, much of the scholarly, policy, and public discussion on the issue remains unchanged. Discussions often fail to distinguish between targeted and comprehensive measures and continue to concentrate exclusively on whether sanctions are able to change the behaviour of targets. Rarely is consideration given to other ways in which sanctions may affect the target or, for example, how they could influence the international norms they are being used to enforce. Explanations of how sanctions should influence a target remain focused on the political outcomes (gain) resulting from economic sanctions (pain), with the implicit assumption that more pain will yield greater gain. The perception that sanctions tend to be ineffective is also widely held, particularly in contrast with expectations about the use of military force. Given the reliance of international actors on targeted sanctions, it is important that conceptual, analytical, and empirical knowledge of sanctions keeps pace with these developments.

Much of the material included in this chapter updates information previously published in *The Effectiveness of United Nations Targeted Sanctions – Findings from the Targeted Sanctions Consortium (TSC)*, T. Biersteker, S. Eckert, Z. Hudáková, and M. Tourinho, The Graduate Institute, Geneva, November 2013.

In the broader context of international sanctions, UN sanctions play a particularly important role. Although unilateral and/or regional sanctions are often important, only those sanctions imposed by the UN Security Council under Chapter VII of the UN Charter are universally applied and legally binding. This is crucial, given that other countries and their commercial entities invariably diminish the impact of unilateral or regional restrictive measures. In addition, UN sanctions carry a legitimating power of their own. Because of the broadly acknowledged authority of the UN Security Council to address international peace and security challenges, it is common that when they impose additional unilateral or regional sanctions, states will make reference to the legitimacy of their actions on the basis of sanctions imposed by the UN Security Council.[1] For better or for worse, the mere characterization by the Council of an issue as a threat to international peace and security brings substantial attention to the issue at hand and often contributes to the stigmatization of international actors.

In fact, targeted sanctions have been increasingly utilized by the United Nations to address a broad range of challenges to international peace and security – to counter terrorism, prevent conflict, consolidate peace agreements, protect civilians, support democracy (or oppose non-constitutional changes of government), improve resource governance, and limit the proliferation of nuclear weapons. In the often-politicized environment of the UN Security Council, sanctions are at the same time political tools employed to address these challenges to international peace and security and subject to political bargaining among its members. In addition, by the time the Security Council acts, the situation is frequently dire or deteriorating, with violence having already occurred or security threats imminent. Apart from sanctions, the UN has a range of options at its disposal, from diplomatic pressure to referral to legal tribunals, or to the use of force. UN targeted sanctions are frequently *the* tool of choice, however, because military intervention is not appropriate, too costly or ineffective, and diplomatic efforts may be insufficient.

The UN's exclusive use of targeted measures when it imposes sanctions provokes a number of important questions. How do targeted sanctions compare to comprehensive sanctions in terms of effectiveness and humanitarian impact? Why are sanctions consistently employed, when there is a widespread perception that they are generally ineffective? What impacts, both intended and unintended, do they have? How do they relate to other

---

[1] On the legitimacy of the UN Security Council, see I. Hurd, *After Anarchy: Legitimacy and Power in the United Nations Security Council* (Princeton: Princeton University Press, 2007). On legitimacy more broadly, T. M. Franck, *The Power of Legitimacy Among Nations* (Oxford: Oxford University Press, 1990).

policy instruments, such as diplomatic efforts, referrals to legal tribunals, or the threat and/or use of force? How well are they coordinated with other measures within the UN system (such as mediation or peacekeeping)? How do UN targeted sanctions interact with other sanctions regimes imposed at the regional or national level? How are UN targeted sanctions designed and implemented? How can they be evaded, and what are the enforcement challenges? How have they evolved over the course of the last twenty-five years? Is there any evidence of institutional learning or improved effectiveness over time? These are some of the questions this volume addresses.

Understanding UN targeted sanctions

Targeted sanctions differ from comprehensive sanctions in that they are discriminating policy measures. Rather than being applied indiscriminately on an entire country and its population (as comprehensive sanctions are) with resultant harmful humanitarian consequences, targeted sanctions are focused on specific individuals, entities, sectors, and/or regions of a country. Targets can include designated individuals, selected firms or business entities, political parties, non-state actors, or regimes (such as the Taliban in Afghanistan or the *de factos* in Haiti). Travel bans and asset freezes are commonly imposed on individuals, while firms likewise may be subject to asset restrictions. Individuals prominently associated with ruling political parties and regimes often face combinations of both types of targeted measures. Targeted sanctions can also be imposed on a sector of activity (such as diplomatic activities) or restrict trade with an entire sector of an economy. Sectoral targeted sanctions include arms embargoes, commodity bans (e.g. on oil, diamonds, or timber), transportation bans, and more general financial sector restrictions. Finally, sanctions may be targeted on a region of a country, such as a province or sub-regional territory, or on the territory under the control of a proscribed rebel group. While targeted sanctions vary in the degree of discrimination (as elaborated in more detail later in this chapter), they differ from comprehensive sanctions in that they are not imposed indiscriminately on an entire population. This does not mean that they do not have any unintended humanitarian consequences (as discussed in Chapter 9), but targeted sanctions are *a priori* more normatively acceptable than comprehensive sanctions, which inflict costs on innocent civilians rather than on those directly responsible for some proscribed behaviour.[2]

---

[2] This assumes, of course, that the imposition of sanctions is legitimate, as opposed to the argument that the Council should focus more on diplomacy and/or non-coercive measures.

Targeted sanctions differ in more than magnitude or degree, however. Targeted measures are qualitatively different from comprehensive sanctions, which are an 'all or nothing' policy instrument which halts all international economic and commercial transactions with a country. In this sense, comprehensive sanctions are not a flexible or agile policy instrument, and are intended to isolate the target completely. By contrast, targeted sanctions can be manipulated in response to target behaviour, increasing restrictions or providing encouragement, as deemed necessary.[3] Like comprehensive sanctions, they should be seen as policy instruments that exist within a larger bargaining framework between senders and targets. Unlike comprehensive measures, however, they can be applied in an incremental manner and be ratcheted upward or downward in response to actions taken by targets, or to changes on the ground. Targeted sanctions are inherently more adaptable than comprehensive sanctions and can be more easily calibrated to influence or affect targets. As elaborated in more detail in Chapter 2, targeted sanctions operate according to a different logic.

This volume analyses United Nations sanctions. UN sanctions are often combined with other international sanctions measures – regional sanctions, and autonomous or unilateral measures by individual states – that in some cases have a greater impact on targeted entities.[4] To the extent possible, we attempt to isolate the independent influence of UN targeted sanctions in our analysis, as elaborated in more detail in Chapter 10. We also address systematically the relationship between UN and other sanctions regimes at the regional and national levels in Chapters 3, 5, and 8. As described above, we chose UN targeted sanctions as our primary object of study because they are the most legitimate, the only universal and mandatory sanctions measures, and are widely used as a fundamental instrument of collective security to address international peace and security challenges.

Our analysis of UN targeted sanctions expands beyond consideration of economic statecraft alone.[5] Like most other scholars working on international sanctions, we examine the application of restrictive economic measures, but we expand the scope of analysis to include diplomatic measures, as well as restrictions on the external political activities of non-state entities. We also include arms embargoes, drawing empirically

---

[3] This distinction between comprehensive and targeted sanctions could be seen as analogous to the classic distinction introduced by Thomas Schelling between the use of 'brute force' and force used to 'compel' an adversary. See T. Schelling, *Arms and Influence* (New Haven, CT and London: Yale University Press, 1966).

[4] This is the kind of analysis that would be undertaken in a case study of a particular country or by an International Relations scholar attempting to generalize about sanctions in general, without distinguishing between their different sources.

[5] D. A. Baldwin, *Economic Statecraft* (Princeton: Princeton University Press, 1985).

from the larger menu of sanctions measures developed by the UN Security Council over the past twenty-five years. Particular attention is given to the institutional mechanisms developed in the course of the last two decades for the improved design, enforcement, and accountability of the measures.

In various ways, targeted sanctions are more complex than comprehensive sanctions. They entail decisions about whom to target, how to limit indiscriminate unintended consequences, and often, a strategy for how to suspend or lift them in an incremental manner as the situation on the ground changes. Targeted sanctions are also more difficult to design and implement than comprehensive sanctions. To maximize effectiveness, they require a sophisticated and detailed knowledge of a country's economy and its political economy. Designing measures that most directly affect the political leadership responsible for decision-making (and in the process, avoiding humanitarian impact to the extent possible) requires detailed knowledge of a country's internal political dynamics. This is far more complicated than imposing blanket sanctions on an entire country. In addition, without a detailed understanding of the inner workings of highly localized conflict economies, it is difficult to know how, where, and when sanctions such as commodity bans are likely to have a constraining effect on a proscribed rebel group. Despite this complexity, however, it is important to note the frequency with which they have significant effects, as elaborated in more detail in Chapters 8 and 10.

Targeted sanctions are designed in New York, but implemented by individual Member States in their respective capitals around the world. The complexity of their design can lead to disconnections between policy intentions and consequences. Ministries of Finance or Economics in capitals responsible for implementation may interpret the measures more broadly or narrowly than intended by the diplomats negotiating the measures in the Security Council. Individual financial institutions responsible for the freezing of assets or the blocking of transfers call upon local officials for guidance as to whether or not to block a particular transaction or account. This inevitably leads to different interpretations, not only across national jurisdictions but potentially among officials from the same government, with important consequences for the scope and impacts of the measures imposed. This issue is taken up more extensively in Chapter 12.

Targeted sanctions share with comprehensive measures the challenge of rational design by a highly politicized body,[6] but they differ in the

---

[6] S. Chesterman and B. Pouligny, 'Are Sanctions Meant to Work? The Politics of Creating and Implementing Sanctions Through the United Nations', *Global Governance*, 9 (2003), pp. 503–18.

difficulty of implementation. As elaborated in more detail in Chapter 7, targeted sanctions require an institutional infrastructure within the UN, including separate sanctions committees for each country's sanctions regime, UN Secretariat staff support, and investigative monitoring assistance from Panels of Experts.[7] Detailed personal identifying information needs to be provided for individual designations, and the lists of sanctioned parties need to be kept current by the sanctions committees for sanctions to be effective and maintain their legitimacy. Implementing states, for their part, face the difficult challenge of translating Chapter VII UN Security Council measures into domestic law, communicating the information to relevant parties for action (to domestic financial institutions or customs officials), monitoring potential violations, and enforcing penalties against sanctions evaders. Simply banning all transactions, as was done with comprehensive sanctions, is far easier to implement.

This means that the implementation of targeted sanctions is more costly, not only for both the UN and Member States, but also for private sector entities required to enforce the measures. There has been a significant increase in the administrative support required of the UN Secretariat to service sanctions committees. Panels of Experts have become routine in nearly all ongoing UN country sanctions regimes (in ten of the fourteen in operation when this book was completed), which also entail additional short-term contract costs for the UN. The complexity of implementing the measures has forced many Member States to expand their enforcement capacity, particularly with regard to financial sanctions. Private sector financial institutions – from traditional banking to insurance firms – report that compliance has been one of the few employment growth areas within the firm during the past decade.

While there are increased costs, there are also some important benefits associated with the move to targeted sanctions by the UN. First, in contrast to comprehensive sanctions, they can be more readily and subtly combined with other policy instruments such as diplomacy, mediation, legal referrals, peacekeeping, and threats of the use of force. Second, as already described earlier, they are easier to calibrate (ratchet up or down) in a general bargaining situation between the UN Security Council and

---

[7] On the monitoring role of panels of experts, see A. Vines, 'Monitoring UN Sanctions in Africa: The Role of Panels of Experts', in Trevor Findlay (ed.), *Verification Yearbook 2003* (2003), p. 247; A. Vines and T. Cargill, 'The Impact of UN Sanctions and their Panel of Experts: Sierra Leone and Liberia', *International Journal*, 64 (2009–2010); A. J. Boucher and V. K. Holt, *Targeting Spoilers? The Role of United Nations Panels of Experts* (Washington, DC: Henry L. Stimson Center, 2009), pp. 1–207.

targets. Third, they do not lead inexorably to broad, non-discriminating, harmful humanitarian consequences.

The targeted sanctions consortium data and analysis

The research and analytical framework of the Targeted Sanctions Consortium differs from other initiatives to assess and evaluate sanctions in several important respects. It responds to a challenge faced by all analyses of international sanctions: how to address changes in sanctions regimes over time. For example, UN sanctions on Somalia have been in place for over twenty years, but their intent was very different when first imposed in 1992 from what they seek to achieve today. During this period, the fundamental objective of the sanctions has changed, the context is significantly different, the types of sanctions imposed have varied, and the initial targets are no longer relevant. If one treats sanctions country cases as a single unit for analysis, it is impossible to grasp analytically the nuances and important variations in any regime over time.

For this reason, the Targeted Sanctions Consortium (TSC) analysis breaks down the broader sanctions country regimes into different episodes – periods in which the sanctions regime remains stable in terms of purposes, types, targets, and context.[8] Sanctions episodes, then, not sanctions country cases, are the core unit of analysis, thereby enabling a more accurate evaluation of the different measures taken by the Security Council to achieve its purposes over time.

The collection and organization of the data used in this research project has developed in three stages. First, groups of regional and sanctions specialists (both scholars and practitioners) developed detailed case studies for all of the major UN targeted sanctions regimes imposed in the last two decades. Second, on the basis of this information, and conducting additional research when necessary, the editors of this volume designed and coded quantitative and qualitative databases to facilitate comparative and comprehensive analyses of UN targeted sanctions. Third, the qualitative and quantitative databases were once again sent to country and sanctions specialists, scholars, and practitioners with the goal of clarifying potential misunderstandings and improving the overall quality of the data.

---

[8] We define a sanctions episode from the vantage point of the sender in terms of significant modifications of the sanctions regime. Operationally this would include a major expansion of designees or lists of proscribed items, the addition of new types of sanctions, a significant relaxation of existing measures, changes in the target designated, or changes in the stated objectives of the sanctions (e.g. from counter-terrorism to non-proliferation). This builds upon but adapts the analytical framework proposed by M. Eriksson in *Targeting Peace: Understanding UN and EU Sanctions* (Farnham, UK: Ashgate, 2011).

As a result, the TSC quantitative and qualitative databases used to inform the chapters in this volume include the entire universe of UN targeted sanctions imposed since 1991, or twenty-three different country regimes broken down into sixty-three case episodes for comparative analysis. All individual episodes have been coded for 296 variables relevant to the issues addressed in this volume, ranging from measures of political will in the Security Council to the different evasion tactics used by targets. Throughout the book, authors make reference to specific case episodes (or EPs) to illustrate different aspects of their argument. A complete list of all country cases and episodes, including their different objectives, types, and targets, is available in Appendix 1. Figure 1.1 summarizes and displays the scope of the project.

It should be noted that unlike many large databases, we have not relied on large numbers of research assistants to undertake the quantitative coding. Each critically important evaluation of the effectiveness of the UN targeted sanctions has been made by the three editors of this volume on a deliberative, consensus (and/or exhaustion) basis. The detailed factual coding of information about each episode (considered for the evaluation of effectiveness in the episode) was made by at least two of the three authors of this chapter, and all of the coding decisions (along with copies of executive summaries of each of the cases) have been sent to the head of the original team of authors of the detailed qualitative case studies, to other country or sanctions experts, and in some cases to UN Panel of Experts members for their evaluation and corrections, as necessary. This significantly increases the reliability of the data by enhancing inter-coder reliability and fact-checking, and ensuring a fairly strict process-oriented coding scheme. As a result of this process, the data provided are more sensitive to the history and politics involved in the implementation of targeted sanctions as policy tools.[9] Details about the definitions of different concepts referred to in the discussion in the remainder of this chapter and the book as a whole can be found in the Codebook contained in Appendix 2.

The analytical choice of using case episodes as a unit of analysis comes with important methodological consequences. For the purposes of statistical analysis, it is not always possible to assume the independence of the different case episodes. While there are sometimes major continuities within a single country case, including the same regional context, the same key targets, or the same key players internationally, there are often significant discontinuities within larger country sanctions regimes, especially those that remain in

---

[9] This is something recommended by J. Kirshner in 'Economic Sanctions: the State of the Art', *Security Studies*, 11 (2002), p. 169.

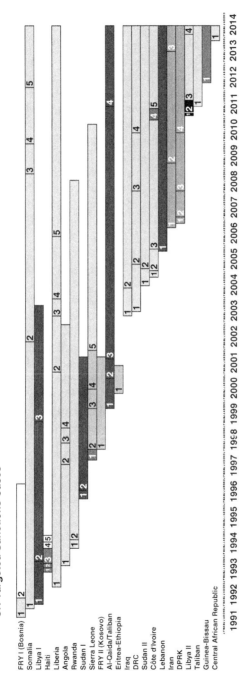

UN Targeted Sanctions Cases

FRY I (Bosnia)
Somalia
Libya I
Haiti
Liberia
Angola
Rwanda
Sudan I
Sierra Leone
FRY II (Kosovo)
Al-Qaida/Taliban
Eritrea-Ethiopia
Iraq
DRC
Sudan II
Côte d'Ivoire
Lebanon
Iran
DPRK
Libya II
Taliban
Guinea-Bissau
Central African Republic

1991 1992 1993 1994 1995 1996 1997 1998 1999 2000 2001 2002 2003 2004 2005 2006 2007 2008 2009 2010 2011 2012 2013 2014

Primary Objectives

Cease hostilities / Peace enforcement
Counter-terrorism
Democracy
Non-proliferation
R2P
Comprehensive sanctions episodes

Figure 1.1 Scope of TSC research

place for a long period of time. For example, the combination of different types of targeted sanctions being applied frequently changes as the Security Council attempts to increase (or relieve) pressure on targets. The targets of sanctions also change, either because the sanctions have been in place for a long time (as in Somalia) or because the sanctions become increasingly targeted over time (as in Angola). Sometimes the territory over which the sanctions apply is variable (as in Angola and the DRC), and the Security Council even changes its core objectives (as it did in the current sanctions regimes in Libya and Somalia). There are instances in which nearly all of these components have changed from one episode to another (e.g. primary objectives, types of sanctions, and targets). Thus, we contend that there is sufficient variation across different case episodes to warrant their comparison as distinct units of analysis.[10] At the same time, we are mindful of the methodological challenges and refrain from making causal claims (as opposed to correlational observations) throughout the volume.

This research makes a contribution to the 'sanctions effectiveness' debate by expanding analytically the understanding of the purposes of sanctions.[11] As discussed more thoroughly in Chapters 2 and 10, the literature addressing the effectiveness of international sanctions historically considered sanctions to 'work' or 'not work' based on the extent to which they coerced a target to change its behaviour.[12] There are, however, sometimes other purposes of the UN Security Council in imposing targeted sanctions. For example, the UN sanctions targeting Al-Qaida were not intended to coerce a change of behaviour of the group directly (since no actual demands were made of the group in the relevant resolutions after 2001), but rather they sought to make the group's activities more difficult by constraining its access to resources. At other times, sanctions are used to send a strong message to a target (stronger than verbal condemnations, because they entail costs to both target and

---

[10] The focus on country cases as a unit of analysis in most large-N studies does not fully solve the problem of statistical independence, since different country sanctions regimes are embedded in highly interdependent regional settings, as illustrated by the West African conflict cases – Sierra Leone, Liberia, and Côte d'Ivoire, the DRC conflict, the conflicts in Eastern Africa, and the spillover from Libya to the Central African Republic.

[11] This expansion builds upon but adapts in several important respects the typology proposed by F. Giumelli in *Coercing, Constraining and Signaling: Explaining and Understanding International Sanctions After the End of the Cold War* (Colchester: ECPR Press, 2011). Unlike Giumelli in his 2011 book, we do not assume that the different purposes are mutually exclusive, but that the senders of sanctions often intend to accomplish different purposes simultaneously.

[12] See notably G. Hufbauer, J. Schott, K. Elliott, and B. Oegg, *Economic Sanctions Reconsidered*, 3rd edn (Washington, DC: Peterson Institute for International Economics, 2007) and R. Pape, *International Security*, among many others cited in Chapters 2 and 10.

sender), often concerning a violation of an international norm. For instance, when the Security Council imposed sanctions prohibiting the export of luxury items to the Democratic People's Republic of Korea (DPRK), it was hardly constraining the activities of the regime or anticipating that the measures would result in the termination of its nuclear programme, but rather was signalling the unacceptability of its actions contrary to international non-proliferation norms. While an immediate resolution to the threat of international peace and security is always desirable, in thirteen of the episodes analysed, *no* specific demands for behavioural change (i.e. policy coercion) were made in the relevant UN resolutions.

Therefore, in the analytical framework employed in the volume, sanctions are understood to have three different purposes: to coerce a change in a target's behaviour; to constrain a target from engaging in a proscribed activity; or to signal and/or stigmatize a target or others about the violation of an international norm. Sanctions with a coercive purpose seek to change the behaviour of targets, often requesting them to fulfil a set of demands explicitly stated in the UN Security Council resolutions or asserted by a relevant actor (e.g. Secretary-General, conflict mediators). Coercion often takes place in a scenario of political bargaining, in which senders attempt to change the incentives for the target to coerce it to change its activities.

Constraining sanctions attempt to deny a target access to essential resources needed to engage in a proscribed activity (e.g. financing, technical knowledge, materiel), raising its costs or forcing a change in strategy. This is often the case with commodity sanctions, which target a consequential sector of the economy to deny targets the resources needed to carry out their proscribed activities.

Signalling and stigmatizing sanctions publicly assert the target's deviation from an international norm, producing at the same time an articulation or reframing of the norm and a statement of its practical applicability in that case. In the sanctions literature, aspects of signalling have long been considered a relevant dimension of sanctions practice. In her classic 1972 article on sanctions against Rhodesia, Margaret Doxey argued that the target's knowledge about both the norm and the penalty were essential for evaluating the effectiveness of sanctions. In what she termed 'the communication factor', she emphasized the importance of 'the extent to which norms and penalties are comprehended'.[13] In the TSC framework, in addition to the 'communication' aspect of signalling (clarity and strength of the message), we examine also the social-normative dimension of the

---

[13] M. Doxey, 'International Sanctions: a Framework For Analysis With Special Reference to the UN and Southern Africa', *International Organization*, 26 (1972), pp. 527–50, at 535.

Table 1.1 *The purposes of UN targeted sanctions*

Purposes	Principal purpose		Purpose	
	Frequency	%	Frequency	%
Coerce a change of behaviour	35	56	50	79
Constrain target behaviour	26	41	59	94
Signal and/or stigmatize target	2	3	63	100

signal, by considering the degree to which the target has been stigmatized for proscribed behaviour by some relevant social community.[14]

Table 1.1 indicates the distribution of 'purposes' in all sanctions episodes considered in this volume. While constraining and signalling are significant purposes present throughout the cases, it is clear that the senders of targeted sanctions, in this case the UN Security Council, continue to consider coercion as the principal purpose of the sanctions imposed.

It is important to note that these different purposes may be directed simultaneously to more than one audience, aiming for example at a rebel faction, its key supporters, as well as to domestic constituencies in sanctions sending states. Furthermore, although these differing purposes typically coexist within a sanctions regime and its different episodes, being aware of their distinct aspects is important in the evaluation of targeted sanctions.

These purposes are often interrelated. For example, sanctions may be designed to constrain a target's access to military resources in order to force a change in the cost–benefit calculation of engaging in warfare. On the surface, constraining and signalling could also be interpreted broadly as an indirect attempt of coercion, analogous to Herbert Simon's conception of bounded rationality and sub-goals,[15] where coercion is seen as the principal objective and constraint and signalling are considered as 'sub-goals' of sanctions (to assist in the achievement of coercion). If one looks at the *mechanisms* through which each combination of sanctions measures is intended to work, however, it is clear that they operate differently from each other. Sanctions with coercive purposes seek most immediately to change the target's *policy objective*. Constraining sanctions aim at impairing the *operational capacity* of the target in the conduct of its

---

[14] On stigma in international relations, see R. Adler-Nissen, 'Stigma Management in International Relations: Transgressive Identities, Norms, and Order in International Society', *International Organization*, 68 (2014), pp. 143–76.

[15] H. Simon, *Administrative Behavior*, 4th edn (New York, NY: The Free Press, 1997).

policies. Signalling sanctions work by highlighting the absence of broad *international social acceptability* of the target's policy.

To add to the complexity of analysis, it is also possible that a given sanctions measure coerces an individual at one level of analysis in order to constrain the activities of a group operating at a different level. This is the case of the Al-Qaida sanctions regime, in which asset freezes are imposed on individuals and entities in order to constrain the operations of the larger group. While in the final analysis the three different purposes seek to address a threat to international peace and security (that is always presumably resolvable though a 'change of behaviour', understood broadly), these three sanctions mechanisms operate under different working logics and, for analytical reasons should be treated separately.

International norms are central to the understanding of UN targeted sanctions regimes. Because the affirmation of an international norm is embedded in the signalling aspect of every episode, sanctions function as a central mechanism for the strengthening and/or negotiation of international norms. This means that debates on the establishment of sanctions regimes are often inextricably linked with political attempts to establish and/or refute norm-precedents in different domains.

Inside the Security Council, negotiation over the normative aspects of the objective of sanctions has at times damaged the optimal design of sanctions regimes. Elsewhere, because the legitimacy of sanctions as a tool is often associated with the legitimacy of the norm it seeks to enforce, the appetite for implementation is affected by the conflation of these two distinct elements.

Of the sixty-three sanctions episodes included in the TSC database, all of them signal specific international norms. While the primary norms signalled tend to be directly associated with the respective objective of each sanction regime (e.g. prohibition of armed conflict, nuclear non-proliferation, responsibility to protect), other norms such as the prohibition of the use of child soldiers, sexual and gender-based violence, and even the established authority of regional organizations are also often signalled. The invocation of these norms has important consequences not only for the specific case in question, but also for the establishment of political and legal precedents in international society.[16]

Political objectives

Targeted sanctions are used by the UN Security Council to address various threats to international peace and security. From demanding

---

[16] I. Johnstone, *The Power of Deliberation: International Law, Politics and Organizations* (Oxford University Press, 2011).

Table 1.2 *Norms signalled by UN targeted sanctions*

Norm signalled	Principal norm		Norm	
	Frequency	%	Frequency	%
Prohibition of war/armed conflict	32	52	36	57
Counter-terrorism	9	15	15	24
Non-constitutional change in government	7	11	15	24
Non-proliferation	7	11	8	13
Improved governance (e.g. natural resources/security sector)	4	6	9	14
Protect population under R2P	2	3	4	6
Support judicial process	1	2	21	33
Human rights	1	2	28	44
Authority of regional arrangements	0	0	23	37
Authority of the UN Security Council	0	0	7	11

Note: Percentage calculated from valid cases only; non-applicable and missing data excluded.

the extradition of criminal suspects to the support of regional peacemaking efforts, to countering nuclear proliferation or terrorism, sanctions are frequently a tool of choice. For analytical purposes, it is useful to categorize and differentiate sanctions regimes based on the general political objective they seek to achieve.

To date, more than half (59 per cent) of the UN targeted sanctions episodes have sought to address problems associated with armed conflict. That parties to a conflict should cease hostilities, engage in the negotiation of a peace settlement, enforce a peace agreement, and respect human rights are frequent goals of Security Council efforts to address conflict. Countering terrorism has also been an important objective of UN targeted sanctions since 1992 – accounting for 14 per cent of the cases of targeted sanctions episodes. Supporting democracy, often through the restoration of an elected government, similarly represents a goal in about 10 per cent of the cases, from the effort to restore the Aristide regime in Haiti in the early 1990s to the response to the military coup in Guinea-Bissau in 2012, including in the interim specific episodes in Sierra Leone and Côte d'Ivoire.

Since 2006, UN sanctions have been used to slow nuclear proliferation activities. Sanctions targeted at Iran and the DPRK, constitute about 11 per cent of the episodes in which the UN has imposed targeted sanctions. The remaining cases (7 per cent) refer to the application of targeted sanctions for three different objectives: support of judicial process (e.g.

Table 1.3 *Objectives of UN targeted sanctions*

Objectives	Objective		Primary objective	
	Frequency	%	Frequency	%
Armed conflict	42	67	37	59
Cease hostilities	31	49	–	–
Peace enforcement	31	49	–	–
Support peace building	10	16	–	–
Negotiation of peace agreement	8	13	–	–
Human rights	22	35	0	0
Democracy support	17	27	6	10
Counter-terrorism	15	24	9	14
Good governance	8	13	1	2
Support judicial process	6	10	1	2
Non-proliferation	7	11	7	11
Support humanitarian efforts	4	6	0	0
Protect population under R2P	2	3	2	3

Note: Percentage calculated from valid cases only, non-applicable and missing data excluded.

following the Hariri assassination in Lebanon (2005)); support for better governance of natural resources in Liberia (2006); and the protection of civilians under Responsibility to Protect (R2P) in Libya (2011).

Other objectives have also been included as part of the rationale for the imposition of UN targeted sanctions. Human rights concerns are routinely invoked, though never as the primary objective, and occasionally, the provision of humanitarian relief and the establishment of new laws and institutions for the management of resources have also been included in resolutions as additional rationales for sanctions regimes.

Types of targeted sanctions

Targeted sanctions can be categorized into six broadly different types. Individual/entity sanctions (most often asset freezes and travel bans) are applied to individuals and corporate entities (companies or political parties). Diplomatic sanctions are restrictions on the diplomatic activity of a governing body, and they refer to measures such as the limitation of accredited personnel, travel, and general suspensions from intergovernmental organizations. Arms embargoes, the most frequently applied UN sanction, include the general or limited suspension of international arms or proliferation-related dual-use goods to a specific country or region. Commodity sanctions limit trade in specific resources in the targeted country or region; to date these sanctions are applied to valuable natural

resources such as diamonds, timber, oil, charcoal, and wildlife.
Transportation sanctions refer to prohibitions on international transit of
carriers (by sea or air) from or to the targeted state. Targeted sanctions
may also be applied to core economic sectors, which have a broader
impact on the economy, including financial sanctions (e.g. investment
ban, limitations of banking services, and sovereign wealth funds).

It is useful to think about these different types of sanctions on a continuum, with the most "targeted" measures on one end and the relatively
more "comprehensive" ones on the other. The variation from one end to
the other of the continuum is based on how discriminating the measure is.

Table 1.4 *Types of UN targeted sanctions*

Type of Sanctions	Frequency	%
Individual sanctions	47	75
Travel ban	34	54
Asset freeze	40	63
Asset freeze and transfer	3	5
Diplomatic sanctions	13	21
Revision of visa policy	6	10
Limiting travel of diplomatic personnel	11	17
Limiting diplomatic representation	5	8
Limiting number of diplomatic personnel	5	8
Sectoral sanctions	60	95
Arms imports embargo	55	87
Aviation ban	11	17
Arms export ban	11	17
Proliferation-sensitive material	7	11
Shipping	3	5
Oil service equipment	2	3
Commodity sanctions	26	41
Diamonds exports ban	11	17
Petroleum imports ban	8	13
Timber exports ban	3	5
Luxury goods	3	5
Charcoal exports ban	1	2
Other	5	8
Financial sector sanctions	6	10
Investment ban	1	2
Diaspora tax	2	3
Central Bank asset freeze	2	3
Financial services	1	2
Sovereign wealth funds	2	3

Individual/entity targeted sanctions (e.g. travel ban, assets freeze; most discriminating)

Diplomatic sanctions (only one sector of government directly affected)

Arms embargoes or proliferation-related goods (largely limited impact on fighting forces or security sector)

Commodity sanctions other than oil (e.g. diamonds, timber, charcoal; tend to affect some regions disproportionately)

Transportation sanctions (e.g. aviation or shipping ban; can affect much of a population)

Core economic sector sanctions (e.g. oil and financial sector sanctions; affect the broader population and therefore are the least discriminating of targeted sanctions)

Comprehensive sanctions (nondiscriminating)

Figure 1.2 Types of targeted sanctions and degrees of discrimination (or relative "comprehensiveness")

For instance, although both are sanctions on a sector of the economy, an oil embargo affects the entire population of a country considerably more than, for example, an arms embargo or diplomatic sanctions. This makes oil embargoes relatively more "comprehensive" in the continuum.[17]

Unintended consequences

Unintended consequences are a critical aspect to consider when thinking about targeted sanctions. Although targeted sanctions do not have the same degree of unintended impact as comprehensive sanctions, it would be a mistake to assume that they do not result in some unintended consequences, both negative and, sometimes, positive. Indeed, they are found in 94% of the case episodes for which reliable data are available.

Among the many possible unintended consequences considered in this study, the increase in corruption and criminality was most frequently observed (58%). The strengthening of authoritarian rule in the target (35%) and the diversion of resources (34%) were also often identified.

---

[17] It should be noted that many of these targeted measures have collateral or unintended consequences on other sectors. Diplomatic sanctions may embarrass elites; arms embargoes may weaken police and security services more generally; while commodity sanctions may cast a shadow over entire industries, harming credit and employment.

Table 1.5 *Unintended consequences*

Unintended Consequences	Episodes	
	Frequency	%
Indications of unintended consequences	48	94
Increases in corruption and/or criminality	31	58
Humanitarian consequences	24	44
Decline in the credibility and/or legitimacy of the UN Security Council	19	37
Strengthening of authoritarian rule	19	35
Resource diversion	18	34
Increases in human rights violations	14	26
Strengthening of political factions	13	25
Increases in international enforcement capacity in different issue domains	11	20
Harmful effects on neighboring states	10	19
Increase in international regulatory capacity in different issue domains	10	19
Widespread harmful economic consequences	8	19
Rally round the flag effect	7	13
Significant burden on implementing states	5	9
Reduction of local institutional capacity	4	8
Strengthening instruments of security apparatus of senders	4	8
Increase in the growth of the state role in the economy	4	8
Human rights implications for sending states	1	2
Enhanced stature of targeted individuals	0	0
Other	5	10
Total	**63**	**100**

Note: Percentage calculated from valid cases only, non-applicable and missing data excluded.

Negative humanitarian consequences, historically the most intensely debated topic concerning comprehensive sanctions, were observed in 44% of the episodes studied. Also importantly, the legitimacy and authority of the Security Council was harmed in more than one third of the cases (37%).

It is important to note that while many unintended consequences could be anticipated and are avoidable, some are not and should be considered as the "costs" of the tool in the policy-making process. Of course, as will be further discussed in Chapter 9, awareness of the potential unintended consequences during the design of sanctions may help in the selection of the most appropriate measures, as well as in the development of strategies to mitigate their broader side-effects in the population.

Evasion/coping strategies

Sanctions are prohibition norms[18] that create powerful incentives for evasion, and there is evidence of evasion or coping strategies in over 90% of the cases of UN targeted sanctions. Targets commonly devise means of evading the measures, from employing black market contractors (who charge a premium for their services) to using safe havens, disguises of identity, or front companies. At the same time, targets are likely to utilize a variety of adjustment strategies to cope with the impacts of sanctions. Stockpiling of critical materials is likely if sanctions are threatened in advance, while diverting trade through third countries,

Table 1.6 *Evasion and coping strategies employed by targets of UN sanctions*

Evasion/Coping Strategies	Frequency	%
Indications of evasion/coping strategies	52	91
Evasion	45	80
Black market contractors	37	69
Safe havens	23	43
Disguise of identity, forged documents	16	31
Informal value transfer systems	13	25
Front companies	15	28
Denial of inspection	14	24
Disguise vessels	14	26
Reliance on family members	6	12
Coping strategies	49	82
Diversion of trade through third countries	46	79
Stockpiling supplies	32	60
Diversify sources of funds or investment	19	32
Alternative value sources	8	14
Import substitution, new technology	9	15
Coerce/pressure major trade partner not to enforce sanctions	6	11
Shifting terms/subject of debate (diplomatic)	6	11
Other evasion/coping strategies	4	8

Note: Percentage calculated from valid cases only, non-applicable and missing data excluded.

[18] E. Nadelmann, 'Global Prohibition Regimes: the Evolution of Norms in International Society', *International Organization*, 44 (1990), pp. 479–526.

diversifying investment partners, and developing new technologies or industries that may be made economically viable the longer the sanctions remain in place.

Relationship to other policy instruments

Sanctions do not exist in isolation. As Chapter 4 illustrates, no UN targeted measures have been imposed without the presence of other policy instruments seeking to achieve similar or related objectives. Concomitant diplomatic negotiations occurred more than 97% of the time, and peacekeeping forces, many authorized by the UN, are on the ground in 62% of the episodes. Some military force (i.e. limited strikes and operations, robust military force, no-fly zones, or naval blockades) was used 52% of the time and legal tribunals were present in 46% of the cases.

In 90% of the episodes, UN sanctions were supplemented by other sanctions in the form of regional (AU, ECOWAS, EU) or unilateral measures. In 74% of the regimes, other sanctions preceded the initial imposition of UN sanctions on the country. Often resulting from a request of a regional body that has already imposed individual sanctions (travel ban or assets freeze) on targets, UN measures often complement or universalize pre-existing sanctions. More recently, UN sanctions resolutions have been used as a basis for more extensive, coordinated multilateral and unilateral sanctions (against Iran and DPRK), which have

Table 1.7 *Other policy instruments employed with UN targeted sanctions*

Other Policy Instruments	Frequency	%
Diplomacy (pressure and/or negotiations)	61	97
Legal tribunals	29	46
ICC/ICJ	14	22
Special courts and tribunals	19	30
Peacekeeping operations	39	62
Threat of use of force	16	25
Use of force	33	52
Limited strikes and operations	18	29
Robust military force	22	35
No-fly zone	1	2
Naval blockade	2	3
Covert	7	11
Cyber-sabotage	4	6
Targeted assassinations	7	11
DDR/SSR	27	43

Table 1.8 *Relationship between UN and other sanctions regimes*

Other Sanctions	Frequency	%
Regional sanctions in place during the episode	43	68
EU	33	52
AU	2	3
OAS	1	2
ASEAN	0	0
ECOWAS	11	17
Unilateral sanctions in place during the episode	41	65
US	40	63
UK	19	30
Other	9	14
Sanctions regimes in neighbouring countries	34	54

created controversy within the Council and some confusion in terms of implementation.

Thus, UN targeted sanctions are better understood if seen in the context of these other contemporaneous policy instruments. Because these efforts are inherently interconnected, the planning, implementation, and evaluation of targeted sanctions should be considered in terms of what they provide to, how they benefit from, or when they are harmed by other initiatives.

The effectiveness of UN targeted sanctions

The measurement of the effectiveness of UN targeted sanctions has been subject to considerable debate in the literature and was a key objective of the TSC research reported in this volume. Our analysis indicates that sanctions are effective in coercing, constraining, or signalling a target on average about 22% of the time.[19] As described in greater detail in Chapter 10, the effectiveness of sanctions is measured as a function of two variables: policy outcome and the UN sanctions contribution to that outcome. Policy outcome is evaluated on a five-point scale, with 1 representing least effective and 5 most effective, and UN sanctions contribution is measured on a six-point scale, with 0 representing a negative contribution and 5 representing

---

[19] This is calculated on the following basis: a total of thirty-eight case episodes have been evaluated as effective (five in coercing, sixteen in constraining, and seventeen in signalling) out of a total of 172 possible (sixty-three case episodes times three purposes minus seventeen cases of non-applicable objectives; thirteen in coercion and four in constraint). 38/172 = 22.09%. This implies valuing the three distinct purposes of sanctions equally.

Table 1.9 *Sanctions effectiveness distribution*[1]

	Effective (%)	Mixed (%)	Ineffective (%)
Coerce	10	10	80
Constrain	27	17	56
Signal	27	29	44

[1] For the general evaluation criteria for effectiveness and episode specific coding decisions, see Appendix 2.

UN sanctions as the most important contribution to the outcome. We only consider UN measures effective when the policy outcome is evaluated as a 4 or 5 and when the UN sanctions contribution to that outcome is at least a 3, meaning they reinforce other measures.

The pattern is more interesting and informative, however, when the analysis is broken down into the different purposes of sanctions (i.e. to coerce a change in behaviour, constrain the activities of a target, or send a powerful signal), described earlier. Here we find that targeted sanctions are much more effective in constraining or signalling a target than they are in coercing a change in target behaviour. They are effective in coercing a change in behaviour only 10% of the time. By contrast, they are effective in constraining target behaviour (increasing costs and inducing changes in strategy) almost three times as frequently, or 27% of the time. They are as effective in sending signals to target audiences, which they also do 27% of the time. Table 1.9 displays the frequency distribution and associated percentages of each category of purpose of targeted sanctions.

Thus, when evaluating the effectiveness of targeted sanctions, as described, it is useful to differentiate between the different purposes of sanctions. They are clearly more effective in accomplishing some policy goals (constraining and signalling) than others (coercing a change in behaviour), and routinely should be evaluated as such. At the same time, different observers may choose to value the three distinct purposes of sanctions differently, given that they may consider some purposes more difficult to achieve than others. For this reason, in this volume we have chosen to use this data in disaggregated form most of the time, unless explicitly stated otherwise.

It is crucial to note still that the assessment of effectiveness does not consider the unintended consequences, economic costs, or harmful effects that may have accompanied each of these "effective" episodes. As Chapters 10 and 12 elaborate, it is possible that a measurement including these elements in the calculation of effectiveness would reach different results.

The results observed thus far demonstrate the analytical advantages of moving away from a nearly exclusive preoccupation with the ability of sanctions to coerce a change in behaviour to include also their ability to constrain actors (i.e. reduce their capacity to engage in proscribed activity) or to send a signal about prevailing norms. It provides the basis for more nuanced assessments of the functioning and effectiveness of UN targeted sanctions, which are based on more precise descriptions of what they are actually intended to accomplish.

Plan of the book

The chapters in this book are based on an original comparative analysis of the entire universe of UN targeted sanctions imposed over the past twenty-five years. Since 1991, twenty-three different country sanctions regimes have been imposed by the UN Security Council, yielding a total of sixty-three distinct sanctions episodes (our core unit of analysis). As already described, the qualitative and quantitative databases were constructed from original, detailed country case studies that facilitated the systematic, comparative, assessment of the impacts and effectiveness of UN targeted sanctions. The book is not organized by country case studies, as is common in much of the sanctions literature.[20] Rather, each chapter draws on the extensive empirical material contained in the two comparative databases that have been constructed in the course of the project. Leading scholars of sanctions and seasoned policy practitioners, all members of the Targeted Sanctions Consortium, reflect comparatively across all twenty-three country regimes. This is the first time these two databases have been systematically and comprehensively examined and analysed.

In Chapter 2, Francesco Giumelli explores the literature on the purposes of sanctions, arguing that it is excessively focused on coercion as the principal purpose of sanctions. Drawing on his previous research concerning the three different purposes of sanctions, Giumelli distinguishes between coercion, constraint, and signalling as core purposes of sanctions, describes the approach taken by the Targeted Sanctions Consortium, and reflects on its adaptation of his categories. He details how the different purposes function and describes the distribution of purposes, the primary purposes of sanctions, and the targets of UN sanctions across the twenty-three cases. He stresses the importance of

[20] See especially D. Cortright and G. A. Lopez, *The Sanctions Decade: Assessing UN Strategies in the 1990s* (Boulder, CO: Lynne Rienner Publishers, 2000) or their subsequent volume, *Sanctions and the Search for Security: Challenges to UN Action* (Boulder, CO: Lynne Rienner Publishers, 2002).

identifying relevant constituencies for sending an effective signal and discusses how sanctions shape international norms. He also describes how the different purposes of sanctions are associated with different types of sanctions, norms signalled, and general objectives.

In Chapter 3, Michael Brzoska and George Lopez analyse the process of decision making at the UN Security Council and how it is related to the design of targeted sanctions. They discuss patterns of UN Security Council voting and explore the paradox that unanimity on the Council is not clearly associated with effective sanctions. They elaborate on recent developments in targeted sanctions that target leadership to protect civilians and democracy and draw on the comparative databases to explore the relationship between types of sanctions, types of targets, and sanctions effectiveness.

The contextual setting of UN targeted sanctions is explored in Chapter 4, where Paul Bentall examines the relationship between UN sanctions and other policy instruments, such as diplomacy, legal referrals, and the use of force. Bentall notes that sanctions are never used in isolation and develops a concept of policy weight to analyse the relative degree of reliance on sanctions, as opposed to other policy instruments. He finds a correlation between the number of UN sanctions and the number of other policy instruments employed, and he concludes with a discussion of how UN targeted sanctions interact with peacekeeping operations, the use of force, and legal referrals.

Andrea Charron and Clara Portela discuss the relationship between UN sanctions and sanctions imposed by regional organizations, particularly the African Union (AU) and the European Union (EU), in Chapter 5. They stress the importance of regional sanctions and the increased frequency with which these two regional organizations in particular impose sanctions of their own, emphasizing that sanctions are not exclusively a policy tool used by "the West". Charron and Portela describe the general division of labour between the UN and regional organizations. While the majority of UN sanctions are focused on resolving armed conflicts, the AU concentrates on using sanctions against parties responsible for non-constitutional changes of government. The AU routinely imposes sanctions on its own members, and they are often more extensive in scope than UN targeted sanctions. The EU, by contrast, concentrates on supporting democracy, rule of law, and human rights, particularly in countries outside of Europe.

In Chapter 6, Alix Boucher and Caty Clement describe the multiple challenges of coordination within the UN system and beyond. They distinguish among the different objectives of UN targeted sanctions and argue that not all sanctions regimes are created equally. The UN Security Council appears to be more concerned with counter-terrorism and non-proliferation than with armed conflict, which is reflected in UN internal resource allocations. They explore the application of targeted sanctions to support peace processes and discuss the wide range and large number of different UN actors involved in conflict cases, arguing for greater coordination between UN sanctions committees and other UN bodies.

Chapter 7 focuses on the implementation of UN targeted sanctions. Rico Carisch and Loraine Rickard-Martin discuss indicators of implementation at both international and national levels. Explaining how the expansion of sanctions actors, instruments, and mandates add complexity and makes more difficult effective implementation of UN sanctions, they analyse how greater technical skills and expertise are required. Recommendations for improved coordination and sharing of information among actors, enhanced awareness and understanding of mutually reinforcing roles, proactive assistance from the Secretariat to support implementation functions of sanctions committees and Panels of Experts, capacity assistance for Member States and other actors, as well as a systematic and comprehensive review of sanctions implementation are ways in which implementation of UN targeted sanctions can be strengthened.

Kimberly Elliott analyses the direct and indirect impacts of targeted sanctions in Chapter 8. Elliott discusses the principal types of impact, differentiating between economic, political, and psychological impacts of the sanctions. She relates different types of targeted sanctions to anticipated impacts, paying particular attention to the degree of discrimination of different targeted sanctions. She also discusses how the challenges of implementation can affect the level of impact (including the ease of evasion of sanctions). Elliott explores the difficulties of determining the contribution of targeted sanctions to broad impacts and concludes with a discussion of the challenges of keeping targeted sanctions targeted.

In Chapter 9, Mikael Eriksson discusses the unintended consequences of UN targeted sanctions. He explores how to think about unintended consequences and differentiates between negative and positive unintended consequences. Following a review of the literature on unintended consequences, Eriksson examines data on different types of unintended consequences, including some of the counter-intuitive findings from the quantitative database. He develops a framework for assessing unintended consequences, discusses human rights implications, provides examples of institutional learning, and offers suggestions for future research.

Chapter 10, by the volume's editors, Thomas J. Biersteker, Marcos Tourinho, and Sue Eckert, proposes a new way to think about evaluating the effectiveness of UN targeted sanctions. Following a review of conventional approaches in the literature, they describe the methodological innovations of the TSC approach to the analysis of sanctions effectiveness, in which effectiveness is a function of policy outcome and UN sanctions contribution to that outcome. They argue that it is important to differentiate among the different purposes of sanctions and elaborate on the TSC findings that UN targeted sanctions are more effective in constraining and signalling than they are in coercing a change in behaviour of the target. They conclude with suggestions that future evaluations of sanctions effectiveness also take both unintended consequences and costs of implementation into consideration.

Peter Wallensteen examines institutional learning in targeted sanctions in Chapter 11. Wallensteen describes broad trends in the effectiveness of UN targeted sanctions over time, concluding that there is some evidence of improved effectiveness for each of the principal purpose of sanctions. He also considers trends within individual country sanctions regimes and observes that effectiveness tends to increase over time. Wallensteen also surveys institutional improvements that have taken place in UN processes of decision making, implementation, and monitoring over time.

Finally, Chapter 12 concludes with a discussion of what has been learned through the TSC framework and analysis of how sanctions work, notes contemporary challenges, and proposes policy recommendations as well as potential areas for future research.

This edited volume is the first and most comprehensive scholarly product of a more than five-year collaborative project. In the chapters that follow, members of the Targeted Sanctions Consortium from both the policy and scholarly worlds make extensive use of the two large databases that have been created as a result of this research. They draw on both the quantitative data assembled about each country sanctions regime and each episode within them for comparative statistics, and also on the qualitative database of detailed, narrative summaries of each of the cases and case episodes for illustrative examples. The qualitative database is being published in a separate volume and is also available in SanctionsApp.[21]

While the quantitative data enable systematic comparison, the qualitative data contain rich narrative information drawn upon by our authors throughout the volume. Appendix 1 at the conclusion of this volume contains a list of all of the UN targeted sanctions country regimes in chronological order and identifies each episode within them. When authors make reference to a country sanctions regime, they describe it

---

[21] T. Biersteker, S. Eckert, Z. Hudáková, and M. Tourinho, *SanctionsApp*, Computer software, *Apple App Store*, 21 June 2013.

in terms of country name, such as the Iran sanctions or the sanctions on Al-Qaida. When they make reference to a specific episode of a country regime, it is either episode x or EPx of a particular country sanctions regime. If there are different sanctions regimes imposed on the same country over time, such as in the cases of the former Yugoslavia, Libya, and Sudan, they are differentiated by decade or purpose of the sanctions, such as Sudan in the 1990s or Sudan over Darfur, or Libya in the 1990s versus Libya in 2011.

2   The purposes of targeted sanctions

Francesco Giumelli

In order to deal with security challenges, the Security Council of the United Nations has resorted to sanctions on numerous occasions in recent years ranging from conflict resolution to human rights promotion.[1] At the same time, sanctions have evolved from a comprehensive form, namely complete trade embargoes, to a more limited form wherein targets of sanctions are often individuals and non-state entities.[2] The intense activity by the Council has brought new interest in understanding how sanctions work and what they are supposed to achieve, but the scholarly and policy debate remains focused on whether sanctions should attempt to change the behaviour of targets,[3] to contribute to a behavioural change,[4] and to achieve political objectives.[5]

The scholarly and policy debate has also not adequately explained the continued use of sanctions, despite the fact that the perception of this foreign policy instrument was often negative. David Baldwin suggested that the problem lay with scholars talking about different things, rather than talking about the sanctions themselves.[6] The diversification in the use of targeted sanctions further underscores the need for more useful

---

[1] This was also noted in D. Cortright and G. A. Lopez, *The Sanctions Decade: Assessing UN Strategies in the 1990s* (Boulder, CO: Lynne Rienner Publishers, 2000).

[2] D. Cortright and G. A. Lopez, *Smart Sanctions: Targeting Economic Statecraft* (Lanham, MD: Rowman & Littlefield Publishers, 2002).

[3] R. A. Pape, 'Why Economic Sanctions Do Not Work', *International Security* 22 (1997), pp. 90–136; D. A. Baldwin and R. A. Pape 'Why Economic Sanctions Still Do Not Work', *International Security*, 23 (1998), pp. 189–98.

[4] G. C. Hufbauer, J. J. Schott, and K. A. Elliott, *Economic Sanctions Reconsidered*, 2nd edn (Washington, DC: Peterson Institute for International Economics, 1990); G. C. Hufbauer et al., *Economic Sanctions Reconsidered*, 3rd edn (Washington, DC: Peterson Institute for International Economics, 2007).

[5] D. Cortright and G. A. Lopez, *Economic Sanctions: Panacea or Peacebuilding in a Post-Cold War World?* (Boulder, CO: Westview Press, 1995); J. F. Blanchard and N. M. Ripsman, 'Asking the Right Question: When Do Economic Sanctions Work Best?', *Security Studies*, 9 (1999), pp. 219–53; J. Hovi, R. Huseby, and D. F. Sprinz, 'When Do (Imposed) Economic Sanctions Work?', *World Politics*, 57 (2005), pp. 479–99.

[6] D. A. Baldwin, 'The Sanctions Debate and the Logic of Choice', *International Security*, 24 (1999/2000), pp. 80–107.

analytical tools, confirmed by the fact that the measures imposed on Al-Qaida were analysed in ways essentially similar to the sanctions applied to North Korea, Libya, or Sudan. In fact, each of these sanctions regimes has very specific characteristics that are scarcely engaged in the literature. If we are to understand sanctions, the reasons behind their imposition need to be clear: namely, what are the different purposes of sanctions?

This chapter intends to investigate the purposes of targeted sanctions and to outline a typology that allows for a more precise comparison across time and space. In this work, 'purpose' refers specifically to the way in which sanctions intend to influence targets, which differs from its objective, that is the policy goal senders broadly want to achieve. The behavioural change criterion – the idea that sanctions are imposed to change the behaviour of targets – still dominates the debate. Sanctions are expected to impose an economic burden on targets, prompting them to change their behaviour in order to avoid the costs of sanctions. Although this expectation was termed the 'naïve theory of sanctions' by Johan Galtung already in 1967, it still drives much of the debate about sanctions today.[7] This pain-gain approach, namely the belief that targets would want to avoid the economic pain imposed by sanctions in exchange for the political gains sought by the senders, would be useful if all sanctions imposed economic costs and there was always something that targets could do to please senders, but this is often not the case. When sanctions do not have material impact, then they are often disregarded as symbolic, as if the only burden were economic. Moreover, it is often assumed that a sanctioning event concerns only senders and targets, while the larger audience is often forgotten. In a nutshell, the pain-gain approach (or the 'naïve theory') oversimplifies sanctions regimes, and alternative attempts to deal with this shortcoming have fallen short of providing useful analytical tools.[8]

The Targeted Sanctions Consortium builds upon and adapts a framework I introduced to look at how sanctions can influence their targets, with multiple and differing purposes, through coercion, constraint, and signal/stigmatization.[9] As described in Chapter 1, *coercion* is the attempt by sanctions to change the behaviour of targets, *constraint* is the effort to reduce the capacity of targets to achieve their objectives (through restricting access to essential resources), and *signalling/stigmatization* occurs

---

[7] J. Galtung, 'On the Effects of International Economic Sanctions: With Examples from the Case of Rhodesia', *World Politics*, 19 (1967), pp. 378–416.
[8] Baldwin, 'The Sanctions Debate and the Logic of Choice'; Hufbauer, Schott, and Elliott, *Economic Sanctions Reconsidered*; Hufbauer et al., *Economic Sanctions Reconsidered*.
[9] F. Giumelli, *Coercing, Constraining and Signaling. Explaining UN and EU Sanctions after the Cold War* (Colchester: ECPR Press, 2011).

when sanctions signal targets (and the broader international community) about international norms. The multipurpose framework applied to the TSC empirical database helps to shed light on a number of aspects that have so far been unexplored. For instance, besides appreciating the very existence of different purposes, coercion, constraint, and signalling/stigmatization play different roles according to the specific crisis and context in which they are applied, the norm justifying their imposition, and the design of the sanctions measures.

The application of the *coerce, constrain, and signal* framework contributes to the creation of an improved common ground for discussion in the sanctions field. This is evident if one looks at the effectiveness debate in the 1990s, when Hufbauer, Schott, and Elliot and Pape discussed the effectiveness of international sanctions in the pages of the journal *International Security*. There, they maintained that sanctions 'worked' or 'did not work' based on very different measures of success. While Hufbauer, Schott, and Elliot were referring to different purposes of sanctions, Pape focused exclusively on the coercive one, or as stated by Baldwin, they were talking about different things. The tripartite conceptualization narrows the gap between the two approaches and sheds light on the different purposes of sanctions.

This chapter is divided in four sections. First, the theoretical framework is explained and illustrated, with the purposes of coercion, constraint, and signalling/stigmatization discussed at length. The second part describes the TSC database and how the different purposes of sanctions are distributed empirically. The third part analyses the connections between the purpose of sanctions and a number of other relevant aspects of crises such as the type of conflict, the norms, and the type of sanctions involved. Finally, the conclusion summarizes the main argument of the chapter, reiterates the importance of moving forward in the sanctions debate, and highlights the TSC project's role in this endeavour.

The purpose of sanctions: coerce, constrain, and signal

The imposition of sanctions is most often described as an attempt by the sender to change undesired policy behaviour of the target through the infliction of some economic pain. This simplification has been often criticized because sanctions episodes have a degree of complexity that goes well beyond the bilateral relations between senders and targets. Yet, there has been a lack of theoretical development towards the creation of frameworks that would permit more precise comparisons across time and space.

Johan Galtung's 1967 characterization of sanctions identified the shortcomings of looking at sanctions through the lenses of the pain-gain approach. He defined this causal link as 'naïve' because the imposition of sanctions triggers a number of inadvertent effects which can strengthen targets, such as 'adaptation to sacrifice, restructuring the economy to absorb the shock, smuggling [and the fact that] the collectivity is threatened, that there is no identification with the attacker, and that there is a firm belief in one's own values'.[10] Galtung famously labelled these latter elements the 'rally-around-the-flag' effect.

Although attempts were made in the scholarly literature to address the issues raised by Galtung, an alternative paradigm has yet to replace the dominant understanding of sanctions heavily influenced by the behavioural change paradigm.[11] In the literature, important arguments have been made about the multiple policy objectives of sanctions, the need to look at what sanctions are intended to accomplish,[12] and the way they influence targets.[13] For instance, James Lindsay's work represents an important attempt to elaborate a typology of sanctions objectives by discriminating among five categories of aims: compliance, subversion, deterrence, international, and domestic symbolism.[14] Other classifications relate to sanctions as denial instruments,[15] namely to deny goods or benefits to targets; as symbolic instruments[16] imposed to uphold international norms; and as punitive measures for undesirable

[10] Galtung, 'On the Effects of International Economic Sanctions: With Examples from the Case of Rhodesia', p. 393.

[11] F. Giumelli, 'How EU Sanctions Work: a New Narrative', in *Chaillot Paper* (Paris: EU Institute for Security Studies, 2013).

[12] J. Lindsay, 'Trade Sanctions as Policy Instruments: a Re-examination', *International Studies Quarterly*, 30 (1986), pp. 153–73; L. J. Brady, 'The Utility of Economic Sanctions as a Policy Instrument', in D. Layton-Brown (ed.), *The Utility of International Economic Sanctions* (New York: St. Martin's Press, 1987); K. R. Nossal, 'International Sanctions as International Punishment', *International Organization*, 43 (1989), pp. 301–22.

[13] J. Barber, 'Economic Sanctions as a Policy Instrument', *International Affairs*, 55 (1979), pp. 368–70; A. L. George, D. K. Hall, and W. E. Simons, *The Limits of Coercive Diplomacy; Laos, Cuba, Vietnam* (Boston, MA: Little Brown, 1971), p. xi; R. Haass, *Economic Sanctions and American Diplomacy* (New York: Council on Foreign Relations, 1998); W. H. Kaempfer and A. D. Lowenberg, *International Economic Sanctions: a Public Choice Perspective* (Boulder, CO: Westview, 1992), p. 7; V. L. Schwebach, 'Sanctions as Signals: A Line in the Sand or a Lack of Resolve?', in S. Chan and C. A. Drury (eds.), *Sanctions as Economic Statecraft: Theory and Practice* (Basingstoke: McMillan Press, 2000), p. 203.

[14] Lindsay, 'Trade Sanctions as Policy Instruments: A Re-Examination'.

[15] Barber, 'Economic Sanctions as a Policy Instrument'.

[16] Schwebach, 'Sanctions as Signals: A Line in the Sand or a Lack of Resolve?'; J. Fearon, 'Signalling Foreign Policy Interests: Tying Hands versus Sinking Costs', *The Journal of Conflict Resolution*, 41 (1997), pp. 68–90.

behaviours.[17] While sanctions can indeed serve these objectives, either directly or indirectly, there were limitations in how these frameworks operationalized the analysis of sanctions in comparative terms. In particular, categories were established based on different levels of analysis, combining political objectives (subversion and symbolism) with the way in which sanctions attempt to influence targets (deterrence and compliance). In addition, the fact that the signalling dimension was relegated to 'symbolism' underplays the importance of actions in creating and producing norms in the international system. In this sense, it is unclear if these approaches truly replaced the pain-gain narrative so often applied in academic and wider policy debates.

The debate on whether sanctions are effective suffers from the same fallacies. On the one hand, there are scholars who look at whether targets change their behaviour after sanctions have been imposed, which itself is a derivation of the pain-gain approach. On the other, the behavioural change criterion is seen as oversimplifying the effectiveness debate and implies that sanctions should be assessed in other ways, but an overall framework has not emerged before now.

Initially, the 'naïve' approach contributed to the negative perception of sanctions as foreign policy tools. It was not unusual to find studies on sanctions based on the presumption that sanctions do not work.[18] This general wisdom was challenged by Hufbauer, Schott, and Elliot with their database of 115 cases suggesting that sanctions were effective 34 per cent of the time.[19] The third edition of their study published in 2007 confirmed the overall assessment of eighty cases of sanctions out of 211 being effective.[20] While some argue that Hufbauer, Schott, and Elliot underestimated the sanctions effectiveness rate since they did not consider sanctions that were threatened but not imposed which could make targets change their behaviour before sanctions were adopted,[21] others maintain that a more accurate analysis of the data set would lead to a less than 5 per cent effectiveness rate.[22]

[17] Nossal, 'International Sanctions as International Punishment'.
[18] For reviews, see D. W. Drezner, 'The Hidden Hand of Economic Coercion', *International Organization*, 57 (2003), pp. 10–1; E. S. Rogers, 'Using Economic Sanctions to Control Regional Conflicts', *Security Studies*, 5 (1996), pp. 43–72; Baldwin, 'The Sanctions Debate and the Logic of Choice'; M. P. Doxey, *International Sanctions in Contemporary Perspective* (Basingstoke: Macmillan, 1987), p. 92.
[19] Hufbauer, Schott, and Elliott, *Economic Sanctions Reconsidered*.
[20] Hufbauer et al., *Economic Sanctions Reconsidered*.
[21] Drezner, 'The Hidden Hand of Economic Coercion'.
[22] Pape, 'Why Economic Sanctions Do Not Work'; Pape 'Why Economic Sanctions Still Do Not Work'; K. A. Elliott, 'The Sanctions Glass: Half Full or Completely Empty?', *International Security*, 23 (1998), pp. 50–65.

Others departed from the behavioural change approach and rather focused on the conditions under which sanctions are effective. This group, admittedly diverse, maintain that while sanctions may not be a *panacea* to solve international disputes, they can be useful under certain conditions.[23] Hovi, Huseby, and Sprinz suggest that sanctions work only when the negotiation process fails because the target underestimates the real intention of the sender,[24] and Blanchard and Ripsman believe that the effectiveness of sanctions is linked to the cost of non-compliance: if compliance is more harmful than non-compliance, then the target is not likely to yield.[25] In more general terms, others have maintained that sanctions can achieve only limited results as tools of foreign policy as '[we cannot ask] the pistol to inflict damage of which only the cannon is capable'.[26]

A number of analyses challenge the behavioural change approach by looking at other aspects of sanction cases that go beyond the direct relationship between senders and targets. Attention has been paid to the need of imposing sanctions as an effort from the sender side to satisfy the demands arising from domestic constituencies, indicating that sanctioning is a foreign policy instrument used to 'feel good' rather than to 'do good'.[27] Others have considered the domestic impacts of sanctions, reflecting on what sanctions cause in the targeted society[28] and in terms of human rights violations.[29]

A theoretical framework to supplant or at least supplement the pain-gain approach was needed to compare cases of sanctions across time and space, but the complexities of the problem have hindered the development of analytical tools that would yield new explanatory power. An effective starting point would be to acknowledge that not all sanctions are equal, so that different sanctions would lead to different expectations

---

[23] Hovi, Huseby, and Sprinz, 'When Do (Imposed) Economic Sanctions Work?'; Blanchard and Ripsman, 'Asking the Right Question: When Do Economic Sanctions Work Best?'; Cortright and Lopez, *Economic Sanctions: Panacea or Peacebuilding in a Post-Cold War World?*.

[24] Hovi, Huseby, and Sprinz, 'When Do (Imposed) Economic Sanctions Work?', p. 480.

[25] Blanchard and Ripsman, 'Asking the Right Question: When Do Economic Sanctions Work Best?', p. 225.

[26] M. S. Daoudi and M. S. Dajani, *Economic Sanctions: Ideas and Experience* (London: Routledge and Kegan Paul, 1983), p. 168.

[27] E. H. Preeg, *Feeling Good or Doing Good with Sanctions: Unilateral Economic Sanctions and the US National Interest* (Washington, DC: Center for Strategic & International Studies, 1999).

[28] E. D. Gibbons, *Sanctions in Haiti: Human Rights and Democracy under Assault* (Westport, CT: Praeger, 1999); M. B. Pedersen, *Promoting Human Rights in Burma. A Critique of Western Sanctions Policy* (Plymouth: Rowman & Littlefield Publishers, 2008).

[29] T. G. Weiss et. al., *Political Gain and Civilian Pain: Humanitarian Impacts of Economic Sanctions* (Lanham: Rowman & Littlefield Publishers, 1997).

of what they can achieve under specific conditions. For instance, the behavioural change approach implies that targets change their behaviour to avoid bearing the material costs imposed by sanctions, but this view contains three fundamental fallacies. First, it takes for granted that targets are capable of complying with the demands associated with sanctions. For instance, the Taliban in Afghanistan and Qadhafi in Libya arguably could not satisfy the demands of the international community without terminating their political activity. Second, sanctions are presumed to have a material impact so targets would change their behaviour, but the case of Lebanon clearly shows that sanctions can be imposed with no material impact. Third, the sole objective of sanctions is to change the behaviour of targets. These three assumptions are rarely all present or valid at the time of sanctions imposition. Senders often formulate demands that cannot be met by targets, and sanctions do not always have a direct material impact on targets, but this does not necessarily translate into ineffective sanctions.

Instead, the empirical data show that sanctions can and do acquire very different forms, considering their type (travel bans, economic restrictions, etc.), their impacts, and the overall objective of their imposition, among many other issues analysed in this volume. Thus, there was a need for concepts and analytical instruments powerful enough to consider these complexities and embark on a more precise discussion about what sanctions are for and, consequently, how they can and should be evaluated.

Introducing the TSC approach to the purposes of sanctions

One of the unresolved problems in the scholarly literature is how to distinguish the different purposes of sanctions. The typology adopted by the Targeted Sanctions Consortium uses the word 'purpose' instead of objective with the intent of referring to what sanctions are supposed to do (how they influence targets) as opposed to the political objective of senders, which is what senders want to achieve by using all policy instruments at their disposal. In brief, senders impose sanctions to coerce, constrain, or signal/stigmatize targets and audiences in international relations. This classification is derived from the literature on power. Therefore, a brief discussion on how the concept of power is used precedes an overall presentation on what coercing, constraining, and signalling mean in the use of UN targeted sanctions.

The decision to impose sanctions is an exercise of power, which can be implemented differently and defined in the context of different purposes (and distinct functioning logics). Power is exercised in three primary ways.[30] First, power can be considered in the classic definition as A makes B do whatever B would not do otherwise. Taken directly from the works of Dahl, Baldwin, and Lasswell and Kaplan,[31] this concept of power differentiates between power and influence, an important distinction useful to this analysis. The second dimension of power captures the ability to preclude certain outcomes (the so-called 'agenda-setting power' outlined by Bachrach and Baratz).[32] Finally, the third dimension of power refers to the situations in which there is no open conflict, but power would affect the potential causes of conflicts to prevent them from erupting. In other words, this dimension of power works with a different internal logic than the previous two, since it neither coerces an actor to act in a specific way nor does it modify their agenda, but rather it shapes the interests and the knowledge of the actors.[33]

The TSC project looks at sanctions by considering the multiple and differing purposes of targeted sanctions. Sanctions can influence targets through coercion, constraint, and signalling, elaborating on the tri-dimensional conceptualization of power as mentioned above.[34] These three aspects of power in international relations can be defined as winning conflicts, limiting alternatives, and shaping norms – sanctions can coerce ('win conflicts'), constrain ('limit alternatives'), and signal ('shape norms') in international relations.

The first is labelled as *coercive* because the objective is to change the behaviour of targets by imposing a cost on some misconduct in order to affect targets' costs/benefits calculation in a way that change of behaviour becomes more likely.

The second, identified as *constraining*, acts by altering the possibilities available to targets by shaping their agenda through making it more difficult for the target to engage in proscribed activities (through con-straining access to essential resources such as funds, arms, sensitive goods, thereby raising costs and forcing changes in strategy).

---

[30] F. Berenskoetter and M. Williams (eds.), *Power in World Politics* (London, New York: Routledge, 2007), pp. 1–22.

[31] R. Dahl, *Who Governs? Democracy and Power in an American City* (New Haven: Yale University Press, 1961); D. A. Baldwin, 'Power and International Relations', in W. Carlsnaes, T. Risse and B. A. Simmons (eds.), *Handbook of International Relations* (Thousand Oaks, CA: SAGE Publications, 2013), pp. 273–97; Harold Lasswell and Abraham Kaplan, *Power and Society: A Framework for Political Inquiry* (New Haven: Yale University Press, 1950).

[32] Berenskoetter and Williams, *Power in World Politics*, p. 7.

[33] M. Barnett and R. Duvall (eds.), *Power in Global Governance* (Cambridge: Cambridge University Press, 2005).

[34] Giumelli, *Coercing, Constraining and Signaling. Explaining UN and EU Sanctions after the Cold War*.

Finally, sanctions contribute to shape international norms, as the very decision to resort to sanctions reinforces the value of norms that discipline behaviours of actors in the international system. Signals can be directed at targets and audiences, either domestic or international, and stigmatize or isolate targets for violating international norms.

There have been other attempts to formulate typologies of how sanctions influence targets, but not all of these three aspects were present. For instance, dichotomous typologies were elaborated maintaining that sanctions can pursue substantive or symbolic goals[35] and expressive or instrumental motives.[36] A tripartite typology of coercing, denying, and punishing has been employed in the study of air power,[37] representing a useful model for the analysis of sanctions. The three forms of power – coercing, constraining, and signalling – had not been considered and included in a single typology until recently.

Coercive sanctions refer to cases of restrictive measures imposed to increase the probability of making a target behave in a way that it would not otherwise do. In other words, the sender intends to change the behaviour of the target and sanctions attach a cost to certain acts in order to affect the target's costs/benefits calculation. In this category, anticipated positive outcomes include actual behavioural change of the target, greater probabilities of a behavioural change, and the improvement of the bargaining position of the sender versus the target. Coercion contains a voluntary aspect in the sense that targets' compliance with senders' demands should not threaten their political (and sometimes physical) existence. Targets should be able to comply with the demands placed on them, and should do so because they deem it more preferable than non-compliance.

Constraining sanctions attempt to thwart a target's ability to pursue its policy. Whereas coercive sanctions require action to meet demands of the sender, constraining sanctions do not require a target to do something, but rather are intended to impede its objectives. Coercive sanctions aim at convincing the target that a specific course of action is in its best interest, while constraining sanctions lack the persuasive element and seek to limit the options available to targets. In other words, if coercive sanctions are successful, targets do not embark in unwanted behaviour despite having

---

[35] Doxey, *International Sanctions in Contemporary Perspective*, p. 10; D. Shambaugh, E. Sandschneider, and Z. Hong (eds.), *China-Europe Relations. Perceptions, Policies and Prospects* (London, New York: Routledge, 2007), p. 13.
[36] Galtung, 'On the Effects of International Economic Sanctions: With Examples From the Case of Rhodesia', p. 412.
[37] R. A. Pape, *Bombing to Win: Air Power and Coercion in War* (Ithaca, NY: Cornell University Press, 1996).

the capabilities to do so, while if constraining sanctions are successful, then targets cannot embark in unwanted behaviour because they do not have the capabilities any longer. In this category, expected positive outcomes include slowing of the target's plans, increasing the costs, or lowering the marginal utility gained, and a change of strategy from the target. In contrast to coercive sanctions, constraining sanctions are often imposed when there is no space for negotiations, and the final objective is to detain, weaken, or defeat targets. This is, for instance, the case of terrorist groups or of dictators who commit massive human rights violations – cases in which senders would be less willing to compromise or accept any negotiations with targets. When looking at the evolution from comprehensive to targeted sanctions, constraining sanctions are increasingly employed in cases where targets are not willing to comply with established international norms. As in national legal systems, laws prohibiting certain forms of behaviour are not ineffective just because crimes continue to be committed. In fact, such laws limit unacceptable behaviour by complicating and making more difficult actions that are contrary to the rules, even though such acts may still occur. Similarly, targeted sanctions are not ineffective because terrorist attacks still occur or because civil wars do not end, but they are useful and also effective in limiting the capabilities of the target to act.

Finally, signalling sanctions refer to the communicative function performed by the very act of resorting to sanctions. This category has often been presented as a residual one in the analysis of sanctions, but this study has taken a different standpoint on it. Signalling incorporates both signalizing and stigmatizing. Sanctions send signals to targets, and they are placed in this category because they do not impose a direct material cost on targets and therefore function according to a different logic. However, sanctioning is also an act of stigmatization that reinforces international norms. The TSC project identifies norms motivating the imposition of sanctions, identifying those applying to each sanctions episode, and determining which is most important. These norms include proscriptions against nuclear proliferation, terrorism, engaging in war or armed conflict, non-constitutional change in government, and human rights violations (such as the use of child soldiers, treatment of minorities, gender-based violence, and ethnic cleansing). They also include prescriptions for the protection of civilians under R2P, the authority of the UN Security Council, the authority of regional arrangements, and improved governance (of natural resources and/or the security sector).

This category should be understood broadly, given the number of actors that are affected by the signals. Signalling sanctions may convey a message either to a domestic and/or an international audience since, for instance, senders may want to please a domestic constituency about a specific crisis, such as in the case of Haiti in the early 1990s. They may also simultaneously want to send a message to other international actors about what could be expected from the Security Council in similar cases, a concern evident in the non-proliferation cases. Here, effectiveness is determined by whether a message is sent and received, and by the social consequences imposed by other actors in the international system, regardless of how exactly targets behave.

This conceptualization was at the foundation of the qualitative advances in determining sanctions effectiveness developed by the TSC project. More is said in a later chapter of this volume on this aspect, but it would suffice here to say that sanctions effectiveness is measured in relation to these three dimensions, since concentrating on behavioural change alone would provide only a partial view of what sanctions can achieve. The three purposes of sanctions are not mutually exclusive, but they refer to different forms of power at play when sanctions are imposed.

The three purposes at work

The three purposes are often pursued simultaneously and 'may be directed simultaneously to more than one target, aiming for example at a rebel faction, as well as its key supporters and domestic constituencies in sanctions sending states'.[38] Considering the three purposes simultaneously is an important novelty in studying sanctions, as it recognizes that sanctions are indeed characterized by different dimensions and that the complexity and evolution of a situation can justify the persistence of multiple and changing purposes of sanctions. The different purposes at the same time can also be influencing different targets in different ways in order to, for instance, favour a specific political balance. This would be the case in post-conflict situations, when individuals and non-state entities are targeted to constrain their capacity to destabilize peace processes or be coerced to cooperate with a new regime. Valuable cases are the post-2003 situation in Iraq, when a list of over 300 targets was prepared by the Security Council in order to support the institution building efforts of the new government, but also in Côte d'Ivoire and in Liberia, where sanctions were kept in place to deter spoilers. Here the border between coercing and constraining is very thin.

---

[38] T. Biersteker, S. Eckert, M. Tourinho, and Z. Hudáková, *The Effectiveness of United Nations Targeted Sanctions: Findings from the Targeted Sanctions Consortium (TSC)* (Geneva: the Graduate Institute, 2013), p. 13.

Second, as described in Chapter 1, the TSC adopted the concept of 'episode', recognizing that broader country sanctions regimes could be composed of different phases, or episodes, which could have different purposes. This idea, combined with the distinction between three different purposes, helps to capture a dynamic of sanction cases that is crucial to understanding effectiveness.[39] Conditions under which the Security Council imposes sanctions change over time, therefore analysis should include multiple episodes to understand the dynamics of sanctions and their multiple and sometimes changing purposes over time. Using episodes as a unit of analysis permits a dynamic evaluation of sanctions and captures different phases of a conflict, when, for instance, signalling would be dominant during the initial episode, as in the case of Haiti, and coercion might be followed by constraining efforts after the UN Security Council realizes that there is little chance of a change of behaviour from the target.

The distinction between the different purposes of targeted sanctions is useful to clarify specific cases. In 1999, the UN imposed sanctions on the Taliban regime in an attempt to coerce it to extradite Osama bin Laden and associates for trial following the bombing of the US embassies in Kenya and Tanzania, and the Security Council subsequently decided to extend the sanctions to Al-Qaida members and associates the following year after the Taliban's refusal. This case describes well the rationale for distinguishing between the purposes of sanctions; the initial attempt was to *coerce* the Taliban to turn over bin Laden and his associates for trial, whereas the post-9/11 episodes (episodes three and four) were devoted to *constraining* the activities of Al-Qaida itself, since it was highly unlikely that they would be coerced by sanctions to change their behaviour.

A decade later, the UN Security Council separated the two regimes: one directed at terrorist activities of Al-Qaida (the fourth and current episode identified in the TSC project to date) and the other at the Taliban (establishing a new TSC country case regime in 2011). The reason for the split was that the Al-Qaida relationship with the Taliban had changed dramatically over the years, as had the UN's purposes in imposing sanctions on each of them. Al-Qaida sanctions remained roughly the same, that is, constrain supporters of the group from financing them through formal sector financial institutions, while the sanctions on the Taliban attempted to limit their ability to engage

---

[39] F. Giumelli, 'The Restrictive Measures of the European Union. Developing Analytical Categories to Understand Functions and Utility of EU Sanctions', *The International Spectator*, 45 (2010), pp. 131–44.; M. Eriksson, *Targeting Peace: Understanding UN and EU Targeted Sanctions* (Farnham, UK: Ashgate, 2011).

in hostile activities (constrain) and to coerce some of them to break away (the so-called 'good' Taliban) and consider joining the government in some kind of coalition arrangement in the post-2014 period. A similar differentiation took place in the listings in Liberia and Côte d'Ivoire, as the list included both individuals who could be willing to cooperate with the UN under specific conditions and others who had no intention to do so. These cases demonstrate the utility of a multi-purpose framework capturing how sanctions attempt to influence world events.

Another example would be to expect constraint to gain importance following a coercive phase of a sanctions regime. This is particularly evident in the cases where a conflict has moved into a post-conflict, peace-enforcement phase, as in Sierra Leone, Liberia, and possibly in Côte d'Ivoire. Also, between 2006 and 2010, sanctions were intended to coerce Teheran into compromise on its nuclear ambitions, but the Security Council's enhanced implementation and enforcement of sanctions shifted the primary purpose of sanctions to constraining the capacities of Iran to acquire components to advance its nuclear programme.

Acknowledging that sanctions can achieve different purposes also highlights that, if improperly designed, the different logics may work at cross purposes and lead to contradictory results. This occurred, for instance, in the initial phase of the UN sanctions on the military junta in Haiti, when the second round of sanctions was interpreted as the Council's inability to act due to lack of agreement among the permanent members. The initial sanctions in Angola and the arms embargo on Serbia could also be interpreted similarly, indicating that sanctions were imposed because of a lack of political will from the international community to intervene militarily. In the case of the former Yugoslavia in the 1990s, not only did the sanctions not stop the violence but they threatened the existence of the weaker party in the conflict. In such instances, signalling helped to undermine both the coercive and con-straining elements of the sanctions.

Coercive sanctions allowing wrongdoers to maintain positions of power may negatively affect the image of senders. For instance, delisted individuals in Afghanistan included former warlords. Although the Security Council intended to delist a few individuals for the sake of the overall stability of the country, by doing so, it ran the risk of being criticized for lifting sanctions too early or for negotiating with former Taliban. Constraining sanctions could also undermine the possibility of coercion, since a change of behaviour may become less likely when the denial of certain technology antagonizes the target and radicalizes parties in conflicts.

Table 2.1 *The different purposes of sanctions*

	Episodes	
Purpose	Frequency	%
Coerce a change of behaviour	50	79
Constrain a target's behaviour	59	94
Signal or stigmatize a target	63	100

The purposes of UN targeted sanctions: an empirical description

The descriptive overview of the TSC database confirms that sanctions are not always the same and the classification according to their purpose does capture an important variation in the use of UN targeted sanctions. The TSC database is composed of twenty-three country sanctions regimes, broken up into sixty-three case episodes, which include 296 variables per case. This chapter analyses the distinct, but often simultaneous, coercive, constraining, and signalling purposes by episode by examining the database according to this categorization (see Table 2.1).

The first noticeable element is the simultaneous presence of different purposes in all sixty-three sanctions episodes. Whereas sanctions used to be assessed by looking primarily at their coercive form of power, recognition of the potentially constraining and signalling intentions underscores that evaluation of sanctions' effectiveness needs to consider the variety of effects that imposing a travel ban, or a financial freeze, among others, could have on different targets.

The principal purpose of UN targeted sanctions episodes, in 56 per cent of the cases, turned out to be coercion. This is somewhat counterintuitive if compared with deductive reasoning and my previous research. In my previous analysis, I had reached the conclusion that constraining should be the most relevant purpose of the Security Council, because sanctions were commonly adopted when a crisis had reached intractable levels and negotiation had become impossible. Coercive sanctions are more likely when targets are clearly identified and when there is a plausible hope for a negotiated settlement, whereas constraining sanctions come into play usually when the parties cannot find an agreement and when stopping the violence becomes the primary concern. The TSC project has shown, however, that the Security Council's primary objective is to change the behaviour of targets in 56 per cent of the episodes, to constrain them in 41 per cent of the episodes, and to signal only in 3 per cent of the episodes. The low level of signalling as primary purpose does not weaken the typology; it actually confirms it. First, sanctions are considered an almost-hard policy instrument and their imposition nearly always involves a signalling dimension, even though it is not the primary purpose. The communicative dimension of signalling may be pursued with other policy instruments, such as active bilateral or regional diplomacy. The second reason is that there are sanctions imposed with the main purpose of signalling. This is an important finding as many would argue that sanctions are always imposed with the objective of changing the behaviour of targets. Having signalling sanctions in the data set challenges this assumption. It is difficult to determine the intentions of policymakers engaged in the complex decision-making processes of the United Nations. Agreement in the Security Council is dependent on P5 consensus, and resolutions are often the product of a political compromise. Nevertheless, the justifications they present in the texts of the Security Council resolutions give indications of their primary purposes. Even though it is rarely the primary purpose of sanctions, signalling is often accomplished by the *very act* of the Security Council in moving to address international crises. Table 2.2 summarizes the entries for this variable.

The multipurpose framework allows us to discriminate among the different targets of sanctions in the different episodes, and it provides us with some interesting insights. For instance, governments or government leaderships are targeted by coercive sanctions in 66 and 64 per cent of the case episodes, respectively, while rebel factions were targeted in 42 per cent of the cases. When sanctions are meant to constrain certain actors, the picture begins to change. While the government is still near the top of the list of targeted actors (at 51 per cent), the focus of sanctions also includes terrorist groups, family members, facilitators, and other individual targets. To this extent, there seems to be an open intent to

Table 2.2 *The principal purpose of sanctions*

Principal Purpose	Episodes	
	Frequency	%
Coerce	35	56
Constrain	26	41
Signal	2	3
Total	63	100

thwart the operability of certain ruling groups/elites by extending the circle of targets in order to undermine capabilities rather than to persuade governments and their leaders to change policy.

Finally, all sanctions involve a signalling component, but in this instance, while governments and government leaderships remain the main targets of signalling, regional and global constituencies also emerge as important targets of signalling (in 49 per cent and 43 per cent of the episodes, respectively). This is consistent with previous findings, as constituencies are targeted even though they are usually secondary targets. Sometimes this decision may be considered as ancillary to a complex strategy, but under certain conditions, signals by the Security Council to strengthen its legitimacy or to uphold norms may be of equal importance to changing the behaviour of certain actors. Table 2.3 summarizes the range of targets for coercion, constraining, and signalling sanctions.

A different picture emerges if primary targets are analysed. Primary targets of sanctions are predominantly governments, their leaders, and rebel factions, which is not surprising, considering the type of conflicts the Security Council usually addresses (described in more detail in Chapter 3). When constraining and signalling dimensions are considered, the Council tends not to discriminate between different parties, indicating a broader influence that sanctions can have beyond merely changing behaviour, but also in restricting access to crucial resources or creating a system of incentives to stabilize critical situations. It is also relevant that

Table 2.3 *Targets of sanctions*

	Purpose					
	Coercion (n=50)		Constraining (n=59)		Signalling (n=63)	
Sanctions Target	Frequency	%	Frequency	%	Frequency	%
Government	33	66	30	51	38	60
Government leadership	32	64	24	41	34	54
Rebel faction	21	42	26	44	27	43
All parties to the conflict	10	20	19	32	22	35
Terrorist group	2	4	8	14	8	13
Leadership family members	7	14	18	31	13	21
Facilitators of proscribed activity	11	22	21	36	22	35
Individual targets	18	36	31	53	30	48
Key regime supporters	5	10	9	15	11	17
Domestic constituencies	0	0	0	0	14	22
Regional constituencies	6	12	8	14	31	49
Global constituencies	1	2	1	2	27	43

Table 2.4 *Primary targets of sanctions*

Primary Sanctions Target	Purpose					
	Coerce		Constrain		Signal	
	Frequency	%	Frequency	%	Frequency	%
Government	17	34	4	7	10	16
Government leadership	14	28	17	29	12	19
Rebel faction	12	24	17	29	14	22
All parties to the conflict	5	10	15	25	9	14
Terrorist group	0	0	2	3	0	0
Facilitators of proscribed activity	0	0	2	3	2	3
Individual targets	0	0	1	2	0	0
Domestic constituencies	0	0	0	0	1	2
Regional constituencies	2	4	1	2	8	13
Global constituencies	0	0	0	0	7	11
Total	**50**	**100**	**59**	**100**	**63**	**100**

wider audiences (such as regional constituencies) may be primary targets of signalling sanctions. This implies two things: first, audiences are important because the effects of sanctions go beyond the relationship between senders and targets; they also contribute to determining acceptable standards of behaviour in international affairs. Second, if signals matter, then the threat of imposing sanctions can play an important role and observing audiences is important in this assessment. Table 2.4 indicates the primary targets of UN sanctions.

Further affirmation of the importance of signalling emerges from the TSC's identification of the norms articulated in Security Council resolutions imposing sanctions, as already described in detail Chapter 1. The analysis of the TSC database indicates that the framework adds analytical quality to existing approaches to sanctions. Looking at the different ways in which sanctions influence their targets and the fate of international events contributes to closing the gap between flawed assessments of the effectiveness of sanctions and their increasing use by the Security Council in the recent past. Enhanced analytical value also produces more nuanced policy expectations, thanks to the acknowledgement that sanctions can take different forms and play different roles under different circumstances.

The three purposes in context

Understanding the multiple purposes of sanctions is only the first step towards a greater comprehension of how the foreign policy instrument works. The categories are even more useful if we consider the three purposes contextually, including the interplay with other policy instruments, the role of sanctions within the range of foreign policy tools senders possess, and the relationship between the influence on targets and the norms supported by the imposition of sanctions.

First, purposes should be related to the larger policy objectives. It should be noted that there are only two cases, Lebanon and Guinea-Bissau, in which signalling is the principal purpose of sanctions, the first involving counterterrorism, and the second opposition to a non-constitutional change of government. The coercive aspect in civil wars focuses on parties not cooperating with the international community or negotiated peace agreements, so the Security Council's purpose is to coerce targets to 'fall back in line'. These cases include Angola, Côte d'Ivoire, the DRC, and Libya. Meanwhile, constraint may be used to prevent or undermine spoilers from prolonging violence and undermining democratic processes. In twenty-six episodes where constraint was the principal purpose, the objective of the Security Council was to eliminate defiance by preventing certain actors from operating and engaging in proscribed activities. Sanctions episodes imposed against Liberia, Somalia, Côte d'Ivoire, and the Former Republic of Yugoslavia fall under this category. Coercion, which is the principal purpose in thirty-five episodes, is slightly more often applied than constraint for non-proliferation (Iran and North-Korea) and counterterrorism (Al-Qaida, Libya, and Sudan). If we analyse the objective of opposing non-constitutional change of government, however, coercion is the principal purpose in two-thirds of the case episodes, as shown in Table 2.5

Table 2.5 *Principal purpose and primary objective*

Primary Objective	Principal purpose			Total
	Coerce	Constrain	Signal	
Non-proliferation	5	2	0	7
Counterterrorism	7	2	0	9
Armed conflict (cease hostilities, negotiation of settlement, peace enforcement, support peace building)	18	19	0	37
Democracy support	4	1	1	6
Good governance, human rights, humanitarian relief, or support judicial process	0	1	1	2
Protection of civilians	1	1	0	2
Total	35	26	2	63

Table 2.6 *Principal purpose and sanctions type*

Sanctions Type	Principal purpose		
	Coerce	Constrain	Signal
Individual (47)	25	20	2
Diplomatic (13)	12	1	0
Sectoral (60)	34	26	0
Commodity (26)	14	12	0
Financial sector (6)	2	4	0

Looking at the type of sanctions imposed is useful as it shows that both coercion and constraint rely on similar means to accomplish their results with individual, sectoral, and commodity sanctions. Comprehensive sanctions were used in three instances only (FRY episode 2, Haiti episodes 4 and 5) and have not been imposed by the UN since 1994.

Coercive sanctions appear to make more elaborate use of individual, sectoral, and commodity sanctions. The three types of sanctions were used in Angola (episodes 2, 3, and 4); Liberia (episodes 2 and 3); Sierra Leone (episode 1); Côte d'Ivoire (episodes 3 and 4); and Al-Qaida/Taliban (AQT) (episode 2). Individual and sectoral sanctions appear more frequently than others in the database, not only when it comes to coercive sanctions but also in the case of constraining ones. Sectoral sanctions were always imposed in the twenty-six episodes when constraint was the principal purpose (for instance in Somalia episodes 1, 2, and 5; Rwanda episode 2; Iraq episode 1 and 2; and Iran episode 4), whereas individual sanctions were imposed in twenty episodes (among others, Sierra Leone episodes 3, 4, and 5; AQT episodes 3 and 4; DRC episode 3; and DPRK episode 2). Financial sector sanctions were imposed only on six occasions (Somalia four and five, Iran four, DPRK three, Libya in 2011 two and three). Table 2.6 presents the summary of the distribution of purpose with sanctions type.

A quick look at the underlying norms supported by UN sanctions suggests that the normative aspect is prevalent in many sanctions cases. Both coercion and constraint are used to enforce the prohibition of war/armed conflict (Angola, Côte d'Ivoire, DRC, and Liberia among others), and to promote democracy, good governance, and human rights (for instance, in Côte d'Ivoire, Haiti, and Libya in 2011). The TSC database indicates that non-proliferation, Responsibility to Protect, and the authority of the Security Council lay in the lower part of the rankings, if

Table 2.7 *Principal purpose and norms signalled*

Norm Signalled	Principal purpose		
	Coerce (35)	Constrain (26)	Signal (2)
Non-proliferation (8)	5	3	0
Counterterrorism (15)	8	7	0
Prohibition of war/armed conflict (36)	19	17	0
Support democracy/Oppose non-constitutional change of government (15)	8	6	1
Improve governance (9)	3	6	0
Human rights (28)	11	17	0
Protect population under R2P (4)	1	3	0
Authority of the UN Security Council (7)	3	4	0
Authority of regional arrangements (23)	10	12	1
Support judicial process (21)	11	9	1

we consider both coercion and constraint (Côte d'Ivoire, DRC, Libya in 2011, Liberia, and Sierra Leone), which appear to have a similar frequency across the database as shown in Table 2.7.

One of the weaknesses in previous analyses of sanctions is that they overlooked the larger context, not only in relation to the type of crisis but also in relation to knowing whether sanctions were used in isolation or in coordination with other policy instruments. The TSC project has found, in fact, that sanctions are never imposed in isolation from other policy initiatives. There has been an attempt to establish a connection between the primary purpose of sanctions with the threat of, or actual use of, force by senders. Sanctions can also be used along with the deployment of civilian or military personnel, the management of covert operations by individual states, the legal referral to international criminal courts, active negotiations, or other diplomatic activities. Sanctions are always used in combination with other foreign policy instruments.

From this perspective, it is interesting to see how coercion is usually associated with a more intense use of institution-building initiatives related to peace operations (for instance, in Somalia episodes 3 and 4; Liberia episodes 1, 2, and 3; Angola; and Sudan over Darfur, episode 2), or disarmament, demobilization, and reintegration (DDR) programmes (Sierra Leone episode 2 and Côte d'Ivoire episodes 1, 3, and 4). The second most frequent use of coercive sanctions occurs with some use of force (Taliban episodes 1 and 2; or Somalia episodes 3 and 4), and the threat of force is also frequent (for instance, Haiti episode 1, and Libya in

2011, episode 1, among others). However, coercive sanctions are always associated with significant diplomatic pressure.

Constraining sanctions reflect a similar pattern, also considering the fact that there are twenty-six instances where constraint was the principal purpose of sanctions versus thirty-five where coercion was the principal purpose. When it comes to the threat of using force, constraining sanctions were used in FRY in the 1990s' episode 1; FRY over Kosovo episode 1; with AQT episodes 3 and 4 and a few others. Some kind of force was used in Somalia, Liberia, Rwanda, Kosovo, AQT episode 4; and Libya in 2011 (episodes 2 and 3) with a naval blockade and no-fly zone being used only in the case of Libya in 2011, episode 2. Constraining sanctions were combined with referrals to international courts (for instance, in the DRC episode 3; Kosovo episode 1; Libya episodes 2 and 3; AQT episodes 3 and 4; and Sierra Leone episodes 4 and 5). Covert operations undertaken unilaterally by individual states are more likely in constraining sanctions than in coercive sanctions (AQT episodes 3 and 4; Iran episode 4; and Somalia episode 5). This becomes intuitive following the analytical framework created above, since the idea of constraining is linked to the senders' attempts to reduce the operational capabilities of targets. Table 2.8 presents the summary of the matrix between the primary purpose of sanctions and other foreign policy instruments.

Greater analytical value can be obtained in a number of ways by looking at the purposes of sanctions, rather than at their objectives or forms. Possibly, the clearest example of this added value comes from looking at the effectiveness of sanctions. This will be treated more extensively in Chapter 10 of this volume by Thomas J. Biersteker, Marcos Tourinho,

Table 2.8 *Relations between principal purpose and other foreign policy tools*

Other Foreign Policy Tools	Principal purpose		
	Coerce	Constrain	Signal
Threat of force (16)	7	8	1
Force (limited strikes and operations, robust military force, no-fly zone, naval blockade) (33)	16	17	0
Peacekeeping operations and/or DDR (40)	20	19	1
Covert (cyber-sabotage, targeted assassinations) (7)	2	5	0
International Criminal Court (ICC), International Court of Justice (ICJ), or other courts and tribunals	16	12	1
Significant diplomatic pressure or negotiation (61)	35	24	2

and Sue Eckert, therefore it is sufficient to mention here that the multi-purpose TSC approach highlights a different perspective on sanctions that departs from the negative assessment from previous empirical assessments that concentrate primarily on behavioural change. At the same time, the assessment is analytically and methodologically rigorous. This is why the TSC elaborated an integrated approach in evaluating effectiveness by combining the overall policy outcome with the sanctions' contribution to it. The TSC analysis suggests that sanctions can be effective policy instruments when considering the full range of influence that they can have as an instrument of power.

Conclusion

Sanctions have been used throughout history as an instrument of foreign policy. This has been the case not because they are the silver bullets that some sanctions advocates might like to believe in. In recent decades, the emergence of targeted sanctions has further improved this evaluation. Despite the complexities, targeted sanctions can yield positive results without the shortcomings, uncertainties, and the costs of military operations, and the TSC research confirms this assessment by looking at the experience of the United Nations. The TSC methodology, by modifying the three-purpose framework to evaluate the effectiveness of UN targeted sanctions, accentuates the need for both policymakers and scholars to move beyond behavioural change as the sole criterion for assessing sanctions and for considering additional means by which sanctions influence their targets.

This approach hopefully will contribute to more realistic expectations concerning the purposes and results of UN targeted sanctions, and, therefore, will enhance understanding and utilization of the instrument. It is important to appreciate not only the multiple purposes sanctions can achieve but also the fact that the three purposes can be applied simultaneously, but with differing emphases under different circumstances. Discussions of effectiveness may then be dominated less by expectations of changes in targets' behaviours and more by how sanctions can constrain and stigmatize in different operational contexts.

3   Security Council dynamics and sanctions design

Michael Brzoska and George A. Lopez

In 2003 David Malone pointed out that the Security Council as a deci-sion-making body had become both more operational and more profes-sionalized after 1990, as the complexities of issues in peace and security before the United Nations increased throughout the decade. Prominent among the tools of choice for the Council in dealing with international crises – or in UN language, 'threats to international peace and security' – was the imposition and maintenance of economic sanctions.[1] Andrea Charron has noted the Council's resort to targeted sanctions involved organizational learning and included the evolution of language and scope of purpose to be more consistent across cases. Thus, the sanctions regimes which had emerged by 2010, she argued, could be classified into four distinct thematic areas: ending violence, promoting democracy and human rights, dealing with terrorism, and controlling nuclear proliferation.[2]

In the course of this evolution, Susan C. Hulton documented that the Council became more organizationally focused and cooperative as a decision-making body, and the Council's relatively frequent imposition of sanctions would appear consistent with this pattern. One of her more significant findings for the period 1992–2003 was the declining use of the veto and increased dialogue and cooperation among the Permanent Five (P5) Security Council members, and among the P5 nations and elected Member States. In particular, she notes the dramatic increase in outreach and interaction of the Council members as they receive substantive brief-ings on a variety of issues and an increased volume of information from the Secretariat, UN agencies, and non-governmental organizations.[3]

---

[1] D. M. Malone (ed.), *The Security Council in the 21st Century* (Boulder, CO: Lynne Rienner, 2004).

[2] A. Charron, *UN Sanctions and Conflict: Responding to Peace and Security Threats* (London: Routledge Press, 2011).

[3] S. C. Hulton, 'Council Working Methods and Procedures', in D. Malone (ed.), *The UN Security Council: From the Cold War to the 21st Century* (Boulder, CO: Lynne Rienner, 2004), pp. 237–51.

More recent analysis and our own direct observations also verify increased degrees of informal dialogue, as well improvements due to the information and technological upgrading that UN staff and branches received during this time period. A number of the discrete Council sanctions votes and the general momentum to continued recourse to sanctions were aided by one of the Council's own creations, the Informal Working Group on General Issues of Sanctions, which, from 2000 to 2007, held ongoing seminars, produced various non-papers on sanctions trends and techniques, and documented both best practices and new recommendations for improving sanctions design and effectiveness.[4]

The meetings of the Group and other Member State–sponsored seminars and reports led to increased transparency and improvements in the real substantive knowledge held by Council Members of increasingly complex sanctions and evasion techniques. Annual retreats for new Council members that addressed these issues provided a more focused confidence and air of debate about Council tools like sanctions, and their relationship between Council action and the other activities taking place in a thematic issue like terrorism or ending civil violence.

While less studied by scholars, it is clear that the P5 have been increasingly active in both formal and informal ways in the past several years, as the questions before them have become more complex.[5] Within the Council itself, hardly any controversial case which may demand Council action comes to it without already being vetted, discussed in prior, closed door meetings and alternatives formed by those sitting at the table. Even when a Member State demands that the Council respond quickly and take action, various members of the P5 begin a process by floating ideas in varied informal meetings or in a 'non-paper' format which later may emerge as the basis of a working draft resolution. It is during this white paper and pre-draft resolution stage that some of the more fiery and contentious discussions among council members take place.[6]

---

[4] J. Weschler, 'The Evolution of Security Council Innovations on Sanctions', *International Journal*, 10 (2009), pp. 31–43; A. Vines, 'The Effectiveness of UN and EU Sanctions: Lessons for the Twenty-First Century', *International Affairs*, 88 (2012), p. 873.

[5] D. L. Bosco, *Five to Rule Them All: The UN Security Council and the Making of the Modern World* (Oxford University Press, 2009) makes this general argument. A more nuanced view which also examines the Council's struggle with the use of force appears in N. Krisch, 'The Security Council and the Great Powers', in V. Lowe, A. Roberts, J. Welsh, and D. Zaum (eds.), *The United Nations Security Council and War, the Evolution of Thought and Practice since 1945* (Oxford University Press, 2008), pp. 133–53.

[6] Direct observations of George A. Lopez October 2010–11 as a member of the UN Panel of Experts for the sanctions on North Korea.

This is not intended to give the impression that formal Council discussion and action is scripted or pro forma. But in light of the diversity, volume, and potential contentiousness of particular issues, much more goes on in a very structured way behind the scenes among delegations and others than was the case in the 1990s.[7] This directly affects the question of national commitments to vote for or against or abstain regarding sanctions resolutions and the degree of political will that a state on the Council may bring to enforcing and monitoring sanctions once they are imposed.

These developments lead to two insights that inform this chapter. First, if the casting of symbolic votes for sanctions resolutions ever existed in Council action, it has evolved more directly into what the Targeted Sanctions Consortium project labels as signalling. As noted in Chapter 2, while signalling is rarely the primary purpose of UN sanctions, it is frequently an important element of episodes. Second, as important as it is to be able to sketch the voting patterns of states when sanctions resolutions come to the Council, the vote may tell us only part of the story. Thus, our quantitative analysis using the TSC data will be augmented by some commentary useful for understanding particular situations.

Council dynamics as assessed by voting

The TSC data set gives us the ability to study voting patterns on sanctions resolutions and to link them to the different purposes of sanctions: to coerce, constrain, and/or signal. Below we use the data to assess whether the trends we note in the scholarly literature and the thematic shifts in ideas that would give rise to sanctions are borne out empirically in the actions of Security Council – both in the voting patterns of the P5 and in non-permanent Member States. Correlating votes with effectiveness by type of sanctioning purpose provides some insight into the intentions and commitments of Council members, especially regarding whether sanctions imposition is simply a reaction in emerging global crises to the imperative 'to do something'.

We begin by examining the strongest indicator of the political will of the Council – how often there was unanimity of voting in the Security Council? In forty-eight of the sixty-three sanctions episodes in the database (76 per cent), all members of the Security Council voted in favour of

---

[7] See J. Prantl, 'Informal Groups of States and the UN Security Council', *International Organization*, 59 (2005), pp. 571–2; T. Whitfield, 'Groups of Friends', in D. Malone (ed.), *The UN Security Council: From the Cold War to the 21ˢᵗ Century* (Boulder, CO: Lynne Rienner, 2004), pp. 311–24.

the resolution mandating the sanctions at hand. Did such commitment of purpose help make sanctions effective? The surprising (or, disappointing) answer is, no. Of the five targeted sanctions episodes considered to be effective in coercion, three showed no unanimity in the Security Council. These are Somalia, episode 4; Libya in the 1990s, episode 3; and Sierra Leone, episode 4. Overall, the percentage of episodes coded as effective in coercing a change in target behaviour constitutes a relatively small percentage of the total number of unanimous decisions of the Council (only 4 per cent), compared to the percentage of times the Council was divided (20 per cent), as noted in Table 3.1. For instance, in the case of Libya in the 1990s, episode 3, France and the United States judged the provisions of the relevant resolution as too lenient and had wanted them to be stronger. But since they also wanted sanctions imposed on Libya in this case, they thus abstained. In the Sierra Leone, episode 4, case, all permanent members of the Security Council voted in favour, but Mali abstained.

Of the sixteen cases classified as being effective in constraining for which there are relevant data, there was a dissenting vote or an abstention in four cases, or in one-fourth of all episodes. In all but one of these episodes (Sierra Leone, episode 4), China abstained (Libya in the 1990s, episode 1 and episode 2), joined by Russia in one case (Libya in 2011 episode 2). In the case of signalling, where such a show of common action should count most, the percentage of episodes coded as effective is much higher when there was unanimity in the Security Council than when there was none (88 per cent compared to 12 per cent). Two episodes (Somalia, episode 4; and Sierra Leone, episode 4) were coded as effective, even though there was no unanimity in the Security Council.

These numbers imply that unanimity in the Security Council is not as important for explaining the effectiveness of UN sanctions as might be expected. This pattern also holds if we focus on the permanent members and examine reservations instead of voting (Table 3.1). This appears to be in contrast to signalling, where we observe that the number of episodes classified as successful and which do not have the full support of the Security Council, and in particular the Permanent Five, is more in line with the view that unanimity in the Security Council matters.

The impression gained from the data presented here corresponds to claims and some findings in the scholarly debate on the importance of a broad consensus for sanctions success. Based on differing data sets for sanctions, some authors have found that a broad consensus increases the likelihood of effectiveness, while others have found powerful state

Table 3.1 *Frequency table on variables related to political will and effectiveness of sanctions*

	Coercion		Constraint		Signalling		
	Effective (*n*=5)	Non-effective (*n*=45)	Effective (*n*=16)	Non-effective (*n*=43)	Effective (*n*=17)	Non-effective (*n*=46)	N
Unanimity in SC	2	34	12	35	15	33	48
Dissent in SC	3	11	4	8	2	13	15
Support by all P5	2	29	12	30	13	30	43
Support by less than all P5	3	16	4	13	4	16	20
Leadership by United States	0	24	10	20	7	24	31
Leadership by other P5	3	25	5	26	5	28	32
Leadership by other country	1	5	1	3	2	4	6
Missing data	1	8	4	7	5	6	10
Significant NGO pressure	3	12	7	9	7	9	16
No significant NGO pressure	2	33	9	34	10	37	47
Western leadership* with consensus	2	7	3	7	3	7	10
Western leadership* without consensus	0	2	0	2	0	2	2
Other	3	36	13	34	14	37	51

* Significant NGO pressure and resolution drafting led by United States, France, or United Kingdom, or joint.
Note: numbers refer to numbers of sanctions episodes.

leadership, especially from the United States, as more important to effectiveness.[8]

Our findings, based on the TSC database, point towards more complex patterns of sanctions effectiveness. Thus we find that among members of the Security Council, leadership in drafting a sanctions resolution from a non-US permanent member has the highest likelihood of success in coercion and signalling. However, with respect to constraint, US leadership is associated with the highest proportion of episodes classified as successful (Table 3.1); this points to the important yet problematic role of the United States as the most powerful, but often resented, actor in the UN.

The adoption of sanctions is sometimes argued to reflect the domestic policies, particularly in 'Western' liberal democracies. The relevance of non-governmental organizations' (NGOs) pressure in sanctions resolution also seems to have some confirmation in the data (see Table 3.1). While the number of cases with significant NGO pressure is low, significant NGO pressure is associated with higher rates of success in coercion, constraining, and signalling. The data show that NGO pressure predominantly, but not exclusively, works through Western permanent members. The proportion of sanction episodes classified as effective is somewhat reduced, when only those sanctions episodes are included in the data, where France, the United Kingdom, or the United States took the lead in drafting a sanctions resolution.

We can augment what the data reveal about the political will of the P5 regarding sanctions by comparing the initial discussions among Council members regarding the contours of the sanctions to be brought to the Council with the robustness of a Security Council sanctions regime that emerges as a result of these discussions at the time of a vote. In at least four cases – Yugoslavia, Rwanda, Liberia (until 2001), and Sudan/Darfur – one or more members of the P5 had vested ideological or economic interests in the manner in which UN sanctions were constructed and which actors were targeted. The various debates resulted in little or no reduction in the killings, because the Council acted late, and then imposed a limited and weakly enforced arms embargo that was not integrated with other more powerful financial or commodity sanctions.[9]

---

[8] D. W. Drezner, 'Bargaining, Enforcement, and Multilateral Sanctions: When Is Cooperation Counterproductive?', *International Organization*, 54 (2000), pp. 73–102; and N. A. Bapat and T. C. Morgan, 'Multilateral versus Unilateral Sanctions Reconsidered: A Test Using New Data', *International Studies Quarterly*, 53 (2009), pp. 1075–94.

[9] A. J. Boucher and V. K. Holt, *Targeting Spoilers: The Role of United Nations Panels of Experts* (Washington, DC: Henry L. Stimson Center, 2009).

Despite pleas of 'never again', the failure of the international community to use sanctions or other means to prevent ethnic cleansing in Bosnia in 1992 or genocide in Rwanda in 1994 was repeated with regard to Darfur a decade later. Without question, the Darfur case serves as a glaring example of very few sanctions imposed too late and without the broad targeting of a substantial number of elites that would maximize their effectiveness. Despite near global condemnation of the Sudanese regime for its actions against the citizens of the Darfur region from 2003 through 2008, a rather watered-down set of financial asset freezes and travel restrictions were imposed against only two Sudanese government officials in a series of Security Council resolutions. A draft Security Council resolution targeting more than thirty persons responsible for killings and brutal actions in the region faced serious opposition. Ultimately the final resolution that was adopted designated only four individuals, two on each side of the conflict. Most of this backtracking was due to the unwillingness of the Chinese and Russians to support more extensive sanctions. The UN debate over sanctions continued for so long prior to their adoption that whoever was to face financial penalties surely avoided them.[10]

Moving a bit beyond the data of sanctions voting but remaining in the realm of the context in which Council sanctions decisions are taken, it is important to document that the Council has also taken patterned and consistent action in more narrowly defined issue areas related to broader peace and security goals. This is particularly true in areas of advancing humanitarian law to protect civilians, which formed the basis for the principle of Responsibility to Protect (R2P), which then served as the springboard for the sanctions and more dramatic military action in Libya and Côte d'Ivoire in 2011.[11]

Thus, the passage of Resolution 1265 on the protection of civilians in armed conflict (1999) becomes particularly noteworthy as the Security Council recognized that civilians comprise the vast majority of casualties in armed conflicts, and must be protected. This validation of humanitarian law regarding the protection of civilians (PoC) clearly provided the basis for a number of sanctions regimes aimed directly at shielding innocent populations from harm. It also established a pattern of designating as targets of sanctions militant non-state actors (both groups and their

---

[10] See G. A. Lopez, 'Enforcing Human Rights through Economic and Other Sanctions', in D. Shelton (ed.), *The Handbook Of International Human Rights Law* (Oxford University Press, 2013).

[11] A. dos Reis Stefanopoulos and G. A. Lopez, 'Sanctions and the Responsibility to Protect', in M. Serrrano and T. G. Weiss (eds.), *Rallying to the R2P Cause? The International Politics of Human Rights* (New York, NY: Routledge, 2013).

individual leaders) like irregular armed groups, death squads or parami-
litary forces which preyed on the civilian population, as well as those who
bankroll them.[12]

Complementary issues were acknowledged in Council resolutions on
women, peace and security (1325, 1960), children (1612), the protection
of humanitarian workers (1502), conflict prevention (1625), and sexual
exploitation (1820). A significant factor that gave these sanctions 'more
teeth' than their predecessors was the priority given to the PoC concept in
the work of many UN missions, including operations in Afghanistan
(UNAMA), Central African Republic (MINURCAT), Côte d'Ivoire
(UNOCI), Darfur (UNAMID), Democratic Republic of Congo
(MONUC), Haiti (MINUSTAH), Liberia (UNMIL), and Sudan
(UNMIS).[13]

In 2006, the protection of civilians agenda advanced considerably at
the UN when the Security Council in Resolution 1674 made its historic
first reference to the newly endorsed construct called Responsibility to
Protect (R2P). As with SCR 1265, this resolution acknowledged that
civilians make up the majority of casualties in violent conflicts and under-
scored the responsibility of all states to protect populations from four
heinous human rights violations: genocide, war crimes, ethnic cleansing,
and crimes against humanity.[14]

Sanctions which target leadership to protect civilians and democracy

The evolution of PoC to R2P as a new potential rationale for Council
action very much coincided with the drive for more sanctions precision of
design and targeting. It also led to the development of new techniques and
rationales for sanctions regimes and the manner in which their effectiveness was increased by the effective investigations and reporting of Panels
of Experts.[15] The sanctions regime imposed on Liberia exemplifies how

[12] Security Council Report, *Cross-Cutting Report on Protection of Civilians in Armed Conflict* (New York: Security Council Report, 2011).
[13] On the importance of sanctions and other aspects of UN operations in conflict zones being 'in sync', see D. Cortright et al., *Integrating UN Sanctions for Peace and Security*. Report prepared for the Canadian Office of Foreign Affairs, 2010. www.sanctionsandsecurity.org/wp-content/uploads/Integrating-UN-Sanctions-for-Peace-and-Security.pdf.
[14] The Global Centre for the Responsibility to Protect. *The Relationship between the Responsibility to Protect and the Protection of Civilians in Armed Conflict* (New York: the CUNY Graduate Center, 2011), p. 2.
[15] M. Notaras and V. Popovski, *The Responsibility to Protect* (Tokyo: United Nations University, 2011).

the Council can move from an ineffective, stand-alone arms embargo to employing a range of targeted sanctions instruments.

More than a decade of diverse sanctions culminated in protective measures that targeted those actors who were responsible for attacking peacekeepers and humanitarian workers, those who were impeding the delivery of humanitarian aid during the war, and those who undermined the peace process and emergence of democratic institutions as the war ended. Replacing weak, initial sanctions measures, the UN Security Council adopted Resolutions 1521 (2003) and 1532 (2004), thereby establishing a more stringent arms embargo on the forces of former President Charles Taylor, as well as extended financial and travel restrictions on Taylor and his supporters who represented a threat to the peace process in Liberia. In addition, certain trade restrictions for timber and diamonds were levied.[16]

Based on the findings of the Panel of Experts and the work of the UN mission, some of the sanctions were lifted following the election of Ellen Johnson Sirleaf. Those targeting timber were removed in 2006 (SCR 1689) followed by those of diamonds in 2007 (SCR 1753) after it was clear that the financial profits from these industries no longer flowed to conflict actors. The remaining sanctions were meant to target actors that might disrupt the democratic process in the country. Thus, the sanctions were increasingly preventive, protecting the new government and Liberian people from potential violent spoilers, leading some to refer to these protective measures as 'Sanctions for Peace', a label which more recently was used to protect the national reconciliation process in Côte d'Ivoire.[17]

Tables 3.2 and 3.3 examine the areas where PoC, R2P, and respect for humanitarian law are invoked in sanctions resolutions. The data in the TSC cases indicate that sanctions targeted at the leadership of a targeted entity are effective in the same number of episodes as sanctions that are not targeted on the leadership. However, the proportion of sanctions episodes coded as effective is lower when coercing the leadership[18] in a targeted country was an explicit objective than where this was not the case. This holds for all three categories of coercion, constraining, and signalling (Table 3.2).

---

[16] For a more complete analysis of these sanctions and cases, see Stefanopoulos and Lopez, 'Sanctions and the Responsibility to Protect', p. 19.

[17] That being stated, by 2013 both the Liberia regime and the Cote d'Ivoire ones had come under critique by then serving and recently past non-permanent members of the Council due to the unwillingness of the United States to move to bring the sanctions and its targeting to an end.

[18] Composed of government leadership, leadership family members and key regime supporters, as coded in the TSC database.

Table 3.2 *Frequency table on variables related to sanctions aiming at leadership of targeted entity and effectiveness of sanctions by purpose*

	Coercion		Constraint		Signalling		
	Effective (n=5)	Non-effective (n=45)	Effective (n=16)	Non-effective (n=43)	Effective (n=17)	Non-effective (n=46)	n=63
Objective: Coercion of leadership*	3	32	8	24	8	27	35
Coercion of leadership* not an objective	2	13	8	19	9	19	28
Objective: signalling to leadership*	3	35	12	28	13	31	44
Signalling to leadership* not an objective	2	10	4	15	4	15	19
Direct political impact	5	22	15	17	15	19	34
No direct political impact	0	20	1	22	1	24	25

* Leadership defined as government leadership, leadership family members, or key regime supporters.

Table 3.3 *Frequency table on variables related to sanctions aiming at leadership of targeted entity and political impact of sanctions*

Objective:	Direct political impact (*n*=34)	No direct political impact (*n*=25)	Indirect political impact (*n*=18)	No indirect direct political impact (*n*=39)	*n*
Coercion of leadership*	16	18	10	24	35
Coercion of leadership* not an objective	11	2	6	6	15
No coercion	7	5	2	9	13

* Leadership defined as government leadership, leadership family members, or key regime supporters.

This result is particularly striking when compared to the proportions of successful sanctions episodes that actually had a political impact in the targeted country. As might be expected, political impact is strongly correlated with sanctions effectiveness, on all three measures (Table 3.2).

However, as seen in Table 3.3, the objective of coercing the leadership in a country decreases both direct and indirect political impact of sanctions. These results suggest that the idea of driving a wedge into the leadership of a targeted country does not, on average, improve the chances of attaining the desired objectives.

The same forces that make it less likely that coercive sanctions achieve their objectives also affect these targeted sanctions. But it is the case that in the limited times where coercive sanctions are effective, their success appears to be due to the significant political impact of the measures (Table 3.2). Thus the economic pain of the sanctions does translate to some political pain as well, with the Charles Taylor and Qadhafi cases being exemplars of this impact. This warrants a brief comment about the Libyan case.

Despite reservations on the part of some Council members, Resolution 1970 passed with remarkable unanimity and speed. The timely adoption of the resolution came after the defection of Libyan UN ambassador Mohammed Shalgham, and as a result of his powerful and emotional appeal to Security Council members to impose sanctions in response to the atrocities committed by Qadhafi.[19] Also Council thinking was influenced by two developments that provided the teeth of enforcement just days before the resolution actually passed. The first was the endorsement by Member States in the region for sanctions, supported by regional actors like Council of the League of Arab States.[20] The second was the extensive reach of national sanctions imposed by the United States and the European Union that had already locked down the bulk of the assets of the Qadhafi regime and family, setting the stage for Security Council action.

Despite the effectiveness of these strong measures it soon became clear that more stringent actions were needed in order to protect the lives of Libyan civilians, specifically in Benghazi, which Qadhafi had vowed to raze. In March 2011, Resolution 1973 expanded existing sanctions and authorized a no-fly zone and a ban on all Libyan flights. The resolution also established a Panel of Experts to evaluate the enforcement of these

[19] 'UN Security Council Unanimously Passes Sanctions against Gadhafi', *Deutsche Welle*, 26 February 2011, www.dw.de/un-security-council-unanimously-passes-sanctions-against-gadhafi/a-14876262.

[20] UN sanctions frequently follow regional measures already in place. Among the twenty-three sanctions regimes, twelve were preceded by autonomous sanctions by regional organizations. By far the largest number (nine) pertains to sanctions by the European Union.

measures. Arab support, critical to obtaining US consent to a military intervention, was quickly provided when the Council of the League of Arab States called for a no-fly zone and the League of Arab States, Qatar, and the United Arab Emirates (UAE) pledged to contribute to the North Atlantic Treaty Organization (NATO) and international effort in Libya.[21] Thus, Resolution 1973 made it clear that 'all necessary measures' other than an occupying force could be used to protect civilians.[22]

Do differences in types of sanctions matter?

A critical, if not fundamental, question for sanctions research and policy is whether targeted sanctions matter in leading to effectiveness. In the scholarly realm, the continued critique of targeted measures is that they are, in fact, of little consequence in reducing unanticipated negative impact and in having only limited effectiveness.[23] The advantage of the TSC data here – with the important distinctions among the three sanctions goals – is telling. But before delving into the question of effectiveness, we will detail the frequency of differing types of sanctions (Table 3.4).

Arms embargoes are by far the most popular kind of sanction, both as single sanctions and in combination with other types of sanctions, followed by individual sanctions (financial and/or travel related). Arms embargoes are present in all sanction episodes, when the objective of sanctions is coded as 'Negotiations over peace agreements'. In the latter category, aviation bans and diplomatic sanctions are found particularly frequently. When the objective is 'cease hostilities' and/or 'non-proliferation', arms embargoes are almost always present (one exception is Iran, episode 1). All non-proliferation sanctions include individual sanctions. Overall, while illustrating the variability of the mix of sanctions, the links between the objectives of sanctions and the combination of sanction types make sense.

The database contains no case where a single type of sanction has been coded as effective on its own. It is rare to use only one type of targeted sanction, with the exception of arms embargoes. The most frequent combination is individual sanctions and arms embargoes with forty-three episodes, and a coercion success rate of 16 per cent. While adding

---

[21] 'Italy, France Sending Troops to Advise Libyan Rebels', *CNN News*, April 20, 2011, www.cnn.com/2011/WORLD/africa/04/20/libya.war/index.html.

[22] As Council debates in 2012 and 2013 revealed, the interpretation by China, Russia, and some Member States that NATO exceeded what was authorized in actions in coercing the Libyan governmental leadership had a significant negative impact on potential Council action, particularly sanctions, against President Assad of Syria.

[23] See J. Gordon, 'Smart Sanctions Revisited', *Ethics & International Affairs*, 25 (2011), pp. 315–35; and D. W. Drezner, 'Sanctions Sometimes Smart: Targeted Sanctions in Theory and Practice', *International Studies Review*, 13 (2011), pp. 96–108.

Table 3.4 *Frequency table on variables related to types of sanctions and effectiveness of sanctions by purpose*

Type of sanctions	Coercion		Constraint		Signalling	
	Effective (5)	Not effective (45)	Effective (16)	Not effective (43)	Effective (17)	Not effective (46)
Individual sanctions (47)	5	31	15	30	16	31
Diplomatic sanctions (13)	1	11	7	3	6	7
Aviation bans (11)	1	9	6	3	3	8
Arms embargoes (57)	5	39	16	40	17	40
Commodity sanctions (26)	2	15	11	15	14	12
Financial sector sanctions (6)	1	3	1	5	2	4
Individual and arms sanctions (43)	5	27	15	27	16	27
Individual, arms and commodity sanctions (23)	2	12	11	12	13	10
Any four of the above (13)	1	9	7	5	6	7

Note: numbers refer to numbers of sanctions episode.
Source: TSC database.

more and more sanctions does not automatically lead to more effective-ness, commodity sanctions, when added to a package, does have an impact (with individual sanctions and arms embargoes: 14 per cent).

Yet in the case of constraining and signalling, some different patterns emerge. For constraining, the more types of sanctions contained in a sanc-tions package, the better (indicated by the increase of effective episodes for four or more sanction types from 47 to 58 per cent). For signalling, a combination of arms embargoes, individual sanctions and commodity sanc-tions has the highest rate of success (57 per cent) due mostly to the inclusion of commodity sanctions, which increased the sanction effectiveness by 20 per cent. The overall impression from the data is that the combination of types of sanctions has achieved a remarkable rate of success with respect to the broader objectives of constraining and signalling.

In a number of ways the data are not as positive, particularly when the purpose is coercion. Some recent adaptations and improvements in arms sanctions design and implementation made by the Council in connection to the wider United Nations system may lead to different data patterns in the future. Recognizing the importance of demobilization of arms and ending the reach of illicit networks, to the success of its missions, special envoys, and peacekeeping units in conflict zones, the Security Council has sought to link the arms embargo enterprise in more dynamic ways to these other ongoing operations. This began in 2005 with Security Council-mandated (SCR 1584) cooperation between the Liberia Sanctions Committee and Panels of Experts and those of Côte d'Ivoire, an issue further discussed in the chapter by Boucher and Clement in this volume. Their shared investigations led to tracing arms flows across a number of neighbouring countries that had evaded the earlier reach of sanctions. This increased cooperation and knowl-edge sharing led to plugging some of the leakages in the embargoes. In the Democratic Republic of Congo and Liberia, UN arms embargoes have been revamped to allow support for emerging and effective national Armed Forces as each of those nations moved closer to peace and democratization. The UN Development Programme through its Rule of Law and Security Programme has taken on an increased role to monitor and train national forces as arms embargoes wind down so as to prevent the entry of new arms into the country that might supply remaining dissidents.[24]

To overcome the problems resulting from inadequate implementation of arms embargoes, the Security Council adopted a number of policy innovations. The language and technical terms employed in the Council's arms embargo resolutions became more precise. Arms embargo resolu-tions included prohibitions not only against the supply of arms and

---

[24] Cortright, *Integrating UN Sanctions for Peace and Security.*

ammunition but also against training, military cooperation, and various support services, including air transportation. This refinement of terms and broadening of covered items helped to close loopholes and reduced the ambiguities that previously impeded enforcement. More vigorous efforts were also made to monitor compliance with arms embargoes. Member States were encouraged to criminalize violations of UN arms embargoes and strengthen export control laws and regulations. These initiatives helped to create a firmer foundation in the domestic law of Member States for penalizing companies and individuals convicted of violating UN arms embargoes.[25]

In 2004 the Security Council began to employ more standardized mandate language in arms embargoes designed to strengthen their effectiveness. The Council directed UN peacekeeping forces in the Democratic Republic of Congo and Côte d'Ivoire to assist with the monitoring of arms embargoes in these countries. This added significant new responsibilities to the mission of UN peacekeepers in these countries. In the cases of Liberia, Côte d'Ivoire, the DRC, and even in Sudan, Security Council resolutions have mandated explicitly the cooperation of missions in the field with newly specified sanctions. Thus, the often referenced embarrassment that UN Blue Helmets look the other way as arms merchants conducted their prohibited business is now the exception, rather than the norm.[26] They have been authorized to enforce sanctions in fourteen out of twenty-five (56 per cent) of sanctions episodes that began in or after 1999 where both arms embargoes and peacekeeping operations were present. For the sanction episodes beginning earlier, the share was two out of thirteen (15 per cent).

Another insight into political will: sanctions enforcement

The query 'do these measures have any teeth?' asks if the measures are sufficiently strong to coerce a target and will these restrictions as designed be enforced by Member States so that they have a chance at maximum success? We know from the data presented above that certain combinations of targeted measures have the best track record of success. Below we analyse some variables that provide insight into measures the Council can adopt to improve the chances of effective enforcement (Table 3.5).

---

[25] G. A. Lopez and D. Cortright, 'Sanctions as Alternatives to War', in C. J. Coyne and R. L. Mathers (eds.), *The Handbook on the Political Economy of War* (Northampton, MA: Edward Elgar Publishing, 2011), pp. 534–70.

[26] In four of the five episodes coded as effective with respect to coercion in the TSC database, peacekeeping forces were an actor (Côte d'Ivoire, episode 3; DRC, episode 2; Sierra Leone, episode 4; Somalia, episode 4). They had mandates to enforce sanctions in three of these episodes (not in Somalia, episode 4).

Table 3.5 *Frequency table on variables related to enforcement provisions and effectiveness of sanctions*

	Coercion		Constraint		Signalling		
	Effective (n=5)	Non-effective (n=45)	Effective (n=16)	Non-effective (n=43)	Effective (n=17)	Non-effective (n=46)	n
All measures* in place	2	9	3	10	3	10	13
Most (4) measures* in place	2	10	6	13	7	12	19
Some (3) measures* in place	0	7	2	6	3	5	8
Few (0, 1 or 2) measures*	1	19	5	14	4	19	23
Panels of Experts or Monitoring Team in place	4	18	10	19	11	18	29
No panel in place	1	27	6	24	6	28	34
Individuals designated	4	21	10	25	12	23	41
Individuals not designated	0	5	0	4	0	5	17
Other (N/A or missing data)	1	19	6	14	5	18	17

(a) Presence of Sanctions Committee, Panel of Experts/Monitoring Team, designations of individual sanctions, Member State reporting requirements, and Sanctions Committee guidelines.
(b) *Source:* TSC database.

Important measures include the formation of a sanctions committee, the adoption of guidelines for the committees' work, Panels of Experts/ Monitors, the designation of individuals to be targeted, and the requesting or requiring of Member State reports on sanctions implementation in the text of a resolution.

Clearly, across the different episodes of Council sanctions in the TSC data, more such measures in place increase the likelihood of sanctions being effective, with respect to coercion, constraint, and signalling (Table 3.5). Among the measures, expert panels are particularly important. Success rates of episodes with panels in place are significantly greater than those where no panel is operational (coercion: 18 to 4 per cent, constraint: 34 to 20 per cent, signalling: 38 to 18 per cent). No doubt this explains the now standard recourse to panels for each sanctions resolution and their continued renewal.

Blending TSC data with rapidly changing events

In this chapter we have demonstrated the convergence between the general literature on sanctions about Security Council decision-making with some of our own UN experiences and the TSC data. For the most part, the empirics validate the literature both by proving some widely held sensibilities but also by illustrating the degree to which we should have confidence in these generalizations. We have tried to bolster the data with a discussion of some Security Council trends in areas related to sanctions, such as the emergence of the Protection of Civilians and the Responsibility to Protect. We complemented this with some further details about the contours of particular sanctions cases. At the very least, this chapter – and the other chapters in this volume using the TSC data – meet squarely the critique of some scholars who have long maintained that claims about targeted or smart sanctions cannot be subject to systematic testing due to lack of anything but impressionistic data.[27]

In conclusion, we are aware of a number of areas yet to be explored in our core themes. Most importantly, we recognize that neither our chapter nor the data can capture what became the very palpable tensions among the P5 members which have arisen since 2011 regarding UN action and intervention – via sanctions or other means – in severe conflicts like Syria. In 2012 this meant that two major resolutions applying R2P principles as warranting sanctions against the Assad regime were defeated by a combined Chinese and Russian veto. At the same time, the same states that

---

[27] As argued by D. W. Drezner, 'Sanctions Sometimes Smart: Targeted Sanctions in Theory and Practice', *International Studies Review*, 13 (2011), pp. 96–108.

are so diametrically opposed on Syria were able to reach unprecedented agreement on a new round of strong sanctions on North Korea in March 2013 in Resolution 2087. And all indications are that China is playing a larger than usual role in enforcing these restrictions. The latter will be captured by the data as they continue to develop, and the authors anticipate this documenting of political will should be consistent with the findings and discussion presented here.

4   United Nations targeted sanctions and other policy tools: diplomacy, legal, use of force

Paul Bentall

The interaction between sanctions and other policy instruments is alluded to or explicitly mentioned in some existing work on sanctions. For example, Cortright and Lopez refer to it in their prescriptions on 'Setting the Policy Framework'.[1] Hufbauer, Schott, Elliott, and Oegg's analysis uses sender state's or coalitions' 'companion policies' as a variable,[2] while Doxey refers to senders' 'complementary strategies' to sanctions.[3]

The Targeted Sanctions Consortium data set allows further study of this issue, of which this chapter is an initial attempt. It is divided in two sections. The first addresses some general questions about the interaction between targeted sanctions and other policy instruments. The second section looks more closely at how UN targeted sanctions have interacted with force, diplomacy and negotiation, and judicial processes.

General questions: what, when, and why?

This section looks at three questions in order to identify general patterns in the interaction between targeted sanctions and other policy instruments:

(a) Which other policy instruments accompany targeted sanctions, and how often?

(b) Are sanctions' effectiveness affected by the number of accompanying policy tools?

(c) To what extent does the Security Council rely on targeted sanctions, as opposed to other policy instruments, in pursuing its policy goals?

The views in this chapter are the author's and do not necessarily reflect those of the Foreign and Commonwealth Office.
[1] D. Cortright and G. A. Lopez, *The Sanctions Decade: Assessing UN Strategies in the 1990s* (Boulder, CO: Lynne Rienner Publishers, 2000), p. 223.
[2] G C. Hufbauer, J. J. Schott, K. A. Elliott, and B. Oegg, *Economic Sanctions Reconsidered* (Washington, DC: Peter G. Peterson Institute for International Economics, 2007), p. 175.
[3] M. P. Doxey, *International Sanctions in Contemporary Perspective* (New York: St. Martin's Press, 1996), p. 124.

Other policy instruments

The data set shows that UN targeted sanctions have been used alongside twelve other policy instruments that seek, in the main, to achieve similar or related policy objectives: threats of and actual use of force (limited strikes, robust military force, no-fly zones, and naval blockades); peace-keeping; DDR; covert action (cyber-sabotage and targeted assassinations); legal processes (the ICC, the ICJ, and other tribunals); and negotiations and diplomacy. This is variously seen in all of the data set's twenty-three targeted sanctions country regimes and sixty-three episodes.

Frequency

In no episode are UN targeted sanctions used alone. They are always accompanied by at least one other policy instrument. The extent to which this reflects purposeful Security Council decision-making is addressed later in the chapter. But for now it is sufficient to note that, to date, UN targeted sanctions are always a complement to, or are complemented by, other policy tools.

Targeted sanctions most frequently accompany negotiations and diplomacy. This occurs in 97 per cent of the sanctions episodes. The second most frequent combination is with peacekeeping, in around 62 per cent of episodes. Force is used, to some degree, alongside UN targeted sanctions in about 52 per cent of episodes and use of force is threatened in 25 per cent of the episodes. Targeted sanctions are used simultaneously with limited military strikes in roughly 29 per cent of episodes, robust military force in about 35 per cent, naval blockades in approximately 3 per cent, and no-fly zones in around 2 per cent. Legal processes are present alongside targeted sanctions in 41 per cent of episodes, ICC or ICJ in 22 per cent, and other international courts or tribunals in 30 per cent of episodes. Covert action is used (according to public sources) in about 11 per cent of episodes.

That the Security Council uses targeted sanctions so frequently alongside diplomatic negotiations and with peacekeeping is unsurprising. Both activities dominate its work. The Council sponsors negotiations; it sets their boundaries, legitimizes their outcomes, assists implementation, and/or otherwise interacts with the parties involved. It has significantly expanded its use of peacekeeping.[4] The Council, therefore, deciding to accompany its regular activities of peacemaking and peacekeeping with a key policy

---

[4] See www.un.org/en/peacekeeping/operations/surge.shtml.

		Number of other policy instruments in play							
		1	2	3	4	5	6	7	8
Number of Sanctions Measures Imposed**	Sus*		Haiti (2)	Libya I (3)					
	1		Ethiopia Eritrea (1) Sudan I (1)	FRY I (1) Liberia (1) Guinea Bissau (1)	Somalia (1) Somalia (2) Rwanda (1)	Rwanda (2) DRC (1)			FRY II (1)
	2	Iran (1)	Sudan I (1) AQT (1) Lebanon (1)		Angola (1) Sierra Leone (2) Sierra Leone (3)				
	3	Iran (2)	Haiti (1) Sudan I (2)	Sierra Leone (1) Sudan II (2) CAR (1)	Sierra Leone (5) DRC (2) Côte d'Ivoire (2) Somalia (3)	Sierra Leone (4) Côte d'Ivoire (1)	DRC (3) AQT (4) Taliban (1)	DRC (4)	
	4	Iran (3)	Iraq (1) Iraq (2)	Libya II (1) Haiti (3)	Côte d'Ivoire (3) Côte d'Ivoire (5)	Liberia (2)	Côte d'Ivoire (4)		
	5		AQT (2)	Libya I (1)		Liberia (3) Liberia (4) Liberia (5) Somalia (4)			
	6	DPRK (1) DPRK (2)			Angola (2) Iran (4)	AQT (3)	Somalia (5)		
	7	DPRK (3)		Libya I (2)			Libya II (2)		
	8				Libya II (3)				
	9				Angola (3) Angola (4)				

*Suspended

**Refers to the number of sanctions measures imposed, not the number of individual targets.
Note: Sanctions episodes that are effective in at least one of its purposes (coerce, constrain, signal) are shown in bold. Sanctions that are ineffective in all of their purposes are marked in grey.

Figure 4.1 Effectiveness by number of sanctions measures and other policy instruments

tool – sanctions – intuitively makes sense. More surprising, perhaps, is the frequency with which targeted sanctions have been used alongside force, as they are widely portrayed as alternatives (such as when Kofi Annan described sanctions as the 'necessary middle ground between war and words').[5]

Figure 4.1 shows by episode how often the Council uses combinations of numbers of sanctions measures and numbers of other policy instruments. Neither strongly consistent patterns of combinations nor a

---

[5] See. K. Annan, *In Larger Freedom: Towards Development, Security and Human Rights for All* (New York, NY: United Nations, 2005), p. 109.

'typical' sanctions episode emerge. However, there is a tendency for the Security Council to impose three or four different types of sanctions measures accompanied by three or four other policy instruments.[6] This occurs in eleven episodes. The average number of types of sanctions measures as well as other policy instruments imposed per episode is roughly four.[7]

Sanctions' effectiveness

These figures can be compared against the data set's findings of sanctions' effectiveness in coercing, constraining, and/or signalling, to see if sanctions tend to be more or less effective when accompanied by higher or lower numbers of other policy instruments.

Three points emerge. First, there is some correlation between the number of targeted sanctions measures imposed and effective sanctions episodes. Of the twenty-four episodes where sanctions are shown to be effective in coercing, constraining, or signalling (including those where sanctions were suspended), sixteen involve average, that is, four or higher, numbers of sanctions measures. No effective episode involves less than three sanctions measures imposed.[8] Similarly, a large proportion of effective episodes involve an average or higher number of other policy instruments at play, that is, four or more. (This occurs in seventeen out of twenty-four episodes, with twelve episodes having an above average number of sanctions measures and only one effective case using less than three policy instruments.)

Second, the opposite tendency seems to occur in the data set's twenty-two episodes where targeted sanctions are deemed ineffective across all purposes (indicated in grey in the figure). Here there is some correlation between ineffective episodes and below average numbers of sanctions measures imposed, and below average numbers of other policy instruments being used (nineteen and eleven episodes, respectively).

So there is some correlation between the effectiveness of targeted sanctions and the numbers of sanctions measures imposed, combined with the number of other policy instruments being used simultaneously. Effective episodes tend to have higher numbers of both. This could

[6] The Security Council often imposes as well a single sanctions measure, that being the case in 11 episodes. The use of two or five policy instruments in addition to sanctions is also frequent, having taken place 10 times.

[7] The total number of measures imposed across all episodes, excluding suspended measures, is 222. The total number of other policy instruments used is 230.

[8] A possible exception is the third episode of the Libya regime in the 1990s, an effective episode in which no sanctions were in place (seven measures had been suspended).

suggest that other policy instruments can reinforce targeted sanctions' effectiveness. Or alternatively, that the higher number of sanctions being imposed and other instruments being used simply reflects the importance that the Security Council and others attach to a particular problem, and hence their greater willingness to ensure all instruments are effective (i.e. it could be a measure of 'political will').

But this correlation should not be overstated. It provides no 'magic formula': x number of sanctions plus y numbers of other policy instruments providing z effectiveness. Because, and thirdly, there is no strong pattern suggesting that, over the course of a sanctions regime (i.e. looking sequentially at their episodes), increasing the number of targeted sanctions imposed and the number of other policy instruments used necessarily makes sanctions effective. While this was the case, for example, in the Liberia regime, and during parts of the Somalia and Haiti regimes, the episodes of the sanctions regime on Iran and Sudan over Darfur remained consistently ineffective despite increases in the types of sanctions imposed and other policy instruments used. The Sierra Leone and DRC regimes combine elements of both dynamics.

Purposes and 'policy weight'

The data set also shows some general patterns in the interaction between targeted sanctions and other policy instrument as they relate to the purposes to which sanctions are employed. These help indicate the relative reliance that the Security Council places on sanctions, as opposed to other policy instruments, when trying to achieve its overall policy goals by using a mix of tools – what could be described as the 'policy weight' that sanctions are expected to bear.

There is some correlation between the number of policy objectives the Security Council seeks to achieve through targeted sanctions – an indication of the relative complexity of the problem being addressed – and the number of other policy instruments employed alongside those sanctions.

In general terms, the more complex a situation, with targeted sanctions being used for multiple purposes, the more likely targeted sanctions will be accompanied by a higher-than-average number of other policy instruments. Invariably, this tends to be where sanctions address conflicts (e.g. the DRC, Côte d'Ivoire, Libya in 2011, and Liberia sanctions especially and in the Somalia and Sierra Leone regimes' later episodes). Here sanctions pursue a range of objectives – cessation of hostilities, enforcing peace agreements, human rights, good governance, democracy and peacebuilding support – and are accompanied by a higher-than-average number of other policy instruments. In these cases, it seems the Security

Council does not regard targeted sanctions as the primary means for addressing the situation. The complexity of the problems involved and the inherent dynamism of the conflicts being addressed dictate that the Council, and others, deploy a mix of policy instruments. The policy weight carried by targeted sanctions within this mix necessarily ebbs and flows, but is rarely central to the overall policy effort.

The opposite seems to apply in less complex situations. Where UN targeted sanctions are accompanied by only one other policy instrument, there tends to be a correspondingly small number of policy objectives at stake. DPRK and the Iran sanctions' first three episodes are good examples of this. UN sanctions have few objectives – countering state-sponsored terrorism, non-proliferation, supporting a judicial process – and are accompanied only by diplomacy and negotiation. On Iran, more policy instruments are added in the fourth episode, with no change in the number of policy objectives. But still, the overall number of other policy instruments being used remains below average. The same happened in the sanctions on Libya in the 1990s, where a single policy objective (counterterrorism) was accompanied by a relatively small number of other policy instruments. Sudan over Darfur is the exception, with targeted sanctions having been used for multiple objectives but accompanied by relatively few other policy instruments.

It seems that when used to counter state-sponsored terrorism and for non-proliferation, UN targeted sanctions have carried a greater policy weight than when used for conflict management, as fewer other instruments are in play. With more policy tools being used in conflict situations alongside targeted sanctions, the sanctions seem to be, necessarily, less central to the Security Council's overall approach. Targeted sanctions are not privileged in these cases, but deployed as one component of a larger mix of policy tools.

Unsurprisingly, the data set's results on sanctions' contribution to policy goals seem to bear out this distinction. In the regimes dealing primarily with state-sponsored terrorism and non-proliferation, the sanctions were deemed to have made a major contribution to the outcome (in coercing, constraining, and/or signalling) 39 per cent of the time, although they were not effective in all of these instances. In all of these cases, the sanctions were accompanied by only one, two, or three other policy instruments. In all episodes where more policy instruments are in play, and which mostly deal with conflict, the sanctions record a major contribution only 14 per cent of the time.[9]

---

[9] There are 12 episodes dealing with state-sponsored terrorism and non-proliferation, where sanctions are accompanied by one, two, or three other policy instruments (i.e. below average). These episodes provide a possible 33 scores for the sanctions' contribution in coercing, constraining, or signalling. In 39 per cent of these episodes, sanctions'

Notwithstanding the specifics of each sanctions regime, two possible reasons explain this difference in the policy weight carried by targeted sanctions in non-proliferation and counterterrorism regimes than in conflict cases.

First, in the non-proliferation and state-sponsored terrorism cases (Iran, DPRK, Sudan in the 1990s, Libya in the 1990s), the interests of the P5 states and key regional powers are particularly at stake. All these cases involve adversaries of the United States (Iran, DPRK, Libya, Sudan), and/ or its key allies (Republic of Korea, Japan, Egypt), as well as allies of China and/or Russia. All are concerned with regions of the world – the Middle East, North Africa, and the Korean Peninsula – where great power competition has been significant. Alternatives to sanctions, such as force, in these cases are and were therefore particularly risky in global and regional security terms because of who would have been involved. P5 and regional players' interests therefore dictate that, in these cases, there are (or were) few realistic policy alternatives to diplomacy backed by sanctions. This has been much less so in most of the conflict cases, where P5 interests particularly have been less directly engaged.[10]

The second explanation relates to the nature of the issues the sanctions address. Conflicts and post-conflict situations are inherently dynamic and complex. In trying, first, to help cease hostilities and then build a sustainable peace, the Security Council and other external players face a range of policy problems, but also have a range of policy tools available. Hence these cases are characterized by a greater mix of targeted sanctions and other policy instruments; with the Council pursuing multiple and changing goals as conflicts develop. The non-proliferation and state-sponsored terrorism cases tend to involve fewer issues and protagonists, and overall are less inherently dynamic. The Council's demands of those it targets with sanctions are established early, and remain fairly constant.

Conclusions

To recap, therefore:
(i) UN targeted sanctions have always been used alongside at least one other policy instrument.

contribution scored 4 (a 'major contribution, necessary, but not sufficient'). In 36 per cent the contribution was 3 ('modest'). By comparison, the 35 episodes involving four or more other policy instruments provide a possible 96 scores for sanctions' contribution, and 14 per cent of these were 4: 'major contribution.' The remaining 16 episodes, which have a variety of objectives, have an average of 2.6 additional policy instruments associated with it.
[10] See D. L. Bosco, *Five to Rule Them All: The UN Security Council and the Making of the Modern World* (Oxford University Press, 2009), p. 4 on the Security Council as an instrument of conflict resolution and of great power relations.

(ii) There is some correlation between employing a higher-than-average number of targeted sanctions and a higher-than-average number of other policy instruments and the effectiveness of sanctions. However, the relationship is not causal. There is no strong pattern showing that, over the course of a sanctions regime, increasing the number of sanctions and the number of accompanying policy instruments necessarily makes sanctions more effective.

(iii) Generally, the more complex the situation being addressed by the Security Council, the more likely that targeted sanctions are used as one of a broad mix of policy instruments. These tend to be for conflicts and post-conflict situations. Where the situation is less complex, with just one or two policy goals, targeted sanctions tend to be accompanied by fewer policy instruments (and in some cases only one). These have so far been cases of non-proliferation and state-sponsored terrorism.

(iv) Targeted sanctions therefore carry more policy weight in some cases than in others: less so in the Security Council's approach to conflict management; more for non-proliferation and state-sponsored terrorism.

How do they interact?

The aforementioned conclusions do not show *how* targeted sanctions interact with other policy instruments. That is what the chapter's second section will try to do, in relation to targeted sanctions and the use of force, negotiations and diplomacy, and judicial processes. It cannot do so in great detail. Instead, it will try to categorize the different ways in which they interact so as to draw out some broad conclusions about Security Council behaviour. It will also try to see if these other policy tools affect sanctions' effectiveness.

At the outset, however, agency needs addressing. This chapter has portrayed the Security Council as a unitary actor, purposefully deploying sanctions and other policy tools to pursue its objectives. While this does not detract from the general patterns identified so far, it is deficient in at least two ways when looking at how and why targeted sanctions have been deployed with other policy instruments.

First, this is because some policy tools identified in the data set are used by others and not by the Security Council (e.g. the Council cannot deploy covert measures). So in looking at how targeted sanctions and other policy instruments have been deployed, the rest of the chapter will focus on those over which the Council has control, showing how the Council *consciously* deploys targeted sanctions alongside other policy tools.

Second, viewing the Security Council as a unitary actor gives a mis-leading sense of coherence to the Council's decision-making. The mix of targeted sanctions and other policy instruments that the Council employs in any situation ultimately reflects the interplay of political forces within the Council. As mentioned in Lopez's and Brzoska's chapter, this mix results from political bargaining between Council members, rather than a careful weighing of each type of sanction and other policy tools against solidly agreed goals, or necessarily based on Council members' agreed understanding of how and why the sanctions and other policy instruments will actually interact. The Council always grapples simultaneously with its own internal political dynamics and those of the situations it addresses.

Targeted sanctions and the use of force

Targeted sanctions have been used alongside the robust use of force and limited military strikes in thirty-two of the sixty-three sanctions episodes; roughly 51 per cent.[11] Add the threat of force and the figure rises to thirty-nine episodes, that is, almost two-thirds of episodes. In only seven of the twenty-three sanctions regimes is force absent as an international policy response: Libya in the 1990s, Sudan in the 1990s and 2011, Lebanon, Ethiopia-Eritrea, DPRK, and CAR. Four of these regimes deal with state-sponsored terrorism and proliferation and not conflict, regimes identified earlier where targeted sanctions carry the heaviest policy weight.

But how do targeted sanctions and the use of force fit into the Security Council's approach to problems? Are they alternative or complementary tools? And what is the impact on sanctions' effectiveness?

These questions are answered by looking at the two scenarios in which targeted sanctions and the use of force play out, covering most of the episodes in which targeted sanctions and robust force and military strikes occur.

The first scenario is where the Security Council imposes targeted sanctions while also authorizing or otherwise blessing the use of robust force by international 'coalitions of the willing' and/or regional organizations, that is, the sanctions regimes on Somalia (where Unified Task Force (UNITAF) was, and African Union Military Observer Mission in Somalia (AMISOM) is now, authorized to use force), Haiti (the Multinational Force in Haiti (MNF)), Côte d'Ivoire (Operation Licorne), and for the AQT, Taliban, and the 2011 Libya regimes (NATO and its allies).

---

[11] Somalia episodes 1–5; Liberia episodes 1–5; Angola episodes 1–4; Rwanda episode 2; Sierra Leone episodes 1–4; FRY over Kosovo episode 1; AQT episodes 3 and 4; DRC episodes 1, 3, and 4; Iraq episodes 1–2; Côte d'Ivoire episodes 1 and 4; Taliban episode 1; Libya in 2011 episodes 2 and 3.

The Security Council has tended in these cases to mandate force after first imposing sanctions, although the time lag between each has varied across the sanctions regimes. Over Libya in 2011, the alignment of political support in the Council behind the use of force and the urgency of the situation meant the Council waited just under three weeks between imposing targeted measures and authorizing the use of force to enforce a no-fly zone and to protect civilians.[12] In other cases the time lag was longer. On Somalia, for instance, it was about eleven months between the arms embargo's imposition and UNITAF's authorization. The time lag in the AQT regime was about two years (1999 and 2001).[13]

In Liberia, Sierra Leone, and Côte d'Ivoire, the Security Council imposed targeted sanctions after it had already authorized or otherwise blessed the use of force by Economic Community of West African States (ECOWAS) and Operation Licorne. Indeed, the immediate trigger for sanctions' imposition in Côte d'Ivoire was the attack on and retaliation by the French (Licorne) forces on 6 November 2004, with UN targeted sanctions following nine days later.

In the second scenario – involving most of the remaining examples of targeted UN sanctions being used alongside robust or targeted military strikes – the Security Council has used sanctions that end up supporting governmental military forces and their allies in conflicts. The Council did not, therefore, authorize the force itself, but used sanctions knowing that other actors would or were likely to use it.

The targeted sanctions against National Union for the Total Independence of Angola (UNITA) are a good example of this scenario. Initially aimed in 1993 at coercing UNITA into ceasing hostilities, abiding by the Lusaka Accord and accepting the 1992 election results, by mid 1998, the expansion of the sanctions (adding travel, diplomatic, aviation, financial, and diamond-related sanctions to the arms embargo and petrol-related measures) and improvements in their enforcement had eroded UNITA's military capacity. This occurred at a time when it and the Angolan government had arguably decided to seek a military solution to the conflict; hence, the sanctions helped isolate UNITA, to the Angolan government's political and military advantage.[14] Targeted sanctions acted similarly in Sierra Leone and the DRC. The sanctions shifted from targeting all parties (in the general arms embargoes) to favouring the respective governmental forces (and their allies) by targeting their

---

[12] UN Security Council resolutions 1970 (2011), 1973 (2011).

[13] Initial sanctions following the East African embassy bombings in 1998 were significantly broadened after 9/11.

[14] This took place in episode 3, in which targeted sanctions were effective in constraining and signalling.

military opponents – the Revolutionary United Front (RUF) in Sierra Leone, and opponents of the DRC peace agreement.[15] Here the Security Council consciously backed one side, as distinct from the Yugoslav arms embargo, which initially but inadvertently favoured the Serb forces.[16]

In responding to conflicts, therefore, the Security Council does not necessarily seem to consider targeted sanctions an alternative to force. Rather, the Council has used targeted sanctions to complement the use of robust force and targeted military strikes, either when expressly authorizing it (by an international coalition or organization) or when backing force used by others (mainly governments). While this was not always the Council's intention from the outset in all instances, its position often evolved so that sanctions and the use of force became aligned. In effect, the Council took sides in the conflict, pushed by the conflicts' changing political and military dynamics interplayed with the politics within the Council itself.

The targeted sanctions concerning Darfur (Sudan over Darfur), however, are an exception. The Security Council members' competing interests have ensured that the sanctions have continued to apply relatively equally to all parties in Darfur. All are covered by the arms embargo, while competing P5 interests dictated that those targeted by the individual travel ban and asset freeze listings also came from all conflicting parties.[17] Consequently, the sanctions do not favour any particular actor. The Council has not authorized force (beyond UNAMID's limited mandate), nor reached a point where it wishes to use sanctions to complement force being used by others. The Council has not taken sides, and its relatively weak sanctions reflect that.

Sanctions' effectiveness when accompanying force

So, while targeted sanctions can complement the use of force, does that affect the effectiveness of sanctions in coercing, constraining, and/or signalling?

The picture is mixed. The data set shows that, of the twenty-four sanctions episodes that are effective in coercing, constraining, and/or signalling, fifteen (roughly 63 per cent) also involve the use of robust force and/or limited military strikes (nine episodes in relation to robust force, eight to limited military strikes, and two episodes having both).[18] But of the data set's thirty-nine ineffective sanctions episodes, seventeen

---

[15] DRC episodes 2, 3, and 4; Liberia episodes 2 and 3.   [16] FRY in the 1990s, episode 1.
[17] UN Security Council resolution 1672 (2006).
[18] Somalia episode 4; Liberia episodes 2–5; Angola episodes 3 and 4; Sierra Leone episodes 1 and 4; AQT episodes 3 and 4; DRC episode 3; Côte d'Ivoire episode 4; Libya in 2011 episodes 2 and 3.

(roughly 44 per cent) involve the use of robust military force and/or limited strikes.[19] It is useful to recall in this context that of the thirty-eight instances of effective sanctions (in the twenty-four episodes mentioned above) only five were so in coercing a target to change behaviour. The majority of effective sanctions episodes were successful in constraining (sixteen) or signalling (seventeen).[20]

Of the episodes where sanctions are accompanied by robust force, over a third (41 per cent) are effective (nine episodes out of twenty-two).[21] They are most frequently effective in signalling (seven of the nine episodes), in constraining (six episodes), or both (four episodes). Targeted sanctions accompanied by the robust use of force are effective in coercing in only two episodes (episodes 4 of the Somalia and of the Sierra Leone cases). When combined with limited military strikes, targeted sanctions are effective in eight of the eighteen relevant episodes (roughly 44 per cent), some of which overlap with episodes involving the robust use of force.[22] The targeted sanctions are effective at constraining and signalling in six of the episodes, and coercing in one (Somalia episode 4).

Given this mixed picture it is difficult to argue that combining the robust use of force or limited strikes with targeted sanctions significantly increases the chances of those sanctions being effective. Where there is a correlation, however, the sanctions' effectiveness tends to be strongest in constraining and signalling. There is little to suggest that sanctions are more likely to be coercive when used alongside force. This intuitively makes sense, as it is reasonable to assume that targeted sanctions are unlikely to be more coercive than military force when employed together.[23] Greater effectiveness in constraining and signalling fits more easily with the idea suggested earlier, of the Security Council using targeted measures to complement the use of force of which it approves, and targeting those of whom it disapproves.

It is important to acknowledge, however, that this discussion of effectiveness of targeted sanctions when used with force has not considered the question of unintended consequences, the risks of which can increase when force is employed. So policymakers should not draw overly

[19] Somalia episodes 1, 2, 3, and 5; Liberia episode 1; Angola episodes 1 and 2; Rwanda episode 2; Sierra Leone episodes 2 and 3; FRY over Kosovo episode 1; DRC episodes 1 and 4; Iraq episodes 1 and 2; Côte d'Ivoire episode 1; Taliban episode 1.
[20] For coercion, constraint, and signal as the purposes of sanctions, see Chapter 2 by Francesco Giumelli.
[21] Somalia episode 4; Angola episodes 3 and 4; Sierra Leone episodes 1 and 4; AQT episodes 3 and 4; DRC episode 3; Côte d'Ivoire episode 4.
[22] Somalia episode 4; Liberia episodes 2–5; AQT episode 4; Libya in 2011 episodes 2 and 3.
[23] In other words, that sanctions would record a higher contribution to the coercion of the target. See also R. A. Pape, 'Why Sanctions Do Not Work', pp. 97–8.

simplistic and narrow policy prescriptions from some of the data set's findings on targeted sanctions' effectiveness.

Threats of force

In sixteen episodes across ten country regimes (FRY in 1990s, Haiti, FRY over Kosovo, AQT, DRC, Côte d'Ivoire, Iran, Taliban, Libya in 2011, and Guinea-Bissau), targeted sanctions were also accompanied by threats of force. In the main, these threats have come from forces mandated by the Security Council or by government forces – NATO's threat against Serbia over Kosovo being an exception. The correlation between the effectiveness of sanctions in coercing, constraining, and/or signalling and the threat of the use of force is reasonably strong. Of the sixteen episodes involving the threat, eight are effective (50 per cent).[24] However, in all but three cases (Haiti, Iran, and Guinea-Bissau), over the course of the sanctions regimes force came eventually to be used (in 1994 the MNF in Haiti deployed peacefully despite being authorized to use force). So even though in many of these cases the sanctions were quite effective, the effect of their use in combination with the threat of force was not such that it meant force was not ultimately used. Arguably, the sanctions did not reinforce the threat sufficiently. Or the sanctions and threat simply operated in parallel. This is a point that is possibly borne out by the fact that, of the eight effective sanctions episodes involving the threat of force, most are effective in constraining (five episodes) and signalling (four episodes, either singularly or together), rather than in coercing (only one episode).[25]

Targeted sanctions and diplomacy/negotiation

UN targeted sanctions are used most frequently alongside diplomacy and negotiation. The combination occurs in all of the data set's targeted sanctions regimes, and in 97 per cent of its episodes. In looking at how targeted sanctions have interacted with negotiations, three categories emerge: first, in those situations where the targeted sanctions become embroiled in ongoing diplomatic process and negotiations, with the Security Council in effect using targeted sanctions to help the processes of reaching an agreement; second, and more frequently, where the Council uses targeted sanctions to support implementation of an existing agreement (most often a peace agreement in conflict); and third, where

---

[24] Haiti episode 1; AQT episodes 3 and 4; DRC episode 3; Côte d'Ivoire episodes 3 and 4; Libya in 2011 episodes 1 and 2.
[25] Côte d'Ivoire episode 3.

the targeted sanctions and diplomatic processes operate in parallel, seemingly without meaningful interaction.

Sanctions central to negotiations

The first category, where negotiations are central to the problem being addressed, includes Libya in the 1990s, Iran, DPRK, Sudan in the 1990s, and Taliban regimes, and initially on Haiti.[26] In these regimes, sanctions become, or became, embroiled in negotiation processes. On Libya in the 1990s, negotiations eventually involved the United States, United Kingdom, France, and Libya, with some UN, Organization of African Unity (OAU), and Arab League participation. For Haiti it was the US-brokered Governors Island negotiations; on Sudan in the 1990s, the OAU mediation of the demand that Sudan extradite terrorist suspects to Ethiopia; while on Iran and DPRK the focus is the 'E3 plus 3' and 'Six party talks', respectively. It is also interesting to note that these cases involve few other policy instruments being used alongside targeted sanctions, negotiation, and diplomacy. Hence, sanctions carry a heavy policy weight, suggesting that their relative effectiveness had, or has, a more direct bearing on the policy's overall success.

In that regard, Libya in the 1990s is an interesting case. Arguably, the diplomatic process and negotiations came to constitute themselves around the question of sanctions and especially of their lifting. The Security Council, backed by targeted sanctions, set the terms of the negotiation in support of British, French, and US demands. Libya responded with a diplomatic and legal campaign to delegitimize and erode political support for the sanctions, especially among the OAU and the Arab League. In September 1997 the Arab League threatened to relax sanctions' enforcement, and in June 1998 the OAU threatened to stop implementing the sanctions unless the dispute was settled by that September.[27] This changed the bargaining process. The United States and the United Kingdom, faced with declining support for sanctions, proposed a compromise whereby *inter alia* the Lockerbie suspects were extradited to a Scottish Court, sitting in The Hague. This was accepted.[28] Just as Arab League and OAU support for sanctions was politically

---

[26] On how the comprehensive FRY sanctions affected negotiations on the Yugoslav conflict, see D. Cortright and G. A. Lopez, *The Sanctions Decade: Assessing UN Strategies in the 1990s*, p. 81, and Report of the Copenhagen Round Table on UN Sanctions in the Case of the Former Yugoslavia S/1996/776, p. 13.

[27] On Libya's strategies to undermine the legitimacy of sanctions, see I. Hurd, *After Anarchy: Legitimacy & Power in the United Nations Security Council* (Princeton: Princeton University Press, 2007), chapter 6.

[28] Cortright and Lopez, *The Sanctions Decade: Assessing UN Strategies in the 1990s*, p. 118.

important, so conversely was their threat of non-implementation. In effect, therefore, the Council's targeted sanctions brought the Arab League and the OAU more directly into the Lockerbie negotiations beyond the main protagonists (Libya, France, the United Kingdom, and the United States), and gave them leverage over those protagonists. The result was a virtuous circle of incentives for all parties to compromise, vindicated by the subsequent prosecution of the Lockerbie suspects, the payment of compensation to victims, and resolution of the UTA flight 772 affair. Interestingly, the 1990s Libya regime's first two episodes were effective in constraining, rather than coercing.

The other cases in this first category, however, have been less success-ful. The UN targeted sanctions on Iran and DPRK, combined with US, EU, and others' bilateral sanctions, have helped encourage Iran and DPRK, periodically, to participate in talks.[29] But, at the time of this writing, in neither case have sanctions been sufficient to effect a settle-ment and force compliance with the Security Council's demands. The targeted sanctions seem to have influenced Iranian and North Korean tactical approaches to negotiations, but not forced a strategic policy change. As 'The Iran Project's' analysis of the Iran sanctions (UN and others') stated, 'Tehran has indicated a willingness to settle some issues ... but as a partial precondition Tehran has insisted on a relaxation of sanctions'.[30]

On Haiti, the imposition of targeted sanctions led quickly to the 'de facto' Haitian regime concluding the Governors Island Agreement, but again, as it transpired, as a tactical ploy to secure sanctions' suspension and to buy time.[31] In the 1990s Sudan case the sanctions were ineffective and had little impact on the diplomatic process and negotiations. The jury remains out on the Taliban sanctions.

On Iran, DPRK, Haiti, and possibly the Taliban where targeted sanc-tions have interacted with negotiations, it has been in getting parties to the negotiating table. But sanctions have not ensured that those negotiations are successful, in terms of securing Security Council demands. The bargaining process between senders and target seen in the 1990s Libya case has not yet been replicated elsewhere. Instead, the targeted sanctions have affected mostly targets' tactical, rather than strategic, decision-making. Given that in most of these cases sanctions carry a heavy policy

---

[29] Iran episode 4; DPRK episode 1.   [30] The Iran Project (2012), p. 64.
[31] There is a parallel with the comprehensive UN sanctions against Rhodesia. The Rhodesian regime accepted the Lancaster House negotiations and resultant agreement in part to get sanctions lifted. Ian Smith mistakenly believed this would then allow Rhodesian forces to prosecute their war against the Patriotic Front more successfully. M. Preston, *Ending Civil War: Rhodesia and Lebanon in Perspective* (IB Tauris, 2004).

weight, the implications are potentially significant if they are unable to enforce a successful negotiation.

Implementing agreements

The second (more common) category of interaction between sanctions and diplomacy and negotiation is where targeted sanctions are used, not so much to help convene a negotiation, but rather to support implementation of a peace agreement and/or peace process. The Angola, Sierra Leone, DRC, Côte d'Ivoire, Liberia, and Somalia have all been in part aimed at, or became focused on, helping implement and/or enforce a peace agreement. Hence, in this category targeted sanctions are related to conflict management. As shown earlier, in these situations targeted sanctions tend to be deployed as part of a wider mix of policy instruments, and as such, carry less weight in ensuring a successful policy. The targeted sanctions are more likely, therefore, to support other instruments – peacekeeping forces, DDR, use of force, etc. – and hence follow, rather than drive, the diplomatic processes and negotiations. The implications of their relative effectiveness are therefore arguably less acute for the overall success of the Council's approach.

Generalizing conclusively about the role of targeted sanctions in the implementation of agreements is difficult.[32] As in the first category in this section, they have occasionally helped secure tactical concessions, such as UNITA's acceptance of the 1994 Lusaka Protocol. But on the whole, where sanctions have made a contribution they tended not to have been singularly decisive in securing implementation of peace agreements. Rather, targeted sanctions have supported implementation by seeking to isolate groups opposing an agreement (e.g. as in the DRC), sometimes reinforcing military reverses in the process (e.g. as with UNITA); reducing external support (e.g. for the RUF and Al Shabaab); and in deterring potential 'spoilers' (e.g. in Liberia, Sierra Leone, Côte d'Ivoire). The effective episodes in these sanctions regimes, therefore, tend to be so in constraining and signalling, thus reinforcing sanctions' complementary, supportive role.

It is noteworthy that, in a number of cases where it was supporting implementation of an agreement, the Security Council's position evolved such that it identified a particular group or groups as blocking progress and amended the sanctions accordingly. A number of sanctions regimes have been changed at key points when the Council has more clearly

---

[32] On sanctions and peace agreement implementation, see A. Charron, *UN Sanctions and Conflict: Responding to Peace and Security Threat* (London: Routledge, 2011), and particularly Appendices A to C.

backed one side in a conflict, usually the relevant government. In Somalia, for example, the creation of Somalia's Transitional Federal Government's in 2004 led, in part, to targeted sanctions being imposed on its opponents and on members of Al Shabaab, and, eventually, secondary sanctions on Eritrea over its interference in Somalia. Following the election of President Kabila in 2006, the Council focused the DRC sanctions more against rebel armed groups outside the DRC peace process. The Council's imposition of secondary sanctions against Liberia over its aid to the RUF marked a shift in the Council's approach to the Sierra Leone conflict. Similarly, from late 1998 the Council explicitly cited UNITA and Jonas Savimbi in particular as the obstacle to peace in Angola. It also targeted Laurent Gbagbo and his supporters following their rejection of the 2010 Côte d'Ivoire presidential election results. In all these examples the congruence of Council members' interests and events on the ground allowed the Council to shift its response to diplomatic processes and negotiations by more expressly falling in behind the government concerned against its opponents. This helped the Council achieve policy coherence with the targeted sanctions by more easily aligning with other policy instruments. Targeted sanctions' relative adaptability, as compared to comprehensive measures, has helped the Council in this regard as targeted sanctions can be more easily changed to fit the Council's policy goals.

Sanctions and negotiations in parallel

Targeted sanctions can therefore play a role in convening negotiations and also implementing agreements. But in some cases, comprising a third category of interaction, they have operated alongside diplomacy and negotiations only in parallel, with little or no impact. This was seen particularly in the Rwanda, AQT, Ethiopia-Eritrea, and the 1990s Libya and Sudan sanctions regimes. The 2011 Libya targeted sanctions initially reinforced the Qadhafi regime's diplomatic isolation following Libya's AU and Arab League memberships being suspended. But the AU's and the Arab League's policy prescriptions diverged. The league called for forceful action (a no-fly zone), whereas the AU tried to mediate and proposed a ceasefire. But as force came to supersede diplomatic efforts (three weeks after the sanctions' imposition), the targeted sanctions came to reinforce military, rather than diplomatic, action. Similarly, the Sudan over Darfur sanctions seem to have had little influence on the Darfur negotiations, possibly due to the way they are targeted, which, in turn, reflects divisions with the Security Council. The Ethiopia–Eritrea arms embargo was imposed too late to influence the negotiation of the

Algiers Agreement and then the formal peace agreements in June and December 2000, and lapsed soon thereafter.

Targeted sanctions and judicial processes

In over 46 per cent of the data set's episodes, UN targeted sanctions have been used alongside national, international, and with the Special Court for Sierra Leone (SCSL) 'hybrid' judicial processes. Sanctions have interacted with these processes in three ways. They have been used as a means of enforcing national judicial decisions, and to accompany international and hybrid war crimes tribunals. And in a significant development, judicial processes have also been used by targets to counter the effects of sanctions.

National judicial decisions

The 1990s Libya and Sudan, and initially the AQT targeted sanctions were aimed at enforcing national court decisions seeking the extradition of terrorist suspects: the Lockerbie suspects' extradition from Libya to Scotland, the extradition to Ethiopia of those suspected of trying to assassinate Egypt's president Mubarak, and the Taliban sending Osama Bin Laden and some associates to face prosecution in the United States for the bombing of its embassies in Kenya and Tanzania. The Lebanon sanctions, imposed in 2005 to support the United Nations International Independent Investigation Commission, Lebanon (UNIIIC), now accompany the Special Tribunal for Lebanon (STL), which was created in 2007.[33]

Targeted sanctions' record in supporting these judicial processes is not strong. The 1990s Libya sanctions were successful and the suspects were extradited. But the 1990s Sudan targeted sanctions were ineffective, with the extradition issues resolved diplomatically. The AQT sanctions neither secured Bin Laden's extradition nor deterred AQ's subsequent attacks on the United States on 11 September 2001. No one has been listed under the Lebanon sanctions regime, nor have any of those indicted by the STL been surrendered.

War crimes trials

A larger set of episodes (twenty) see targeted sanctions used alongside international and hybrid war crimes processes: the International Criminal Tribunal for the former Yugoslavia (ICTY, involving the Kosovo

---

[33] The STL is of an 'international character' but applies Lebanese law.

sanctions), the International Criminal Tribunal for Rwanda (ICTR, Rwanda sanctions), the SCSL (the Sierra Leone and Liberia sanctions), and the ICC (the Sudan over Darfur, 2011 Libya, DRC, and Côte d'Ivoire sanctions).[34] Interestingly, the effectiveness of targeted sanctions when employed alongside these different war crimes processes is quite striking. Of the twenty sanctions episodes, twelve are deemed effective,[35] that is, 60 per cent of this group of episodes and half of all the data set's twenty-four effective episodes. Again, sanctions' effectiveness here rates more in signalling (eight out of twelve episodes) and constraining (nine episodes) – mostly simultaneously – than in coercing (only three episodes).

Does this strong correlation show a profound interaction between sanctions and these war crimes processes, and a strong Security Council strategy in this regard?

Again, the answers are mixed. First, the use of sanctions alongside these judicial processes has not always reflected conscious Security Council decision-making. The ICTY's creation pre-dated the Kosovo sanctions regime,[36] while the Council mandated the ICTR and the SCSL after it had imposed sanctions on Rwanda and Sierra Leone.[37] So the Council chose to use sanctions alongside these three judicial processes. This was also the case for the two situations the Council referred to the ICC: Darfur in 2006 and Libya in 2011 (especially so over Libya, with Resolution 1970 (2011) simultaneously imposing targeted sanctions and making the referral). The ICC's involvement in the DRC and Côte d'Ivoire, however, followed self-referrals. The Court's jurisdiction was engaged without Security Council involvement, with targeted sanctions therefore being used coincidentally alongside these ICC cases.

Nor does the Security Council seem to have a clear strategy in how it seeks to use targeted sanctions with judicial processes. On Rwanda and Kosovo the Council did not use sanctions specifically to support the ICTR or ICTY.[38] Libya in February 2011, however, was different. Security Council Resolution 1970 (2011) imposed targeted sanctions

---

[34] DRC episodes 1–4; Sudan over Darfur episode 2; Côte d'Ivoire episodes 4 and 5; Libya 2011 episodes 1–3; Liberia episodes 2–5; Sierra Leone episodes 4 and 5; Lebanon episode 1; Rwanda episodes 1–2; FRY over Kosovo episode 1.

[35] DRC episodes 2 and 3; Côte d'Ivoire episode 4; Libya 2011 episodes 1–3; Liberia episodes 2–5; Sierra Leone episodes 4 and 5.

[36] UN Security Council resolution 827 (1993).

[37] See UN Security Council resolutions 955 (1994) and 1315 (2000).

[38] Nor did the Council use the comprehensive FRY sanctions to support the ICTY. It lifted the sanctions fully in 1996 to underpin the Dayton agreement, well before the ICTY had completed its work. The ICTY's most active phase came after the sanctions had been lifted. See R. Kerr, *The International Criminal Tribunal for the Former Yugoslavia: An Exercise in Law, Politics, and Diplomacy* (Oxford University Press, 2004), chapter 7.

on Muammar and Saif Qadhafi and Abdullah Al-Senussi, among others. They were indicted by the ICC prosecutor four months later. Here the ICC referral, the subsequent indictments, and the targeted sanctions' effectiveness in signalling were reinforcing.[39] The judicial processes and targeted sanctions pulled logically in the same direction in isolating the Qadhafi regime.

The Darfur case is different still. The Security Council was divided over the initial ICC referral. (Resolution 1593 (2005) received eleven votes, with only two of the P5 – France and the United Kingdom – supporting.) Controversy followed the ICC's subsequent indictment of Sudan's president Bashir, and the question of states' cooperation with the Court has become contested. The Council has been unable, however, to use targeted sanctions to address these problems. The way the sanctions are targeted means that there is little interaction with the ICC processes. They operate in parallel, with neither supporting the other.

Similarly, in the DRC and Côte d'Ivoire cases the interaction between the ICC and targeted sanctions does not seem significant. As already shown, their use together is coincidental. Some of those listed under the DRC regime, however, have been indicted by the ICC, with a number being indicted and listed for allegedly recruiting child soldiers.[40] Laurent Gbagbo was also listed under the Côte d'Ivoire targeted sanctions a few months before his ICC indictment was unsealed in November 2011. But given the time lag between these listings and indictments, it would be wrong to suggest that the listings necessarily led to the indictments. As with the Libya case, however, the ICC's involvement in the DRC and Côte d'Ivoire reinforce the overall signalling – and for some of the ICC's indictees, the constraining effect – of sanctions.[41] Similar processes played out with the SCSL.

It is perhaps worth considering, therefore, if the Security Council referring a situation to the ICC constitutes a new type of targeted sanction. Douglas Cantwell's work certainly shows key similarities between ICC referrals and targeted sanctions.[42] Referrals signal concern to multiple audiences and can reinforce norms. Indictees' activities become constrained. They are also potentially coerced. But it is difficult to argue that in referring a situation to the ICC, the Council is using a targeted measure aimed at influencing targets' behaviour. As Cantwell also notes, while the

---

[39] Libya 2011 episodes 1 and 2.
[40] E.g. Thomas Lubanga, Germain Katanga, Ngudjolo Chui, Bosco Ntaganda.
[41] DRC episodes 2, 3, 4; Côte d'Ivoire episodes 4 and 5.
[42] Douglas Cantwell, 'Sanctioning Justice: The Security Council and the International Criminal Court among Words and Wars' (Master's thesis, the Graduate Institute, Geneva, 2012), chapter 2.

Council refers the problem to the ICC, it is the prosecutor and Court which decide who, if anyone, is indicted and for what (i.e. they pick the targets). Furthermore, the Council cannot set criteria for lifting ICC indictments or ending cases. At most it can suspend a case, using its prerogatives under Article 16 of the ICC Statute. Although to date it has not done so. (The Council has not agreed AU requests that it defer the ICC's Darfur and Kenya cases.)[43] The power to end indictments and cases rests with the ICC. And unlike the Council when it imposes and lifts sanctions, ICC decisions are not based on a political assessment of the indictees' future behaviour, or that since their indictment. The Council therefore cedes control and agency when referring a situation to the ICC. And the potential bargaining process between sender and target – a feature of targeted sanctions and inherent in the prospect of their lifting – is not replicated between indictees and the ICC. The ICC and Council could potentially work at cross-purposes, the former pursuing justice and the latter peace, which has led some to question whether an ICC referral helps or hinders the Council's primary role.[44]

Courts as a defence against targeted sanctions

Finally, there are instances where targets have tried to use courts to get sanctions lifted. The Libyan government sought an ICJ ruling on the Lockerbie and UTA 772 extradition requests, to pre-empt their consideration by the Security Council, and then to erode the legitimacy of the Council's subsequent decision to impose targeted sanctions (the 1990s Libya regime).[45] The ICJ claimed jurisdiction in February 1998, but the case subsequently lapsed following the Lockerbie suspects' extradition.

Some of those targeted by the AQ sanctions have challenged them in European and other courts on 'due process' and human rights-related grounds. In both the 1990s Libya and AQ sanctions, the court cases have served to blunt the sanctions' effectiveness in signalling. In reaction to the AQ-related cases, the Security Council, from July 2005, has incrementally reformed its procedures for listing and delisting individuals and entities under the AQ regime.[46] The most recent 'due process' innovation was the creation and subsequent strengthening of an Ombudsperson

---

[43] The AU Permanent Observer's letter of 21 July 2008 to the Security Council President (S/2008/481), and AU Assembly resolution Assembly/AU/Dec.334 (XVI).
[44] See, for example, Russian comments in the Security Council debate of 17 October 2012 (S/PV.6849).
[45] Hurd, *After Anarchy*.
[46] See T. J. Biersteker and S. Eckert, *Addressing Challenges to Targeted Sanctions: An Update of the "Watson Report"* (Geneva: The Graduate Institute, 2009), Annex C, p. 56.

through which delisting requests can be channelled.[47] However, the ECJ, in its *Kadi II* judgement, argued that the Ombudsperson provided insufficient legal protection to the person being listed.[48]

Judicial challenges continue to pose a significant challenge to UN targeted sanctions, and in so doing are bringing legal concerns to bear on the Security Council's political decision-making processes in an unprecedented way.

Conclusions

This chapter has tried to identify which policy tools have been employed alongside UN targeted sanctions, when, and why. In doing so, it introduced the idea of policy weight: the extent to which targeted sanctions can be relied upon to deliver the overall policy goal compared with the reliance on other tools being simultaneously employed for the same ends. In some cases targeted sanctions bear, or have borne, a heavy policy weight, as only one other policy tool or few tools have been used alongside them. In these situations the challenge for the Security Council in achieving its policy objectives is directly linked to the sanctions' effectiveness. Where targeted sanctions bear less policy weight, because they are used as part of a broader mix of policy tools, the challenge for the Council is not only effectiveness but also coherence, ensuring that the policy tools align. This seems most likely to occur where the interplay between Council members' interests and the situation and politics on the ground allows the Council definitively to take sides in a dispute. Invariably this has occurred in conflict and post-conflict situations, with the Council usually backing a government against its opponents.

The chapter also looked at how targeted sanctions interact with the use of force, diplomacy and negotiation, and judicial processes. In trying to show the variety of interactions, it has illustrated ways of categorizing Security Council behaviour in using targeted sanctions alongside these other policy tools to see if the Council itself has clear strategies in this regard. It has shown that at times targeted sanctions and these other policy tools operate in parallel, without much interaction, and, in the case of some judicial action, as a brake on sanctions. But this chapter has also shown that, in many instances, targeted sanctions interact in a complementary way with these other policy tools, mainly by constraining and signalling. Identifying if and how these complementarities can work in each context is, of course, the challenge to policymakers, but also one for further and more in-depth study.

---

[47] UN Security Council resolutions 1904 (2009), 1989 (2011), 2083 (2012).
[48] See p. 133 of the ECJ Judgement C-584/10P www.curia.europa.eu.

5   The relationship between United Nations sanctions and regional sanctions regimes

Andrea Charron and Clara Portela

One of the most notable developments in the sanctions landscape over the past couple of decades has been the proliferation of sanctions imposed by regional organizations. Of the sixty-three United Nations sanctions episodes studied by the consortium, forty-three involve regional organizations, in some cases a multiplicity of them. In twelve sanctions regimes, regional sanctions preceded the UN sanctions, and in ten cases, unilateral sanctions preceded UN sanctions. In fact, only six episodes are of stand-alone UN sanctions. This suggests that states subject to sanctions are increasingly targeted by a combination of UN and regional measures.

This development is interesting for several reasons. First, the use of sanctions outside of the framework of the UN has illustrated the willingness of regional organizations to employ coercive measures within their regions, even in the case of organizations created fairly recently. From this vantage point, it is symptomatic of the rise of regional governance. Second, in the past, sanctions had been criticized by Third-World leaders as a tool to impose a Western agenda on them. Indeed, many regional organizations in the developing world emerged as post-colonial projects with the explicit aim of shielding sovereign governments from external interference.[1] The fact that some regional organizations now employing sanctions most frequently are located outside of the Western world is indicative of these measures' growing legitimacy and usefulness as foreign policy tools. In addition, the increasingly frequent resort to sanctions signifies that some regions in the developing world, which have been traditionally at the receiving end of sanctions, are taking ownership of their security governance.

Despite the proliferation of sanctions adopted by regional arrangements, little attention has been devoted to them or to their relationship

---

[1] E. Hellquist, 'Regional Organisations and Sanctions against Members: Explaining the Different Trajectories of the African Union, the League of Arab states, and the Association of Southeast Asian Nations' (KFG working paper series, Freie Universität Berlin, 2014), http://userpage.fuberlin.de/~kfgeu/kfgwp/wpseries/kfg_wp59_a.htm.

with UN sanctions.[2] To date, research has focused primarily on regional organizations as implementers of UN sanctions – an issue that has gained currency especially following successful legal challenges to legislation giving effect to UN blacklists of individuals.[3] But important questions as to the interrelationship between regional and UN sanctions exist – such as whether they complement or conflict with each other, and whether regional organizations follow the lead of UN sanctions or set the stage for the UN to act. This chapter explores the relationship between mandatory sanctions imposed by the UN Security Council, on the one hand, and regional organizations, on the other. In particular, we consider the timing and sequencing of sanctions, the compatibility of objectives pursued, and the nature of the sanctions imposed.

We focus in this chapter on regional organizations in Africa and Europe, because in comparison with other regional organizations, they have imposed the largest number of sanctions regimes. Three African regional organizations are considered: the African Union, the Economic Community of West African States, and the South African Development Community. Most UN sanctions regimes in the post–Cold War period have been imposed against African states and actors, but these sanctions differ from those sanctioned by the African organizations in terms of objectives, measures, and targets. The European Union has a rich and long-standing sanctions practice and constitutes one of the most prolific senders of sanctions. The EU imposes sanctions on about twice as many countries as the UN. In the time frame from 1990 to 2013, the UN wielded sanctions against twenty states, while thirty-five states were affected by EU sanctions during the same period (see Table 5.4). Regional organizations elsewhere have also imposed sanctions: The Organization of American States (OAS) applied sanctions against Haiti in the early 1990s to protest the military coup that ousted President-elect Aristide. The Arab League suspended Egypt's membership from 1979 to 1989 and more recently, Libya in 2011 and Syria in 2012. By contrast, Association of Southeast Asian Nations (ASEAN) continues to reject the notion of sanctions: it has never imposed sanctions, neither externally nor internally, and it vocally condemned the imposition of Western sanctions against its Member State Myanmar, causing considerable friction in its

---

[2] C. Portela, *European Union Sanctions and Foreign Policy* (London: Routledge, 2010); M. Eriksson, *Supporting Democracy in Africa* (Stockholm: FOI Swedish Defence Research Agency, 2010).

[3] E. Drieskens and C. Boucher, 'Researching the European Union at the United Nations in New York: Current Trends and Future Agendas', in K. E. Jorgensen and K. Laatikainen (eds.), *Handbook on Europe and Multilateral Institutions* (London: Routledge, 2012); M Heupel, 'Multilateral Sanctions against Terror Suspects and the Violation of Due Process Standards', *International Affairs*, 85 (2009), pp. 307–21.

relations with Western partners.[4] Due to the low incidence of sanctions by these regional organizations, the present chapter focuses on African and EU sanctions and their relationship to UN sanctions.

UN sanctions

UN sanctions are used to target often intractable conflicts with a myriad of measures against a number of targets. Although this is hardly acknowledged in the literature, regional organizations do not merely follow the UNSC lead. Instead, it is the regional efforts, especially African regional efforts in the form of negotiated peace agreements, missions, and calls for action, that are the springboard for UNSC sanctions.

For the UNSC, the trigger for sanctions is the definition of a case as a threat to or breach of international peace and security as per Article 39 of the UN Charter. In practice, this has meant that the Council has applied sanctions to deal with a host of crises, often of a humanitarian nature.[5] If we look more closely at the twenty-three UN country sanctions regimes explored by the consortium, fourteen target an African state – mostly sub-Saharan[6] – and one a European state, the former Yugoslavia. Broken down by episodes, it means that forty-three of the sixty-three episodes (or 68 per cent) of sanctions targeted an African conflict of some variant and thirty-one of sixty-one episodes for which there are data have some EU involvement.

Of the fourteen UN sanctions regimes imposed on African countries, ten were in response to civil conflict (Angola, Côte d'Ivoire, DRC, Liberia, Libya in 2011, Rwanda, Sierra Leone, Somalia, Sudan over Darfur, and CAR). Two regimes addressed the interference of one state in another – Djibouti and Somalia captured under the Somalia sanctions and the interstate war between Ethiopia and Eritrea. Two others addressed state support to international terrorism: Libya in the 1990s on account of Libyan authorities' implication in the destruction of Pan American flight 103 and Union de Transports Aériens flight 772, and Sudan in the 1990s due to Sudanese involvement in the assassination attempt against former Egyptian president Hosni Mubarak in 1996. The sanctions regime imposed against Guinea-Bissau addresses an unconstitutional change in government: following the military coup of April 2012,

---

[4] See S. Boisseau du Rocher, 'The European Union, Burma/Myanmar and ASEAN', *Asia Europe Journal*, 10 (2012), pp. 165–80.

[5] Refer to variables 18–20 in the Targeted Sanctions Consortium's database. Protection of human rights, protection of population under R2P, and support to humanitarian efforts account for twenty-one of the sixty-two episodes or 34 per cent of the episodes but rarely do they represent the primary objective.

[6] Libya (2xs), Somalia/Eritrea, Liberia, Angola, Rwanda, Sudan (2xs), Sierra Leone, DRC, Côte d'Ivoire, Ethiopia/Eritrea, Guinea-Bissau, and CAR.

Table 5.1 *Primary objective of UN African sanctions (episodes)*

Primary Objective	Episodes	
Counterterrorism	5	Libya in the 1990s (1–3), Sudan in the 1990s (1–2)
Good governance	1	Liberia (5)
Democracy support	3	Sierra Leone (1), Côte d'Ivoire (4), Guinea-Bissau (1)
Armed conflict (cease hostilities, negotiation of settlement, peace enforcement. support peacebuilding)	32	Somalia (1–5), Liberia (1–5), Angola (1–4), Rwanda (1–2), Sierra Leone (2–5), Ethiopia-Eritrea (1), DRC (1–4), Sudan over Darfur (1–2), Côte d'Ivoire (1,2,3,5), Libya in 2011 (3), CAR (1)
Protection of civilians under R2P	2	Libya in 2011 (1–2)
Total	43	UN African episodes out of a total of 63 UN episodes

the Council unanimously adopted mandatory travel sanctions against five members of the newly installed military junta.

By episode, the breakdown for the primary objective of UN sanctions on African countries is shown in Table 5.1. In most cases (i.e. thirty-two of the forty-three episodes), UN sanctions are dedicated to addressing armed conflict. In other words, when faced with a conflict in Africa, 74 per cent of the time or nearly three times out of four, the UNSC is focused primarily on ending hostilities.

Armed conflict, UN sanctions, and Africa, therefore, are inextricably linked. The UNSC, however, tends to focus its sanctions on dealing with the *effects* of violent conflict (i.e. is it destabilizing the region? Is the level of violence increasing? Are the terms of peace agreements violated? Have negotiations ended?) more than it focuses on the *roots* of violence (is the fighting a result of ethnic rivalry or a coup? Is it competition for scarce resources?). Surprisingly, despite the amount of attention the UNSC has devoted to theme-based resolutions on violence and women, the promotion of human rights, and good governance, they are the primary objective of sanctions in only one of all the UN sanctions episodes: Liberia. This is true if one also reviews the breakdown for the principal norm signalled. The overwhelming norm advanced via the application of UN sanctions is the prohibition of war in thirty-three of the forty-three African sanctions' episodes. Acute events obstructing the democratic process such as coups do not normally prompt UN sanctions. This is entirely consistent with the principle and purposes of the Charter and the sanctioning history of the UNSC, which focuses on the avoidance of interstate conflicts.

African regional organizations

The UN and African regional organizations use sanctions differently. The UN applies sanctions for a range of objectives against numerous targets, whereas African regional organizations employ sanctions for one consistent reason: unconstitutional change of government. The African Union, Economic Community of West African States, and Southern African Development Community target exclusively unconstitutional changes in government with a suspension of membership. This development is mainly a function of these organizations' mandates as reflected in their constitutional texts. The AU, launched in 2002, is the successor to the Organization of African Unity. While its fifty-four Member States remain committed to the goal of African unity, they have added the goals of economic integration and maintenance of peace and security to their mandate.[7] ECOWAS is a group of fifteen countries, founded in 1975, with a mission to promote economic integration in all fields of economic activity. SADC began in the early 1970s with a goal of liberating southern Africa. The current organization was formed in 1992 with a focus on economic integration of its fifteen Member States. The adoption of a 'democracy clause' was pioneered by the Commonwealth of Nations, which in 1995, agreed on a provision authorizing a collective response to grave breaches of democratic standards, notably coups. Each of the African organizations adopted codes inspired by the democracy clause, prescribing that in cases of an unconstitutional change of government, the organizations shall suspend the membership of the state in question.

Article 30 of AU's 2002 Constitutive Act states as follows: 'Governments which shall come to power through unconstitutional means shall not be allowed to participate in the activities of the Union'. Similarly, as Article 45(1) of ECOWAS' Protocol on Democracy and Good Governance sets out, 'In the event that democracy is abruptly brought to an end by any means or where there is massive violation of Human Rights in a Member State, ECOWAS may impose sanctions on the State concerned' in the form of a suspension of membership. Article 33 of the Treaty of SADC calls for sanctions in the event of an unconstitutional change of government. Sanctions apply to the state even if its intended signal is meant for the *de facto* coup leaders. The result is that the African regional organizations target different states from UN sanctions, as summarized in Table 5.2.

---

[7] Morocco is the only African state that is not a member of the AU.

Table 5.2 *African states sanctioned between 1990 and 2013*

Organization	UN	AU	ECOWAS	SADC
Number of African states sanctioned	13	10	7	1
Number of Member States	193 (54 African)	54	15	15
Per cent of states sanctioned	7 (24 if Africa only)	19	47	7
Which states	Angola, CAR, **Côte d'Ivoire**, DRC, Eritrea (twice), Ethiopia, **Guinea-Bissau**, Liberia, Libya (twice), Rwanda, Sierra Leone, Somalia, Sudan (twice)	CAR, Comoros, **Côte d'Ivoire**, Guinea, **Guinea-Bissau**, Madagascar, Mali, Mauritania, Niger, Togo	**Côte d'Ivoire**, Guinea, **Guinea-Bissau**, Liberia, Mali, Niger, Sierra Leone	Madagascar
Most sanctioned state	Sudan (twice), Libya (twice), Eritrea (twice)	Guinea-Bissau (twice), Mauritania (twice)	Guinea-Bissau (twice)	

Note: States sanctioned by three or more organizations are in bold face.

Only Côte d'Ivoire, Sierra Leone, and Guinea-Bissau have been subject to both UN and African regional sanctions simultaneously and for the same reason, that is, unconstitutional change of government. In the cases of Côte d'Ivoire and Guinea-Bissau, regional sanctions preceded the UN measures, but the sanctions applied differed. Both states were suspended from the AU and ECOWAS, whereas the UN applied travel and financial sanctions against individuals for their refusal to accept electoral results in Côte d'Ivoire and a travel ban against the perpetrators of the coup in Guinea-Bissau. There has been one other case in which states were subject to both UN and ECOWAS sanctions: Sierra Leone immediately after the 1997 coup. In that case, the measures applied and the intended targets were remarkably similar. ECOWAS applied an arms embargo, petroleum products ban, and travel and financial sanctions against the military junta that had staged the coup.[8] Citing the measures applied by ECOWAS, the UN also applied an arms embargo and petroleum ban against the state and a travel ban against the coup leaders.[9] In all other cases, the UN did not apply sanctions for unconstitutional changes of government, for example in the cases of Madagascar or Togo. The UN has condemned unconstitutional changes of government or refusal to accept electoral results in fifteen episodes, ten of them in Africa. This kind of breach constitutes the *principal* norm signalled for seven sanctions episodes, four of which are African cases (Sierra Leone episode 1, Côte d'Ivoire episode 4, Libya in 2011 episode 3, and Guinea-Bissau episode 1).

Given the number of cases of unconstitutional changes of government which African regional organizations sanction but that the UNSC does not, one is tempted to believe that the UN focuses on conflicts different from those on which the African regional organizations concentrate. However, this reading would be incorrect. In fact, to assist their efforts to negotiate peace agreements, send missions, and call for action, African regional organizations have requested a number of UN sanctions regimes on their continent. Indeed, when it comes to Africa in the post–Cold War era, sanctions activity by the UNSC has almost always interacted with a regional initiative of some sort: as many as thirty-eight out of the forty-three episodes of UN sanctions against African states were imposed in support of African organizations' efforts.

Because the drafters of the UN Charter were non-prescriptive in the scenarios that could be subject to sanctions, the UNSC has applied sanctions to address different security challenges including dealing with terrorism and the proliferation of nuclear weapons in addition to humanitarian crises. It has also made ample use of its flexibility by choosing

---

[8] S/1997/695: Annex II.   [9] S/RES/1132 (1997), paras 6 and 5, respectively.

different targets (states, non-state actors, individuals, and entities) and using different measures (arms embargoes, travel bans, financial asset freezes, diplomatic measures, and bans on the sale of natural resources). For example, twenty-five of the thirty-four UN travel bans were against actors in Africa, and fifteen of the twenty-five natural resource sanctions episodes were imposed against African states. Government leaders and their family members, rebel factions, parties to the conflict, and terrorists are all targets of sanctions in addition to traditional states, particularly in the case of arms embargoes. All of the UN African sanctions involved an arms embargo except in the case of Sudan in the 1990s and Guinea-Bissau. By contrast, African regional sanctions rarely apply arms embargoes, while asset freezes on key individuals are becoming more common.

The most significant difference lies in the objectives triggering sanctions. For African organizations, an unconstitutional change in government results in sanctions. Coups d'état are a recurrent problem in Africa – for example, out of the fifteen ECOWAS Member States, only Cape Verde has never suffered a coup.[10] Because of the instability coups generate, signalling abhorrence of such events is an African regional goal. Following the lead of the Commonwealth of Nations and the AU, African regional organizations have made the transparent and fair transfer of power a priority. Therefore, coups and other unconstitutional changes of government trigger the response in most African organizations of a suspension of membership that is lifted as soon as constitutional order has been restored. In recent occasions, additional measures of travel and financial bans have been imposed on coup leaders.

In contrast, the UNSC's first response is usually a resolution condemning the coup, recognizing the efforts of African organizations, and awaiting their outcome. For example, the Security Council passed Resolution 1876 in 2009 condemning the coup in Guinea-Bissau, but did not impose sanctions until 2012, as did the AU, ECOWAS, and the EU. Instead, it extended the mandate of the United Nations Peacebuilding Support Office in Guinea-Bissau (UNOGBIS) and called for 'enhanc[ed] cooperation with the African Union, the Economic Community of West African States, the Community of Portuguese-speaking Countries, the European Union and other partners in their efforts to contribute to the stabilization of Guinea-Bissau'.[11] For the coups in Madagascar in 2005, Comoros in 2007, and Guinea in 2008, for example, no UN sanctions were applied,

---

[10] H. Ben Barka and M. Ncube, 'Political Fragility in Africa: Are Military Coups D'états a Never-Ending Phenomenon?', *African Development Bank* (2012), pp. 1–16.
[11] S/RES/1876 (2009), para 3(j).

while the AU, ECOWAS, and/or SADC wielded sanctions. When the UNSC does sanction states that are subject to unconstitutional changes of government, like Côte d'Ivoire in 2010, the UNSC had sanctions in place already and was sanctioning to mitigate the impact of the wider civil war when former president Gbagbo refused to step down after losing the election. The exceptions are Sierra Leone in 1997 and the latest coup in Guinea-Bissau in 2012. In both cases, UN sanctions were adopted in support of the engagement by the AU, ECOWAS and/or the Community of Portuguese Speaking Countries (CPLP) to restore constitutional order. These cases represent a deviation from the general UN sanctioning pattern.

Whereas the UN and African regional organizations apply sanctions in different scenarios, the number of times that regional efforts act as touch-stones for UNSC measures like sanctions is underappreciated in the literature. Generally speaking, the African conflicts have first been the subject of a peace agreement negotiated by a regional organization or an informal group of neighbouring states that is backed by a UN or UN-blessed mission prior to the application of UN sanctions (especially for sanctions regimes applied in the late 1990s and 2000s). Indeed, thirty-eight of the forty-three UN African sanctions episodes or 88 per cent feature some form of regional involvement and four UN African sanc-tions' country regimes were preceded by African sanctions. The resump-tion of fighting remains the UNSC's main reason for the application of sanctions against African states; thus, when this happens, UN sanctions signal support for the previously applied regional efforts. Sanctions usually consist of an arms embargo followed later by travel bans and (often) financial measures. Natural resource sanctions are increasingly utilized in addressing the financing of African conflicts.[12] These UN sanctions regimes often last for decades, with sanctions' measures renewed year after year as the Council assesses the conditions required for termination. The measures are often 'tweaked' in response to events on the ground – certain sanctions may be terminated in recognition of progress in some areas, while other sanctions remain in place until all conditions are met – many of which often include free and fair elections. The question of how to bring sanctions regimes to closure continues to be a challenge.

European Union

The European Union has its origins in the European Economic Community created in the 1950s. At its inception, the European

---

[12] A. Charron, *UN Sanctions and Conflict: Responding to Peace and Security Threats* (London: Routledge, 2011).

Economic Community was tasked with the creation of a common market and lacked a mandate in foreign policy. However, over time, Member States started to coordinate their policies on international affairs on a purely intergovernmental basis. Because their trade policies were integrated, they established a practice of implementing UN sanctions jointly rather than through separate national legislation. From the early 1990s onwards, the Member States started agreeing on sanctions autonomously, that is, in the absence of a UNSC mandate. Over the years, the frequency of sanctions imposed under this autonomous practice of the EU has increased steadily.[13]

Today, the European Union comprises twenty-eight members.[14] The organization includes a mandate for intergovernmental cooperation in the field of foreign policy, the so-called Common Foreign and Security Policy (CFSP), which constitutes the legal framework under which sanctions are adopted. The objectives of the CFSP include the support of democracy, the rule of law, human rights, and the principles of international law, as well as the preservation of peace, the prevention of conflicts, and the strengthening of international security, in accordance with the purposes and principles of the United Nations Charter (Treaty on European Union 2010). Table 5.3 illustrates the primary objectives of case episodes in which UN and EU sanctions overlap. Separately, the EU also imposes sanctions on African, Caribbean, and Pacific countries in the framework of the development cooperation relationship it entertains with these countries under the ACP-EU Partnership Agreement, also called Cotonou Convention. The interruption of cooperation is foreseen in response to breaches of democratic principles, human rights, and rule of law under Article 96 of the Cotonou Convention.[15]

The EU imposed autonomous sanctions in forty-three of the sixty-three episodes of UN targeted sanctions, that is, in 68 per cent of them. In a number of cases, the EU was involved either before or in the early stages of UN sanctions episodes, such as Sudan over Darfur, the Federal Republic of Yugoslavia twice, in the 1990s and over Kosovo, Libya in 2011, Guinea-Bissau, the DRC, and the anti-terrorism regimes of Al-Qaida/Taliban. In four cases, the EU had not been involved initially, but became active later during the regime. This was the case with Liberia,

---

[13] Seth Jones *European Security Co-Operation* (Cambridge: Cambridge University Press, 2007).

[14] Austria, Belgium, Bulgaria, Croatia, Cyprus, Czech Republic, Denmark, Estonia, Finland, France, Germany, Greece, Hungary, Ireland, Italy, Latvia, Lithuania, Luxembourg, Malta, Netherlands, Poland, Portugal, Romania, Slovakia, Slovenia, Spain, Sweden, and the United Kingdom.

[15] Portela, *European Union Sanctions and Foreign Policy.*

Table 5.3 *Primary objective of UN sanctions with EU additional measures*

Primary Objective	Episodes	
Counterterrorism	9	Libya in the 1990s (1–3), Sudan in the 1990s (1–2), Al-Qaida (1–4)
Good governance	1	Liberia (5)
Democracy support	3	Sierra Leone (1), Guinea-Bissau (1), Côte d'Ivoire (4)
Armed conflict: cease hostilities, negotiation of peace settlement, peace enforcement, and/or support peacebuilding	23	FRY in the 1990s (1), Somalia (3–5), Liberia (4), Sierra Leone (2–5), FRY over Kosovo (1), Ethiopia/Eritrea (1), DRC (1–4), Iraq (1–2), Sudan over Darfur (1–2), Taliban (1), Libya in 2011 (3), Côte d'Ivoire (3; 5)
Non-proliferation	6	Iran (2–4), DPRK (1–3)
Protection of civilians under R2P	2	Libya in 2011 (1–2)
Total	44	case episodes in which UN and EU sanctions overlap

Source: TSC database.

Somalia, Côte d'Ivoire, and Iran. In the remaining cases (Haiti, Angola, Rwanda, Lebanon, and CAR), the EU did not take independent action at any stage of the UN sanctions effort. In some instances, the EU imposed sanctions where it had no direct diplomatic involvement in the management of the crisis: Ethiopia/Eritrea, Sierra Leone, Sudan in the 1990s, and Libya in the 1990s (Table 5.4).

In theory, the objectives for which EU sanctions are imposed should differ from those pursued by UN sanctions: UN sanctions are adopted primarily in order to address situations endangering international peace and security, notably violent conflict, while EU sanctions typically pursue the promotion of democracy and human rights. This 'division of labour' emanates from the international legal nature of the objectives pursued. The abstract goal of maintaining international peace and security enjoys universal legitimacy, to the extent that the UN Charter recognizes its paramount importance and empowers the UNSC to address conflict situations by adopting sanctions, or even authorizing the use of force. Some UN members argue that the adoption of mandatory UN sanctions makes it unnecessary for other actors to adopt unilateral measures; however, other states wishing to go beyond the measures authorized by the Council consider UN sanctions a 'floor' upon which unilateral or regional sanctions are based. UNSC sanctions are typically applied in interstate conflicts – which correspond to the breach of peace the drafters of the Charter initially had in mind. In practice, the UNSC has

Table 5.4 *States sanctioned by the UN and the EU between 1990 and 2013*

Organization	UN	EU
Number of states affected by sanctions	20	35
Identity of states	Afghanistan, Angola, Central African Republic, Côte d'Ivoire, DPRK, DRC, Eritrea, Ethiopia, Federal Republic of Yugoslavia, Guinea-Bissau, Haiti, Iran, Iraq, Lebanon, Liberia, Libya, Rwanda, Sierra Leone, Somalia, Sudan	Burma/Myanmar, Belarus, Burundi, CAR, Comoros, Côte d'Ivoire, DRC/Zaire, Equatorial Guinea, Ethiopia, Eritrea, Federal Republic of Yugoslavia, Fiji, Gambia, Guatemala, Guinea, Guinea-Bissau, Haiti, Indonesia, Kenya, Liberia, Libya, Madagascar, Malawi, Mali, Mauritania, Moldova, Niger, Nigeria, Rwanda, Sierra Leone, Sudan, Syria, Togo, Uzbekistan, Zimbabwe

Note: The table features only state actors, excludes autonomous sanctions regimes which supplement UN sanctions such as the EU sanctions against Iran, and excludes the category of 'informal' sanctions, adopted in the absence of a legal act, which encompasses the arms embargo against China alongside measures against Cuba (Portela 2010).
Source: Portela (2005, 2010) and own elaboration.

also used sanctions for objectives less directly connected to interstate conflicts: the condemnation of apartheid, and after the cold war, increasingly to address intra-state conflicts, the proliferation of weapon of mass destruction (WMD), and to counter terrorism.[16] By contrast, the protection of human rights and the promotion of democracy are more distant from the core mission of the UNSC, and the Council tends to refrain from initiating action in these areas.[17] The desirability of promoting democracy through these means does not enjoy universal recognition, but despite this, the UN has still imposed sanctions primarily in support of democratic processes in nearly 10 per cent of the targeted sanctions episodes. In these cases, it usually follows the lead of regional organizations, however.

Individual states or regional organizations are more likely to condemn and impose sanctions in response to grave human rights violations or interruptions of the democratic process, as in Mali, Belarus, Togo,

[16] Charron, *UN Sanctions and Conflict: Responding to Peace and Security Threats.*
[17] M. Brzoska, 'Sanktionen Als Instrument der Europäischen Außen- und Sicherheitspolitik', *Friedensgutachten* (2006), pp. 247–55.

Zimbabwe, or Burma/Myanmar. Indeed, the EU follows a declared policy of imposing sanctions in support of democracy, human rights, and good governance.[18] It is not always possible to clearly distinguish sanctions applied in support of democracy from those imposed in support of human rights. In EU practice, both are intertwined: the sort of human rights violations to which the EU responds with sanctions are often closely connected to the democratic process, such as breaches of the freedom of association, of speech, and of demonstration.[19] The linkage of breaches of the democratic process with human rights might be motivated by a desire to enhance the legitimacy of the restrictive measures by presenting them as violations of universally agreed norms.

While the 'division of labour' applies to much of the practice of the UN and EU, we still find an overlap in the field of peace and security. As we can observe in Table 5.3, as many as twelve countries were at the receiving end of European sanctions due to conflict-related concerns. This overlap comes about for several reasons. First, because the UNSC is often slow to react to international crises, and sometimes remains deadlocked due to the veto threat of some of its permanent members, the EU has imposed unilateral sanctions in situations of violent conflict. This was the case with the former Yugoslavia: the EU was the first to impose an arms embargo on Yugoslavia shortly after bellicosities commenced in 1990. The embargo was made universal and mandatory by the UNSC some six months later. Similarly, the EU imposed an arms embargo against Sudan as early as 1994 in response to the attacks against civilians perpetrated by government forces, some ten years before the UN applied its own measures on account of the situation in Darfur. In this regard, the close interconnection between EU and UN practice benefited from the fact that two EU members – the United Kingdom and France – are simultaneously members of the P5. In both cases, the European members of the UNSC actively promoted the adoption of mandatory sanctions. A current example concerns the sanctions against Syria in response to the use of violence against civilians: the EU only imposed unilateral measures after consensus at the UNSC proved impossible to achieve.

Second, the EU has been more cautious than the UN about resuming the supply of weapons and related technology in post-conflict situations. Thus, after the UN lifted sanctions against Libya and the former Yugoslav republics, the EU maintained its unilateral embargo. One

[18] KEEP Council of the European Union (2004) 'Basic Principles on the Use of Restrictive Measures (Sanctions)', Council Doc. 10198/1/04 REV 1, Brussels, 7 June 2004, p. 2.
[19] C. Portela, 'European Union Sanctions as a Foreign Policy Tool: Do They Work?', in S. B. Gareis, G. Hauser, and F. Kernic (eds.), *Europe as a Global Actor* (Leverkusen: Budrich, 2012).

example of the closely interlinked nature of UN and EU practice was the establishment of the Sanctions Assistance Missions (SAMs) by the EU in order to aid the enforcement of the UN embargo imposed on the former Yugoslavia during the Bosnian conflict. The fact that the UN sanctions against Libya and the former Yugoslavia in the early 1990s were preceded and followed by EU sanctions corroborates the idea that regional organizations are mostly concerned with security and stability in their vicinity.[20] However, the EU also 'pioneered' sanctions in African crises before the UN became active: it had measures in place in Sudan, DRC, and Ethiopia/Eritrea before the UN levied its own sanctions. Interestingly, it did not impose autonomous measures against Côte d'Ivoire until the UN added the goal of democracy promotion to its sanctions regime.

The fight against terrorism and the proliferation of WMD are well-represented objectives among European sanctions, in particular if compared with the breakdown of African regimes. Every sanctions regime imposed by the UN to counter terrorism or proliferation was accompanied by EU measures. These objectives only made their way into the motivations warranting UNSC measures after the end of the Cold War, and its practice has been gradually acquiring robustness. The UNSC adopted measures against states sponsoring terrorism in the early 1990s, expanding its action to terrorist suspects after the US embassy bombings in East Africa in 1998. In the field of terrorism, the EU sanctions 'pioneered' UN practice in the sense that it had imposed counterterrorism sanctions against Syria and Libya already in the 1980s, largely following US leadership. The objective of nuclear non-proliferation has been added later: non-proliferation objectives were part of the comprehensive sanctions imposed against Iraq after its withdrawal from Kuwait. However, stand-alone targeted sanctions regimes in support of non-proliferation objectives have only been imposed in 2006 against North Korea and Iran. Here, the development observed with the EU is highly interesting: the EU did not have any sanctions in place before the UN imposed its own measures. Yet, after the UN levied sanctions, the EU went beyond the requirements of the UNSC resolution, imposing supplementary sanctions.[21] Once again, the EU followed the lead of the United States. However, neither with Iran nor with North Korea are EU sanctions as far-reaching as those imposed by the United States.

This evolution suggests that the imposition of UN sanctions constitutes a 'threshold' in terms of legitimacy. Prior to the imposition of UN

---

[20] C. Portela, 'Where and Why Does the EU Impose Sanctions?', *Politique Européenne*, 17 (2005), pp. 83–111.

[21] B. Taylor, *Sanctions as Grand Strategy* (London: IISS/Routledge, 2010).

sanctions, the EU was often reluctant to follow the lead of the United States in imposing sanctions. Once the UN had imposed some measures, the EU grew more willing to use additional sanctions supplementing UN regimes. Thus, the adoption of sanctions by the UNSC constitutes an 'enabling' condition allowing the EU to decide on extra measures, always following the US lead – even though they still fall short from reaching the level of severity of US restrictions. In the field of the non-proliferation, we witness the opposite scenario from what has been noted with regard to the objectives of stopping violent conflict and fighting terrorism. The EU followed the UN, rather than preceded it.

Interestingly, the nature of the goals the EU intends to advance through the use of sanctions varies from region to region. Most sanctions regimes imposed in sub-Saharan Africa respond to breaches of human rights and democratic rule. Also in Eastern Europe, sanctions are mostly imposed for democracy and human rights promotion. In the Middle East, sanctions used to be connected with the fight against terrorism. Recently, objectives pursued by the EU sanctions have become more diverse: in Iran, sanctions support non-proliferation objectives, and in the aftermath of the Arab spring, the EU has imposed autonomous sanctions in response to violent state repression in Syria and in support of democratic forces in Tunisia and Egypt. In another Arab spring country, Yemen, some observers claim that the threat of sanctions facilitated the peaceful power transition in that country.

The range of sanctions tools employed by the EU is as diverse as that of the UN. Since the mid 1990s, the EU has followed a policy of imposing targeted sanctions rather than comprehensive embargoes, although it did not make this policy explicit until the publication of the 'Basic Principles on the Use of Restrictive Measures' in 2004, which states that 'sanctions should be targeted in a way that has maximum impact on those whose behaviour we want to influence. Targeting should reduce to the maximum extent possible any adverse humanitarian effects or unintended consequences for persons not targeted or neighbouring countries'.[22] Targeted sanctions are designed to focus on the leadership responsible for the objectionable policies the imposer intends to modify, rather than to affect the population of the target country as a whole.[23] Only targeted sanctions are imposed by the EU, as it currently does not feature a single instance of comprehensive sanctions. There are no perceptible differences in the targeting by the UNSC and that by the EU.

---

[22] KEEP Council of the European Union, 'Basic Principles on the Use of Restrictive Measures (Sanctions)', p. 3.
[23] A. Tostensen and B. Bull, 'Are Smart Sanctions Feasible?', *World Politics*, 54 (2002), pp. 373–403.

Interactions between UN sanctions and regional sanctions

The overview provided in this chapter offers useful insights on the relationship between the sanctions practice of regional organizations and that of the UN. First, the regional organizations in Africa and Europe share similar objectives when they employ sanctions broadly supporting democracy. More specifically, they aim to reverse unconstitutional forms of power transfer, which most frequently take the form of coups d'état or refusal to recognize election results. Here, the contrast to the UN practice is clear: as mentioned above, UN sanctions imposed for the promotion of human rights and good governance account for only one of all the African UN sanctions episodes. However, regional organizations have imposed sanctions for peace and security objectives before the UNSC became active: ECOWAS did so in Sierra Leone in 1997, while the EU was the first to impose an embargo on Yugoslavia in 1990. In both cases, these regimes were followed by UN measures. In terms of timing, the imposition of UN sanctions have often been preceded by diplomatic and other efforts by both sets of organizations, which gave way to UN action once their attempts at non-coercive solutions failed.

The division of labour consisting of the UN dealing with the violence of conflicts while regional organizations are active in democracy support is likely to remain blurred in future. The fact that the UN imposed sanctions on Côte d'Ivoire in 2010 (episode 4) and on Guinea-Bissau in 2012 on the basis of interruptions of the democratic process recognizes the linkage between lack of democracy and the likelihood of eruption or recurrence of violent conflict, at least in volatile West Africa. Given that regional organizations have played an *avant-garde* role in the imposition of sanctions, their efforts in the restoration of constitutionally elected governments lead us to regard them as 'pioneers' of democracy support and human rights sanctions.

However, there are also important differences obscured *prima facie* by the division of labour between the UN and the regional organizations. In both cases, sanctions are primarily imposed in response to breaches of the democratic process, typically a coup d'état. The imposition of sanctions by the African organizations is used against their own members and represents a strong resolve to address regional security issues. By contrast, the EU imposes sanctions externally, as part of its foreign policy. In this respect, the EU is rather atypical in comparison to other regional organizations.[24] Often, its sanctions policy is modelled on US sanctions

---

[24] Hellquist, 'Regional Organisations and Sanctions against Members: Explaining the Different Trajectories of the African Union, the League of Arab states, and the Association of Southeast Asian Nations'.

policies, as it reflects shared values and responds to a desire to reinforce US measures. Importantly, the type of sanction is very different: African organizations normally use the traditional diplomatic sanction of suspending the country's membership of the organization, but it has started to use assets freezes, visa bans, and the denial of transport and communications.[25] By contrast, the EU normally imposes the same trio that constitutes standard practice by the UN – arms embargo, travel or visa ban, and assets freeze – although it increasingly employs oil bans and financial sanctions, as witnessed with Iran, Libya, and Syria. In any case, both sets of regional organizations display a trend towards incrementalism in their sanctions practice. It also highlights the fact that EU Member States are endowed with better resources and expertise than African organizations and can, therefore, give effect to more complex sanctions regimes.

Conclusions

Overall, our analysis does not detect any patterns of stark incompatibilities or even competition between the sanctions regimes imposed by the UN and regional organizations. On the contrary, the close interconnections between UN and regional sanctions practices are evident in both cases. Both the EU and African organizations make similar use of their measures: they impose regional sanctions, among others, to draw attention to a situation that requires correction in the hope of attracting the support of the UNSC. The effects of globalization of regional sanctions through the adoption of a UN mandate are significant: it multiplies the efficacy of the measures and, importantly, legitimizes them on a global level. This is particularly remarkable in the case of the African organizations, which have proved ready to take bold measures to suspend members from within the organization, while the EU utilizes sanctions against third states as part of its foreign policy. Perhaps a difference between both sets of organizations is the fact that African organizations pursue the imposition of sanctions by the UNSC as their ultimate objective. The EU, however, also takes advantage of the legitimacy created by the imposition of UN measures to upgrade its unilateral sanctions regime, as witnessed most conspicuously in the case of Iran. The adoption of UN sanctions constitutes a 'threshold' for the EU: before the UN imposes measures, it employed timid measures; after the UN became active, its reticence weakened. Russia, China, and others, by contrast, increasingly

---

[25] Eriksson, *Supporting Democracy in Africa.*

view the adoption of UN sanctions not as a threshold for further measures, but as ceiling of what they consider globally legitimate measures.

In theory, the coexistence of multiple sanctions regimes might have a multiplying effect. However, the fact that different sanctions regimes employed simultaneously by different senders, with different coverage or objectives, sometimes confuses the actors involved. A case in point is Myanmar: private sector operators in both the sender and target countries mistakenly believed that sanctions by the United States and the European Union were identical, while the US measures were far more comprehensive. What remains unexplored is whether simultaneous sanctions regimes by multiple organizations produce synergies or, on the contrary, hinder each other. In other words, if a state like Iran is subject to UN, EU, and US sanctions, even if the measures and objectives are different, does this lead to better policy outcomes or unintended ones? Could the sum total of the targeted sanctions regimes become comprehensive? And to which measures and objectives do the targeted state/actors respond to first? These questions require further study, providing potentially fruitful avenues for future research.

6   Coordination of United Nations sanctions with other actors and instruments

Alix Boucher and Caty Clement

The range of actors and instruments involved with UN sanctions has increased significantly over the past two decades. The growing frequency with which peacekeeping operations, international judicial processes, regional sanctions, and other instruments are employed together with UN targeted sanctions raises issues of coordination and complementarity. With this broad variety of actors comes overlapping mandates that may reinforce sanctions' objectives or undermine them. How these many actors interact with each other directly influences the overall effectiveness of UN sanctions. This chapter examines the range of actors, institutions, and mechanisms both within the United Nations system and outside of it that relate to UN targeted sanctions. After describing the various types of interactions, the chapter provides illustrations of how these entities cooperate (or fail to cooperate), and the ways in which UN sanctions and the activities of other actors either complement or conflict with each other. It concludes with recommendations to enhance the coordination among UN sanctions and related actors.

The modes of interaction among UN sanctions and other actors generally can be characterized as 'cooperation', 'coordination', and 'collaboration'. Most scholarly literature differentiates among the three, with collaboration signifying the most advanced relationship requiring a commitment to shared objectives and missions.[1] Coordination connotes efficiency, valued so as to avoid duplication and overlap, but also implying the consent of those coordinating.[2] Notwithstanding repeated calls for collaboration and better coordination among various actors involved with UN sanctions, most interactions are limited to cooperation at best (and at worse, contradictory

---

[1] See P. W. Mattessich, M. Murray-Close, and B. R. Monsey, *Collaboration: What Makes It Work: A Review of Research Literature on Factors Influencing Successful Collaboration* (St. Paul, MN: Amherst H. Wilder Foundation, 2001), pp. 59–61, adapted from the works of Martin Blank, Sharon Kagan, Atelia Melaville, and Karen Ray, for a discussion of the elements entailed in cooperation, coordination, and collaboration.

[2] A. Wildavsky, *Speaking Truth to Power: The Art and Craft of Policy Analysis* (Boston, MA: Little, Brown & Company, 1979).

or conflicting actions). The aspirational goal of coordination between UN sanctions and other instruments and actors remains desirable, but in practical terms, cooperation is often the most that can be achieved.

The wording of the relevant UN Security Council resolutions, the political environment in which the sanctions operate, and the specific actors involved influence how various actors interact. Since the imposition of sanctions is fundamentally a political act, cooperation or coordination among actors either within the UN or between UN and outside entities is not a simple administrative or technical issue. It is itself political as well, shaped by a variety of institutional factors and dynamics. This explains why the call for 'more coordination' as a basic element of efficiency is likely to remain limited without significant changes by and in the Security Council. The nature of cooperation entailed in UN sanctions regimes likewise varies considerably, from leveraging personal connections to cooperation that is expressly required by a Security Council resolution. Such mandates can lead to formal institutional cooperation, including the signing of specific agreements both between UN actors themselves, as well as with other international organizations. However, even in cases where cooperation is mandated by a resolution, formal mechanisms are extremely rare, and in practice often depend on the initiative of the individuals involved.

Cooperation and coordination around UN sanctions generally occur in four venues, among: (1) UN sanctions actors (sanctions committees, expert panels, the Secretariat, and Security Council); (2) other specialized UN agencies (e.g. UN peacekeeping and political missions, Special Representatives of the Secretary-General (SRSGs), human rights entities, and judicial processes); (3) international institutions involved with specific functional issues (e.g. Financial Action Task Force (FATF), International Police (International Criminal Police Organization) (INTERPOL), International Civil Aviation Organization (ICAO), and World Customs Organization (WCO)), and (4) regional bodies, national institutions, and non-governmental organizations. The following sections will address these four areas of interaction.

Sanctions are first and foremost a political instrument employed in support of wider political objectives (associated with threats to international peace and security), which are unique to each case. As such, they are modified according to progress or setbacks in the political developments in each particular context. UN sanctions are therefore part of the larger toolkit of instruments the UN Security Council uses to influence the behaviour or signal certain actors, typically used together with diplomatic initiatives (97 per cent of episodes), political or peacekeeping missions (62 per cent), and in some cases a judicial process (46 per cent).

Security Council mandated interaction

The Security Council often mandates interactions between sanctions regimes and other actors, most frequently between expert panels and Member States or relevant international organizations. Table 6.1 summarizes and illustrates these mandates, and Appendix A at the end of this chapter provides greater detail on cooperation requirements of UNSC resolutions with regard to specific sanctions regimes. While all the African country sanctions regimes require cooperation with co-deployed peacekeeping missions, cooperation between expert panels is much weaker, despite the fact that weapons and other embargoed commodities circulate between targeted countries.[3] Only half (three) of the African regimes and the global counterterrorism regime formally require cooperation with other panels. Cooperation with related international entities and organizations is often referred to in resolutions (e.g. the Kimberley Process regarding sanctions on diamonds, and the FATF for financial sanctions) but remains largely *ad hoc* and limited.

The Council has required cooperation for political reasons, for instance, when it believes states are directly involved in a conflict, supporting belligerent parties, or when business intermediaries (e.g. trading companies) and natural resources fuel conflicts. The UNSC has called for enhanced coordination between sanctions regimes, ranging from secondary sanctions to greater cooperation between expert groups. Secondary sanctions imposed against a third state (usually a neighbouring country) for failing to comply with or engaging in egregious violations of UN sanctions have proven effective in achieving sanctions objectives.[4]

Sanctions regimes in West Africa have been considered as part of a regional strategy, as combatants and natural resources have long circulated among Liberia, Sierra Leone, and Côte d'Ivoire. The Sierra Leone panel found that responsibility for sanctions violations lay with Liberian authorities and recommended the imposition of secondary sanctions on Liberia and the creation of a new panel for Liberia.[5] When the Group of Experts on Côte d'Ivoire was created, it worked cooperatively with the Panel on Liberia and vice versa. In early June 2012, when seven Nigerian

---

[3] C. J. Chivers, 'A Trail of Bullets Casings Leads from Africa's Wars Back to Iran', *The New York Times*, 11 January 2013.

[4] Secondary sanctions were imposed against Liberia in 2001, when then president Charles Taylor supported the rebel group RUF in Sierra Leone, as well as against Eritrea in 2009 for its support of Al Shabaab in Somalia.

[5] In 2001, UNSCR 1343 imposed secondary sanctions on Liberia for its support of the RUF in Sierra Leone. Once the RUF became a political party, the rationale for the embargo shifted towards governance and management of natural resources. The Liberia panel was tasked to monitor a fully fledged sanctions regime with an arms embargo, individual sanctions, and sanctions on diamonds and timber.

Table 6.1 *Summary of UNSC Coordination/Cooperation mandates*

Sanctions regimes/ mandates	Targeted state	Other states in the region	Expert panels	PK mission	CT entities	WMD entities	Other UN entities	Functional IOs	Regional orgs
Somalia	X	X		X					
Liberia	X		X	X				X	
DRC	X	X	X	X			X		
Côte d'Ivoire	X	X	X	X			X	X	X
Sudan II	X			X			X	X	X
Libya II	X			X	X		X	X	
Iran	X	X			X	X	X		
DPRK	X	X				X	X		
Al-Qaida/Taliban			X		X		X	X	X
Guinea-Bissau	X	X		X			X		X
CAR	X	X	X	X			X	X	X

peacekeepers were killed while deployed to the peacekeeping mission in Côte d'Ivoire, cooperation between the two expert groups ensured the swift identification and subsequent arrest of those who had ordered the attack. UN sanctions in the African Great Lakes region constitute another example of the threat of secondary sanctions. In 2007, building on a dormant arms embargo remaining from the 1994 Rwandese genocide, the Security Council threatened to reactivate sanctions when claims of Rwandese support were documented by empowering the DRC Group of Experts to handle investigations in Rwanda. Through a set of diplomatic and financial donor pressures, Kigali eventually moved to put CNDP leader Laurent Nkunda under house arrest in Rwanda. The dormant Rwandese sanctions regime was formally lifted in 2008.

UN sanctions actors

Cooperation among the different actors within the UN directly responsible for sanctions – the Security Council, sanctions committees, Panels of Experts, and the Secretariat – has neither been well understood nor widely debated, until relatively recently.[6] When the UNSC imposes a sanctions regime, it typically (in 74 per cent of the episodes) establishes a sanctions committee.[7] Panels of Experts or Monitoring Teams were established to monitor implementation in 57 per cent of the cases, but were established at the outset of the first episode in only 13 per cent.[8] Sanctions committees and expert groups thus play critical roles in explaining the measures and acting as the primary interface between the UN system and Member States. Other chapters address in greater detail the role of UN sanctions actors, but the effectiveness of a sanctions regime can be enhanced by the quality and level of involvement of its Sanctions Committee chair. As discussed in Chapter 7 by Rico Carisch and Loraine Rickard-Martin, Ambassador Robert Fowler of Canada, who chaired the Angola sanctions committee in 1999 and 2000, is often cited as a model for effective committee leadership in naming and shaming sanctions' violators and establishing expert panels as merit-based independent

---

[6] The 2014-15 High Level Review of UN Sanctions focused on enhancing the implementation of UN sanctions through improved integration and coordination of UN and external institutions and instruments (www.hlr-unsanctions.org/). See also the 2010 report, *Integrating UN Sanctions for Peace and Security* by D. Cortright et al. at http://sanctionsand security.nd.edu/news/42167-integrating-un-sanctions-for-peace-and-security/).

[7] Only two sanctions regimes failed to create sanctions committees – FRY and Sudan, both in the 1990s.

[8] Panels of experts or monitoring teams were added during the second episode in seven cases (30 per cent) and towards the end of the sanctions regime in three cases (13 per cent). Panels were not established at all in ten of the twenty-three regimes (43 per cent).

bodies.[9] Sanctions committee chairs convey to Member States the importance the Council places on sanctions regimes; an active chair traveling to the region can positively influence both coordination and implementation.

Within the Security Council, Member States' involvement with the content and working methods of expert panels has also increased in recent years. Because some Member States have attempted to block reports critical of certain states' implementation, panels have been forced to limit dissemination of controversial material, which are often confined to confidential annexes. In 2012, the United States reportedly blocked the release of the DRC expert panel report, which criticized Rwanda's role in funding and managing the M23 rebellion. The report was released only after Rwanda provided a detailed response which could be released with the panel's report. Similarly, China reportedly objected to the content of the Sudan panel's report that claimed Chinese ammunition was found in Sudan in violation of the arms embargo.[10] The panel's original report was leaked to the press and a much less contentious report was published later as an official document.

Moreover rules related to sanctions committees' documentation and evidence reportedly have compromised expert groups' independence and ability to report factual information.[11] The Secretariat's requirements that the non-proliferation expert groups privilege information provided directly by states and construe their responsibilities in a restrictive manner serve to limit cooperation and even interaction with certain actors. Taking the general approach that if cooperation is not required by the mandate, it is not permitted at all is problematic for the continued utility of expert panels.[12] UN expert panels' reports are essential in providing information and recommendations to refine sanctions policies as well as following up on sanctioned individuals. Such was the case with the Angola, Sierra Leone, and Liberia panels, which played crucial roles in contributing to the establishment of the Kimberley process. The Sierra Leone panel in particular recommended the imposition of secondary sanctions on Liberia. Similarly, the DRC Expert Panel on Natural Resources recommended the creation of a sanctions committee. The subsequent DRC Arms Embargo Expert Group recommended due diligence procedures for private companies involved in trading natural resources. More recently, the Somalia panel, by repeatedly recommending the measure, played an essential role in the Council's decision to impose a charcoal embargo on Somalia and secondary sanctions on Eritrea.

[9] This example is discussed more extensively in Chapter 7.
[10] Author interviews, former expert panel members.
[11] Author interviews, former expert panel members.
[12] Author interviews, former expert panel members.

Primacy of counterterrorism and non-proliferation sanctions regimes

Most UN sanctions are aimed at ending armed conflicts or supporting peacebuilding efforts in Africa. The number of sanctions episodes that have armed conflict, peace-related, and/or democracy support as their main objectives (68 per cent) significantly outnumbers those for counterterrorism (14 per cent) and non-proliferation (11 per cent) purposes. However, there is an inverse relationship between the number of sanctions regimes and the means placed at their disposal, with the Council devoting more attention and allotting greater financial and human resources to counterterrorism and non-proliferation regimes, despite their relative infrequency. As detailed in Appendices B and C regarding funding for panels of experts, despite variations over time and across regions, sanctions regimes addressing conflict mitigation, democracy support, or good governance (e.g. Côte d'Ivoire, DRC, Liberia, Libya, Somalia/Eritrea, and Sudan) received only 40 per cent ($9 million) of the funding, compared to the counterterrorism and non-proliferation regimes ($22 million) in 2012–2013.

The same distinction is visible in other forms of support. Sanctions regimes related to peace enforcement and peacebuilding in Central and West Africa are typically supported by a single staff member at UN headquarters, and expert panels typically have no more than five to six members. In contrast, non-proliferation regimes are supported by eight-member panels, which in turn receive support from several staff each, while the Al-Qaida and Taliban sanctions regimes are assisted by twelve experts on the Monitoring Team.

This contrast in political support for sanctions regimes is also visible in the frequency with which the UNSC has listed individuals and entities. In the counterterrorism regime, the number of designations exceeded 500 at its peak; there were 113 individuals and entities listed for Iran (since September 2009). The African sanctions regimes, however, have far fewer designations, with only thirty-nine for the DRC (since May 2010) and a high of fifty-eight in Liberia (December 2003–June 2006); the other conflict/governance regimes had fewer than twenty designations. Moreover, Al-Qaida sanctions also benefit from access to the Office of the Ombudsperson for delisting requests. The inability for individuals to challenge their listing by other sanctions committees is a source of contention between sanctions actors and those targeted, raising questions as to the fairness and credibility of UN sanctions, since only those designated by the Al-Qaida regime may avail themselves of this due process mechanism.

Another distinctive aspect of the non-proliferation regimes is the degree to which P5 members have insisted on the appointment by the

Secretary-General of 'national representatives' on the expert panels, and an active role in vetting the content of the experts' reports. This is in sharp contrast to the Central and West African regimes, for which the Department of Political Affairs has more independence in identifying and appointing experts, and where expertise, rather than national origin and presumably political adherence to national policy goals, plays more of a role in the appointment.[13]

Specialized UN agencies

Beyond those actors directly responsible for designing and implementing UN sanctions, a host of other UN players interact with sanctions regimes; these range from peacekeeping and special political missions to SRSGs, mediators, human rights, and humanitarian actors, among others (Table 6.2). The most frequent interaction of sanctions and

Table 6.2 *Specialized UN agencies interacting with sanctions*

	Episodes	
Actors Involved	Frequency	%
Conflict related		
Peacekeeping forces	39	62
Peacekeeping mission in neighbouring country	31	52
Special Representative of Secretary-General (SRSG)	42	67
Functional SRSG	25	40
Disarmament, demobilization and reintegration (DDR)	27	43
Office for the Coordination of Humanitarian Affairs (OCHA)	33	52
UN High Commissioner for Refugees (UNHCR)	36	57
Human Rights Council/Commission	18	30
UN Development Programme	16	27
World Food Programme	13	22
Terrorism related		
UN Office on Drugs and Crime (UNODC)	8	13
Justice related		
International Court of Justice (ICJ)/International Criminal Court (ICC)[a]	14	22

Note: Percentage calculated from valid cases only; non-applicable and missing data excluded.

[a] Although it operates in close coordination with the UN, the International Criminal Court is not a part of the UN system.

[13] Author interviews, former expert panel members and UN Secretariat officials.

country-based missions concerns UN peacekeeping missions (in 62 per cent of sanctions episodes) but they have a fragile and uneven relationship.[14] UN missions are essential to the successful work of expert panels, as they depend on such assistance to secure flights, vehicles, situation reports, military observers and troops for information, logistical support, and security. But the degree of support that experts receive often depends on how they are perceived by the mission and its leadership. In Liberia, for example, the arms panel preceded the mission and benefited from its expertise, but cooperation remained informal and based on personal relationships among experts, the mission staff, and leadership. The notable exception in which coordination was formalized between the expert panel and mission is Côte d'Ivoire, which formed a dedicated embargo support cell. Tasked with monitoring the sanctions, the embargo cell provided ongoing logistical and administrative support to the Panel of Experts and often conducted joint investigations. This is in marked contrast to other missions which often have a single (sometimes very junior) officer tasked with providing basic administrative support and collecting information from across the mission to share with experts. In Côte d'Ivoire, for instance, cooperation greatly improved when a former expert panel member headed the embargo cell.[15]

While the international community uses both expert groups and peacekeeping missions as tools to address conflict situations, they are perceived very differently. Peacekeeping missions typically see their role as supporting the post-conflict transitional authorities, while sanctions are often negatively perceived as punitive, even when they are in fact designed to support the transitional authorities against potential spoilers. Angolans, for example, generally viewed sanctions as such even though they only targeted UNITA rebels. Similarly, during the transition in the DRC, authorities considered the arms embargo punitive despite the fact it was aimed only at non-signatories of the 2002 Global and All Inclusive Peace Agreement.[16]

Moreover, UN peacekeeping missions tend to have different views regarding the utility and purpose of UN sanctions. For peacekeeping missions with mandates to assist in the monitoring of sanctions (45 per cent of episodes) – in particular by monitoring an arms embargo or by observing and monitoring actions that could lead to individuals being

[14] Boucher, *UN Panels of Experts and UN Peace Operations: Exploiting Synergies for Peacebuilding*.
[15] Author interview.
[16] Boucher, *UN Panels of Experts and UN Peace Operations, Exploiting Synergies for Peacebuilding*, pp. 17–20.

listed based on their role in certain human rights abuses – sanctions represent either an additional resource drain/obligation or, more positively, a reinforcement of the peacekeeping mandate. A 2010 DPKO-DPA effort to develop basic guidelines for cooperation between Panels of Experts and peacekeeping missions produced an initial set of instructions, but they were poorly distributed and applied; the result is that tensions persist between some panels and peace operations.[17] At times, sanctions have also been used as inducement for building institutional capacity. In the case of Liberia in particular, the UNSC set clear conditions for lifting sanctions with co-deployed peacekeeping missions having a mandate to build institutional capacity. Even with an explicit mandate to contribute to sanctions implementation, the missions and UN country teams often fail to leverage information contained in panel reports for their own strategic planning and Council-mandated implementation.[18]

Special Representatives of the Secretary-General are frequently (67 per cent of episodes) involved with sanctions but often have conflicting views regarding sanctions. Most understand sanctions as an integral part of the Council's peacebuilding strategy, but at the same time, accept that they can complicate relationships with local authorities.[19] Indeed, SRSGs reported hearing numerous complaints from host government officials about how the sanctions negatively affect them. When expert panels highlight government human rights abuses or the failure to manage resources properly, local officials also reportedly complain to SRSGs about the impact such assessments have on their ability to govern. SRSGs therefore must walk a fine line representing multiple Security Council objectives, including supporting sanctions. In some cases, SRSGs actively contribute to sanctions discussions because consultations on peacekeeping and other mandates and sanctions resolutions are now increasingly linked. Renewal schedules have been rationalized so that they occur at similar intervals, facilitating an overall Council discussion of these instruments to ensure they are as complementary as possible.[20]

Human rights and humanitarian actors affiliated with the United Nations also have mixed views on sanctions. The United Nations Development Programme along with the Office for the Coordination of Humanitarian Affairs (52 per cent of episodes) and the UN High

[17] *Ibid.*, pp. 29–32. The guidelines provide expectations for peace operations' support to expert panels in three categories: logistics and administration, security, and substantive support.
[18] *Ibid.*, pp. 33–8.
[19] Although it operates in close coordination with the UN, the International Criminal Court is not a part of the UN system.
[20] Author interviews, former panel members, UN Secretariat officials, and member state officials.

Commissioner for Refugees (57 per cent) frequently are involved in countries subject to sanctions. Tensions between humanitarian actors and sanctions actors have at times been quite significant; in particular many humanitarian actors continue to harbour negative perceptions of sanctions, based on their experience with the comprehensive Iraq sanctions in the 1990s. Some humanitarian workers note that sanctions have impacts on their ability to help those affected by conflict, either by restricting their ability to bring in certain kinds of materiel to affected areas or by limiting access to needy communities. Humanitarian actors nonetheless acknowledge that when known human rights abusers (e.g. perpetrators of sexual violence or child recruitment) are sanctioned, this sends a strong signal in support of human rights norms.[21] Strong cooperation between the UN SRSG on Sexual Violence in Conflict and the DRC arms embargo panel contributed to listing Mai Mai Cheka for widespread sexual abuse and child recruitment in 2011. However, humanitarian actors in the DRC still believe too few actors have been targeted, rendering individual sanctions less meaningful because known abusers are either not listed or if listed, no steps towards implementation have been taken.[22] In 2010, humanitarian actors were embarrassed when the UN Monitoring Group on Somalia reported that three key World Food Programme contractors had diverted substantial amounts of food aid for personal enrichment, as well as in support of armed militias and radical Islamists.[23]

With regard to international judicial proceedings, UN sanctions increasingly target perpetrators of violence that could be considered crimes within the jurisdiction of the International Criminal Courts or other tribunals. The intersection of these two different systems highlights the need for better awareness of respective mandates and ways to cooperate and share information. Issues involving information and standards related to criminal investigations and proceedings, coordination among field and headquarter investigators, and differentiating between sanctions and court proceedings are overlapping areas that would benefit by greater cooperation and closer contacts.

International functional institutions and mechanisms

A range of international bodies and mechanisms not generally part of the UN system increasingly interact with UN sanctions regimes (Table 6.3).

[21] Author interviews, humanitarian officials.   [22] Author interviews, UN officials.
[23] UN Monitoring Group on Somalia, Report of the Monitoring Group on Somalia, submitted in accordance with resolution 1853, S/2010/91, 10 March 2010.

Table 6.3 *International institutions/mechanisms and UN sanctions*

	Episodes	
Actors Involved	Frequency	%
Proliferation related		
International Atomic Energy Agency (IAEA)	9	14
Other proliferation-related actors (e.g. E3+3, Six Party, NSG, etc.)	7	11
Terrorism related		
International Bank for Reconstruction and Development (IBRD)/ International Monetary Fund (IMF)	11	17
Financial Action Task Force (FATF)	8	14
Counter-terrorism Implementation Task Force (CTITF)	3	5
Counter-Terrorism Executive Directorate (CTED)	3	5
Other terrorism-related actors	5	9
Conflict related		
Kimberley Process	8	13
Other conflict-related actors (ICRC, INTERPOL, IMO)	15	25

Note: Percentage calculated from valid cases only; non-applicable and missing data excluded.

In most cases, institutional mandates do not necessarily refer to or require cooperation with sanctions institutions and personnel, but the tools and mechanisms offered are complementary or even essential for effective implementation of UN sanctions. Targeted interactions with these entities generally occur on an as-needed-basis, often initiated by an expert panel, but enhanced cooperation and information sharing could be beneficial in leveraging relevant expertise and resources to promote a more integrated approach to UN sanctions.

One area with significant potential for cooperation concerns weapons and ammunition tracing. Different databases coexist and many are incomplete. INTERPOL, for instance, makes its database available to expert groups, but it only covers stolen weapons or those used to commit a crime. In 2013, when similar munitions cartridges were found in Côte d'Ivoire, the DRC, Niger, and Afghanistan, experts shared information and linked the ammunition to Iran. This successful investigation raised the issue of knowledge management within UN sanctions regimes and the need to ensure that such information is not missed in the future.[24] Sanctions

---

[24] In 2011, a former member of the Côte d'Ivoire panel developed a tracking system to trace weapons and ammunition investigated in conflict contexts. See J. Bevan and G. McDonald, 'Weapons Tracing and Peace Support Operations: Theory or Practice?', Briefing Paper Number 1 (Geneva: Small Arms Survey, May 2011).

committees and expert groups also have worked closely with transport organizations in order to track weapons flows. Institutions such as the International Maritime Organization, the International Civil Aviation Organization, and regional organizations such as the Agency for the Security of Aerial Navigation in Africa and Madagascar have had interactions with sanctions committees but they are largely *ad hoc*. Cooperation is not institutionalized and is based largely on personal relationships or even on the presence within experts groups of personnel who previously worked for these organizations. Another important source of relevant information is the World Customs Organization, but again, systematic interaction is lacking. INTERPOL has agreements with ten of the fifteen sanctions committees, and 526 INTERPOL-UN Special Notices have been issued to facilitate implementation of travel bans and assets freezes.[25]

Sanctions regimes have long attempted to mitigate conflict funded by natural resources, collaborating closely with non-UN actors such as the OECD, as well as the Extractive Industries Transparency Initiative. The effort to control the diamond trade and establish a process for governments to certify the provenance of diamonds eventually became the Kimberley Process Certification Scheme (KPCS), which the Security Council first endorsed in 2003.

The DRC Group of Experts contributed to developing a systematic initiative to curb conflict by regulating the trade in natural resources through due diligence procedures.[26] The creation of the DRC committee and the corresponding expert panel in 2004 provided new impetus for mechanisms to address trade in natural resources. Indeed, the group found that weapons were routinely exchanged for natural resources or benefits yielded from their trade. Since 2007, the DRC Group of Experts has worked with the OECD to develop due diligence procedures. While the effort originally met with resistance from some Member States, public pressure eventually led to the endorsement of due diligence guidelines for

---

[25] Originally called for in UNSCR 1617, the INTERPOL Special Notices are useful in making specific information, such as photographs or physical descriptions of persons listed, accessible to more than 25,000 authorized users in INTERPOL's global network of national police, immigration, and border-control authorities.

[26] The first DRC expert panel on natural resources was not mandated by sanctions and could only report findings, and name and shame rather than suggest that Member States enforce recommendations. Civil society organizations' attempts to use the OECD soft law to produce more effective action all failed. When the panel's report was first published, some Western Member States wanted to use the opportunity to strengthen the OECD's voluntary standards as encapsulated in the Guidelines for Multinational Companies. But at the time, they did not attempt to strengthen hard law within the DRC (e.g. mining code) or the region. The panel contributed to confusing Member States when its reports included lists of people and companies that had not complied with the voluntary OECD standards.

companies exploiting and trading minerals from the DRC in UNSCR 1952.[27] Further attempts have been made to translate due diligence into hard law at the DRC Ministry of Mines and the International Conference on the Great Lakes. Due diligence procedures have been adopted elsewhere (e.g. Section 1502 of the US Dodd–Frank Wall Street Reform and Consumer Protection Act concerning conflict minerals) and expanded to other industrial sectors, notably to the International Members of the Tin Industry and the World Gold Council.[28]

The Financial Action Task Force has long interacted with UN sanctions regimes. An intergovernmental body that promotes legal and regulatory measures to combat money laundering, terrorism financing, and illicit finance, FATF standards have developed into *de facto* global standards for the implementation of financial sanctions and assessment of national compliance systems. The Security Council endorsed these guidelines in various resolutions, but they remain limited to counterterrorism and non-proliferation sanctions, and do not apply to conflict-related financial sanctions. Relevant sanctions regimes (Iran, DPRK, and Al-Qaida) cooperate closely with the FATF, including on specific recommendations (notably recommendations 6 and 7 on the financing of terrorism and weapons of mass destruction). Although they are soft law, the banking and financial industries generally adhere to FATF's standards, as do states, which are likely to comply, since adverse assessments could affect their credit rating.[29] However, no specific FATF measures address financial support linked to mass atrocity crimes, threats to international peace and security, or jeopardizing democratic processes; financial institutions may therefore be more reluctant to exercise restraint in these fields. While interactions between UN sanction committees and international financial institutions are infrequent, direct engagement and extension of FATF standards to conflict-related financial sanctions could enhance implementation of UN sanctions.

Regional bodies, national authorities, and non-governmental organizations

Regional sanctions can complement UN sanctions, although the multiple layers of sanctions can be confusing to various actors. As discussed in Chapter 5, the European Union most frequently imposes

[27] The UNSC has remained reluctant to designate any individual or entity based on violations of the guidelines, despite repeated recommendations by the expert group.
[28] For more, see E. Carisch and L. Rickard-Martin, 'Sanctions and the Effort to Globalize Natural Resources Governance' (Berlin: Friedrich Ebert Stiftung, 2013).
[29] For details on the FATF recommendations, see www.fatf-gafi.org/topics/fatfrecommendations/.

Table 6.4 *Regional actors and UN sanctions*

	Episodes	
Regional Actors	Frequency	%
ECOWAS	16	25
AU	37	59
OAS	3	5
EU	31	51
NATO	11	17
Arab League	14	22
OIC	17	28
OSCE	4	7
Other	14	24

Note: Percentage calculated from valid cases only;
non-applicable and missing data excluded.

sanctions, in 52 per cent of UN sanctions episodes, and is directly involved in 51 per cent of them. The African Union, in contrast, is involved in 59 per cent of all UN sanctions episodes but imposes autonomous sanctions in only 3 per cent of them. Table 6.4 describes the involvement of regional actors in UN targeted sanctions episodes.

Once adopted by the Security Council, UN sanctions must be implemented by Member States; Council decisions, although binding, are not self-implementing. Thus, each Member State must have adequate legal authority and regulatory mechanisms to give effect to UN sanctions. Private sector firms then need to understand and comply with limitations on sanctioned goods and services in order for the measures to be effective. Chapter 7 addresses further the importance of systematic engagement with the private sector to enhance the implementation and effectiveness of UN sanctions.

Cooperation with non-governmental or public–private organizations is typically not institutionalized and often based on personal contacts or the fact that UN expert panel members formerly worked for the NGOs involved. This form of cooperation, however, provides an important opportunity for raising awareness and enhancing implementation of UN sanctions. This was particularly the case for conflict minerals, the Kimberley Process, and due diligence procedures.

Sanctions in support of political transitions

Even if direct coordination among sanctions actors and mediation efforts remains limited – indeed negotiation of a peace agreement is mentioned as an objective of sanctions in only 13 per cent of cases – sanctions have become versatile tools to adapt to changing political and security situations. They have evolved significantly and are a far cry from the early sanctions on Haiti, for example, which were unduly maintained.

The political nature of sanctions accounts for considerable variation in their application by Member States. When political will exists in the Security Council, sanctions can be implemented and enforced swiftly (e.g. the counterterrorism sanctions and the Libyan sanctions in 2011). Over the past decade, sanctions have increasingly been employed to support peace and stabilization processes, rather than merely stop the fighting. In Liberia, Côte d'Ivoire, the DRC, and Somalia, sanctions regimes are now aimed at protecting the transition and maintaining peace after agreements have been signed and elections have brought new leaders to power. The Council increasingly uses sanctions to address the threat of potential spoilers.

As such, UN sanctions are being employed in a flexible manner to support political processes in several ways, such as by threatening sanctions, promising the lifting of certain sanctions according to specifically defined criteria, changing the geographical scope, or by selectively delisting certain targets. In 2003 in Liberia, the UNSC laid out conditions for sanctions to be lifted: a 'transparent, effective and internationally verifiable Certificate of Origin regime for Liberian rough diamonds', full authority and control over timber producing areas, and a transparent financial management system that would help 'ensure that government revenues are not used to fuel conflict'.[30] In 2010, due diligence procedures were added to the DRC sanctions for companies involved in trading minerals (e.g. cassiterite, coltan, wolframite, and gold) in an attempt to end protracted conflicts over resources. In 2011, the UN sanctions that paralyzed Libya's financial sector were substantially modified when transitional authorities took over. In 2012, to protect the new Somali transitional authorities, the UNSC imposed an embargo on charcoal, which the Monitoring Group had identified as a key revenue source of Al Shabaab.[31] Specifying potential targets also sends strong positive or negative political signals. Negative signals were used in Angola, where

---

[30] See United Nations UNSC Resolution 1521, S/RES/1521 (2003), 22 December 2003, para 5; Resolution 1579, S/RES/1579 (2004), 21 December 2004, especially paras 10–12; and Resolution 1607, S/RES/1607 (2005), 21 June 2005. For more, see A. J. Boucher, W. Durch, S. Rose, and J. Terry, *Mapping and Fighting Corruption in War-Torn States* (Washington, DC: Henry L. Stimson Center, 2007), pp. 53–5.

[31] UN Security Council Resolution 2036 (2012) and Report of the Monitoring Group on Somalia, S/2012/544, 13 July 2012.

the UNITA rebellion was specifically targeted by sanctions, and against Al Shabaab and Eritrea seen as undermining the 2008 Djibouti Agreement on Somalia.[32] Positive reinforcing signals concerning counterterrorism sanctions resulted when the Al-Qaida and Taliban regimes were split in 2011 during track II negotiations with the Taliban. Similarly, in the DRC, after the Global and All Inclusive Peace Agreement was signed in late 2002, the arms embargo included exemptions for signatories of the peace agreement.

The scope of sanctions may also be modified. While early DRC sanctions only covered the eastern portion of the country, by 2005, with the transition and military integration far behind schedule, the UN extended its arms embargo to the entire country. After the elections in 2008, sanctions were again scaled back to the east of the country. Similarly, the UNSC-established conditions for the lifting of sanctions on Côte d'Ivoire also aimed at supporting peace; these conditions included holding peaceful and fair elections and participating in the peace and reconciliation process.[33] After elections were held in 2011 and former president Gbagbo was removed from power, the new Ivorian authorities, including the Permanent Representative of Côte d'Ivoire, welcomed the sanctions, arguing that they would provide incentives for continuing democratization, maintaining a schedule for parliamentary elections, and security sector reform in Côte d'Ivoire, as well as containing spoilers.[34] Sanctions continue because they provide an accountability mechanism for achieving these objectives.

Challenges of greater cooperation

While UN resolutions often mandate cooperation between various actors involved in sanctions monitoring and implementation, in practice, the Security Council does little to promote greater cooperation among the many actors and institutions. As a result, most cooperation is *ad hoc*, relying on personal relationships, and lacking in formal guidelines, memoranda of understanding, and systematic information sharing or coordination. This lack of institutionalized mechanisms to promote and encourage cooperation among sanctions and other UN and international institutions reduces opportunities to leverage complementary mandates. The TSC database indicates that in 86 per cent of the episodes, UN sanctions complement the activities of other multilateral actors, and

---

[32] Al Shabaab was a splinter group of the Islamic Courts which only formally affiliated with Al-Qaida in 2012.
[33] UN Security Council Resolution 1572 (2004).
[34] See records of the meetings of the Security Council, S/PV6525, 28 April 2011.

conflict with them in only 9 per cent of the cases. While this appears to be a positive indication of the complementarity of sanctions with other instruments, it fails to capture the missed opportunities represented by the absence of greater cooperation and coordination that could enhance the effectiveness of UN sanctions. When failure to cooperate emerges out of obstacles imposed by the Council, political will on the part of Member States will be required to change the political dynamics. However, when a failure to coordinate stems from a lack of understanding of sanctions and awareness of various mandates, the lack of tools to facilitate coordination, or inadequate resources to promote cooperative efforts, it is imperative that the relevant actors – the Security Council and Member States – address the problems.

The current UN sanctions' institutional framework faces three challenges that urgently need to be addressed: (1) internal knowledge management, (2) outward communication, and (3) a better understanding of the nature of sanctions institutions. The fact that these challenges are well known, but largely have been ignored, raises serious questions as to the degree to which Member States actually intend sanctions to be an effective tool or whether they are political window dressing, allowing Member States to appear to act without truly being committed to their objectives.[35]

Knowledge management within and across country sanctions regimes is important in a system where at least two of the three key components (the sanctions committee and the Panel of Experts) have a high turnover in personnel. Diplomats of P5 members regularly rotate, sanctions chairs change every two years with elections to the Council, and experts face a four-year term limit. The Secretariat's role in ensuring the continuity both within sanctions regimes and across regimes is therefore crucial. While the first issue is essentially technical, the second is more political. Within the same sanctions regime, keeping track of documentation, requests to states, and contacts with the relevant stakeholders requires systematic management and continuity, which has been addressed by assigning a Secretariat political officer to the committee and expert group.[36] Managing the significant amount of complex information requires an efficient and usable archive of information, something the Secretariat attempted to put in place but which experts criticized as unwieldy, difficult to use, and lacking in functionality for effective

---

[35] Chesterman and Pouligny, 'Are Sanctions Meant to Work? The Politics of Creating and Implementing Sanctions through the United Nations'.

[36] It is worth noting the comparative dearth of support Africa-focused panels receive, in part because of lack of funding for relevant positions in the Sanctions Branch.

cross-referencing. Some of the most successful recent breakthroughs on data cross-checking came from such a matching process between various sanctions regimes tracing weapons and ammunition back to Sudan or Iran. Contrary to popular belief, INTERPOL does not provide a solution, since it relies on the good will of Member States to act and does not maintain a comprehensive database. While the Secretariat is aware of the need to strengthen continuity and coordination between successive panels and committees, cross-panel information sharing is contentious, particularly when findings are controversial and information sharing and cooperation are actively discouraged unless expressly mandated by the Security Council.

Outward communication entails the development and better dissemination of clear guidelines from the Council to Member States concerning sanctions implementation and enforcement responsibilities. Member States should ensure that such guidance is distributed within relevant ministries, and ultimately to the private sector (as appropriate), and that national authorities are able meet their compliance obligations. This requires greater communications and, especially, capacity building and technical assistance training within Member States. Sanctions objectives are often poorly communicated externally either because Member States (the targeted country as much as UNSC members themselves) misunderstand their obligations or because relevant country missions have no understanding or training. Currently this educational role falls *de facto* on the shoulders of the expert panels, whose role has come to entail information gathering in addition to educating the various stakeholders on the nature of the sanctions and their ensuing obligations. Mechanisms such as Côte d'Ivoire's embargo cell within the mission could be mainstreamed and tasked with proactive communications in-country with both government officials and international actors. Sanctions training for Member States (particularly for officials from targeted states and their neighbours) and missions would be beneficial. Since sanctions, as well as related due diligence requirements, are likely to become more prevalent, private companies would also benefit from such training and outreach activities. A user-friendly website, allowing for transversal searches and regular updates on sanctions (again, requiring an integrated database and matching system of individuals/entities, entities, weapons, financial transactions, etc.), could result in a mechanism that facilitates panel reports and tracks implementation to promote more effective implementation of UN sanctions.

The uncertain institutional basis to support sanctions can result in suboptimal conditions that compromise the effectiveness and independence of expert panels. Time-limited contractual arrangements are viewed as inadequate by experts, as they are considered temporary consultants or 'experts on mission' and provided with a UN *laissez passer* to facilitate travel.[37] Within the UN, this diminished status undermines the ability to attract high-quality experts and often elicits reluctant and piecemeal information sharing from UN and other institutions.

As noted, not all sanctions regimes are created equally; disproportionate support for terrorism and non-proliferation sanctions conveys a hierarchy within sanctions regimes. Greater support for and cooperation among conflict-related sanctions regimes is possible if Member States demonstrate necessary political will to use sanctions to address such challenges. An important step to this end would include the creation or extension of specific FATF recommendations aiming at ending conflict and restoring peace and democracy.

Finally, double standards continue to apply to the enforcement of sanctions, resulting in resentment among states whose cooperation is essential. Paradoxically, weak states with limited institutional capacity bear the brunt of enforcement efforts, while more developed states with greater capabilities have a relatively lighter compliance burden (even when their large international corporations are involved). Few international corporate entities from developed countries are designated on the sanctions lists even when financial support for targeted individuals may originate from such entities or when they are the destination for sanctioned minerals. Experience has shown that it is politically easier to list firms in fragile states, with a relatively low capacity for implementation, than it is to designate companies based in countries where state capacity is significantly higher, but the risk of litigation is also much higher. Trafficking in conflict-fuelling commodities, financial support for illegal armed groups, and trade in weapons and ammunition can only be addressed by targeting the entire network from supply to demand.[38]

Conclusion

Increasing the quality and frequency of interactions between UN sanctions regimes and other UN and international actors requires more systematic engagement and cooperation. Synergies should be explored with

---

[37] As such, they receive no benefits such as medical insurance or paid leave. See A. J. Boucher and V. K. Holt, *Targeting Spoilers: The Role of United Nations Panels of Experts* (Washington, DC: Henry L. Stimson Center, 2009), p. 48.

[38] An attempt at targeting the entire supply-and-demand chain has been pursued through the judicial system after failure to do so through the OECD focal points and confidential annex to the DRC group of experts' reports. See K. Manson in Nairobi, J. Shotter in Zurich, and J. Farchy, 'Swiss Investigate Congo Gold Bought by Biggest Refiner', *Financial Times*, 4 November 2013.

relevant organizations and mechanisms that move beyond personal relationships and *ad hoc* agreements to create strategic partnerships and specific cooperation agreements. To break down barriers to cooperation, more cross-cutting discussions of sanctions implementation issues should be conducted. Greater understanding and cooperation of relevant actors at all levels – within the UN system, with related international institutions, among regional organizations, and Member States (including regulatory authorities and the private sector) – should be promoted through regular interaction and engagement. Building the capacity of Member States and UN officials through training to understand better their obligations for monitoring and enforcement of UN sanctions is essential. Improving coordination and cooperation among the range of actors and instruments involved with UN sanctions is possible, but will require political will on the part of the Security Council and Member States to provide the necessary leadership and support to the actors involved.

Appendix A *Sanctions regimes and resolution mandates*

Sanctions regime	Resolution cooperation mandates
	Africa conflict cases
Somalia/Eritrea (e.g. S/RES/2060, paras 9, 16)	• AMISOM (the AU force deployed to Somalia) to help the Monitoring Group implement its mandate. • Enhanced cooperation, coordination, and information sharing between the Monitoring Group, humanitarian organizations in Somalia/the region; all states in the region, the TFG, international, and subregional organizations.
Liberia (e.g. S/RES/2025 and S/RES 2079)	• Panel to work with the Kimberley Process Certificate Scheme. • The panel to cooperate with counterparts for the DRC and Côte d'Ivoire. • UNMIL to cooperate with the panel.
DRC (e.g. S/RES/2021 (2011) and S/RES/2078 (2012)	• MONUSCO and the Group to cooperate with each other. • The Group and Member States to cooperate with each other. • The Group to cooperate with the Liberia and Côte d'Ivoire panels, especially on natural resources.
Côte d'Ivoire (e.g. S/RES/2045 (2011) and S/RES/2102 (2012)	• UNOCI, the French forces and the Group of Experts to cooperate. • Requests the KPCS to cooperate with the group. • Welcomes continued cooperation with the Liberia panel. • Urges all states, relevant United Nations bodies and other organizations, and interested parties, to cooperate fully with the 1572 Committee, the Group of Experts.
Sudan (e.g. S/RES/2025)	• Requests the panel coordinate with UNAMID and the Joint AU/UN mediation. • Requests all UN bodies' full cooperation with the panel.
Libya (e.g. S/RES/2017, S/RES/2040, and S/RES/2095 (2013)	• Requests cooperation with Libya Sanctions Committee, the panel, Counterterrorism Executive Directorate (CTED), UN bodies (including ICAO) to assess small arms threats and help with border security.

- Member States, UN bodies, UNSMIL, the Libyan government, to cooperate to stem the proliferation of weapons.
- All states, relevant United Nations bodies, including UNSMIL, and other interested parties, to cooperate fully with the committee and the panel.
- UNSMIL and the Libyan government to support panel investigatory work inside Libya.
- Welcomes the important role of the region through the active leadership of the Economic Community of Central African States (ECCAS), in particular the mediation by the Congo.
- Stresses the urgent need to deploy throughout the country an increased number of BINUCA's human rights monitors in order to implement fully its mandate to monitor, help investigate, and report to the Council on violations of S/RES/2134 (2014) international humanitarian law and of abuses and violations of human rights committed throughout the CAR.
- Emphasizes the need for strong coordination and information-sharing between BINUCA, the African Union-Regional Task Force (AU-RTF), and the MISCA in the context of their protection of civilians' activities and counter-LRA operations.
- Encourages ECOWAS to continue its mediation.
- Requests the Secretary-General to be actively engaged in this process, in order to harmonize the respective positions of international bilateral and multilateral partners, particularly the AU, ECOWAS, CPLP, and the EU, and ensure maximum coordination and complementarity of international efforts, with a view to developing a comprehensive integrated strategy with concrete measures aimed at implementing security sector reform, political and economic reforms, combating drug trafficking and fighting impunity.

Central African Republic (e.g. S/RES/2181; S/RES/2134; and 2127)

Guinea-Bissau (e.g. S/RES/2048)

Nuclear non-proliferation

- Requests all states and UN entities to cooperate with the panel.
- Requests Member States, UN bodies, and interested parties to cooperate with the panel.
- Calls upon relevant international, regional, and subregional organizations to designate and provide the 1540 Committee by 31 August 2011 with a point of contact or coordinator for the implementation of Resolution 1540 (2004).

Iran (e.g. S/RES/2049)
DPRK (e.g. S/RES/2050)
1540 Committee/Group of Experts (e.g. S/RES/1977 (2011)

Appendix A (*cont.*)

Sanctions regime	Resolution cooperation mandates
	• Encourages them to enhance cooperation and information sharing with the 1540 Committee on technical assistance and all other issues of relevance for the implementation of Resolution 1540 (2004).
	• Reiterates the need to continue to enhance ongoing cooperation among the 1540 Committee, the UNSC Committee established pursuant to Resolution 1267 (1999), concerning Al-Qaida and the Taliban and the UNSC Committee established pursuant to Resolution 1373 (2001), concerning counterterrorism.

Counterterrorism

Al-Qaida (Monitoring Team for S/RES/1267 and 1989), for example, through S/RES/2083	• Welcomes continuing cooperation between the committee and INTERPOL, the United Nations Office on Drugs and Crime, in particular, on technical assistance and capacity-building, and all other United Nations bodies, and encouraging further engagement with the Counter-Terrorism Implementation Task Force (CTITF) to ensure overall coordination and coherence in the counterterrorism efforts of the UN system.
	• Reiterates the need to enhance ongoing cooperation among the committee, the Counter-Terrorism Committee (CTC), and the committee established pursuant to Resolution 1540 (2004), as well as their respective groups of experts.
	• Requests the Secretary-General to make the necessary arrangements for the groups to be co-located as soon as possible.
	• Encourages the Monitoring Team and the United Nations Office on Drugs and Crime, to continue their joint activities, in cooperation with the Counter-Terrorism Executive Directorate (CTED) and 1540 Committee experts to assist Member States in their efforts to comply with their obligations under the relevant resolutions.
Counterterrorism Committee (Resolution 1373) and its Counter-Terrorism Executive	• CTED to intensify cooperation with relevant international, regional, and sub-regional organizations with a view to enhance Member States' capacity to fully implement Resolution 1373 (2001) and Resolution 1624 (2005) and to facilitate the provision of technical assistance.

Directorate (CTED), for example S/RES/1963

- Reiterates the need to enhance the ongoing cooperation among the CTC, the committee established pursuant to Resolution 1267 (1999), and the committee established pursuant to Resolution 1540 (2004), as well as their respective groups of experts, including through, as appropriate, enhanced and systematized information sharing, coordination on visits to countries, and participation in workshops, on technical assistance, on relations with international and regional organizations and agencies, and on other issues of relevance to all three committees.
- Recalls Resolution 1904 (2009), which requests the Secretary-General to make the necessary arrangements for the groups to be co-located as soon as possible.
- CTED to continue joint activities, in cooperation with the 1267 Monitoring Team, the 1540 committee experts, and the United Nations Office on Drugs and Crime to assist Member States in their efforts to comply with their obligations under the relevant resolutions.
- Welcomes and encourages CTED's continued active participation in and support of all relevant activities under the United Nations Global Counter-Terrorism Strategy, including within the CTITF.

Appendix B *UN funding for Panels of Experts on Africa: 2004–13*[1]

Activity & cost in US dollars	2004–05	2006–07	2008–09	2010–11	2012–13
Monitoring Group on Somalia and Eritrea					
Salaries/staff cost, 2 administrative staff, 5 local level in 2012–13, 1 P3, and 1 professional administrative staff	100,300	115,300	95,000	113,100	417,200
Panel fees, 4 members (4 members, 1 consultant in 2010)	1,275,700	556,200	702,300	875,800	1,142,100
Panel travel		361,100	419,000	416,200	588,400
Operational/logistical support (including staff travel, office space and security)	84,200	153,500	116,200	150,100	331,500
Total	1,460,200	1,186,100	1,332,500	1,555,200	2,479,200
Panel of Experts on Liberia					
Panel fees (5 experts in 2004–05, 4 experts in 2006–07, 3 experts in 2008–09, 3 experts in 2010), travel	1,306,900	1,243,100	422,200	385,800	315,000
Support, assessing socioeconomic impact of sanctions (includes travel to remote areas)		26,200	348,000	350,900	n/a
Operational/logistical support, including travel, consultants, and information technology requirements	31,700	49,400	26,800	20,700	317,200
Total	1,338,600	1,318,700	797,000	757,400	632,200

	Group of experts on the DRC				
Salaries/staff costs, 1 mid-level officer	74,400	85,000	148,800	148,800	156,900
Panel fees for 5 members, 5 consultants	805,500	615,600	699,900	622,700	480,00
Panel travel		630,700	742,300	562,600	703,400
Staff travel (for the mid-level officer)	42,100	61,000	54,700	65,400	70,000
Operational/logistical support (includes local travel)	47,400	31,200	51,000	52,800	123,100
Total	969,400	1,423,500	1,695,800	1,452,300	1,533,400
Panel of Experts on Sudan					
Salaries/staff costs, 2-mid-level officers, and 1 administrative staff (local); 1 mid-level officer and 1 administrative staff in 2010 and 1 mid-level officer in 2012–13		276,300	170,300	135,900	127,200
Panel fees for 4 members (5 members, 1 consultant, 1 translator in 2010)		706,200	911,700	919,600	599,100
Panel (and consultant) travel, panel and staff travel in 2012–13		689,800	752,400	572,400	530,300
Operational/logistical support, including consultants, translators, and travel in 2012–13		151,300	51,000	111,200	351,600
Total		1,823,600	1,695,800	1,739,100	1,609,000
Group of Experts on Côte d'Ivoire					
Salaries/staff costs, 1 mid-level officer		113,700	148,800	137,700	130,500

Appendix B (cont.)

Activity & cost in US dollars	2004–05	2006–07	2008–09	2010–11	2012–13
Panel fees for 4 members, 1 consultant (5 members, 1 consultant in 2010, 5 members in 2013)		538,300	583,300	525,200	502,700
Panel travel		473,700	459,800	505,300	653,800
Consultant travel/staff travel		77,400	75,500	75,500	50,000
Operational/logistical support		20,500	30,500	27,700	46,400
Total		1,223,600	1,297,900	1,271,400	1,293,400
Panel of Experts on Libya					
Salaries/staff costs for 2 positions (1 mid-level officer and one administrative officer)				235,500	165,400
Panel fees, 8 members and then 5 members)				1,018,100	505,500
Panel travel				1,075,000	643,000
Staff travel				144,600	63,300
Other operational/logistical support				123,800	77,600
Total				2,597,000	1,456,800
TOTAL: Panels monitoring of sanctions in Africa	**3,768,200**	**5,772,400**	**5,621,400**	**9,373,400**	**9,004,000**

[1] These tables build on Boucher and Holt, *Targeting Spoilers: The Role of United Nations Panels of Experts*; and Boucher, *UN Panels of Experts and UN Peace Operations: Exploiting Synergies for Peacebuilding*. The data for these tables can be found in the following documents (all have the same name): United Nations, *Estimates in Respect of Special Political Missions, Good Offices and Other Political Initiatives Authorized by the General Assembly and/or the UNSC*, Report of the Secretary-General, Addendum, A/59/534, Add.1, 23 November 2004. A/61/525/Add.2, 7 November 2006; A/63/346/Add.2, 11 September 2008; A/64/349/Add.2, 11 September 2009, A/66/354/add.2, 12 September 2011, A/67/346/Add.2, 31 August 2012.

Appendix C *UN funding for monitoring implementation of counterterrorism and non-proliferation mandates: 2004–13*

Activity & cost in US dollars	2004–05	2006–07	2008–09	2010–11	2012–13
Analytical and monitoring support for Al-Qaida/Taliban					
Salaries/staff costs for 12 positions to support the team and in 2012–13, the Office of the Ombudsperson	1,072,300	1,137,700	1,211,000	1,211,000	1,397,500
General temporary assistance				57,200	38,700
Monitoring team fees (8 members)		1,357,900	1,508,400	1,554,000	17,178,400
Monitoring team travel and Ombudsperson travel in 2012–13	1,725,800	437,400	552,800	509,000	644,800
Travel, the committee and staff	401,400	272,900	307,300	307,300	142,800
Other operational and logistical support	404,800	442,900	384,200	332,400	445,900
Total	3,604,300	3,648,800	3,963,700	3,970,900	4,388,100
Counterterrorism Executive Directorate (CTED)					
Salaries/common staff costs for 34 positions, 2004–05; 35 positions, 2006–07; 35 positions, 2008–09 and 38 positions, 2010, 41 positions in 2012–13	4,877,200	5,412,700	6,033,500	6,830,600	6,714,800
General temporary assistance with database analysis and other consultancies	190,400	303,400	No data	No data	
Travel costs for CTED	963,800	798,900	870,000	870,000	1,055,200
Facilities and infrastructure (office rental in 2007)		875,900	882,400	970,000	993,500
Communications	856,900	149,800	98,000	71,000	51,400
Information technology		65,300	72,200	137,900	91,200

Appendix C (*cont.*)

Activity & cost in US dollars	2004–05	2006–07	2008–09	2010–11	2012–13
Other supplies and equipment		112,800	32,900	79,200	11,400
Total	6,888,300	7,718,800	7,989,000	8,958,700	8,917,500
Panel of Experts on the Democratic People's Republic of Korea					
Salaries/staff costs for 4 positions				412,000	406,300
Panel fees for 7 members, 1 consultant				1,292,500	1,408.300
Official travel, Panel				837,600	627,800
Official travel, staff				207,900	70,000
Other operational and logistical support				647,700	81,100
Total				3,397,700	2,754,800
Panel of Experts on the Islamic Republic of Iran					
Salaries/staff costs for 4 positions				475,200	429,500
Panel fees for 8 members				1,677,400	1,638,600
Official travel, Panel				700,900	709,900
Official travel, staff				105,700	105,700
Other operational and logistical support				234,400	221,800
Total				3,193,600	3,009,800
Support for 1540 Committee					
Salaries/staff costs for 3 positions (2 mid-level, 1 administrative staff), and 1 of the 8 experts (in the	322,300	598,600	661,900	930,300	707,100

last 2 years); 4 positions and 1 senior officer in 2010; 5 positions in 2012–13					
Fees, 7 experts; 9 experts in 2012–13	1,195,800	1,264,800	1,420,100	1,357,400	1,748,900
Expert travel		82,600	212,300	181,000	181,000
Official travel, committee chair and members, meetings	25,000	57,700	No data	257,300	257,300
Official travel, committee members and staff, outreach		32,700			
Other operational and logistical support	193,200	152,700	166,300	667,900	296,500
Total	1,736,300	2,189,100	2,460,600	3,393,900	3,190,800
TOTAL: Counterterrorism and non-proliferation-related special political missions	**12,228,900**	**13,556,700**	**14,413,300**	**19,721,200**	**22,261,000**

7 Implementation of United Nations targeted sanctions

Enrico Carisch and Loraine Rickard-Martin

The United Nations Charter does not mention the word 'sanctions' nor does it provide any guidance as to how decisions made by the Security Council regarding 'measures not including the use of force' under Article 41 should be implemented. Article 25 states, 'The Members of the United Nations agree to accept and carry out the decisions of the Security Council in accordance with the present Charter.' This has been widely interpreted to mean that Member States are the primary implementers of sanctions. While true, states are not solely responsible for carrying out UN sanctions. In fact, a broad range of UN and other international actors – the Secretariat, sanctions committees, Panels of Experts, regional and international organizations, civil society, and the private sector – share this obligation and play essential roles in implementing UN sanctions.[1]

Misperceptions based on misplaced emphasis on Member States' implementation duties have allowed the UN Secretariat and UN agencies to eschew implementation responsibilities. Failure to recognize and apportion implementation responsibilities to multiple actors, including the Secretariat and UN agencies, has hampered the effectiveness of UN sanctions. In addition, there is insufficient recognition of what should be self-evident: certain types of sanctions, such as assets freezes and others, cannot effectively be implemented without intense collaboration between the sanctions committees, expert panels, the Secretariat, UN agencies,

---

[1] The fact that Article 25 of the Charter mentions only Member States in relation to Security Council decisions has led to misperceptions that Member States are the only implementers of sanctions. An array of actors are responsible for implementing UN sanctions, beginning with the committees established under Article 29 of the Charter, often established by the same resolution that imposes sanctions and creates sanctions-monitoring panels of experts; the UN Secretariat and its agencies; regional and international organizations; civil society; and the private sector. The authors contend that misperceptions concerning Member States' responsibility to the exclusion of others have hampered the effectiveness of sanctions by allowing other actors, including the UN Secretariat and its agencies, to abdicate vital responsibilities.

regulatory institutions of member states, international organizations, and most importantly, banks and other private sector actors.

Targeted sanctions are more complex to implement than comprehensive sanctions and therefore require greater technical skills and expertise. This poses significant capacity challenges for many Member States and other actors within the UN system. Because of the interrelationship between capacity and political will, it is often difficult to determine whether deficiencies in implementation or noncompliance are attributable to the lack of capacity or to an absence of political will. While technical assistance for counterterrorism and non-proliferation sanctions – purposes that enjoy the greatest political unity among the Permanent Five members of the Security Council – has been available, this has not been the case for most other sanctions regimes.[2]

Moreover, implementation is often complicated by the range of tools utilized by the international community in parallel with sanctions. Peacekeeping missions, mediation and other diplomatic efforts, humanitarian assistance, special envoys, and work of specialized agencies are among the many other policy instruments employed in addressing international crises. In some cases, sanctions are accompanied only by diplomatic negotiations or a peacekeeping mission, while in others, the panoply of tools and actors come into play along with sanctions monitoring mechanisms. Coordination and collaboration among these efforts represent ongoing challenges, as discussed in Chapter 6 by Alix Boucher and Caty Clement.

The expansion of sanctions actors, instruments, and mandates adds complexity and makes effective implementation of UN sanctions more difficult. Changes of implementation practices and mechanisms have evolved without deliberate planning as the Security Council responds to unfolding crises under time constraints. Consequently, there has not been a systematic assessment or study of these interactions and the implications for implementation of UN sanctions. In fact, the last comprehensive reviews of UN sanctions date back ten to fifteen years to the Interlaken Process (1998–1999), focused on targeted financial sanctions; the Bonn/Berlin Process (1999–2000), analysing arms embargoes, travel, and aviation-related sanctions; and the Stockholm Process (2001–2003), addressing implementation and monitoring of targeted sanctions. Much has changed in the intervening years, however, to make today's conflict resolution landscape, and therefore implementation of international measures to address it, more complex and complicated.

---

[2] On this issue, see Chapter 6 by Alix Boucher and Caty Clement.

This chapter addresses implementation experiences of the past two decades of UN targeted sanctions, drawing on the TSC database to analyse implementation at both the UN and Member State levels. Overall, it finds that much greater consistency is needed in the praxis of national, regional, and multilateral sanctions implementation efforts. Improved coordination and sharing of information among actors, enhanced awareness and understanding of mutually reinforcing roles, proactive assistance from the Secretariat to support implementation functions of sanctions committees and Panels of Experts, as well as capacity assistance for Member States and other actors are some of the ways implementation of UN targeted sanctions can be strengthened. To focus greater attention on and understanding of the challenges to effective implementation, the authors recommend a comprehensive and systematic review of UN sanctions resulting in recommendations to strengthen implementation and enforcement of UN targeted sanctions.

TSC database and sanctions implementation

A valuable contribution of the Targeted Sanctions Consortium is the data now available regarding implementation of UN targeted sanctions on a comparative basis. Until recently, there was little empirical data focused on sanctions implementation. The twenty-three UN country-based sanctions regimes were evaluated according to 296 TSC variables, of which more than twenty relate to implementation and enforcement of sanctions at two levels – at the UN and international level and at the level of individual Member States.

Effective implementation of sanctions depends on several elements – the Security Council's design of appropriate measures, a Secretariat infrastructure to ensure that Member States are informed of and comply with their obligations, the monitoring of implementation and enforcement by independent Panels of Experts, legal, administrative, and enforcement mechanisms of Member States, and ultimately for certain sanctions, compliance by relevant private sector actors. This is especially important in the case of assets freezes, sanctions on financial institutions, or civil society monitoring of due diligence compliance related to natural resources and corporate supply chains.

The TSC database addresses implementation at two levels: UN/ international, and national implementation by Member States. As noted above, Member States are primarily responsible for the implementation of UN measures, since sanctions must be translated in national regulatory requirements affecting individual companies, exporters, banks, and others. The database approaches national implementation through examples of enforcement (e.g. interdiction, detention) and evidence of specific sanctions implementation. Evidence of implementation is drawn mainly from reports by Panels of Experts and Member States.

Indicators of implementation at the UN level

At the UN level, the database contains the general categories of political will and implementation, which attempt to reflect UN and international dynamics in adopting sanctions. These include the following specific variables: whether sanctions committees are formed, guidelines put into place, designation criteria and enforcement authorities specified in UNSC resolutions, individual sanctions authorized or targets designated, Panel of Experts appointed, reporting requested or required by Member States on implementation, substantive reports received, instances of enforcement reported, and whether a peacekeeping operation has a mandated enforcement role (Table 7.1).

The Security Council, in adopting resolutions imposing sanctions, routinely establishes a committee consisting of all fifteen UNSC members to oversee and assist in the implementation of UN sanctions. Only in two instances involving sanctions against Sudan were there no sanctions committees created at the outset of the regime. Committee guidelines,

Table 7.1 *Indicators of implementation at the UN/international level*

Indicators of Implementation	Episodes			
	%	Frequency	Missing	n
Designation criteria specified (individual sanctions)	98	41	5	42
Sanctions committee formed at the passage of UNSCR	89	56	0	63
Individual sanctions authorized/designated	88	35	7	40
Committee guidelines developed	78	49	0	63
Reporting requested or required, conditional or not	72	44	0	61[†]
Instances of enforcement	63	34	0	61[†]
Enforcement authorities specified	57	35	0	61[†]
Panel of Experts or Monitoring Teams appointed	46	29	0	63
Peacekeeping operations' enforcement role	45	17	0	38[†]

Note: Percentage calculated from valid cases only; non-applicable and missing data excluded. Relevant suspension episodes excluded.

that is, public documentation laying out the operating procedures and generally indicative of the level of activity of committees, were developed in 78 per cent of the episodes; guidelines were not established during early sanctions regimes (e.g. in Haiti, Rwanda, Sudan in the 1990s, and during the first episodes of other sanctions regimes on Côte d'Ivoire, Sudan over Darfur, Liberia, and Iran), as well as during Lebanon, Libya in 2011, and CAR sanctions regimes.

Perhaps the most significant innovation in the past fifteen years regarding the implementation of UN sanctions is the widespread use of Panels of Experts. Authorized by resolution and appointed by the Secretary-General, they are independent investigative teams responsible for monitoring sanctions implementation. Since 1999, such panels have constituted the primary means by which committees learn what is happening on the ground. Panels of Experts focus on sanctions violations and evasion strategies, and provide recommendations as to targets and ways to enhance the effectiveness of the sanctions. They have been appointed in just under half of the TSC episodes (46 per cent), as they were not a common feature of early UN sanctions regimes. It was only since Angolan sanctions committee chair ambassador Robert Fowler championed the innovative mechanism of expert panels that they have become an essential and routine part of the UN's sanctions implementation infrastructure.

Other indicators of implementation in the database concern whether or not individual sanctions (travel ban/asset freeze) are authorized and targets designated. In 98 per cent of all episodes in the data set UNSC resolutions contain specific criteria regarding who is to be designated as subject to the targeted sanctions (e.g. those violating arms embargo and those inciting violence), a necessary condition for identification of targets. Individual sanctions designations are made in 88 per cent of the cases where they are authorized, an innovation not present in the earlier regimes. Sierra Leone and the Al-Qaida sanctions are among the first regimes in which individual sanctions appear in the initial episodes, a practice more common in recent regimes such as Iran and Libya in 2011.

Instances of enforcement of UN targeted sanctions, either through the specification of enforcement authorities in the resolutions (57 per cent), an enforcement role of peacekeeping operations (45 per cent), or other examples of enforcement (63 per cent), also provide a gauge concerning implementation at both UN and Member State levels. For example, specific cases are referenced in the database regarding sanctions committees' actions (e.g. considering exception requests for medical treatment, conditional authorization for the Hajj, exemptions to the assets freeze) as well as Member State actions to freeze assets, suspend contracts, or arrest and sentence those violating sanctions.

Another significant innovation of the past decade is the enhancement of Member State reporting. In 72 per cent of the episodes national reports are requested or required, sometimes conditionally, and constitute critical information to assess implementation efforts.

Reporting on implementation

The principal implementation obligation of Member States contained in sanctions resolutions concerns reporting – requests or requirements to report on the steps taken to implement UN measures. Typically, UNSC resolutions refer to Member States reporting on the legal and regulatory initiatives taken to implement UN sanctions. Of a total of sixty-one episodes, Member States were called upon or urged to report in six episodes, requested to report in twenty-three, conditionally required or requested in nineteen cases, and required in only two episodes, while in eleven episodes reporting was not mentioned.[3]

Sanctions committees received substantive reports (i.e. beyond assertions of compliance but demonstration of active engagement) and responses from states in just under 50 per cent of the episodes for which data are available (46 per cent). What is interesting to note, however, is that most reporting since the 1267 and 1373 committees' procedures in the post–9/11 period are substantive. With unprecedented political will among P5 members and strong compliance by Member States, Al-Qaida sanctions introduced a number of innovations in reporting requirements and formats, as well as offering states in need of implementation assistance the opportunity to request such support. Further innovation was introduced with the development of Implementation Assistance Notices now utilized by several committees, notably Al-Qaida/Taliban and Iran. Greater information and transparency as to specific measures taken by Member States to implement UN sanctions provided by reporting, as well as an enhanced role and basis for oversight by Security Council committees concerning implementation, are important developments to focus greater attention on implementation efforts.[4]

---

[3] The required reporting generally relates to specific instances of reporting, such as in the case of intercepting individuals subject to the travel ban or when sanctioned goods are intercepted or interdicted. In two episodes sanctions had been suspended.

[4] See T. Biersteker and S. Eckert, *Countering the Financing of Terrorism* (New York and London: Routledge Publishers, 2008).

International actors involved in UN targeted sanctions implementation

The range of UN-related actors and mechanisms associated with sanctions has increased significantly over the past two decades. The roles of existing international organizations have expanded, and new mechanisms and entities developed with responsibilities related to sanctions implementation. The roles of these actors are primarily functional – addressing disarmament and non-proliferation issues (e.g. UN Office of Disarmament Affairs, the International Atomic Energy Agency, the Organization for the Prohibition of Chemical Weapons (OPCW)); establishing international standards against money laundering and terrorist financing (FATF); monitoring compliance with international human rights and humanitarian laws (e.g. Office of the Coordinator of Humanitarian Affairs, Office of the United Nations High Commissioner for Refugees, Human Rights Council); establishing international norms and standards for trade, transportation, and travel (International Civil Aviation Organization, International Air Transport Association), and facilitating global collaboration in enforcement (INTERPOL, World Customs Organization).

Within the UN, agencies and departments with traditional roles in international crisis management and conflict resolution (Department of Political Affairs, Department of Peacekeeping Operations, DDR/SSR, Special Representatives of the Secretary-General) increasingly experience overlapping mandates in countries subject to sanctions.[5] International judicial processes such as the ICC and other criminal tribunals, likewise, have become more frequent.

Moreover, regional organizations, especially in Europe and Africa, responsible for promoting regional security increasingly play a role in implementing or enforcing UN measures or imposing their own sanctions, raising issues of coordination and complementarity (see Chapter 5 by Andrea Charron and Clara Portela on regional sanctions regimes). The relationship between UN and regional or unilateral sanctions is particularly important. They appear to be related measures, but most often are independent, and they rarely complement and may sometimes be in conflict with UN sanctions policies. Regional organizations impose sanctions differently and for different reasons, and have no implementation monitoring mechanisms. Only the EU recognizes in practice and in its institutional setup its obligation to implement UN sanctions, in addition to its substantial independent sanctions regimes. The AU, ECOWAS, SADC, as well as the LAS have no institutionalized

---

[5] These include the Department of Political Affairs, the Department of Peacekeeping Operations, and Special Representatives of the Secretary-General, among others.

requirement to implement UN sanctions and in the case of the African sanctions regimes are far more focused on purposes and policy objectives when compared to UN measures.[6] Differences in UN, regional, and unilateral sanctions raise questions about the strength of Member States' consensus concerning implementation. Confusion between the differing layers of sanctions complicates sanctions implementation. The public, many policymakers, and even sanctions implementation professionals often conflate these measures with UN sanctions.

At its core, however, the key UN institutional actors responsible for sanctions are: the Security Council, sanctions committees and their Panels of Experts, and the Sanctions Unit of the Secretariat. The proliferation in the number of these sanctions actors has been a gradual phenomenon. Ten years ago, only three sanctions regimes (Al-Qaida/ Taliban, Liberia, and Somalia) were supported by a Panel of Experts or Monitoring Team, but currently ten of the thirteen sanctions regimes have them.[7] While the TSC database indicates that expert monitoring mechanisms are present in just under half of the episodes (46 per cent), it is important to note that PoEs are now routinely appointed by the Security Council as an essential element in monitoring implementation. An exception is the regime imposed on Guinea-Bissau in 2012 (Table 7.2).

These entities are called on, directed, or otherwise referred to or acknowledged for playing some role as part of the peace and security architecture associated with UN sanctions.

While the sanctions policies of the UN and individual Member States or regional organizations at times reflect divergent political interests, Security Council directives and UN implementing organizations are expected to be complementary. Unfortunately, what should be collaborative interaction between Security Council sanctions implementation and other UN instruments such as peacekeeping and mediation is not well coordinated generally, and at times results in tensions and internal conflicts.

UN Secretariat

The 2003 Stockholm report notes that 'while primary responsibility for implementing targeted sanctions enacted by Security Council resolutions

---

[6] The AU/PSC commissioned the development of a manual on all aspects of AU sanctions implementation in 2012.

[7] Exceptions include sanctions committees dealing with Iraq (UNSCR 1518), Lebanon/ Syria (UNSCR 1636), which authorizes sanctions against those involved in the assassination of former Lebanese prime minister Rafiq Hariri (designations were never made), and Guinea-Bissau (UNSCR 2048).

Table 7.2 *UN/international actors involved in sanctions*

UN Security Council
  Secretariat
  Sanctions Committees
  Panels of Experts/Monitoring Teams
UN specialized agencies/departments/functions
  Peacekeeping (DPKO, PK forces, DDR)
  Special Representatives of the Secretary-General (SRSGs), functionally
  appointed
  Non-proliferation (IAEA, OPCW, 1540 Committee)
  Counterterrorism (CTED, CTITF, UNODC)
  Disarmament (ODA)
  Human Rights (OCHA, HCHR, HRC)
  Other (WFP, ICAO)
Regional sanctions actors
  EU
  AU
  ECOWAS
  Arab League
Judicial processes
  ICC
Article I. International courts/tribunals (ICTY, ICTR)
Other (international/intergovernmental/etc.)
  Informal proliferation actors (NSG, MTCR, AG)
  FATF/IBRD/IMF
  INTERPOL
  Kimberley Process
  Civil Society (private business sector, NGOs)

rests with Member States, effective implementation depends on strong coordination and communication between the UN and Member States'.[8] Such statements go to the heart of widespread misperceptions about the role of the Secretariat and UN agencies that have become an impediment to the UN assuming its full range of responsibilities in sanctions implementation. A 2009 retrospective of the Angola sanctions regime by a former chairman of the Panel of Experts described his experience in the late 1990s as follows: 'In addition to the obviously still troublesome capacity problems in the Secretariat, the Committee and the Panel had to overcome a considerable amount of scepticism on the part of the

[8] P. Wallensteen, C. Staibano, and M. Eriksson, *Making Targeted Sanctions Effective: Guidelines for the Implementation of UN Policy Options* (Uppsala: Department of Peace and Conflict Research, Uppsala University, 2003). Available at: www.pcr.uu.se/researc h/smartsanctions/.

leadership in the Secretariat. I remember being introduced by Ambassador Fowler to one head of department as "Sancho Panza." Obviously the UN official had earlier referred to Fowler's mission as a Don Quixote undertaking, fighting with windmills, giving low odds for success.'[9] More recently, a 2010 study noted ways in which the Secretariat and UN agencies fall short in fully implementing their responsibilities: 'The willingness of [UN] officials to integrate sanctions with other UN operations is often impeded by erroneous and outdated misperceptions about sanctions. . . . High-ranking officials at the UN and in prominent member states may not be aware of their obligations to implement sanctions or of the security benefits that accrue from compliance with Security Council measures.'[10]

The P5 generally considers the Secretariat as a solely administrative body, but E10 members rely on the Secretariat for vital institutional knowledge, advice, and essential support. The sanctions branch in particular is responsible for providing substantive, technical, and administrative support to sanctions committees and expert panels. While the Secretariat clearly 'does not make policy' on sanctions, often the Secretariat has self-limited its role in declining to raise awareness and assist in sanctions implementation. The lack of coordination among various parts of the UN regarding sanctions suffers from a lack of leadership and poses serious challenges to the effective implementation of UN sanctions. The Secretariat's narrow view of its implementation role has limited sanctions' effectiveness; instead of being reactive, the Secretariat needs to provide leadership from its highest officials, in formulating a unified sanctions policy and coordinating all bodies of the UN into a more coherent focused implementation effort.[11]

Various branches of the Secretariat have had to overcome tensions emerging from seemingly contradictory mandates, as the coercive political nature of sanctions at times conflicts with aid agencies or peacekeeping missions that depend on cooperative relationships with governments, some of whom may be targets of sanctions. Part of the tensions can be attributed to the lack of a unified policy that integrates sanctions with other policy instruments and recognizes their mutually reinforcing nature with other UN mandates. Articulation and development of a unified

[9] A. Mollander, *UN Angola Sanctions – A Committee Success Revisited* (Uppsala: Department of Peace and Conflict Research, Uppsala University, 2009).

[10] D. Cortright, G. A. Lopez, L. Gerber, E. Fackler, and J. Weaver, *Integrating UN Sanctions for Peace and Security* (Goshen Indiana: Fourth Freedom Forum and Kroc Center, University of Notre Dame, 2010). Available at: sanctionsandsecurity.nd.edu/.

[11] E. Carisch and L. Rickard-Martin, 'Global Threats and the Role of United Nations Sanctions' (Berlin: Friedrich Ebert Stiftung, 2011), p. 16.

sanctions policy, as well as relevant training, could promote better implementation of multiple mandates.

Particular emphasis on training of SRSGs (who are involved in nearly 70 per cent of the episodes) and their executive staffs would be helpful to ensure better understanding of how to manage the tensions between their mandates with sanctions and other obligations. Sanctions constitute an important element that has been underutilized by SRSGs and UN mediators as a leveraging and bargaining tool in ceasefire or peace negotiations. The UN system-wide sanctions training effort which took place in 2011 and 2012 under the auspices of the Canadian government was a consultative process that included headquarters officials and field personnel, members of expert panels, Security Council member states, and representatives from other countries, regional groups, and others. Without exception, those participating expressed the need for greater training and awareness about sanctions.[12]

Panels of Experts

Panels of Experts play an essential role in providing information regarding implementation of UN sanctions. Experts are usually appointed on the basis of their functional expertise; they are expected to be independent and objective in evaluating facts on the ground, and not subjected to political pressures. Their reports, many of which are extremely detailed and include documentation regarding violations, and their recommendations often form the basis for committee actions to designate additional targets or modify sanctions.

Unfortunately, recent trends in which experts were chosen as representatives of P5 states (a move effectively politicizing the body) may undermine the critical role of PoEs in sanctions implementation. Reports from the Iran and DPRK panels have suffered delays in publication due to concerns among P5 states; some panel members view their mandates in very limited terms. This runs counter to the operational practices of PoEs developed over the past decade and impairs their monitoring. According to some former experts, reporting has been carefully filtered to reflect political messages of the P5, resulting in the lowest common denominator of information. While interesting and no doubt the best that can be accomplished under difficult circumstances, these PoE efforts fall short of what is necessary to promote effective implementation.

---

[12] UN sanctions training pilot conducted in 2011 by the Sanctions and Security Program, Kroc Institute for International Peace Studies (University of Notre Dame), in collaboration with Compliance and Capacity International, LLC, and UN system-wide sanctions training conducted in 2012 by CCI, both projects funded by the Government of Canada.

Member State implementation

Even when the Security Council adopts sanctions and creates a committee and PoE, these measures will have little impact unless given effect through national means. The elements generally required to translate UN mandates into national measures able to be implemented by relevant parties include a legal framework, administrative or regulatory mechanism, development and dissemination of information, compliance initiatives, and enforcement efforts. National-level implementation is reflected in the database through several different variables.

Instances of implementation of UN sanctions at the national level occurred in 76 per cent of the TSC episodes. In particular, individual sanctions such as assets freezes and travel bans requiring specific action on the part of Member States to freeze funds or monitor travel were employed frequently – assets or accounts frozen account for 72 per cent of episodes, while travel bans were implemented in 63 per cent of the episodes they were imposed. Examples include cases such as Liberia and Sierra Leone, where targets complained of being unable to travel to peace talks; in a few other cases, requests for exemptions or actual violations of travel ban were noted.

Diplomatic sanctions have only been utilized against six countries – Afghanistan, Angola, Liberia, Libya over Lockerbie, Sierra Leone, and Sudan in the 1990s – for which information concerning implementation was available only for Sudan (implemented 100 per cent of the time). Landing rights have been denied in the cases of Angola and Al-Qaida/Taliban, representing 86 per cent of the episodes for which information is available where aviation bans have been imposed. Servicing has been denied only in Iran, or 11 per cent episodes where authorized, and cancellation of credit in 86 per cent of episodes, notably in recent cases of Iran, DPRK, and Libya in 2011.

Overall, instances of enforcement were observed in 63 per cent of the episodes, of which interdiction was observed in 42 per cent of episodes and detention of vessels in 33 per cent of relevant cases. Of particular note is that enforcement measures were employed during early UN sanctions (notably the comprehensive cases on the former Yugoslavia and Haiti) and most recently in the form of interdiction and detention in Iran, DPRK, and Libya since 2011, largely as a result of more explicit enforcement language in Council resolutions. This development reflects a growing interest of several Member States in enhancing the quality of UN targeted sanctions implementation and enforcement (Table 7.3).

Table 7.3 *Indicators of implementation at the national level*

Indicators of Implementation	Episodes			
	%	Frequency	Missing	n
Indications of national-level implementation	76	42	6	61
Diplomatic sanctions enforced	100	2	10	12
Landing rights denied	86	6	1	10
Cancellation of credit	86	6	1	8
Accounts and assets frozen	72	24	5	38
Travel ban implementation	63	24	4	42
Interdiction	42	19	13	58
Detention of vessels	33	9	4	31
Servicing denied	11	1	8	17
Instances of enforcement	63	34	7	61
MS (substantive) reports received	46	23	11	61

Note: Percentage calculated from valid cases only; non-applicable and missing data excluded. Relevant suspension episodes excluded.

Member State reporting

Attention to Member States' obligations to implement UN measures goes back many years. In the case of Southern Rhodesia, the first case of UN sanctions, the initial resolution in 1965 did not address reporting. However, when the UK lost patience with the secessionists, the subsequent resolution, United Nations Security Council resolution (UNSCR) 232, adopted under Chapter VII, contained blunt language emphasizing implementation obligations: 'Reminds Member States that the failure or refusal by any of them to implement the present resolution shall constitute a violation of Article 25 of the United Nations Charter.' In contrast, sanctions against apartheid South Africa – a UN sanctions regime that lacked consistent support by the P5 during the more than ten years of its existence – did not call on Member States to report their compliance efforts.

Today, as noted previously, Member States are typically requested or required to report periodically regarding their legal and regulatory initiatives to implement UN targeted sanctions. Yet, sanctions committees received substantive responses in fewer than 50 per cent of the episodes (46 per cent); however, nearly all sanctions imposed since the 1267 committee first requested substantive reporting have followed suit. This is an important development in the evolution of UN sanctions, as national reports provide important information with which to assess Member

State compliance with UN sanctions. Reporting is generally strongest in the counterterrorism and non-proliferation regimes; in contrast, requests to states by sanctions monitors, for example, especially to neighbours of a state subject to an arms embargo, often elicit no response.

In reviewing PoE reports, most Member States provide minimal information in their national implementation reports, particularly when UN sanctions could trigger criminal prosecutions. Many states privilege national discretion and sovereignty over reporting obligations to the United Nations. Similarly, Member States may take action to freeze the assets of individuals and entities or implement measures upon notification of UN designations, but often do not report to the committee or UN sanctions monitors regarding assets frozen or travel blocked.

The reasons for uneven reporting are multifaceted and have not been fully explored. Since the rigorous reporting standards introduced by the Counter-Terrorism Committee's innovative interactive dialogue with Member States on national reports, there have been indications of 'reporting fatigue'. Speculation as to a general 'sanctions fatigue' is not uncommon, as national officials face daunting requirements in reporting and implementing Security Council measures. The Al-Qaida/Taliban Sanctions Committee responded to this concern by streamlining reporting requirements. Recently Member States were requested to complete a Voluntary National Assessment of Implementation Survey; however, most states failed to utilize the voluntary questionnaire to report on implementation efforts under the 1267/1989 regimes. Notwithstanding this experiment, consolidation of Member State reporting on implementation for the range of sanctions regimes should be considered. For example, a master template including all relevant issues as determined by each sanctions regime could be developed. This once-a-year reporting format could be made compulsory for Member States in contrast to current reports, nearly all of which are requested.

An important element of sanctions implementation that is often overlooked concerns the role of the private sector. Most measures would make no sense and be 'unimplementable' if they were dependent only upon government actions. This dilemma is best illustrated in the context of the sophisticated financial and economic measures, especially as part of counterterrorism and non-proliferation sanctions. While bank supervisory agencies are responsible for informing financial institutions about specific measures adopted by the Council, government agencies cannot actually freeze assets – only institutions holding the assets can. Over the past ten years, the financial industry has installed sophisticated internal screening systems to identify potential transactions related to targeted individuals. The use of name recognition software to facilitate private sector compliance has in fact become so efficient that banks have reported blocking assets before some Member States formally notify banks of the sanctions.

Another indication of the essential role of the private sector in sanctions implementation relates to due diligence-based sanctions for conflict minerals sourced in the eastern DRC. Here, too, governments may assist companies in providing certain information, but in the end, sanctions directly affect firms that trade, refine, or use these minerals. If they want to act responsibly, they must implement appropriate due diligence measures in order to minimize the risk of receiving secondary sanctions themselves.

Fundamental to Member States' ability to implement UN sanctions is adequate national administrative and enforcement capacity to give full effect to the measures. The lack of technical assistance focused on sanctions implementation generally (aside from counterterrorism and nonproliferation) remains a challenge for many Member States.

Sanctions implementation experiences

The following section provides an overview of implementation experiences based on selected UN sanctions regimes. This section is not exhaustive of the broad range of implementation-related UN targeted sanctions experiences, but provides narrative accounts of important cases in a typology of some typical implementation practices.

Lack of Security Council attention, coordination, and implementation: Somalia and Côte d'Ivoire

Somalia   The Somalia arms embargo, first imposed in January 1992, remained isolated from other UN-led mediation, humanitarian, and military-backed efforts to protect humanitarian relief. Following the 'Blackhawk Down' incident in 1993, a prolonged period of neglect ensued, that ended only after the 9/11 attacks prompted concern for Somalia's potential as a safe haven for Al-Qaida terrorists. Although a PoE was established in 2003 to monitor compliance with the arms embargo, it was another five years until 2008 (UNSCR 1844) when individual targeted sanctions were authorized, and another year and a half more before designations were first made (2010, eventual listings were mostly individuals and entities associated with Al Shabaab and other Al-Qaida spin-offs). The sanctions were wholly ineffective in coercing, constraining, and signalling until the fourth episode when designations were made and secondary sanctions applied on Eritrea for its support of armed opposition groups.

Côte d'Ivoire   In response to a prolonged period of internal violence and military coups beginning in the 1990s, the UN imposed an arms embargo and individual sanctions (travel ban, assets freeze UNSCR 1572) when the Ivorian Air Force attacked the French military in late 2004. A diamond ban was added in 2005, and in 2006, token targets were designated, but implementation of Côte d'Ivoire sanctions was delayed. Only in 2011 when the incumbent president of Côte d'Ivoire Laurent Gbagbo ignored his election loss to opposition leader Alassane Ouattara did UNSCR 1975 impose meaningful sanctions – a travel ban and assets freeze on him, his wife, and three key supporters, a significant action in which sanctions and referral to the ICC effectively signalled support for the UN-certified electoral results.

Aggressive sanctions monitoring/enforcement: former Yugoslavia

While sanctions against FRY were a mix of comprehensive and targeted measures (the first episode in 1991 included an arms embargo on all parties that was expanded in episode 2 (May 1992) to comprehensive sanctions), the case is notable for the unprecedented degree of sanctions monitoring.

Following establishment of a sanctions committee on Yugoslavia, UNSC resolutions began mention of 'monitoring missions' until, finally, UNSCR 820 'welcomed the role of the international Sanctions Assistance Missions'. Operationally, the SAMs evolved from the European Commission's deployment of customs experts along the borders of countries neighbouring Yugoslavia (Bulgaria, Hungary, and Romania). Eventually the network was expanded to Albania, Croatia, Macedonia, and Ukraine. It was understood that these monitors required adequate communication and intelligence support, and coordination, which were provided from a sanctions assistance mission communications centre (SAMCOMM) in Brussels.

Eventually, as many as 250 professionals, experts, and intelligence personnel would constitute the SAMs and SAMCOMM. The Europeans also developed elaborate procedures to coordinate implementation efforts and appointed an independent International Sanctions Coordinator to oversee the operations. Suspected breaches of sanctions were communicated through a dedicated EU/OSCE Sanctions Liaison Group to the UN Sanctions Committee.[13]

---

[13] The full extent of this effort is described in the Report of the Copenhagen Round Table on United Nations Sanctions in the Case of the Former Yugoslavia that was submitted in a letter by the Chairman of the Security Council Committee established pursuant to Resolution 724 (1991) concerning Yugoslavia, addressed to the president of the Security Council on 26 September 1996.

Despite these unprecedented efforts applied to the enforcement of a comprehensive sanction, violations of the arms embargo and other sanctions still occurred. Conflating monitoring efforts with sanctions compliance, critics began to question the utility of sanctions monitoring. This extraordinary example represents the apogee of sanctions monitoring; the lack of comparable investment of resources in monitoring other sanctions regimes since raises questions regarding the international community's commitment to effective implementation of UN sanctions. In addition to better monitoring, more determined enforcement under Chapters VII and VIII could enhance effectiveness.

Effect of leadership, monitoring mechanisms, and commodity sanctions: Angola

Following years of ineffective sanctions against UNITA, three distinct factors contributed to innovative implementation strategies that contributed to the end of the conflict in Angola: leadership and political resolve by the sanctions committee chair (the 'Fowler Factor'), independent monitoring and enforcement of sanctions that 'named and shamed' violators, and focus on the particular resource of diamonds. These measures constrained, isolated, and stigmatized UNITA, making the third and fourth episodes of the Angolan sanctions relatively effective.

As part of tightened financial measures against UNITA, important changes in Security Council mechanisms were introduced through the leadership of committee chair and Canadian diplomat Ambassador Robert Fowler. From January 1999 to August 2000, he relentlessly focused on the implementation of UN sanctions on Angola and other African war zones. He gained Security Council support for the establishment of the Panel of Experts to investigate violations of sanctions against UNITA. One year later, UNSCR 1295 established a monitoring mechanism for compliance with the UN arms embargo, assets freeze, and diamond trade restrictions, led by respected diplomats of ambassadorial rank and staffed with technical experts. This unprecedented focus on monitoring was reflected in UNSCRs for the first time, along with detailed instructions to Member States regarding information to be provided.

More detailed implementation requirements encouraged end-use documentation for granting of export permits, attention by national financial institutions to identify funds subject to sanctions, and the exercise of due diligence. Diamond industry initiatives to develop and implement a worldwide control system ultimately contributed to the creation of the

Kimberley Process Certification Scheme that was endorsed by the UN General Assembly in 2001, and the Security Council in 2003.

Fowler's determined effort to 'name & shame' violators brought about a sea change in attitudes towards Security Council sanctions among African heads of state supporting UNITA, who became targets of monitoring group reports. Multilateral and bilateral diplomatic pressure increased substantially, particularly on the presidents of Togo and Burkina Faso. President Laurent Gbagbo of Côte d'Ivoire was also identified publicly. Exhorting Member States to enhance their sanctions implementation practices was unparalleled and reflected the importance that the Security Council accorded the thirty-nine recommendations of its PoE – specific actions that were converted into resolution language.

In opening the door to investigations and reporting, Angola's (and eventually the Congo's) illegal diamond trade would move centre stage of the world's attention. Security Council action led to a number of resolutions targeting the export of illegal raw diamonds from Angola, including transhipments via the DRC. The sanctions imposed against Angolan diamond exporters and the threat of sanctions against their illicit trading counterparts in neighbouring Congo prompted both countries to accede to the Kimberley Process.

The targeting of diamonds, and greater awareness of the linkages between the acquisition of arms and revenues from Angola's artisanal diamond mining sector, were also extremely important. Reports by Human Rights Watch and Global Witness called attention to 'diamonds for arms deals' with extensive research and primary accounts from Angola's embattled fields.[14] Efforts by these advocacy groups prompted many governments to support the Kimberley Process.

Complications of judicial proceedings and governance reforms: Liberia

In the TSC database, the fourth episode of the Liberia sanctions (Dec 2003– June 2006, including a travel ban on family members and diamond and timber sanctions) is assessed to be an example of effective constraint. Indeed, the situation addressing Charles Taylor's misconduct in Liberia and Sierra Leone led to an unprecedented combination of measures – individual sanctions (including secondary sanctions), peacekeeping and peace enforcement missions, mediation, international judicial proceedings,

---

[14] *Angola: Arms Trade and Violations of the Laws of War since the 1992 Elections*, Human Rights Watch, November 1994, followed by *Angola Unravels – The Rise and Fall of the Lusaka Peace Process*, Human Rights Watch, September 1999. *A Rough Trade – The Role of Companies and Governments in the Angolan Conflict* was published by Global Witness, 1 December 1998.

financial aid, and management of government functions (controlling natural resources), as well as sanctions on the commodities of diamonds and timber.

Liberia was an important case in which targeted sanctions and international criminal law converged; similar dynamics of prosecutions and threatening or imposing targeted sanctions followed in the DRC, Côte d'Ivoire, Libya in 2011, and most recently Central African Republic regimes. It is difficult to imagine how the coercive power of sanctions can succeed if at the same time a targeted individual faces prosecution and punishment through international judicial bodies for the same conduct. Under such circumstances, there is little reward for modifying behaviour; the lasting impact of criminal prosecution and punishment likely weighs much more heavily compared with the effects of temporary sanctions. The interplay of temporary and coercive sanctions and the lengthy and permanent nature of legal prosecutions is not well understood; the ramifications of how to maintain the coercive and stigmatizing effects of sanctions once the Council refers cases for judicial proceedings have not been thoroughly considered.

The Council's massive sanctions interventions mandated the restructuring of Liberia's timber, diamond, and aviation sectors. The Security Council targeted two of the three major export sectors – diamond and timber exports in 2002 and 2003, respectively. Sanctions forced the closure of the Liberian Civil Aviation registry, effectively grounding the entire civil aviation in the country for a period of time. A precondition for the resumption of the aviation and timber sectors was full restructuring of the government's oversight and significant reform of the affected industries. These draconian measures essentially turned Liberia into a ward of the international community as 50–60 per cent of its income was lost and significant unemployment resulted. The wholesale restructuring required by the Security Council of the Liberian timber, diamond, and aviation management has raised serious questions. The need for research into the unintended consequences of the Liberia sanctions has not been recognized, as costs of the international community's actions received little attention. Notwithstanding significant international investment in Liberia and the fact that ten years have passed since Charles Taylor was expelled, sanctions remain in Liberia, and progress towards effective resource governance has slowed.

Implications of ambiguous language/multilayered sanctions:
Iran and DPRK

Compared to the first non-proliferation sanctions imposed as part of comprehensive measures against South Africa in 1977, today's proliferation-related sanctions on Iran and DPRK are much more sophisticated and detailed. In both cases, the restrictions gradually expanded from an initial arms embargo, assets freeze, and travel ban on government institutions/ officials engaged in nuclear or missile technology development to include relevant private sector entities and companies providing financial or insurance services, logistical support for the transport, insurance or brokering of transportation, or other proliferation-related activities.

UNSC resolutions call on Member States to 'exercise vigilance' for travel, training, exports, or for 'increased vigilance over activities' of banks, cargo inspections – without definition. As a result, Member States interpret poorly defined measures at their national discretion, likely resulting in differing and non-parallel implementation.

UN sanctions provide a baseline or minimal threshold which some states choose to go beyond and adopt more far-reaching measures – as the United States, EU, and other countries have done in the cases of Iran and DPRK. Other states (Russia and China, among others), however, consider UN sanctions as a ceiling reflective of maximal international consensus; additional measures are viewed as distorting the carefully negotiated balance in the Council. The long-term implications of these differing perceptions remain to be seen, but could have consequences for future consensus on new sanctions and for implementation efforts.

Lessons and future initiatives

As discussed in Chapter 11 by Peter Wallensteen, the UN and Member States have benefited from institutional learning over the past two decades of implementing targeted sanctions, but the record remains mixed and concerted institutionalization of the positive practices and lessons is lacking.

Sanctions committees' procedures and guidelines have generally become more consistent across regimes, but a distinction remains between the counterterrorism and non-proliferation sanctions and the other, mostly, conflict regimes. The critical importance of monitoring sanctions by expert panels has been largely recognized and has become standard practice. Some Panels of Experts serve committees in a highly professional manner, reporting on sanctions violations, evasion strategies, and prospective targets, and making recommendations for ways to improve effectiveness. Others, such as the Somalia Panel, have at times been criticized for weak evidentiary standards and methodology, and still others, the DRC Panel, for example, appear to adopt a practice of making recommendations not directed at the sanctions committee, but to a range of other constituents for which the panel has no mandate. State reporting, with the possible exception of the Al-Qaida/Taliban regimes, is infrequent, often fails to meet even minimal requirements, and is spotty on specificity, and also requests by committees for additional information go unanswered. An intensified focus on individual sanctions has promoted more precise targeting and the tailoring of measures for greater efficiency; however, implementation has been made more difficult by lack of political will among Council members. Similarly, the importance of leadership, political resolve, and collaboration among implementation actors – within UN entities, among other international institutions, and with Member States – is increasingly being recognized. The need for well-coordinated, clearly defined sanctions supported by the Secretariat, implemented by states, and efficiently monitored and enforced, is still a work in progress.

Thus, significant challenges to effective implementation remain. Sanctions suffer from inattention or lack of political will by P5 members; division within the UN as to conflicting mandates and misperceptions of responsibilities of sanctions actors; and complications of other peace and security instruments, regional sanctions, and unintended consequences. The result is less-than-optimal implementation of sanctions at best, and ineffective measures at worst.

Previous sanctions processes (Interlaken, Bonn-Berlin, and Stockholm) helped to clarify and standardize implementation mechanisms for targeted sanctions. More than a decade has passed, however, since there has been a concerted focus on sanctions implementation practices. Global threats have changed considerably, with today's conflict resolution landscape being more complex and complicated. Sanctions-related actors, instruments, and mandates have expanded. Institutions both internal to the UN and outside have assumed new roles in assisting states' and their sanctions' implementation efforts. For example, the Financial Action Task Force promotes implementation of financial sanctions in Member States and among financial institutions. Its recommendations are acknowledged as the global standard and were recently expanded to non-proliferation sanctions. Thematic sanctions, in particular those focused on sexual and gender-based violence (SGBV) or children in armed conflict, have gained considerable momentum in part due of the signalling power of reporting by the SRSGs in charge of SGBV or children in conflict, and UNICEF. New arrangements are necessary to manage and accommodate related mandates of the ICC, other tribunals and courts, and also technical agencies for disarmament, the IAEA, and OPCW. While their work can complement and support the implementation of sanctions, more concerted coordination of sanctions and these related institutions, actors, and tools is needed.

In particular, questions remain as to how much support the Secretariat can provide as long as there is insufficient awareness of the roles, responsibilities, and capacity required to manage effectively implementation efforts. Appropriate training is essential to enhance the effectiveness of the Secretariat's skills to support committees and panels, avoid confusion over mandates, promote consistent evidentiary and methodological standards, and assist Member States.

To address these challenges and ensure effective implementation of UN sanctions, we believe that a systematic review of current sanctions policies and implementation practices is necessary. The UN's institutional structure and staffing responsible for sanctions should be assessed, as well as needs for greater coordination, capacity assistance, training, and new initiatives focused on enforcement.[15]

---

[15] Since this chapter was drafted, the recommendation for a systematic review of sanctions implementation practices has become a reality with the 2014-15 High Level Review of UN Sanctions that resulted in the issuance of the HLR-Compendium (see http://www.hlr-unsanctions.org/).

8   The impacts of United Nations targeted sanctions

Kimberly Ann Elliott

Policymakers imposing sanctions expect them to have an impact, whether economic, political, or psychological. What makes UN targeted sanctions different from many traditional sanctions is that UN policymakers want to minimize the negative impacts on ordinary citizens in the target country. In most cases, this means that UN sanctions target individuals or particular activities that are linked to the threat the Security Council seeks to address. In some cases, however, noncompliance by the targeted regime leads to pressures to ratchet up the impacts by expanding sanctions or tightening their enforcement. In these cases, tensions often arise between sanctions that are effective in achieving compliance, or in supporting international norms, yet still have minimal impact on ordinary citizens.

This chapter looks, first, at the types of targeted sanctions that the United Nations employs and the psychological, political, or economic impacts that different sanctions can have. Sanctioning parties can aim targeted measures very narrowly on individual regime leaders or supporters, or they can broaden their aim to encompass whole sectors, such as aviation or finance, or commodities, such as oil, diamonds, or timber. Obviously, the types and severity of the impacts will differ widely as well. The second part of the chapter looks at how impacts can be measured and evaluated. The following sections examine whether different types of impacts are associated with different categories of goals, or with particular unintended consequences. I then discuss the challenges to keeping targeted sanctions targeted and a tentative assessment of the links between impacts and effectiveness. I conclude with suggestions for future research.

Types of targeted sanctions and impacts

Much of the previous research on sanctions focuses on economic measures, and therefore on economic impacts, as the principal path to policy impact and effectiveness.[1] Targeted UN sanctions, however, include travel bans, diplomatic sanctions, and arms embargoes as well, where the principal impact might be political or psychological rather than economic.[2] Moreover, this volume goes beyond the traditional assessment of the effectiveness of sanctions in terms of their ability to *coerce* changes in the target government's policies or behaviour. The research in this volume also examines the degree to which targeted sanctions contribute to *constraining* capabilities that are of concern or *sending signals* to various audiences.

In assessing the multiple purposes for which policymakers use sanctions, it is important to study all the potential impacts of sanctions. Thus, the country case study authors explicitly address, and the Targeted Sanctions Consortium database includes, all three types of impacts—economic, political, and psychological. In addition, impacts can be either direct or indirect. Often, indirect impacts are related to efforts to evade sanctions, such as Iran's increasing use of barter transactions to get around financial sanctions in the later 2000s, or to unintended consequences of sanctions, such as the increased cost of food and medicine in the latter stages of the mid-1990s UN sanctions against Haiti. Chapter 9 by Mikael Eriksson discusses these unintended consequences of sanctions in more detail.

Potential impacts of targeted sanctions

Even within the realm of targeted sanctions, there is a wide continuum of impacts across different types of measures depending on how discriminating they are.[3] Fewer people would feel the impact of narrowly targeted sanctions, but the principal *type* of impact associated with different targeted sanctions could vary as well. Table 8.1 provides a summary

---

[1] That does not mean this research embraces the 'naïve theory' of economic sanctions that economic pain leads to political gain. See, for example, G. C. Hufbauer, J. J. Schott, K. A. Elliott, and B. Oegg, *Economic Sanctions Reconsidered*, 3rd edn (Washington: Peterson Institute for International Economics, 2007); J. Galtung, 'On the Effects of International Economic Sanctions: With Examples from the Case of Rhodesia', *World Politics*, 19 (1967), pp. 378–416; D. W. Drezner, *The Sanctions Paradox: Economic Statecraft and International Relations* (Cambridge University Press, 1999); Weiss et al., *Political Gain and Civilian Pain* (New York: Rowman & Littlefield, 1997).

[2] The TSC authors identify diplomatic sanctions in only thirteen episodes over six country case studies. None of these cases involve diplomatic sanctions alone and the impacts the authors identify do not point to diplomatic sanctions as the source of the impacts, except perhaps in some episodes involving sanctions against the UNITA rebel faction in Angola. For those reasons, I put diplomatic sanctions aside in the analysis that follows.

[3] T. Biersteker, S. Eckert, M. Tourinho, and Z. Hudáková, *The Effectiveness of United Nations Targeted Sanctions: Findings from the Targeted Sanctions Consortium (TSC)* (Geneva: The Graduate Institute, 2013), pp. 16–7.

Table 8.1 *Principal impact expected by type of targeted sanction*

How targeted is the sanction?	Expected impacts		
	Psychological	Political	Economic
More targeted	Travel ban Individual assets freeze	Travel ban Individual assets freeze	
	Arms embargo	Arms embargo Proliferation controls (narrowly defined) Aviation ban	Proliferation controls (broadly defined) Public assets freeze Aviation, other sectoral Commodities
Less targeted			Financial sector

characterization of what kinds of impacts we might expect to see from different types of sanctions.

Travel and assets sanctions that target individuals are potentially the most precise and we might expect that they would have primarily psychological impacts on those targeted, or their supporters. Assets freezes, if effective in catching significant amounts of assets, would also have financial consequences for targets and could have political impacts. But if the targets are individuals, broader economic impact is limited. Discernible economic impact is possible, however, if UN sanctions target *government* assets. In 2011, for example, American and European policymakers caught the Qadhafi regime by surprise and froze some $50 billion in public and private financial assets held in their jurisdictions. The case study authors find evidence of economic, political, and psychological impacts in that instance.

Arms embargoes target the military or other combatants collectively, so they are not as narrow as sanctions targeting specific individuals. They are intended to have political as well as psychological impacts, but these sanctions are targeted on an activity – the arms trade – that would not have significant economic impacts on a country or its general population.

The impacts of export controls on other weapons-related, or proliferation-sensitive, dual-use technologies, equipment, or materials depend on how broadly they are defined and how well they are enforced. If they are narrowly focused, they could have political or psychological impacts with only limited economic impact; but if they encompass a broader range of technologies or materials that are widely used in manufacturing, such export controls might have economy-wide effects.

As we move to somewhat broader sectoral sanctions, the impacts depend on the breadth of the sanctions and the importance of the sector to the target's economy. Aviation bans, such as the one on air travel to and from Libya in the 1990s, could well have psychological or political impacts by making international travel more difficult and costly for elites and they might impede foreign direct investment or certain types of trade – in perishables, for example. But the economic impacts of aviation restrictions are likely to be relatively small in many contexts.[4]

In addition to any psychological or political impacts, other sectoral, commodity, or financial sanctions will typically have an economic impact commensurate with the role of the sector in the targeted country's overall economy. Financial sanctions are potentially the broadest of all, as we saw with the American and European unilateral sanctions on insurance and banking transactions with Iran that severely hampered that country's trade in 2012 and 2013.

Implementation and enforcement challenges reduce impact

The impact of most sanctions will erode over time as targets adjust and find ways to evade them. And there are logistical difficulties involved with the more targeted sanctions – assets freezes and arms embargoes – that often undermine their ability to have any discernible impact at all. For an individual assets freeze to have an impact, for example, the targeted individuals must hold assets abroad, and the assets must be traceable to those individuals, which is often difficult. Many arms embargoes target small arms that are widely available and easy to smuggle across porous borders in areas where intrastate conflicts occur.

Corruption is often an unintended consequence and an obstacle in the effective use of targeted sanctions.[5] In the first year of UN-imposed sanctions, all of the targeted governments, for which data are available, scored in the lower third on Transparency International's Corruption Perceptions Index. In such cases, any overseas assets will often be hidden because they are illicitly gained and that will make them difficult to identify and freeze. In addition, the UN Security Council typically engages in lengthy debate

---

[4] An exception is countries where tourism is important. In such cases, restrictions on transportation to the target, or on the issuance of visas to residents of the sanctioning country who might want to visit the target country, could have severe economic effects. In such cases, however, it may also be difficult to disentangle the effects of the sanctions from the depressing effects on tourism of whatever instability or disturbance triggered the sanctions in the first place.

[5] See Chapter 9 by Mikael Eriksson in this volume.

before members agree to impose sanctions. In the case of liquid financial assets, such delays are deadly because they give targets an opportunity to move those assets to safer locations or to hide them using false names, front companies, and other subterfuges. Of course, there are costs associated with money laundering and hiding assets, but they are less than the cost of losing the full value of the assets and, as noted, officials may well be paying those costs already to hide illicit activities. Moreover, even though corruption levels tended to be high even before sanctions were imposed, the case studies show that sanctions had the unintended consequence of increasing corruption or other criminal activities in thirty-one of fifty-three episodes for which information was available.

Assuming that, against these odds, sanctioning countries can identify and block targeted assets, under what conditions might this tool have an ongoing, significant impact on the target? If targeted individuals can obtain access to *new* income or financial flows, the impact of the sanctions could quickly erode. This would likely be a problem when targeted regimes are corrupt *and* the country has valuable natural resources, such as oil, diamonds, or timber. In those cases, if there are no complementary restrictions on the export of valuable commodities, targeted individuals might replenish their resources rather quickly. They may not be able to deposit or invest that wealth abroad, or they may be able to do so only at higher cost due to the need for secrecy, but that cost may be acceptable. Thus, we see in the western African cases, where access to alluvial diamonds was an issue (Angola, Côte d'Ivoire, Liberia, and Sierra Leone), that assets freezes and travel bans against individuals were accompanied or followed by sanctions on the diamond trade, and in the Liberian case, timber as well.

Arms embargoes are less targeted than sanctions against designated individuals or entities, but they target the military, or rebel factions. Any major impacts would be mainly on those groups, usually with the intent of lowering capabilities and squeezing budgets by raising the price of military hardware. The ultimate objective of these sanctions is typically to prevent conflict or at least reduce the level of violence by denying protagonists the means to carry it out. In theory, timely implementation and vigorous enforcement of an arms embargo might achieve these goals of constraining capabilities. In practice, the obstacles to effective arms embargoes are numerous and they often mean, at least with respect to small arms, that arms embargoes have little constraining impact because of challenges related to

- the sheer volume of small arms in circulation around the world since the end of the Cold War, including within states that have often been in conflict for years before the United Nations imposes sanctions;

- the enormous profit potential involved in moving arms from where they are in surplus to where they are in demand, an incentive that usually increases with sanctions; and
- political opposition by great powers or by neighbours with a partisan interest in the outcome.

These logistical and political challenges are compounded by the fact that nominally even-handed arms embargoes may lead to highly inequitable results on the ground which, in turn, can undermine support for the embargo, as shown in the TSC case study of the sanctions against the Former Republic of Yugoslavia.

Observed impacts of targeted sanctions

In practice, it is difficult to sort out the specific impacts of different types of targeted sanctions because they are rarely used in isolation. There are no episodes where the UN imposed individual assets freezes alone, and in only one case study a travel ban was used in isolation. At the time the case study was prepared, the travel ban, against eleven individuals in Guinea-Bissau following a military coup in 2012, had registered no significant economic, political, or psychological impact and it had not been effective in signalling, constraining, or coercing the government. There is one other case study where the UN Security Council authorized only individual travel and asset sanctions, in this case against individuals suspected of involvement in the assassination of Lebanese prime minister Rafiq Hariri, but the sanctions were never actually imposed and there was little discernible impact in Lebanon. Finally, the case studies show little evidence of any impact on targets when the UNSC imposes arms embargoes in isolation.

Most often, the United Nations uses travel bans and freezes individuals' assets in conjunction with one another and with arms embargoes. Arms embargoes are the most commonly imposed targeted sanction overall, appearing in almost every episode, while individual assets freezes and travel bans are present in 51 to 54 per cent of the episodes studied, respectively. But individually targeted sanctions and arms embargoes are the only sanctions in place in just around a fifth of the episodes. The sanctions in those episodes, which include (usually early stage) sanctions against, among others, Côte d'Ivoire, the Democratic Republic of Congo, Somalia, and the Taliban, usually have political impacts, but economic and psychological impacts are uncommon.

As expected, in cases where broader sectoral sanctions are used, case study authors find evidence of economic, as well as political, impacts in more than half the episodes. The pattern for indirect impacts is similar and it is rare to observe indirect impacts where there is no direct impact.[6] Interestingly, psychological impacts are identified in only a handful of episodes, perhaps because these impacts are difficult to observe. It could also be because of the types of regimes that the United Nations typically targets, as discussed below.

Measuring and evaluating impacts

Measuring the impact of sanctions is never simple, yet the degree of difficulty varies across the different types of impact. In general, economic impacts should be relatively more visible and measurable than psychological impacts, which may not have any external manifestation at all. Political impacts are somewhere in between. But in all cases, there is the challenge of linking any observed impact back to the sanctions and eliminating alternative explanations. In the large number of cases where unilateral or regional sanctions are also present, the need to disentangle the specific impacts of the UN-authorized sanctions compounds the challenge.

Putting attribution aside for the moment, economic impacts are, in theory, tangible and measurable. While the overseas assets of targeted individuals can be difficult to identify, especially if the targeted regime is corrupt, freezing those that are found denies the target access to those resources. And the value of overseas assets, or of foreign trade or financial flows, is quantifiable, which should have some relation to the impact. Even so, it is not easy to measure even the economic impacts of sanctions. Some countries, particularly less developed ones, often do not consistently report economic data to the International Monetary Fund or World Bank, and, even in the best case, there are often long lags before data are available.

When the data are available, assessing economic impacts will *still* be difficult. Modern economies, even less developed ones, are complex entities and the effects of targeted sanctions are often lost in the broader picture. Economies and individuals also adjust over time so researchers have to try and measure the *net* impact of, for example, cutting off diamond exports. What is the impact *after* the target adjusts by finding buyers or suppliers that are not cooperating with UN sanctions? Or by setting up smuggling routes, or developing alternative exports, or hiding financial assets?

Moreover, many things besides sanctions will be going on in an economy, particularly one in conflict, so what part of the observed changes in

---

[6] Evasion and unintended consequences, of course, have important interactions with these impacts. Unintended consequences are analysed in Chapter 9.

economic variables should be attributed to the impact of sanctions? How successful is the target in deflecting the impact of sanctions? Hufbauer, Schott, Elliott, and Oegg[7] develop a crude methodology for trying to estimate the economic cost to the target. They use a sanctions multiplier between zero and one to calculate the *net* welfare impact of economic sanctions based on observed changes in trade or financial flows. But this approach requires having the data and sufficient information about the market environment and broader economic conditions in a country to make informed judgements about potential impacts.

As difficult as that is, tracing political or psychological impacts is even more difficult. For example, feelings of stigmatization due to individual listings or a UN resolution condemning one's government may undermine internal or external support for a regime. However, finding evidence of such psychological effects may only be possible through interviews and that is not always possible.[8] This difficulty could be one reason that psychological impacts are relatively rare in the databases.

Some political impacts, such as street protests, legislative votes, or changes in political or military alliances, are more visible. And for some impacts there are cross-country data sources that could be used, for example, to identify coups or other political events that occur during episodes and might be due to sanctions. But often the political impacts, like the psychological ones, will be more subtle and identifying them will require careful, detailed research on a case-by-case basis.

An additional challenge arises from the fact that many UN sanctions are imposed alongside unilateral or regional sanctions and the latter sanctions often go beyond what is called for by the Security Council. In roughly three-quarters of the regimes, regional or unilateral sanctions are already in place when the Security Council acts. These sanctions often exceed the targeted measures adopted by the UN, making it difficult to disentangle the impact of the UN measures. Beyond the economic impacts, it might be expected that UN Security Council measures would have more legitimacy and broader geographic coverage than unilateral sanctions and, therefore, more political and psychological impact. But those potential effects are difficult to assess given the information available.

Yet another challenge arises from the fact that Security Council resolutions often use hortatory language, such as calling on members to 'exercise restraint' or 'increase vigilance', or to take certain actions to

<hr>

[7] See Hufbauer, Schott, Elliott, and Oegg, *Economic Sanctions Reconsidered*, Appendix C.
[8] The increasing number of, and access to, individuals delisted, and therefore no longer subject to UN sanctions, provides new opportunities for research regarding the psychological impacts of targeted sanctions.

implement sanctions under conditions that are vaguely defined and leave a great deal of discretion to Member States. In such cases, some Member States may choose to interpret the resolution expansively and to impose sanctions that go beyond what other Member States are doing. If more forward-leaning members justify their actions with reference to UN resolutions, should the impact of the broader sanctions be assessed as part of the UN sanctions, or as the impact of extra-UN sanctions?

For example, in the decisions implementing the 2010 ban on new investments in Iran's petrochemical sector and the 2012 boycott on Iranian oil, the European Council referred to the language in UN Security Council Resolution 1929 'noting the potential connection between Iran's revenues derived from its energy sector and the funding of Iran's proliferation-sensitive nuclear activities'.[9] Other parts of Resolution 1929 also refer to the potential for sanctions on trade, financial, or transit transactions to be expanded beyond the specific areas or entities identified in the resolution if the Member State has information that the transaction or activity 'could contribute to Iran's proliferation-sensitive nuclear activities'.

The impacts of the sanctions that are *clearly* mandated in various UNSC resolutions against Iran remain *relatively* targeted. But the additional European sanctions, along with restrictions on the Central Bank and other US sanctions, are rooted in concerns that such revenues contribute to proliferation-sensitive activities in Iran and that the economic impacts of those sanctions since 2012 are deeper and broader than what had gone before. Should those impacts be attributed to the UN sanctions regime? There is an attempt in the Iran case study to disentangle these impacts. But should there be an eventual political settlement of this case, it will be exceedingly difficult to, first, measure and, second, determine the relative contribution of targeted UN sanctions to the outcome.

Finally, neither the quantitative nor qualitative databases of the TSC project consistently report on the *magnitude* of the sanctions' impacts. The quantitative database currently uses a binary variable to indicate whether each type of impact is present or not. But it is likely that the magnitude of the impact also matters for effectiveness. For economic impacts, it should be possible to at least roughly estimate the cost and then give an idea of the magnitude of that cost by comparing it to total exports or national income, or some other objective indicator. But the data are often not available or are available only at highly aggregated levels

---

[9] The decision implementing UNSCR 1929 is available at www.hm-treasury.gov.uk/d/council_decision_413_Repeal_140.pdf and that implementing the oil boycott and other restrictions at www.hm-treasury.gov.uk/d/finsanc_council_decision_1225_35cfsp_230112.pdf.

that give a crude idea, at best, of impact. Objective measures of political impacts are more difficult to identify, and for psychological impacts it may be impossible. Still, some qualitative judgement as to whether these impacts are minor or major would be useful.

Impacts and objectives

I now turn to whether there is any correlation between the types of impacts we observe across episodes and the particular objectives the United Nations is seeking in each. The terms of reference for the case studies on which the TSC databases are based identify seven primary objectives. To make the discussion more tractable, I combine them into five and include democracy support, good governance, and support for judicial processes under the broad heading of support for democracy and good governance (see Table 8.2).

The most striking result, though not one that is particularly surprising, is that regimes or non-state actors involved in terrorism, attacks on civilians, or coups are difficult to stigmatize. Only two of nine sanctions intended to counter terrorism showed signs of psychological impact. Stigmatization was somewhat more common in cases involving violent conflict and the evidence from the case studies suggests that stigmatization often led to the erosion of political support for the sanctions targets. The targeted governments (where they are governments) are also often authoritarian and may simply be impervious to criticism, even by the United Nations. According to the Freedom House assessments of political and civil rights around the world, all of the countries subject to targeted sanctions fell into the 'not free' category for most of the period they were under sanctions. A few countries moved to partly free, but typically only towards the end of the case studies as conflicts or other issues were resolved. And yet, only one in eight episodes involved support for democracy or good governance.

There is support in the case studies for targeted sanctions having political impacts when the peaceful settlement of conflicts or counterterrorism is the goal. Political impacts occur in 58 per cent of these episodes, versus only one in seven when the primary goal is non-proliferation. The political impacts can be negative as well as positive, however. For example, the arms embargo against Sudan over the conflict in Darfur apparently contributed to an increase in the local production of small arms. More often, however, the observed political impacts involved increased strains on the targeted individuals or factions.

The overall impacts observed when the primary goal is support for democracy are difficult to assess because that category is dominated by

Table 8.2 *Primary objectives and direct impacts*

Primary objective type	Type of impact (where evidence available)		
	Psychological (18)	Political (34)	Economic (30)
Non-proliferation (DPRK-3, Iran-4)	3	1	4 (difficult to disentangle from unilateral sanctions)
Counterterrorism (AQT-2;4, Libya I-3, Sudan I-2)	2	5 (including some negative for UN)	5 (mostly minor)
Peaceful settlement of conflicts (37 episodes across 15 cases)	10 (often stigmatization leading to erosion in political support)	20 (some important in reaching resolution; a few negative)	14 (some major due to commodity bans)
Support for democracy, judicial processes, and good governance (Côte d'Ivoire-1, Guinea-Bissau-1, Haiti-3, Liberia-1, Lebanon-1, Sierra Leone-1)	1	6 (3 times in Haiti, equally positive and negative)	5 (large impacts from broad sanctions against Haiti)
Protection of civilians, human rights (Libya II-2)	2	(significant impacts across the board but difficult to distinguish from impact of military intervention and civil war)	

Note: The cases and number of episodes for each are shown in parentheses.

the five episodes that were imposed on Haiti following the coup against the Aristide government (the last two of which were comprehensive sanctions). Not surprisingly, since they were comprehensive, those sanctions had significant economic impacts and a range of unintended consequences, including increased corruption and human rights violations, negative humanitarian consequences, and widespread harmful economic consequences.

Overall, the case studies identify direct economic impacts in just above half of the episodes. But those impacts are spread relatively evenly across the types of objectives, ranging from 38 per cent of episodes involving the peaceful settlement of conflicts to more than half of episodes in the other goal categories. Not surprisingly, the economic impacts that stand out are those associated with cases where sanctions eventually became comprehensive, as in Haiti and the Former Republic of Yugoslavia, or where extensive unilateral or regional sanctions, such as the American and European sanctions against Iran over its nuclear programmes, are imposed alongside UNSC sanctions.

Impacts and unintended consequences

The case studies document a wide range of unintended consequences that occur even with more targeted UN sanctions. The most common of the unintended consequences (see Table 8.3) is increased corruption or criminality, though readers should recall that levels of corruption are relatively high in the targeted countries even before sanctions enter the picture. In these episodes, TSC researchers observe economic or political impacts, or both, in almost all of them. Humanitarian consequences are also relatively common, despite the fact that avoiding this outcome is one of the goals of targeted sanctions. In addition to the twenty episodes with humanitarian consequences and political or economic impacts, there were three episodes targeting Haiti and the Former Republic of Yugoslavia that actually involve comprehensive sanctions and led to such consequences, but are not included in this database. Many of the others in this category involve sectoral or commodity sanctions with the potential to have broader economic impacts than more narrowly targeted sanctions.

Table 8.3 shows other unintended consequences that appear relatively often in the case studies, including strengthened authoritarian rule, increased human rights violations, and resource diversion. Not

Table 8.3 *Impacts and unintended consequences*

	Episodes with impact		
Unintended consequence	Economic alone ($n = 11$)	Political alone ($n = 14$)	Both ($n = 18$)
Increased corruption, criminality	6	6	13
Strengthened authoritarian rule	2	5	9
Increased human rights violations	3	2	6
Resource diversion (e.g. from health to the military)	4	5	6
Humanitarian consequences	5	3	11

Note: Refers to valid cases only, non-applicable and missing data excluded.

surprisingly, unintended consequences are more common when sanctions inflict both economic and political impacts. It is also not surprising that economic impacts are more closely associated with negative humanitarian consequences. It is somewhat more puzzling that economic impacts are relatively more likely to be associated with increased human rights violations, while political impacts are more highly correlated with incidents of resource diversion than economic impacts.

Can targeted sanctions stay targeted?

Sanctions cases typically drag on for years and there is often pressure to ratchet up sanctions in response. Biersteker et al. conclude that UN sanctions remain mostly targeted, but there is also evidence in the databases that the types of sanctions imposed, as well as the impacts, tend to expand over time.[10] The terms of reference for the case studies specify that authors should create new episodes within case studies when there are significant changes in the sanctions regime, such as new UNSC resolutions that tighten, expand, or relax sanctions. So looking at the number of episodes across case studies gives at least some idea of the expansion of sanctions over time.

If we look at seven categories of sanctions identified in the case studies – travel bans, individual assets freezes, arms embargoes, other sectoral sanctions, commodity sanctions, diplomatic sanctions, and financial sector sanctions – the first episode of all the cases, on average, features two of these types.[11] Usually the initial sanctions involve arms embargoes, often combined with some sanctions targeted solely at individuals. Three of the six cases consisting of only one episode – Ethiopia-Eritrea, Guinea-Bissau, and FRY over Kosovo – involve only one sanction, either an arms embargo or travel restrictions. Taliban and CAR sanctions include a combination of three sanctions measures – arms embargoes, travel bans, and individual asset freezes. In the case of Lebanon, travel bans and asset freezes on individuals were authorized, but never imposed.

There were eight episodes where arms embargoes were imposed initially with no other accompanying measures; six of those lasted at least two episodes and in four of those the UN Security Council ratcheted up sanctions in later episodes. Only in Somalia and Rwanda were arms embargoes the sole sanction for even as many as two episodes. Most of the time, arms embargoes alone had no

---

[10] Biersteker, Eckert, Tourinho, and Hudáková, *The Effectiveness of United Nations Targeted Sanctions*, p. 41.
[11] The average number of types of sanctions for all episodes is 3 sanctions.

discernible impact, but in two – Somalia and Sudan over Darfur – the sanctions had perverse political effects that exacerbated the conflicts they were aimed at stopping.

In cases that extend through four or five episodes (eight total), the cases typically involve three or four types of sanctions and only DRC does not have commodity or financial sanctions alongside the more targeted types at any point during the episode. During the first episodes when sanctions are relatively more targeted, evidence of psychological impacts is rare and economic or political impacts are more frequent, occurring in 68 per cent of these early episodes.

Table 8.4 summarizes the number of episodes per case study, providing some indication of the 'ratcheting up' of sanctions, at least when the goal involves the peaceful resolution of conflicts. In all cases involving at least four episodes (unless an episode involved the lifting of sanctions as part of the resolution), there were both political and economic impacts at one point during the regime, and often psychological impacts as well (where information on impacts was available). One plausible explanation is that UNSC feels greater pressure to respond in the midst of violent conflicts and therefore imposes additional sanctions.

Perhaps the most prominent ongoing case of escalating sanctions is the set of UNSC resolutions targeting Iran over its nuclear programme. The case began with relatively narrowly targeted restrictions on products and technologies that might create proliferation concerns, as well as asset freezes on twelve individuals and ten entities linked to Iran's nuclear and missile programmes. The second episode expanded both lists, imposed an arms embargo on arms exports from Iran, and called on international financial institutions to 'avoid' *new* lending to Iran. In the third episode, the UNSC further expanded the existing sanctions, imposed individual travel bans, and called on members to exercise vigilance over various financial activities involving Iran and designated Iranian banks in the event that financial flows might contribute to proliferation sensitive activities in Iran. And the fourth episode continued the pattern of expanding the lists, while adding language on Iranian shipping and the use of enforcement measures, including the inspection and seizure of cargoes that might contribute to Iran's proliferation of weapons of mass destruction. It seems quite likely that we would observe a similar ratcheting process in the case study involving North Korea if not for Chinese opposition to stronger sanctions.

As noted above, however, it is difficult to assess the impact of intensifying the UN sanctions against Iran because the European Union is interpreting the UN resolutions quite broadly and the United States' is going well beyond the resolutions with its financial and other sanctions. The

Table 8.4 *Case studies by number of episodes*

Primary objective	Number of episodes				
	1	2	3	4	5
Non-proliferation			North Korea (ongoing)	Iran (ongoing)	
Counterterrorism		Sudan I	Libya I	Al-Qaida–Taliban (ongoing)	
Peaceful settlement of conflicts	CAR (ongoing) Ethiopia-Eritrea FRY I[a] FRY II Taliban (ongoing)	Iraq (ongoing) Rwanda Sudan II (ongoing)		Angola DRC (ongoing) Liberia[b] (ongoing)	Côte d'Ivoire[b] (ongoing) Somalia (ongoing) Sierra Leone[b]
Support for democracy and good governance	Guinea-Bissau (ongoing) Lebanon (ongoing)		Haiti[a]		
Protection of civilians, human rights			Libya II[c] (ongoing)		

[a] In these cases comprehensive sanctions were imposed following the targeted sanctions episodes described here.

[b] There is one episode in each of these case studies where conflict resolution remained a goal, but support for democracy and/or good governance as part of the process took primacy.

[c] In the last episode, peaceful settlement of conflict became the primary objective.

European Union decided that Iran's oil export revenues were contributing to its proliferation activities and imposed an oil boycott in 2012, in addition to banning EU firms from investing in the Iranian energy sector or providing insurance for Iranian oil tankers. The United States pressured key importers of Iranian oil to reduce their purchases by threatening their access to US financial markets. As of late 2013, severe impacts on the Iranian economy had resulted from these sanctions, reducing oil exports by half and contributing to an inflationary collapse in its currency. But many countries, including some members of the UN Security Council, would not attribute such impacts to UN sanctions. The case study authors carefully attempted to parse the impacts attributable only to UN sanctions, concluding that there were no economic impacts until the third of four episodes and no political or psychological impacts until the fourth. Nevertheless, this case illustrates the challenges of keeping UN sanctions targeted when they involve core national interests of key Security Council members.

Impacts and effectiveness: a tentative assessment

Most of the cases analysed by this project are ongoing and the information on impacts is incomplete in many episodes. In particular, hard data on economic impacts and qualitative data on the magnitude of all types of impacts are missing for most episodes. Therefore, this analysis of impacts and effectiveness should be regarded as preliminary, tentative, and incomplete. Nevertheless, there are some interesting connections.

Table 8.5 shows the type of direct impacts associated with effective sanctions by purpose, and for ineffective sanctions overall. First, psychological impacts alone are never associated with any degree of sanctions

Table 8.5 *Effectiveness by purpose and type of direct impacts*

		Type of direct impact			
		Psychological	Political	Economic	All impacts
	Effectiveness by purpose	Frequency	Frequency	Frequency	Frequency
Effective	Coercion (5)	0/2	1/5	0/3	1/10
	Constraint (16)	0/8	3/15	1/12	7/10
	Signalling (17)	0/9	3/15	1/12	8/10
Ineffective (39)		0/6	8/13	7/12	2/2

effectiveness. Episodes where all three types of impact are present were effective, usually for constraining and signalling, in all but two episodes (Iran and Côte d'Ivoire in the last episodes). And these episodes, not surprisingly, involve a wide variety of sanctions. All combine sectoral, commodity, or financial sanctions with the more targeted arms embargoes and individually targeted measures. Political or economic impacts alone seldom correlate with effectiveness.

Conclusions and avenues for future research

A major contribution of the TSC research is that it systematically analyses all types of targeted sanctions, not just economic measures. It also analyses political and psychological impacts, alongside economic ones. This is important because some targeted sanctions, for example, travel bans, will have little if any economic impact in targeted countries. At the same time, it turns out to be a challenge to assess the impact of different targeted sanctions because they are rarely used in isolation.

A few interesting associations do emerge from the data. One is that the case studies suggest that psychological impacts are relatively uncommon, even when sanctions publicly and prominently target individuals. But it is not clear whether that is because these impacts really are rare or because they are extremely hard to observe. It could also be because terrorists, coup leaders, and human rights abusers are difficult to embarrass.

The evidence also suggests that the more narrowly targeted sanctions – individual travel bans and asset freezes, and arms embargoes – typically have fewer impacts than other types and rarely involve economic impacts. Episodes involving broader sanctions that affect important economic sectors or commodities result in more impacts and unintended consequences; the sanctions in those episodes appear to be more effective at signalling and constraining targets. To make more definitive judgements in these areas, however, the research will need to further assess the relative magnitude of the impacts.

Finally, this chapter only touches the surface of issues that are possible to investigate using the data compiled by the Targeted Sanctions Consortium. These are some of the other questions that would be interesting to explore:

- whether indicators of political will, either at the time resolutions are passed (e.g. the number of abstentions) or when they are implemented (evidence of assets frozen or travel blocked), affect the type or magnitude of impact;

- which types of implementation measures (sanctions committees, Panels of Experts, or reporting) affect impacts;
- whether the cooperation of some regional or other non-UN bodies contributes more than others to certain types of impact; and
- whether impacts are different if the targets are non-state actors rather than governments.

While the analysis in this chapter is tentative, further refinement of the case studies and associated data will allow richer exploration of all these questions and, eventually, firmer conclusions about impacts, unintended consequences, and other factors associated with the effectiveness of UN targeted sanctions.

9   The unintended consequences of United Nations targeted sanctions

Mikael Eriksson

Extensive research has been conducted over the past decades to understand the use of targeted sanctions by the United Nations. While a great deal of the research has appraised sanctions effectiveness, less attention has been invested in critically seeking to understand the unintended consequences of UN targeted sanctions. In an attempt to throw light on this understudied aspect of targeted sanctions, this chapter will look more carefully at the various unanticipated implications of UN targeted sanctions policies related to the threat, decision, adoption, and subsequent implementation of United Nations Security Council resolutions. This will be done with an analysis of the new data introduced in this book.

Unintended consequences of UN targeted sanctions are defined as those observable policy effects not anticipated or simply overlooked by the sender at the time when a decision was made to impose targeted sanctions. An essential criterion for identifying unintended consequences is if the policy implications to impose sanctions went beyond the goal of the UN Resolution establishing the sanctions regime.[1] The definition used here builds on the understanding of unintended consequences applied in similar studies of unintended consequences, that is, unanticipated, overlooked, or perverse side effects of a policy objective.[2] However, unlike conventional perspectives on unintended consequences

---

[1] For an operationalization and definition of the variables used in the data collection process, see the Codebook in Appendix 3 of this book.

[2] There are several studies examining unintended consequences of policy phenomena. See, for instance, M. Zajko, 'Climate Change and Extreme Weather as Risk and Consequence', in A. Mica, A. Peisert, and J. Winczorek (eds.), *Sociology and the Unintended: Robert Merton Revisited* (Frankfurt am Main, DE: Peter Lang, 2012); R. Nordås and S. C. A. Rustad, 'Sexual Exploitation and Abuse by Peacekeepers: Understanding Variation', *International Interactions*, 39 (2013), pp. 511–34; A. Chiyuki, C. de Coning, and R. Thakur (eds.), *Unintended Consequences of Peacekeeping Operations* (New York: United Nations University Press, 2007); E. C. James, 'Witchcraft, Bureaucraft, and the Social Life of (US) IAD in Haiti', *Journal of Cultural Anthropology*, 27 (2012), pp. 50–75; S. Fukuda-Parr, 'Global Goals as a Policy Tool; Intended and Unintended Consequences', *Journal of Human Development and Capabilities*, 15 (2014), pp. 118–31. For a discussion on definitions of unintended consequences and the way to

of social action which essentially consider them undesirable, the definition used here allows the possibility that unintended consequences can be positive or negative and that they can have effects on both the sanctions sending body and the listed target.[3]

There are many good reasons to examine the unintended consequences of targeted sanctions, of which three stand out. First, there has been no systematic study made of the unintended consequences of *targeted* sanctions. While the sanctions scholarship has produced much insight on the unintended consequences of comprehensive sanctions, there has been little systematic data to substantiate or refute similar critiques of targeted UN sanctions.[4] Prior to the Targeted Sanctions Consortium initiative, the unintended consequences of targeted sanctions could only be derived from *ad hoc* testimonies and anecdotal examples from specific sanctions regimes.

Second, this is an important question to examine because the principal rationale for the UN Security Council's shift to targeted sanctions was to counter criticisms of the negative humanitarian consequences resulting from comprehensive sanctions in the 1990s.[5] That is to say, the UN and its Member States wanted to develop a more legitimate policy instrument that was better designed than comprehensive sanctions, with their blunt and undiscriminating effects.

Third, there is a tendency in the popular media to be critical of the effects of targeted sanctions. The UN Security Council – or regional actors such as the European Union or the African Union – are frequently questioned or criticized for pursuing sanctions policies that are 'toothless' or only enforced for 'symbolic' reasons.[6] One way to explain this criticism is that there may exist among some decision-makers a naïve assumption

classify this type of phenomena, see P. Baert, 'Unintended Consequences', *International Sociology*, 6 (1991), pp. 201–10.

[3] See T. Biersteker, S. Eckert, M. Tourinho, and Z. Hudáková, *The Effectiveness of United Nations Targeted Sanctions: Findings from the Targeted Sanctions Consortium (TSC)* (Geneva: the Graduate Institute, 2013).

[4] Important exceptions are M. Eriksson, 'Unintended Consequences of Targeted Sanctions', in C. Daase and C. Friesendorf (eds.), *Rethinking Security Governance: The Problem of Unintended Consequences* (London: Routledge, 2010), pp. 157–75; and T. Biersteker, 'Unintended Consequences of Measures to Counter the Financing of Terrorism', in C. Daase and C. Friesendorf (eds.), *Rethinking Security Governance: The Problem of Unintended Consequences* (London: Routledge, 2010), pp. 127–36.

[5] D. Cortright and G. A. Lopez, *Economic Sanctions: Panacea or Peacebuilding in a Post-Cold War World?* (Boulder, CO: Westview Press, 1995); D. Cortright and G. A. Lopez, 'Are Sanctions Just? The Problematic Case of Iraq', *Journal of International Affairs*, 52 (1999), pp. 735–55; D. Cortright and G. A. Lopez (with J. Wagler, R. W. Conroy and J. Dashti-Gibson), *The Sanctions Decade: Assessing UN Strategies in the 1990s* (Boulder, CO: Lynne Rienner, 2000).

[6] T. Deen, 'Politics: U.N Faulted for Toothless Sanctions in Civil Wars', *Inter Press Service News Agency*, www.ipsnews.net/2010/01/politics-un-faulted-for-toothless-sanctions-in-civil-wars/.

about the possibility of achieving policy perfection. This in turn may be rooted in a tendency to assume 'policy idealism', that is, where policy decisions could be designed to have the exact intended outcome that the senders have in mind.

Translating this to the practice of the adoption and enforcement of targeted sanctions would suggest that decision-makers, often at the UN Security Council level, may have unrealistic expectations of what targeted sanctions can actually achieve. As such, minor deviations from the stated purposes in UN Security Council resolutions typically cause popular frustration and criticisms of the UN for not being policy proficient. Another source of frustration is that targeted UN sanctions are often adopted against targets that have many times carried out hideous crimes against civilians (such as in Rwanda, Libya, and Sudan), engaged in illicit trade in arms (Iran, North Korea), or engaged in undermining democracy (Haiti, Guinea-Bissau, Côte d'Ivoire, Sierra Leone, among others) – as well as on other sensitive matters – which the global public generally demands an adequate and swift response. In the absence of legitimate, accurately targeted, and coercive measures, the global audience may be frustrated by the incapacity of the Security Council. These high expectations are not unique to targeted UN sanctions, as they also apply to other policy instruments of the UN to promote international peace and security. Nonetheless, the critique, in combination with inflated expectations of targeted sanctions, calls for further scrutiny of their unintended effects.

Given that UN targeted sanctions have been in use for more than twenty years, it is important that the scholarly community analyse their key features, including unintended consequences. It would be a mistake to assume that targeted sanctions do not result in significant unintended consequences in some circumstances,[7] and therefore a better understanding of their consequences is essential. More precise counterclaims can then be evaluated using the data and findings of the TSC project.

To design a research framework that can effectively assess the unintended consequences of UN targeted sanctions, this chapter employs a conventional understanding of policy action in combination with the rich empirical data of the TSC (further discussed below). Cross-data comparisons can not only address popular critiques of sanctions but also provide new insights into patterns of use of targeted UN sanctions. This includes the identification of new and emerging trends that can feed into the design of an assessment framework for the benefit of future sanctions regimes.

---

[7] T. Biersteker, S. Eckert, M. Tourinho, and Z. Hudáková, *The Effectiveness of United Nations Targeted Sanctions: Findings from the Targeted Sanctions Consortium (TSC)*, p. 17.

The data treatment in the following sections illustrates examples from different sanctions episodes from the TSC database.[8]

The second part of this chapter continues with a discussion of how to think about targeted sanctions in general and the unintended consequences of sanctions. The third part revisits previous research on the unintended consequences of sanctions and presents a typology of unintended consequences, while the fourth part examines the TSC data to provide empirical substance based on the systematic data generated on all twenty-three sanctions regimes (and sixty-three episodes) of UN targeted sanctions since 1991. The fifth part discusses some analytical challenges in analysing unintended consequences, and the sixth part introduces and applies a framework to analyse the unintended consequences of UN targeted sanctions. The chapter concludes with some reflections on ways to mitigate the unintended effects of sanctions and suggestions on how to advance the study of unintended consequences in the sanctions literature.

How to think about the unintended consequences of targeted sanctions

Sanctions as a policy outcome

There has been a growing trend in recent sanctions literature to overuse the analogy of sanctions as a 'tool', an 'instrument', or a 'device'.[9] Although these are sometimes useful characterizations, it is essential to recall that targeted sanctions are, above anything else, a policy, that is, the outcome of a social action used by a collective of policymakers in an institutional setting to address a specific concern in the global domain. Hence, a policy is a guide for social action towards a specific aim with a preferred and anticipated result as stipulated in a UN Security Council Resolution. The unintended consequence, in turn, is conceived as the outcome of an incomplete policy process. This incompleteness may have occurred for many different reasons. Adding to this, the unintended consequence can present itself very differently (e.g. positively, negatively, pervasively, etc.).

---

[8] As outlined in the introductory chapter of this book, the cases of targeted sanctions have been broken down into more vibrant, telling episodes (e.g. to capture variation within regimes). Previous research has typically evaluated entire country sanctions regimes instead of assessing the policy dynamic that takes place at crucial points within each case.

[9] S. Geoffrey-Leslie, *Imposing Economic Sanctions: Legal Remedy or Genocidal Tool?* (London, Sterling, VA: Pluto Press, 1999).

The study of unintended consequences in the realm of social practices has a long research tradition and goes back to the writings of Weber and Durkheim.[10] The issue has been considered in discussions of causality, consequentialism, or social interconnectedness and is often associated with important works by Robert Merton.[11] As noted by Mica and others, Merton made important contributions to structuring and popularizing scientific thinking on unintended consequences. In his early work on the sociology of the unintended, Merton conceptualized the notion of the 'unintended' around its different manifestations like 'unanticipated' or 'unexpected' consequences of social action, interaction, and collective decisions.[12] He argued that there were different causes for unanticipated consequences (e.g. ignorance/incomplete analysis, analysis errors, conflict of interest, changes of interest and/or values, and 'self-defeating prophecy'). This in turn led to different explanations of social action, social complexity, social biases, ignorance, decision-making incapacities, over-reliance, self-deceptions in moments of social actions, and social coincidences – features that we can also observe in contemporary practices and understandings of UN targeted sanctions. Recent scholarship has advanced Merton's ideas on the unintended,[13] some criticizing him for not 'delivering an authoritative penetrating answer to the question of how they [unintended consequences] are produced'.[14]

A challenge to the analysis of unintended consequences of UN targeted sanctions is to understand to what extent it is possible to anticipate 'unanticipated' or 'unforeseen' consequences in the first place. There are actually many different types of unintended consequences, some of which are possible to identify or deal with *ex-ante*, while other unintended consequences are never foreseen. As mentioned above, unintended

[10] For a starting point see A. Hirschman, *Rhetoric of Reaction: Perversity, Futility, Jeopardy* (Cambridge, MA: Belknap Press, 1991), in particular chapter 2, pp. 11–35.

[11] R. Merton, 'The Unanticipated Consequences of Purposive Social Action', *American Sociological Review*, 1 (1936), pp. 894–904, and *Social Theory and Social Structure* (London: the Free Press, 1949).

[12] Mica, Peisert and Winczorek (eds.), *Sociology and the Unintended: Robert Merton Revisited*, p. 9.

[13] Other key scholars in the field of the sociology of the unintended include J. Elster, 'Mertons Functionalism and the Unintended Consequences of Action', in J. Clark, C. Modgil, and S. Modgil (eds.), *Robert Merton: Consensus and Controversy* (London, New York: Falmer Press, 1990), pp. 129–35; E. Garfield, 'The Unintended and Unanticipated Consequences of Robert K. Merton', *Social Studies of Science*, 34 (2004), pp. 845–53; R. Boudon, *The Unintended Consequences of Social Action* (London and Basingstoke: The Macmillan Press, 1982). For a good overview of more recent scholars see Mica, Peisert, and Winczorek (eds.), *Sociology and the Unintended: Robert Merton Revisited*, pp. 16–21.

[14] Mica, Peisert, and Winczorek (eds.), *Sociology and the Unintended: Robert Merton Revisited*, p. 13.

consequences have been narrowly defined in the sanctions literature as mostly having negative effects, and mainly in conjunction with comprehensive sanctions. Such a view is simply too limited, which is why the definition presented at the outset of this chapter allows for different types of unintended effects.

In the context of UN Security Council action, decision-makers seek to ensure that the policies pursued and the decisions they take have foreseen outcomes, but are aware of possible unforeseen consequences. While side effects usually denote an anticipated implication of a planned policy (e.g. as a result of bad policy implementation), an unintended consequence is likely to occur as a result of bad policy planning not necessarily foreseen by or related to the policy action.[15] A multilateral sanctions policy under Chapter VII of the UN Charter both guides and typically demands a particular policy action for a particular policy outcome.

As noted above, the unintended consequences of targeted sanctions do not have to be exclusively negative, and the unforeseen implications of sanctions regimes have sometimes turned out to be positive. For example, the counterterrorism financing sanctions regime has strengthened many states' capacities to counter money-laundering activities. Thus, the unintended consequences of targeted sanctions include both *negative* outcomes (e.g. strengthening proscribed leadership or political factions, increased corruption and criminality, resource diversion, burdens on neighbouring states) and *positive* outcomes (e.g. increased regulatory and enforcement capacity, enhanced credibility of UN).[16]

The policy of UN targeted sanctions can also be characterized as a more complex policy instrument than some others in international relations. Unlike dispatching assessment teams or establishing UN special envoys, targeted sanctions are carried out in a highly dynamic institutional environment in which the Council (the 'sender') continually engages with the target (the 'receiver') in a multifaceted interaction.[17] This complex and fluid environment of formal and informal power structures (see Chapter 3 by Brzoska and Lopez) entails a range of actors and stakeholders, each with their own unique context-specific rules, norms, and orders. This environment is adaptive and changeable, and there are also the challenges of implementing targeted sanctions by Member

---

[15] An indirect effect by contrast can be a policy implication emerging from either side effects or unintended consequences.

[16] A slightly modified view of unintended consequences based on the Framework for Analysis and Effectiveness in Biersteker, Eckert, Tourinho, and Hudáková, *The Effectiveness of United Nations Targeted Sanctions: Findings from the Targeted Sanctions Consortium* (TSC).

[17] Senders impose sanctions with multiple distinct but parallel purposes. See Chapters 1 and 2 in this volume.

States, sometimes with differing interpretations, and different resources or the political will to implement targeted sanctions.[18] All these aspects suggest that the policy of targeting is extremely complex, something not generally appreciated from an institutional perspective.[19] This underestimation of the complexity, or the overestimation of the ease with which the policy can be implemented, may well be an important contributor to the occurrence of unintended consequences.[20] As a result, a framework for how to assess the unintended consequences of UN targeted sanctions is presented below. The aim is twofold: first, to provide a framework for the assessment of targeted sanctions that can be used in other sanctions assessment studies; and, second, to gain an empirically grounded sense of the problems and challenges in contemporary UN sanctions regimes.

Three generations of research on the unintended consequences of targeted sanctions

The study of targeted UN sanctions has undergone tremendous change in the past twenty years. The usage of targeted sanctions now includes new actors, objectives, implementation areas, and new tools. What during the 1990s were occasionally problematic sanctions practices, as a result of general design, meagre prior experiences, and inadequate follow-up capacity, have now become increasingly hands-on and technical policies. To illustrate this change better, one might consider what I call the first, second, and possibly third generations of unintended consequences of UN sanctions targeting individuals and entities.

The first generation of unintended consequences in the 1990s mainly followed from deficiencies in the design and implementation of targeted sanctions. Problems such as lack of accurate or sufficiently detailed identifiers (e.g. name, birthdate, address, nationality, personal identification number, passport number) for targeted individuals generally have been addressed by sanctions committees, something which helped to limit unintended consequences of this type.

---

[18] For more on aspects of the implementation of UN targeted sanctions, see Wallensteen, Eriksson, and Staibano (eds.), *Making Targeted Sanctions Effective: Guidelines for the Implementation of UN Policy Options*.

[19] Building on a large number of interviews with different institutional actors, inter alia, at UN Department of Political Affairs, the author has previously demonstrated how the institutional administration of sanctions, including UN practitioners' understanding of the sanctions policy, differs quite substantially across bureaucratic divisions. These differences in turn suggest that the complexity is not generally appreciated, see Eriksson, *Targeting Peace: Understanding UN and EU Targeted* Sanctions.

[20] *Ibid.*

The second generation, post 11 September 2001, was dominated by an increase in unintended consequences for private and public actors. For private actors, problems of naming and shaming led to reputational costs for company brands, leading to loss of company value. Panels of Experts paid increasing attention to companies alleged to have circumvented UN targeted sanctions, or to have helped designated entities evade sanctions, at times resulting in 'innocent' companies being branded in a negative way. For some public actors there have been unintended consequences in the form of legal challenges as a result of incorrect listings.[21] The increasing number of court challenges by listed targets has been the subject of significant scholarly analysis, which suggests that the lack of procedural and legal safeguards on central elements of the sanctions process, such as designations, have been an important source of unintended consequences.[22]

The third generation, which we are currently experiencing, is the dramatic increase in unintended consequences for private actors (i.e. occurrences that take place when UN Security Council resolutions have effects on the activities and opportunities of private sector actors). That is, sanctions 'sending-actors' such as the United Nations, the European Union, and the United States are increasingly using sanctions to gain leverage on private actors.

For example, insurance companies are increasingly unwilling to enter into contractual arrangements with shipping companies, fearing that some of the vessels they may have insured may be associated with entities in target states (or associated with target states' decision-makers). Although there may be no formal restrictions on interactions, the mere fear of being associated with an entity in a targeted country may preclude legitimate business, a point made, for example, by numerous companies concerning the Iran sanctions regime. This in turn may lead to loss of

---

[21] For example, millions of US dollars have been paid in compensation to listed entities. The main reasons have been that targets have not received proper statements of reasons for why they have been listed; because of untimely notifications that they have been listed; because of wrongful listing (e.g. listed entities were assumed to be affiliated to terrorism, though they were not; see, for example, the case of Al-Barakaat).

[22] See I. Cameron (ed.), *EU Sanctions: Law and Policy Issues Concerning Restrictive Measures* (Cambridge: Intersentia, 2013); T. Biersteker, 'Targeted Sanctions and Individual Human Rights', *International Journal*, 65 (2009–10), pp. 99–117; M. Heupel, 'Multilateral Sanctions against Terror Suspects and the Violation of Due Process Standards', *International Affairs*, 85 (2009) pp. 307–21; M. Eriksson, *In Search of a Due Process: Listing and Delisting Practices of the European Union* (Uppsala, Department of Peace and Conflict Research: Uppsala University, 2009); G. Porretto, 'The European Union, Counter-Terrorism Sanctions against Individuals and Human Rights', in M. Gani and P. Matthew (eds.), *Fresh perspectives on the 'War on Terror'* (Canberra: ANU E Press, 2008); A. Bianchi, 'Assessing the Effectiveness of the UN Security Council's Anti-Terrorism Measures: The Quest for Legitimacy and Cohesion', *European Journal of International Law*, 17 (2007); E. J. Flynn, 'The Security Council's Counter-Terrorism Committee and Human Rights', *Human Rights Law Review*, 7 (2007), pp. 371–84.

trade, cargoes being uninsured, sailors not being covered by social insurances, and so on.

Compliance concerns may also lead to considerable costs for economic operators. For example, private bankers are increasingly unwilling to transfer money for seemingly legitimate business, if there is even a slight chance that such transfers are destined for actors associated with sanctions, as it would expose them to significant economic penalties from the United States. Private actors also face differing national enforcement systems, trade prohibitions (e.g. on dual-use items), and complicated regulations concerning financial dealings with targets, which may dissuade business. While senders of sanctions such as the Security Council and governments have the capacity to plan for and address the unintended consequences of sanctions, most private sector actors do not, even though they bear what can be considerable economic costs.

While the above mentioned examples highlight a number of negative unintended consequences for private actors, there are also several positive consequences. For example, UN sanctions intended to thwart the financing of terrorism such as those in the Al-Qaida and Taliban regime also have the positive effect of making illicit financial activities more difficult. In general, economic actors may now need to operate more responsibly in the way they conduct business. This has caused private actors such as banks and industries to make sharper distinctions between transparent business and less legitimate business.

In the context of this third generation one may already begin to anticipate and discern new forms of unintended consequences. Today, sanctions regimes are typically established on a country basis, but some entities have been operating in multiple conflict zones (e.g. various front companies and transportation firms to facilitate and engage in the illicit flows of arms, rough diamonds, rebels, conflict-minerals, drugs, and high-value timber).[23] For example, the listed, and now convicted, arms trader Viktor Bout allegedly operated in several countries under UN sanctions such as Angola, Afghanistan, Iraq, Liberia, and Sudan. He was also charged with supporting international terrorism and fuelling other civil wars not subject to UN sanctions (e.g. Colombia and the Revolutionary Armed Forces of Colombia, FARC).[24] Hence, following money trails, criminals, shadow infrastructures, and illicit private operators may prove

---

[23] See, for example, the work of Countering Illicit Trafficking–Mechanism Assessment Projects (CIT-MAP) at the Stockholm International Peace Research Institute, SIPRI.

[24] Bout opportunistically took advantage of surplus Soviet aircraft available relatively cheaply in the immediate post-Soviet era. Based on these he set up a number of enterprises allegedly to be used in various conflict zones. See *United States Attorney's Office* 2012-04-05.

to be the future grounds upon which listings are based. With more aggressive enforcement of such sanctions, new types of unintended consequences are likely to result. In light of this, how should we think conceptually about the phenomenon, and how has the literature treated it?

Literature on sanctions and unintended consequences

As previously discussed, unintended consequences of a policy action can be understood in many different ways. Surprisingly, though, few sanctions studies have engaged themselves with conceptualizing and theorizing unintended consequences. Those studies that exist have mainly focused on negative consequences.

On a conceptual level, unintended consequences 'are a perennial of social action'.[25] In this context, authors like Daase and Friesendorf (building on Baert)[26] define an unintended consequence as an 'effect of purposive social action which is different from what was wanted at the moment of carrying out the act, and the want of which was a reason for carrying it out'.[27] They further suggest that unintended consequences can be understood by using the yardstick of the policy initiators and implementers' own view of what constitutes the unplanned consequences of their policy.[28] The field of sanctions policy analysis is no exception. A number of studies on targeted sanctions have tackled various dimensions of unintended consequences empirically (sector specific, geographic, etc.), though not necessarily treating them in any theoretical or conceptual way. However, as indicated above, there are a number of features of targeted sanctions that make them an empirically rich area of study in the context of their unintended consequences.[29]

For the most part, sanctions scholarship has treated unintended consequences as problems of effectiveness and efficiency; that is, targeted sanctions give cause to a number of problems if not adopted and implemented in an effective and efficient way.[30] Scholars have also looked at

---

[25] Daase and Friesendorf (eds.), 'Introduction: Security Governance and the Problem of Unintended Consequences', p. 1.

[26] Baert, 'Unintended Consequences: A Typology and Examples', pp. 201–10.

[27] Daase and Friesendorf (eds.), 'Introduction: Security Governance and the Problem of Unintended Consequences', p. 9.

[28] *Ibid.*, p. 11.

[29] B. W. Jentlesson, 'Economic Sanctions and Post-Cold-War Conflict: Challenges for Theory and Practice', in P. C. Stern and D. Druckman (eds.), *International Conflict Resolution after the Cold War* (Washington, DC: National Academies Press, 2000), pp. 123–77.

[30] See D. Cortright and G. Lopez (with G. Linda), *Sanctions and the Search for Security: Challenges to UN Action* (Boulder, CO: Lynne Rienner, 2002); D. Cortright and G. A. Lopez, *Smart Sanctions: Targeting Economic Statecraft: Toward Effective and Humane*

different areas and policies of targeted sanctions that have led to unintended consequences and side effects. Biersteker, for example, has written on the unintended consequences of measures to counter the financing of terrorism and the challenges relating to listing and delisting of targeted entities (especially relating to financial sanctions and assets freeze),[31] Andreas has written on the negative implications of sanctions implemented during the war in former Yugoslavia, notably on the increase of criminality in the region,[32] Cosgrove on the consequences of early implementation of UN travel bans on listed individuals and their evasion tactics,[33] Eriksson on some of the unforeseen implications of targeted sanctions on third states[34] (in particular, the negative impact on those listed in terms of livelihood, life conditions, etc.),[35] and Cameron on the legal problems associated with UN and EU listing practices and the partial erosion of the legal human rights paradigm under which the UN operates.[36] However, much of this research focuses on early sanctions regimes that were not as sophisticated as more recent UN regimes in terms of sanctions lists, implementation procedures, and so on. The development of a new framework, in light of the TSC data, will be able to capture different features of unintended consequences, as the data presented below indicate.

Types of unintended consequences

The TSC has worked inductively to identify various types of unintended consequences of UN targeted sanctions.[37] Four categories stand out:

Sanctions Reform (Lanham, MD: Rowman and Littlefield, 2002); G. C. Hufbauer, J. J. Schott, K. A. Elliott, and B. Oegg. *Economic Sanctions Reconsidered*, 3rd ed (Washington, DC: Peterson Institute for International Economics, 2007).

[31] T. Biersteker, 'Unintended Consequences of Measures to Counter the Financing of Terrorism', in *Rethinking Security Governance: The Problem of Unintended Consequences* (Abingdon, Oxon: Routledge, 2010), pp. 127–36.

[32] P. Andreas, 'Unintended Criminalizing Consequences of Sanctions: Lessons from the Balkans', in C. Daase and C. Friesendorf (eds.), *Rethinking Security Governance: The Problem of Unintended Consequences* (Abingdon, Oxon: Routledge, 2010), pp. 102–26.

[33] E. Cosgrove, 'Examining Targeted Sanctions: Are Travel Bans Effective?' in P. Wallensteen and C. Staibano (eds.), *International Sanctions: Between Words and Wars in the Global System* (New York: Frank Cass, 2005), pp. 207–28.

[34] M. Eriksson, 'Unintended Consequences of Targeted Sanctions', in C. Daase and C. Friesendorf (eds.), *Rethinking Security Governance: The Problem of Unintended Consequences* (Abingdon, Oxon: Routledge, 2010), pp. 157–75.

[35] Eriksson, *Targeting Peace: Understanding UN and EU Targeted Sanctions*.

[36] See I. Cameron (ed.), *EU Sanctions: Law and Policy Issues Concerning Restrictive Measures* (Intersentia, 2013); I. Cameron, 'European Union Anti-Terrorist Blacklisting', *Human Rights Law Review*, 3 (2003), pp. 225–56; J. M. Farrall, *United Nations Sanctions and the Rule of Law* (Cambridge University Press, 2007).

[37] For the variables applied to identify unintended consequences of UN targeted sanctions see Appendix 3.

(1) implications for senders/actors, (2) for society, (3) for governance norms, and (4) for systemic rules.

With regard to the unintended consequences for senders/actors, the consortium has paid particular attention to the authoritarian rule of targets; the security apparatus of senders (e.g. the surveillance capacity of the state); certain political factions, or imbuing legitimacy on certain parties; the stature of targeted individuals; and the harmful effects on neighbouring states. Examples include former Ivorian president Laurent Gbagbo's defiant view of the UN, which in turn strengthened his authoritarian rule; an increase in popularity of one of the listed entities of the Côte d'Ivoire sanctions regime; and an undermining of regional state capacity in West Africa as sanctions evasion increased following the Liberia sanctions.

With regard to societal unintended consequences, there were observed increases in corruption and criminality, human rights violations in target states, the capacity to regulate internationally in different issue domains, and the capacity for enforcement in other domains (e.g. financial controls, immigration, customs and borders) – the latter being mostly a positive consequence. Examples include Iran's increasingly innovative practices of using illicit routes to trade in sensitive commodities subject to sanctions, such as energy and arms; and the mobilization of the international community to strengthen international trade regimes in high-value resources, such as rough diamonds (i.e. the Kimberley Process), as was the case in the Angola, Sierra Leone, and Liberia and in the high-quality timber sanctions regime in Liberia.

In terms of governance, illustrations from the various cases include implications for target state capacity, that is, the rally round the flag effect; resource diversion towards security and away from development; a reduction in local institutional capacity; and the significant administrative burden on the implementing states. Examples here include the use of propaganda against UN sanctions in the DPRK to strengthen the rule of Kim Jong-il and Kim Jong-un.

Finally, illustrations of the unintended consequences of UN targeted sanctions for the international system include implications for the UN and the normative order it represents. Examples include the weakening of liberal human rights norms and the negative legitimacy impact on the UN Security Council (e.g. overuse of targeted sanctions, lack of due process for listed actors, etc.). Examples here are linked to the challenges of listing and delisting entities as part of the Al-Qaida and Taliban sanctions regime (e.g. the early listing of Al-Barakaat). Apart from these empirical illustrations, what other types of examples of unintended consequences of UN targeted sanctions can be identified? Here, the analytical framework developed above becomes relevant.

Main findings from the TSC data

Overall, unintended consequences are found in 94 per cent of all case episodes. This is a discouraging finding, but the data include a number of positive unintended consequences. They also indicate that UN targeted sanctions matter and have definite impacts, even if they are not always as precise as intended at the outset. However, they have different implications for different types of threats to international peace and security. Charron finds, for example, that UN sanctions tend to be clustered around concerns related to armed conflict, international norm-breaking, and terrorism.[38]

The most frequently observed unintended consequence of targeted UN sanctions is increased corruption and criminality (58 per cent of the case episodes). This is followed by negative humanitarian consequences (44 per cent of the time), harm to the legitimacy of the UN Security Council (37 per cent), the strengthening of authoritarian rule (35 per cent), and the diversion of resources (34 per cent).[39] By disaggregating sanctions regimes into different episodes, the TSC data enable the identification and analysis of the political dynamics between sender and targets. In total there were nineteen variables in the database that examined different aspects of unintended consequences. In the ensuing section, I have tried to identify patterns of unintended consequences by categorizing all sanctions episodes coded in the same way across a case without variation (i.e. a variable with only 'yes' or 'no' (binary) features for each case). Although this approach has left out some cases where variation may have occurred, I argue that the extreme cases illustrate some of the main challenges that sanctions practitioners confront when designing a sanctions policy.

As shown in Table 9.1, a large majority (94 per cent) of all UN sanctions regimes result in unintended consequences, most often already in the first episode. Only Sudan in the 1990s and Guinea-Bissau did not show any evidence of unintended consequences.[40] The data hence suggest that unintended consequences are unavoidable features of most sanctions practices and are likely to accompany nearly all sanctions.

The question of which sanctions regimes experienced the lowest/highest number of unintended consequences is important, but somewhat problematic to answer in a comparative way, as most regimes consisted

[38] Andrea Charron, *UN Sanctions and Conflict: Responding to Peace and Security Threats* (London: Routledge, 2011).
[39] For definitions of these variables, see Appendix 3.
[40] Initial episodes of Liberia and Sudan sanctions also did not indicate unintended consequences.

Table 9.1 *Unintended consequences of UN targeted sanctions*

Unintended Consequences	Episodes	
	Frequency	%
Indications of unintended consequences	48	94
Increases in corruption and/or criminality	31	58
Humanitarian consequences	24	44
Decline in the credibility and/or legitimacy of the UN Security Council	19	37
Strengthening of authoritarian rule	19	35
Resource diversion	18	34
Increases in human rights violations	14	26
Strengthening of political factions	13	25
Increases in international enforcement capacity in different issue domains	11	20
Harmful effects on neighbouring states	10	19
Increase in international regulatory capacity in different issue domains	10	19
Widespread harmful economic consequences	8	19
Rally round the flag effect	7	13
Significant burden on implementing states	5	9
Reduction of local institutional capacity	4	8
Strengthening instruments of security apparatus of senders	4	8
Increase in the growth of the state role in the economy	4	8
Human rights implications for sending states	1	2
Enhance stature of targeted individuals	0	0
Other	5	10

Note: Percentage calculated from valid cases only; non-applicable and missing data excluded.

of multiple episodes. However, since all sanctions regimes experienced at least two episodes (apart from FRY in the 1990s, Ethiopia-Eritrea, Lebanon, and Guinea-Bissau that only had one episode), the question could be posed by only taking these episodes into account. In doing so, we find that of the remaining eighteen cases, the highest number of unintended consequences for the first episode, that is, Former Republic of Yugoslavia in the 1990s, had nine out of nineteen unintended consequences variables, while Libya sanctions in the 1990s recorded eight out of nineteen variables. Similarly, Libya in 2011 recorded nine types of unintended consequences. The results become more telling if we add episodes one and two together. Then we find that FRY (where the UN imposed a comprehensive sanctions episode after its initial targeted sanctions) stands out as a sanctions regime having most observations of unintended consequences (recording nineteen variables), followed by

Libya in 2011, which involved fairly broad targeted sanctions (recording fifteen variables). That FRY experienced the highest record of unintended consequences comparatively is not that strange, as the sanctions regime, despite having targeted aspects (i.e. list of designated names), was a comprehensive sanctions regime. In addition, they came about at a time when targeted sanctions had not been in practice for very long, suggesting that there were still a number of 'first-generation' types of unintended consequences associated with the sanctions. The high level may also be explained by the fact that both the European Union and the United States were strongly seeking to enforce independent sanctions of their own, hence some of the consequences might be more attributable to these sending actors than to the UN.[41]

With regard to an increase in corruption and criminality as an unintended consequence of targeted UN sanctions,[42] the presence of such effects in all episodes of a country case was found in at least three regimes: FRY in the 1990s, Angola, and the Taliban regime. The Al-Qaida/ Taliban and Libya in 2011 regimes also had criminality effects, albeit with one episode missing information. Considering all episodes, the data indicate that criminality effects were present in 58 per cent of all situations. These are consequential problems involving political will and enforcement capacity that the UN Security Council needs to tackle more directly.

Another significant variable is 'humanitarian consequences' (44 per cent of the cases). However, the data show that such implications can vary a great deal. It is worth noting that it is difficult to assess humanitarian consequences as they can be, particularly in the context of crises, a product of many different things. Moreover, the question of causality poses a challenge. There seldom is a linear relation between a dependent and an independent variable in the sanctions policy practice, and coding social events more generally can rarely catch or perfectly mirror reality.

Analytical challenges

Human rights challenges

There has been much debate in sanctions policy and research in the past decade over questions of human rights, particularly related to the

---

[41] On EU sanctions, see I. Anthony, 'Sanctions Applied by the European Union and the United Nations', in *SIPRI Yearbook 2002 Armaments, Disarmament and International Security* (Oxford University Press, 2002).
[42] This refers to the tendency of sanctions to contribute to a proliferation of illicit means and networks that function in place of previously legitimate channels.

so-called 'War on Terror' and the Al-Qaida and Taliban sanctions lists (for many years these lists were entwined, but they were separated in 2011). A variable addressing the human rights implications for sending states was included to capture potential implications.[43] Interestingly, only one sanctions regime showed negative unintended consequences for sending states: Al-Qaida/Taliban. The results indicate that the legal challenges regarding the Al-Qaida and Taliban lists have been considerable and may have overshadowed the more workable country-based sanctions regimes lists of designations. Another interpretation may be that too little empirical work on the human rights implications of country-based sanctions regimes has been done, and that we have not yet begun to see the problems associated with this variable. There are fewer legal challenges to country-based listed entities of UN sanctions (as distinct from EU sanctions), indicating that the debate on this issue is not yet fully developed.

The data indicate that unintended consequences concerning 'credibility, legitimacy impact on UNSC itself' are present in 37 per cent of the episodes. Twelve sanctions regimes recorded this unforeseen implication for the institution; of these, two stand out – Somalia and Sudan over Darfur – as they recorded this for all episodes. Meanwhile, there were five in which this unintended consequence was not identified.

Regarding the deterioration of human rights in the target state, nearly half of all regimes (43 per cent) indicate an increase of violations or the strengthening of authoritarian rule in the target state, reducing civil liberties of the population. It could be assumed that the more pressure a target regime experienced, the more internal repression it would exert, at least according to the naïve theory of sanctions that Johan Galtung criticized in the 1960s. Another interpretation of the empirical finding could be that there may be many obstacles to obtaining reliable information, given that measurable human rights violations of targeted UN sanctions during civil wars or repression are very difficult to verify. Empirical observations in this regard are neither as accessible nor as clear as one would like.

Target states and unintended consequences

The data suggest that the 'strengthening of authoritarian rule' in the targeted country can be an unintended consequence of targeted sanctions, as it was observed in 35 per cent of the episodes across eight country sanctions regimes. This has been the case, for example, in Libya during

---

[43] This refers to the negative impact on human rights in sending states as a result of imposing and implementing sanctions.

the 1990s and in Somalia. These illustrations are likely explained by the fact that the variable is mostly applicable to situations in which the state is functioning, in contrast to a situation where the state has collapsed into civil war. This is also why Libya in the 1990s, for example, indicated a strengthening of the Qadhafi regime, whereas Somalia, which was undergoing civil war, did not. Similarly, this could explain the low number of cases in which sanctions contributed to a 'rally round the flag effect' in the target state, since there were only seven episodes in which this unintended consequence was observed. Another explanation for a 'strengthening of authoritarian rule' is that this unintended consequence is often observed when the sanctions seek to undermine rebel groups acting against a legitimate government (which the UN may be favouring at the time).

The data suggest that imposing targeted UN sanctions does not enhance the target's standing or credibility; however, the variable is complex as such enhancement could probably be perceived in many different ways, for example, by domestic approval rates in the target state and a further integration of the target into decision-making processes. This is not to suggest that it never occurs. For example, Eriksson gives empirical examples of how specific entities targeted with sanctions were given more support by their followers as a result of their being listed, for example, as was the case in Côte d'Ivoire.[44]

Unintended consequences, target states, and their neighbours

As discussed in Chapter 7, an important aspect of sanctions efficiency is to ensure that implementing states have the necessary and relevant resources to enforce targeted sanctions. As argued in the Stockholm Process manual, the effectiveness of sanctions implementation is likely to increase if the state in which the sanctions are being enforced is given necessary resources.[45] Similarly, supporting neighbouring states' capacity would enhance the effectiveness of sanctions regimes (an idea supported by the experiences from the civil wars in East and West Africa). Taking targeted sanctions implementation seriously requires considerable administrative capacity, which sometimes can become an unintended burden. One variable capturing this unintended consequence is harmful effects on neighbouring states. Most (81 per cent) sanctions episodes, however, did not indicate this type of unintended consequence. One might expect that harmful effects on neighbouring states are closely related to the costs associated with implementing targeted sanctions.

---

[44] Eriksson, *Targeting Peace: Understanding UN and EU Targeted Sanctions*, pp. 88–9.
[45] Wallensteen et al., *Making Targeted Sanctions Effective: Guidelines for the Implementation of UN Policy Options*.

Here, the data demonstrate mixed results. For example, while Al-Qaida, DPRK, and Libya in 2011 suggest there were such unintended consequences, there were no such observations for most of the country sanctions regimes.[46] A tentative explanation for this may be that the more integrated a neighbouring country is with a targeted state, the more costly it becomes to impose sanctions; or, put differently, the more isolated a country is, the less costly. For example, Afghanistan under the Taliban was closely integrated with Pakistan, and Libya with many states around the world through the vehicle of the Libyan Investment Authority's investments and the active regional foreign policy of the Qadhafi regime.

Counterintuitive findings

One might expect that few initial or first episodes of a country sanctions regime would give rise to unintended consequences, since new policy decisions to impose UN sanctions are likely to encounter a complex policy challenge in terms of implementation and target reaction. Unintended consequences are likely to emerge as more policy learning takes place during the course of a sanctions regime. Yet, the majority of the sanctions regimes did show evidence of unintended consequences in the first episodes. This suggests that even mere threats can produce unintended consequences. A possible explanation could be that the sender makes an extra effort to demonstrate resolve during the first episode, a resolve that could backfire in the form of unintended consequences. With regard to 'strengthening of authoritarian rule' of targets, only five sanctions regimes experienced such unintended consequences in the first episodes (Haiti, Angola, Al-Qaida/Taliban, FRY, and Libya in 2011). Another explanation for the occurrence of unintended consequences in the first episodes could be the length of some of the first episodes before systematic follow-ups (and the possible use of additional sanctions) by the sender takes place.

Another counterintuitive finding is that Iran (together with Sudan over Darfur) stands out as experiencing fewer indications of unintended consequences than one would expect given the popular discourse about the Iran sanctions.[47] This appears odd at the outset given that international sanctions on Iran after 2012 approximate a comprehensive sanctions regime. One would have assumed that Iran would stand out by displaying

---

[46] FRY in the 1990s, Libya in the 1990s, Somalia, Haiti, Liberia, Angola, Rwanda, Sudan in the 1990s, Sierra Leone, Ethiopia and Eritrea, Democratic Republic of Congo (DRC), Iraq, Sudan over Darfur, Lebanon, Taliban, and Guinea-Bissau.

[47] See, for example, the research produced by the *National Iranian American Council*, NIAC (www.niac.org).

unintended consequences throughout most of its episodes. However, the principal reason that there are not more unintended consequences identified in the Iran case is because UN sanctions (the focus of the TSC database) remain relatively targeted.

To conclude, there are several unintended consequences that the sender should be able to anticipate. A country experiencing a civil war without clear government control of the territory (such as previous civil war in Liberia) is not likely to experience a 'rally around the flag effect', nor a strengthening of regime. Likewise, one would not expect an administrative burden on a target state (like Sudan or Iran) where there is a strong government with only a small number of its members being listed.

Methodological challenges

There are three principal methodological challenges in gathering and interrogating data on the unintended consequences of targeted sanctions, namely selection bias, validity, and causation. To begin with, the data on which the consortium rests its observations face the problem of selection bias. The selection bias displays itself in two ways, one general and one more specific. The general challenge of selection bias is that all sanctions regimes examined in the TSC database have already been sorted out from a hypothetically larger universe of 'cases' where UN targeted sanctions have not been applied. So in a sense the data are somewhat skewed at the onset of analysis. Cases that arguably would have warranted UN targeted sanctions (such as the armed conflicts in Colombia, Mali, Nigeria, Israel, or Syria) should have been investigated in addition to the cases where UN sanctions were imposed. This selection bias has consequences for generalizations one can make concerning the nature of the unintended consequences of UN targeted sanctions. Although immensely difficult methodologically, as each conflict has its own context and distinctive characteristics, an examination of non-cases and how they have developed without targeted sanctions, but by means of other UN interventions, would be useful. The challenge of selection bias is not unique to the analysis of unintended consequences or to the analysis of sanctions more generally. On the contrary, this methodological challenge is present in many data collection efforts of a similar kind (e.g. the effects of peacekeeping, humanitarian assistance missions, and mediation interventions). One specific selection bias associated with the TSC data is the fact that most of the variables associated with unintended consequences tend to illustrate negative effects. As seen in sanctions literature more generally, positive unintended consequences are less distinct and less amenable to data collection. This challenge has been addressed to a certain extent in the TSC database by identifying *a priori* both positive and negative unintended consequences, codifying both as well-defined variables. A limitation of this approach, however, is that there may well be many more forms of negative and positive unintended consequences of UN target sanctions than identified here.

The second challenge with studying unintended consequences has to do with validity, or how much of the data from which one can draw inferences is generalizable. After all, each sanctions regime is unique and very context specific. Hence, from this aspect one needs to be cautious about the generalizability of the data on unintended consequences. However, the frequency distribution of both the type of unintended consequence and its spatial location, that is, in which type of episode the unintended consequence tends to manifest itself, may at least give an important indication of the nature of unintended effects, which could have important policy implications when designing sanctions regimes.

Finally, there is the challenge of determining causation. As with the more general challenges of studying sanctions from the point of view of efficacy, there are also the challenges of identifying the unintended consequences of targeted sanctions due to their embeddedness with other policy measures. After all, UN targeted sanctions are always employed together with a range of other policy measures, and it is therefore difficult to determine what policy effects are the result of a sanctions regime. As discussed more extensively in Chapter 4 targeted sanctions are embedded with, or linked to, other policy measures such as UN peacekeeping interventions, mediation, third party involvement, and/or the use of force. It is therefore not simple to identify unintended consequences of targeted sanctions. However, the data produced by the TSC have sought to isolate the unintended consequences that have come about as a product of a decision to impose sanctions and would not likely have emerged in the absence of a decision to impose sanctions. Moreover, by employing the concept of sanctions episodes as its unit of analysis, it is easier to observe the dynamic that follows the sender's use of various policy instruments and hence ensure that the main source of a particular unintended consequence is the result of UN targeted sanctions.

Towards a framework for assessing unintended consequences

Given the potential significance of the unintended consequences of targeted sanctions, it is important to develop a policy strategy that could avoid, or at least try to prevent, their occurrence. A systematic assessment framework is most likely the best way for a policy-maker to fend off unintended consequences. Before presenting such a framework, it is worth noting a couple of features of unintended consequences that are usually associated with sanctions regimes, but often overlooked in the research of how sanctions work.[48]

First, a distinction should be made between *positive* and *negative* consequences.[49] As noted above, the unintended consequences of targeted sanctions can strengthen both senders and targets in a sanctions regime, as much as they can cause negative consequences. Most attention is focused on the negative consequences. Thus, it is important that in any assessment of unintended consequences, we should identify both types.

Second, in contrast to *material* consequences (such as consequences for individuals, like loss of income or property, or for companies, such as loss of assets, market shares, capacity to effectively work as an economic operator), *non-material* consequences (such as implications for rules, norms, and orders) can also be affected by the unintended consequences of targeted sanctions. For example, the 'rule of law' can be negatively affected by illiberal practices of UN targeted sanctions, thereby giving rise to various side effects. Another example concerns the stigmatization of third parties associated with the target, such as family members. Although, these types of unintended consequences may sometimes be more subtle and difficult to detect than more direct consequences, they can have just as serious consequences for the sender or the target.

Third, it is generally difficult to get a precise understanding of when unintended consequences arise in the course of sanctions enforcement. For example, criminalization has long-lasting negative consequences leading to favourable conditions for criminal networks to operate (as is usually the case for sanctions regimes that include an arms embargo). Thus, even when targeted sanctions work well on a short-term basis, there

---

[48] For analytical and conceptual purposes, six attributes of unintended consequences can be distinguished: (1) value traits, (2) type of subject/object, (3) quality of impact, (4) type of impact, (5) time-linked consequences, and (6) level of analysis. These attributes could further help us in categorizing the type and implications of unintended consequences.

[49] This goes hand-in-hand with the original terms of reference for the data collection. According to the terms of reference for the data classification on which findings of this book rest:

"Among the possible negative externalities of targeted sanctions are the legacies of corruption and criminality often left by sanctions, the strengthening of instruments of authoritarian rule, as well as their effects on neighbouring states. On the other hand, positive externalities one could expect increased capacity to regulate internationally in different issue domains (such as financial controls) or opportunities for capacity building training for financial controls, immigration, or customs." (For a precise definition of unintended consequences, see Codebook in Appendix 3).

may be other long-term implications. A distinction in this regard could be made between *short-* and *long-term* implications of UN targeted sanctions. Thinking of time-bound consequences then fills an analytically important gap that should be a part of a future policy assessment framework.

Finally, the unintended consequences of targeted UN sanctions can have various effects on different analytical units (levels). For example, differentiating between individual, state/societal, or systemic consequences may be valuable. Far too often the debate on unintended consequences seems to focus on the societal level rather than the individual or systemic level (aside from the community of legal scholars that have done much work on particular cases related to listing practices of sanctions).

In sum, the disaggregation of the unintended consequences of targeted UN sanctions as proposed above suggests that information about unintended consequences can be categorized in a more systematic manner than has been done in the past. The different features suggested here illustrate not only the complexity of sanctions as a policy but also the complexity of their unintended consequences. However, to develop a useful framework for assessing the unintended consequences of targeted UN sanctions, we also need to define the essential components of a sanctions regime. An outline of the key components of a sanctions regime is set out below.

Key assessment components

A UN targeted sanction regime is defined as a situation in which a *sender* (i.e. the UN Security Council) imposes sanctions against selected *target entities* (e.g. private or public actors, 'physical' or legal entities, companies or businesses, rebel groups, third parties, states, regions or a society) or *objects* (e.g. a commodity such as rough diamonds, arms, or timber; or an entire economic sector).[50] An effective sanctions regime requires that senders have the capacity to *enforce* sanctions. Examples of enforcement include capacity to address evasion techniques and overcome implementation challenges. Thus, the implementation, administrative management, and enforcement of sanctions can all lead to unintended consequences. Finally, a little-noticed aspect of sanction regimes that can generate unintended consequences is that they can affect *rules, norms,* and *orders* (e.g. liberal norms, the rule of law, democratic governance). Combining these components into a single analytical scheme on the basis of two axes enables the identification of different types of unintended consequences.

---

[50] As discussed in Chapter 1, in the TSC project a sanctions regime is understood to have multiple episodes.

There are many illustrative examples of the unforeseen implications of sanctions when the dimensions of unintended consequences of UN targeted sanctions are combined with the various features of sanctions regimes. For the purpose of illustrating the rationale of the framework of analysis, I begin by making reference to a number of possible situations of unintended consequences of UN targeted sanctions on the basis of positive and negative, material/non-material, short and long-term consequences, and their implications for different systemic units.

Sender Starting with examples that arise from a combination of positive and negative features of unintended consequences for the sending body, there can be a variety of different forms that unintended consequences can take. Positive examples could include increased legitimacy, following the UN Security Council's decisive action to impose and/or enforce sanctions – a sign of leadership in moments of crisis. Consensus to impose severe political and economic measures against a target can fortify international efforts to resolve a crisis, thus strengthening the legitimacy of the Security Council. For example, the UN Security Council showed considerable unanimity in protecting civilians in Libya in 2011 in the face of violence threatened and perpetrated by Qadhafi. On the negative side, however, the imposition of targeted sanctions too frequently can actually harm sender credibility. The challenge of the overuse of sanctions, and the implications this may have for the UN, is difficult to assess. So far there is little empirical evidence (i.e. global 'opinion polls') that could verify sanctions fatigue, though it is increasingly plausible as sanctions become the instrument of choice. There is some evidence of global sanctions fatigue in the critique of the global south as being over-represented as the target of country-based sanctions regimes (only the two FRY cases and possibly Lebanon are exceptions to the pattern of UN targeted sanctions). Similarly, hyper-vigilance can be criticized when compared to inaction in other conflict or crisis situations (e.g. imposing the UNSCR 1970 regime on Libya in 2011, but not on Syria).

Regarding the material and immaterial implications of UN targeted sanctions for the sender, there are situations in which a Member State might be required to compensate financially a wrongly listed target as a result of their innocence or because it violates a human rights norm. Such a situation would be characterized as one with material consequences. A situation in which the sender experiences an immaterial unintended consequence would be when sanctions undermine the legitimacy or credibility of the UN, for example, as observed in the legal challenges to sanctions of the 1267 (Al-Qaida/ Taliban) committee.[51]

Target If looking for positive and negative unintended consequences from the perspective of listed individuals (i.e. those subject to travel bans and/or assets freezes), there are a number of illustrations. For example, among the positive implications, a listed entity's stature could be enhanced among followers of the targeted regime. If a listed entity were a public official, a positive consequence could come from a strengthening of the target politically. Equally, looking at the consequences for a listed entity from a negative side, a target may be socially isolated and stigmatized. For example, if the target were a public figure, the target might face problems in attracting domestic support and be undermined politically by being perceived as an international pariah by many (e.g. Milosevic in FRY, and Bashir in Sudan over Darfur).

However, targets may also be corporate entities, for which there could be positive consequences (e.g. some businesses gain larger market shares as a result of sectorial sanctions that bar other actors or through enhanced visibility resulting in economic advantage). Society in general might also be strengthened (e.g. giving rise to an economically vibrant, more self-sufficient society in the target state). Negative consequences for the corporate target could entail an undermining of private engagements, leading to a loss of market share and revenue, overburdened organizational resources, and societal tensions if larger parts of the economy are affected. These negative implications should be seen in the context that they were not the goal of the sanctions resolution (i.e. constraining, coercing, or signalling).

In terms of the material and non-material dimensions of the unintended consequences against targets, there may be the loss of employment opportunities and salaries for individuals or larger communities as a result of sectoral or commodity sanctions (e.g. in the case of the Liberia sanctions regime, the imposition of timber sanctions had significant implications in the forestry industry). In terms of non-material dimensions, stigmatization stands out as a frequent consequence for targets that have not been given adequate reasons for why they have been targeted (personal accounts by listed entities in the Liberia sanctions regime provide empirical illustrations of this).[52]

---

[51] As well as their subsequent collapses noted in UNSCR 1333 (2000), 1390 (2002), and 1453 (2002).

[52] Eriksson, *Targeting Peace: Understanding UN and EU Targeted Sanctions;* Wallensteen et al., *Sanctions for Conflict Prevention and Peace Building: Lessons Learned from Côte d'Ivoire and Liberia.*

Combining the short- and long-term implications of sanctions from a target's perspective, there are situations in which the target may temporarily receive much significant international attention (short term) that amplifies the target's outreach capacity (i.e. for the listed target to communicate its propaganda). On the other hand, the longer-term implication could be a situation in which the target can never move beyond stigmatization, even after the sanctions have been lifted.

Enforcement of sanctions

Both the recent literature on sanctions and case examples from the consortium database testify to the positive and negative implications of the enforcement of UN Security Council targeted sanctions. In terms of the positive unintended consequences of enforcement of UN targeted sanctions, there are several examples of sanctions regimes supporting new governance mechanisms, such as border controls (customs ports) and surveillance mechanisms (e.g. air, maritime surveillance). Several regimes have also benefited from new resource governance mechanisms ensuring that natural resources do not fuel conflict. There are also cases of the negative implications of enforcement actions. For example, Haiti and FRY in the 1990s included episodes of comprehensive sanctions, with blunt societal consequences. Moreover, there are examples of how private sector entities have been forced to implement expensive banking screening mechanisms to ensure that targets cannot transfer money. Another example of negative implications is the situation in which listed entities and their associates (Al-Qaida and the Taliban) are driven further underground including a strengthening of criminal groups benefiting from sanctions busting.[53]

The *Stockholm Process on the Implementation of Targeted Sanctions*[54] includes various examples of the material and non-material unintended consequences of the enforcement of UN targeted sanctions. When it comes to material consequences, few if any of the under-resourced international bodies such as INTERPOL or the World Customs Organization have been provided with increased resources to ensure effective sanctions implementation.[55] In terms of non-material resources, various sanctions regimes, most notably those on Al-Qaida and the Taliban, have resulted

---

[53] P. Andreas, *Blue Helmets and Black Markets: The Business of Survival in the Siege of Sarajevo* (Cornell University Press, 2008).

[54] Wallensteen et al., *Making Targeted Sanctions Effective: Guidelines for the Implementation of UN Policy Options.*

[55] Cortright and Lopez (eds.), *The Sanctions Decade: Assessing UN Strategies in the 1990s*; D. Cortright and G. A. Lopez, *Uniting against Terror: Cooperative Nonmilitary Responses to the Global Terrorist Threat* (Cambridge, MA: MIT Press, 2007).

in counterterrorism norms being implemented through legal and administrative regulation at the national level, which have financial consequences for both governments and the private sector.[56] All the examples noted here are also found at the state, regional, and systemic levels, suggesting that there can be unforeseen implications of sanctions at various levels in the international system.

Rules, norms, and orders

Regarding unforeseen consequences affecting rules, norms, and orders, positive implications are similar to the positive enforcement practices noted above. A number of sanctions regimes, the Al-Qaida/Taliban regime in particular, have facilitated the development of international practices to enhance cooperation among its Member States, including strengthening non-military means to address international crises and armed conflict. Through the use of targeted sanctions, the UN Security Council has also opened new avenues for dialogue and engagement with actors that otherwise would have been isolated or excluded from UN deliberations. Previously the Security Council engaged only with Member States, but targeting opens up the opportunity to engage individuals (and courts) and seek accountability that conforms to more general developments under international law. Dealing directly with individuals and decision-makers resonates well with other trends in international relations.[57] On the negative side, there are numerous examples where sloppy implementation of targeted sanctions undermines UN credibility. For example, allowing targeted commodities to cross borders in violation of sanctions, especially when there is UN presence on ground, is problematic. Angola is a clear case in which such violations took place.

There are several short- and long-term illustrations of non-material consequences. Most of these examples would be unforeseen long-term implications, such as a strengthening of rule of law practices (e.g. Chapter VII mandatory legal measures enforcing rule-based sanctions mechanisms). Another example would be the strengthening of other UN peacemaking measures in which sanctions play a role. For example, various UN mediators such as Jan Eliasson (in the case of Sudan over Darfur) or

---

[56] T. Biersteker and S. Eckert, *Strengthening Targeted Sanctions through Fair and Clear Procedures*. Report commissioned by the Governments of Germany, Switzerland, and Sweden (Providence, RI: Watson Institute for International Studies, Brown University, 2006).

[57] See K. Sikkink, 'From Pariah State to Global Protagonist: Argentina and the Struggle for International Human Rights', *Latin American Politics and Society*, 50 (2008), pp. 1–29 for a description of an increase in individual accountability for crimes committed, in a process described as a 'justice cascade'.

Pierre Schori (in Côte d'Ivoire) have used UN targeted sanctions as leverage to achieve their objectives.[58]

Finally, it goes without saying that the non-material unintended consequences of UN targeted sanctions have systemic implications. Most clearly, they have an effect on the way states behave. Even though a target (either a regime or an individual) may never recognize the legitimacy of sanctions, the target still often bargains with the sender to lift sanctions in exchange for changed behaviour (as happened, for example, in the case of Iran and the negotiations over its nuclear programme in 2013).

Final reflections

The changing character of the policy of targeting, the increasing number of listed entities, the blurring of UN targeted sanctions with other sanctions regimes at the national or regional level, and new objectives for sanctions (e.g. against sexual offenders, child recruiters, and against conflict minerals) make targeting increasingly complex.[59] There are a number of factors that can reduce or minimize the unintended consequences of targeted sanctions. Greater experience may lead to institutional learning over time (as considered in Chapter 11). Moreover, improving monitoring systems (e.g. better registers, legal oversight, and financial supervision) could lead to fewer unintended consequences. Coupled with better guidelines and training, the UN could gain better command and anticipate better the policy challenges of unintended consequences.

While the UN can do much more to attempt to address these challenges, there are also a number of structural problems that impede limiting unintended consequences. For example, rotation among the ten elected members of the UN Security Council (the 'E-10') limits potential learning and institutional experience. Another problem is the absence of political will and P5 power interests. Some structural problems could be addressed through adding institutional resources to the UN Secretariat and the sanctions branch, institutionalizing assessment procedures, disseminating information more effectively, and systematically following on Panel of Expert recommendations and proposals.

The sanctions policy instrument is a complex tool. The complexity requires the sender to take sanctions policy seriously (e.g. as seriously as

---

[58] Eriksson, *Targeting Peace: Understanding UN and EU Targeted Sanctions.*
[59] See E. Carisch and L. Rickard-Martin, *Global Threats and the Role of United Nations Sanctions Report* (International Policy Analysis, Friedrich Ebert Stiftung, 2011).

the UN Security Council does when authorizing a UN peacekeeping mission, for example). A legitimate criticism against the UN is that sanctions many times are not as effective as they could be. What could the UN and its Member States then do?

A simple way would be to pay far more attention to some basic elements of the policymaking process. Building on Bridgman, Davis, and Althaus,[60] a policymaking process typically entails issue identification, policy analysis, policy development, consultation, coordination, decision, implementation, and evaluation. For example, while a UN troop deployment is typically backed up with a high degree of analysis and attention to aspects across the policymaking process (often in advance of decisions to deploy), contemporary UN sanctions policies suffer from a general lack of early and credible policy analysis, deficiencies in institutional coordination and information dissemination, weak implementation, and a lack of evaluation/assessment. This is rather surprising given that lives and high politics are usually at stake with the enforcement of sanctions. The contrast between these two policy processes could not be clearer. That is not to say that institutional learning cannot take place. In fact, few UN instruments have been given the amount of systematic scholarly attention that sanctions have.

Without credible policy planning, including all the components of the policy process outlined above, the line between accomplishing a policy's aims and a policy fiasco is very thin. A key component of learning from policy ignominies is a systematic assessment of the use of a policy. Aside from general improvements of decision-making and institutional design of UN targeted sanctions practice, what other recommendations can we distil from the analysis?

First, the findings suggest that careful attention needs to be paid to the interaction among unintended consequences and other UN policy instruments and international bodies. As noted in Chapter 4, sanctions are never a stand-alone measure, and efforts to address negative unintended consequences, such as an increase in corruption and criminality, should be integrated and coordinated with strategies of other agencies such as INTERPOL and the UN Office on Drugs and Crime (UNODC), which have a wealth of experience in tackling these challenges. Stronger cooperation could potentially mitigate some of the unintended consequences of targeted sanctions.

Second, in order to counter the strengthening of authoritarian rule, the UN should utilize enhanced information dissemination practices to

---

[60] C. Althaus, P. Bridgman, and G. Davis, *The Australian Policy Handbook*, 5th edn (Sydney: Allen & Unwin, 2013).

support democracy and human rights.[61] Engaging further in 'multilateral counter-propaganda campaigns' is also crucial to discredit decision-makers in target countries. The UN already has a communication and information service that could take on such responsibilities. Moreover, the UN Security Council needs to improve its internal interactions with the rest of the organization, in order to harmonize the understanding of the organization's sanctions objectives.

Third, with regard to resource diversion, data suggest that the UN should coordinate with other international bodies such as the World Trade Organization and the World Customs Organization. Other initiatives such as the Kimberley Process also address resource diversions in conflict zones.

Finally, there are negative humanitarian consequences of sanctions. Although it comes as no surprise that targeted sanctions have unintended consequences, it does raise questions concerning the rationale of targeting, especially since targeted sanctions were intended to minimize such consequences. A possible explanation for harmful humanitarian effects may be the recent broadening of targeted sanctions – from being targeted on individuals (travel ban, and assets freeze), which are the most discriminating, to relatively indiscriminate measures such as financial sector sanctions as in the case of Libya.[62] One way to overcome and prevent such effects in future sanctions regimes would be to develop formal assessment models that could be employed following the adoption of a UNSCR, but prior to actual implementation of the measures. Recognizing the time pressure in responding to many crisis situations, there will obviously be considerable challenges with this kind of assessment (e.g. identification of targets, likely impacts, unintended consequences, and evasion strategies). Nonetheless, it is important to address unintended consequences. The Office on the Coordination of Humanitarian Affairs (OCHA) has some modelling experience, but it needs to be refined to address the humanitarian consequences of sanctions.[63] However, the task of developing assessment models need

---

[61] See Wallensteen et al., *Making Targeted Sanctions Effective: Guidelines for the Implementation of UN Policy Options;* P. Wallensteen, M. Eriksson, and D. Strandow, *Sanctions for Conflict Prevention and Peace Building: Lessons Learned from Côte d'Ivoire and Liberia* (Uppsala: Uppsala University Department of Peace and Conflict Research, 2006).

[62] See Biersteker, Eckert, Tourinho, and Hudáková, *Effectiveness of UN Targeted Sanctions,* p. 17 for a chart depicting the degrees of discrimination (or relative 'comprehensiveness') of targeted sanctions.

[63] M. Bessler, R. Garfield, and G. McHugh, *Sanctions Assessment Handbook: Assessing the Humanitarian Implications of Sanctions.* United Nations Inter-Agency Standing Committee (New York: United Nations Office for the Coordination of Humanitarian Affairs, OCHA and the Policy Development Studies Branch, 2004).

not be left to the UN alone, since some UN Member States also have the capacity to develop such models of their own.

Future research

One avenue for future research would be to continue assembling additional empirical observations that could add to helping sanctions scholarship understand the implications of the various crises/armed conflicts that have experienced unintended consequences. Second, further investigation is needed to differentiate which type of unintended consequence comes from which type of sender. An increasing number of actors are imposing sanctions and thereby producing different types of unintended consequence (e.g. US, EU, and AU sanctions). Third, further research and data examination of the positive side effects of targeted sanctions is worthwhile. It is fairly easy to look at negative effects, but much more difficult to identify and understand positive unintended consequences and how they contribute to the goals of the United Nations. Finally, the framework presented in this chapter needs to be applied to future sanctions regimes. One potential challenge for such a research path would be to tackle the potentially changing character of what today constitutes a sanctions regime. We appear to be entering another sanctions decade, where traditional blacklisting models and sanctions regimes need to be reconsidered. No longer can sanctions regimes be examined in isolation, but the money-arms-resource trails organized by shadow actors also need to be considered. Trails that transgress borders and undermine legitimate governance structures pose a threat to international peace and security. Hence, using the country sanctions regime as the focus of analysis may be increasingly misleading. This is a challenge that needs future attention, not least if the UN should be able to tackle unintended consequences of UN targeted sanctions.

10 The effectiveness of United Nations targeted sanctions

Thomas J. Biersteker, Marcos Tourinho, and Sue E. Eckert

The effectiveness of sanctions is probably the most frequently debated aspect of the policy instrument. This chapter begins with a review of the conventional wisdom about effectiveness (including the extensive scholarly literature on the subject), some general recommendations for how to think about evaluating effectiveness analytically, and a detailed explanation of how we have evaluated the effectiveness of UN targeted sanctions imposed since 1991. The chapter continues with a comparative empirical analysis of the research results, including detailed correlations of sanctions effectiveness and ineffectiveness with all relevant variables in our database (defined in Appendix 3), and concludes with some recommendations for future assessments of sanctions effectiveness.

Conventional wisdom among policy practitioners, journalists, and the general public holds that sanctions are typically imposed to force a change in the behaviour of targets, and that with a few notable exceptions,[1] they do not 'work' particularly well as a policy instrument. When sanctions are contrasted with other policy instruments, especially the use of military force, few contend that sanctions are more 'effective' than military means. Sanctions are often perceived as a compromise measure between diplomacy and the use of military force (somewhere 'between words and wars'), implying that decision-makers choose policy instruments from a continuum of escalating measures – from diplomacy to sanctions to military force – rather than use them in combination.

Most practitioners and journalists assess the effectiveness of sanctions regimes in broad, national terms, such as 'the sanctions against Iran or Libya,' rather than disaggregating the analysis into different phases of a

---

[1] South Africa is often invoked as an example of sanctions success, although sanctions took a very long time to achieve tangible results and other factors (the end of the Cold War and internal political dynamics) also played an important role. Iran's 2013 return to the negotiating table has been attributed by many to international sanctions imposed on the country since 2012, but the contribution of sanctions to that outcome can be questioned, since Iran offered more generous concessions in 2003, long before the sanctions were extended and the electoral political change in Iran in 2013 is also key.

conflict or dispute, as we have done in this book. When sanctions are applied, it is generally assumed that they function by placing pressure on a target or a broader population, by depriving them of some valued good or goods. Increasing the pressure through comprehensive, broader, or 'crippling' measures is presumed to increase the chances of people rising up and challenging their regime or divisions being induced within regime leadership. As suggested in Chapters 1 and 2, the general logic of how sanctions influence a target remain focused on how political outcomes (gain) can be produced by applying economic sanctions (pain), with the implicit assumption that more pain will yield greater gain.

Scholarly literature on sanctions and sanctions effectiveness

The scholarly literature on sanctions effectiveness tends to replicate much, but not all, of the conventional wisdom just described. The primary focus of leading scholarly analysts of the effectiveness of sanctions has long been on the ability of sanctions to coerce a change in target behaviour. Johan Galtung, Peter Wallensteen, and Margaret Doxey conducted pioneering studies of the sanctions imposed on Rhodesia in the 1960s and described the principal function of economic sanctions in terms of their ability to obtain 'compliance' from a target,[2] 'compliance to the demands of the sender',[3] and a 'desired behavioural result'.[4] Gary Hufbauer, Jeffrey Schott, and Kimberly Elliott talk about the purpose of sanctions in terms of 'policy or governmental change',[5] while Daniel Drezner described 'the hidden hand of economic coercion' and concentrated on the ability of threats of sanctions to yield significant concessions from the target.[6] The same is true of the formal modelling work of Jon Hovi, Robert Huseby, and Detlef Sprinz, who define the effectiveness of sanctions in terms of whether a target yields to a sender's demands.[7] Robert Pape concentrated on the concept of economic coercion for

[2] J. Galtung, 'On the Effects of International Economic Sanctions: With Examples from the Case of Rhodesia', *World Politics*, 19 (1967), pp. 378–416, at 381.
[3] P. Wallensteen, 'Characteristics of Economic Sanctions', *Journal of Peace Research*, 5 (1968), pp. 247–66, at 249.
[4] M. Doxey, 'International Sanctions: A Framework for Analysis with Special Reference to the UN and Southern Africa', *International Organization*, 26 (1972), pp. 527–50, at 529.
[5] G. C. Hufbauer, J. J. Schott, and K. A. Elliott, *Economic Sanctions Reconsidered*, 2nd edn (1990); G. C. Hufbauer et al., *Economic Sanctions Reconsidered*, 3rd edn (Washington, DC: Peterson Institute for International Economics, 2007), p. 158.
[6] D. W. Drezner, 'The Hidden Hand of Economic Coercion', *International Organization*, 57 (2003), p. 643.
[7] J. Hovi, R. Huseby, and D. F. Sprinz, 'When Do (Imposed) Economic Sanctions Work?', *World Politics*, 57 (2005), pp. 479–99, at 485.

political purposes, which he termed 'the traditional understanding of sanctions' and was explicitly critical of David Baldwin's efforts to broaden the concept of economic statecraft to other goals.[8] Moreover, sanctions databases assembled by Hufbauer, Schott and Elliott,[9] Clifton Morgan and Valerie Schwebach,[10] and Christian von Soest and Michael Wahman[11] all emphasize changes in the behaviour of targets in their measures of effectiveness.

A number of sanctions scholars have identified policy goals other than coercion when assessing the effectiveness of sanctions. David Baldwin considered the different purposes of sanctions as an instrument of economic statecraft,[12] Margaret Doxey described both deterrence and norm reinforcement,[13] and James Lindsay proposed a typology differentiating between compliance, subversion, deterrence, and symbolism.[14] Most of the scholarly literature, however, shares Morgan and Schwebach's view that 'the focus of the debate regarding the effectiveness of sanctions is on whether they can enable the sanctioner to achieve its goals of altering the behaviour of the target'.[15]

While sanctions scholars are more likely to identify anecdotal examples of sanctions success than the general public,[16] most contend that sanctions are 'effective' at most only about one-third of the time. Hufbauer, Schott, and Elliott's 2008 edition of *Economic Sanctions Reconsidered* estimated that sanctions were at least partially successful in 34 per cent of the cases they studied.[17] In his critical reanalysis of an earlier version of the Hufbauer, Schott, and Elliott database in 1997, Robert Pape excluded cases in which sanctions coincide with threats or the use of force, concluding that sanctions were effective only 6 per cent of the time.[18] In their significantly larger sample of sanctions cases, Navin

---

[8] R. A. Pape, 'Why Economic Sanctions Do Not Work', *International Security*, 22 (1997), pp. 90–103, at 95.

[9] Hufbauer et al., *Economic Sanctions Reconsidered*.

[10] T. C. Morgan and V. L. Schwebach, 'Fools Suffer Gladly: The Use of Economic Sanctions in International Crises', *International Studies Quarterly*, 41 (1997), pp. 27–50.

[11] C. von Soest and M. Wahman, 'Sanctions and Democratization in the Post-Cold War Era', Hamburg: *GIGA Working Paper*, Number 212 (2013).

[12] D. A. Baldwin, 'The Sanctions Debate and the Logic of Choice', *International Security*, 24 (1999/2000), pp. 80–107, at 88.

[13] Doxey, 'International Sanctions', p. 532.

[14] J. Lindsay, 'Trade Sanctions as Policy Instruments: A Re-Examination', *International Studies Quarterly*, 30 (1986), pp. 153–73, at 157.

[15] Morgan and Schwebach, 'Fools Suffer Gladly', p. 29.

[16] See, for example, G. A. Lopez and D. Cortright, 'Containing Iraq: Sanctions Worked', *Foreign Affairs*, 83 (2004), pp. 90–103 or T. Biersteker, 'Targeted Sanctions and Individual Human Rights', *The International Journal*, 65 (2010), pp. 99–117.

[17] Hufbauer et al., *Economic Sanctions Reconsidered*, p. 158.

[18] Pape, 'Why Economic Sanctions Do Not Work', p. 106.

Bapat and Clifton Morgan concluded that sanctions are effective only about 23 per cent of the time.[19] Large-N studies of sanctions generally include both unilateral and multilateral (UN, EU, or other regional sanctions) measures in their large samples, without necessarily distinguishing between targeted and comprehensive sanctions in their analysis. This can prove to be problematic, since targeted sanctions have a different scope and logic from comprehensive sanctions, as discussed earlier in this volume in Chapters 1 and 2.

Like the popular and public discourse, much of the scholarly literature also assumes that sanctions will inevitably be less effective than the use of military means. Robert Pape asserts that '[m]ilitary conquest, when it occurs, is always a more credible explanation than economic sanctions because the target state's failure to concede before military defeat is in itself evidence of the failure of coercion'.[20] As a result, in his critique of the analysis of Hufbauer, Schott, and Elliott's data, he *a priori* excluded from his analytical consideration of effectiveness any of their cases in which there was a threat or use of military force. This is one of the reasons his overall evaluation of effectiveness is significantly lower than theirs.

Many scholars also share with conventional wisdom the idea that sanctions exist on a continuum between words (diplomacy) and war (the use of force). Peter Wallensteen and Carina Staibano titled their important book on sanctions, *International Sanctions: Between Words and Wars in the Global System*.[21] Hufbauer, Schott, and Elliott place sanctions as a policy instrument between the unsatisfactory alternatives of military force, which would be too disproportionate a response, and diplomatic protestations, often too meagre a response.[22] David Baldwin similarly talks about the menu of choice available to decision-makers and discusses whether sanctions or diplomacy should be considered as substitutes for the use of military force.[23]

In contrast to the approach taken in this book, most of the sanctions literature also shares with the public debate a tendency to discuss sanctions and effectiveness in state-centric, aggregate terms. Most case study collections and virtually all large-N studies examine the effectiveness of sanctions in terms of national units, such as the sanctions against Iran or Liberia. The pioneering studies of targeted sanctions by David Cortright

---

[19] N. A. Bapat and T. C. Morgan, 'Multilateral versus Unilateral Sanctions Reconsidered: A Test Using New Data', *International Studies Quarterly*, 53 (2009), pp, 1075–94, at 1082.
[20] Pape, 'Why Economic Sanctions Do Not Work', p. 97.
[21] P. Wallensteen and C. Staibano, *International Sanctions: Between Words and Wars in the Global System* (London: Frank Cass/Routledge, 2005).
[22] Hufbauer et al., *Economic Sanctions Reconsidered*, p. 9.
[23] Baldwin, 'The Sanctions Debate and the Logic of Choice', pp. 82–3.

and George Lopez were organized around a careful selection of country case studies.[24] The same is true for studies drawing on large-N databases. Hufbauer, Schott, and Elliott's database of economic sanctions, one of the most widely utilized, employs the target country as their core unit of analysis.[25] The codebook for the Threat and Imposition of Economic Sanctions (TIES) database utilized by Bapat and Morgan (among others) requires that a sanctions episode be defined in terms of a sender state and a target state,[26] and von Soest and Wahman's core unit of analysis is country year.[27]

To its credit, however, most of the scholarly community does not subscribe to the conventional wisdom that more civilian pain leads to greater sanctions effectiveness. First criticized by Johan Galtung as the 'naïve theory of sanctions',[28] and discussed more fully in Chapter 2, variations of his argument have reappeared every decade since he first wrote about the subject in 1967. In addition to many of those already cited above, in their review essay on targeted sanctions, Arne Tostensen and Beate Bull argued,

The theoretical underpinnings for the pain-gain formula lie in a cost-benefit analysis calculated by the parties in financial terms, as well in terms of the costs of casualties, political gains and losses, and trade-offs between future human rights gains and immediate violations. However, the transmission assumption and cost-benefit rationale are questionable on theoretical, empirical, and ethical grounds.[29]

Other scholars, most notably Jonathan Kirshner and Risa Brooks, have urged analysts to explore the domestic political economy aspects of sanctioned parties to understand how sanctions function[30] and to examine how they can be manipulated for political gain by targeted parties.[31] Neta Crawford and Audie Klotz explored similar issues related to the

---

[24] See especially D. Cortright and G. A. Lopez, *The Sanctions Decade: Assessing UN Strategies in the 1990s* (Boulder, CO: Lynne Rienner Publishers, 2000) or their subsequent volume, *Sanctions and the Search for Security: Challenges to UN Action* (Boulder, CO: Lynne Rienner Publishers, 2002).

[25] Hufbauer et al., *Economic Sanctions Reconsidered*, pp. 20–32.

[26] T. C. Morgan, V. Krustev, and N. A. Bapat, 'Threat and Implementation of Sanctions (TIES) Codebook', (2006), p. 1.

[27] von Soest and Wahman, 'Sanctions and Democratization in the Post-Cold War Era', p. 13.

[28] Galtung, 'On the Effects of International Economic Sanctions', p. 388.

[29] A. Tostensen and B. Bull, 'Are Smart Sanctions Feasible?', *World Politics*, 54 (2002), pp. 373–403, at 375.

[30] J. Kirshner, 'Economic Sanctions: The State of the Art', *Security Studies*, 11 (2002), pp. 160–79, at 169.

[31] R. Brooks, 'Sanctions and Regime Type: What Works, When?', *Security Studies*, 11 (2002), pp. 1–50, at 2.

adaptability of targeted parties over time in their analysis of how sanctions worked in South Africa.[32]

While the scholarly literature generally has been critical of the pain/gain argument, it shares most of the conventional wisdom with regard to the core purpose of sanctions (to coerce a change in behaviour), the effectiveness of sanctions (generally low), the placement of sanctions on a continuum of policy choice (between words and war), and the analytical focus of sanctions (with countries as the core unit of analysis). Most ignore the varying purposes of sanctions discussed in Chapters 1 and 2, as well as the fact that policy practitioners may simultaneously be pursuing more than one, or indeed all three, of these purposes at any point in time. The focus on states as a unit of analysis is out of step with the move to targeted sanctions, which are just as likely to target non-state actors as the leadership of a government. Most analyses also suffer from the problem of the contingent timing of evaluations, in that the analysis of effectiveness is determined by what is ultimately an arbitrary decision (based on when the country case regime is analysed).

Two recent contributions to the sanctions literature by authors included in this volume begin to address these analytical and methodological problems in their recently published works. Mikael Eriksson has developed the idea of sanctions episodes within a larger country sanctions regime as the unit of analysis to capture the sometimes significant variation that can take place within a single country regime over time. He defines an episode as 'one out of many interventions made by members of the international community in interacting with specific targets' and operationalizes the concept in terms of the sender's 'every decision to implement, broaden or suspend its restrictive measures against a listed entity'.[33] While we have employed Eriksson's idea of sanctions episode as our basic unit of analysis, we have also adapted it to reduce significantly the number of potential episodes within each country sanctions regime, as described in Chapter 1 and in more detail in the next section.

As he outlines in Chapter 2 of this volume, Francesco Giumelli has developed a typology that differentiates between three different purposes of sanctions: coercion, constraint, and/or signalling a target. He defines coercion in terms of an intention to change the behaviour of a target. Constraint is defined in terms of an effort to thwart a target from pursuing some policy, and signalling includes sending a message to one or more

[32] N. Crawford and A. Klotz, *How Sanctions Worked in South Africa* (New York: St. Martin's Press, 1999).
[33] M. Eriksson, *Targeting Peace: Understanding UN and EU Targeted Sanctions* (Surrey, England: Ashgate Publishers, 2001), p. 47.

targets.[34] He defined these different purposes in mutually exclusive terms, which allows him to apply his classification scheme to different sanctions regimes at a given point in time, to describe them as coercing, constraining, or signalling. While we have employed Giumelli's categories in this book, we have adapted them to allow for the possibility of senders simultaneously pursuing more than one purpose, as described in more detail in the section below. We also recognize the deep interrelationships among the different purposes (discussed in more detail in Chapter 1) and the ways in which a sender of sanctions might use constraint or signalling in order to coerce a target, just as coercion of an individual might be used to constrain a targeted group.

Analysing sanctions effectiveness

The analytical framework developed for the purposes of our assessment of sanctions effectiveness addresses two of the challenges identified above. The first, already discussed in Chapter 1, is the methodological problem arising from the fact that sanctions regimes can change significantly over time. As years go by, sanctions regimes often change radically in terms of their purpose, context, target, or type of measure imposed. In a situation of ever-shifting political bargaining, an evaluation that considers the country regime as a single unit of analysis cannot adequately incorporate these changes, and ends up measuring the effectiveness of the entire regime based on the situation in place at the moment of evaluation, something that is often just the latest development in a long and continuing bargaining relationship between sender and target.

For example, if the effectiveness of the UN targeted sanctions regime against Liberia were evaluated as a single unit, it would be apparent that over the long period sanctions have been in place (more than twenty years) the objectives of the UN Security Council have changed multiple times. The Council began by supporting the enforcement of a peace agreement (1992) and later moved to halting Liberian support for the RUF rebel group in Sierra Leone (2001) and currently is trying to contain spoilers of the peacebuilding process in place following the exile and arrest of Charles Taylor (i.e. since 2003). If the evaluation considered only one or the most recent of these multiple (and fairly different) iterations between target and sender, much of the actual impact and effectiveness (or ineffectiveness) of targeted sanctions observable at different times would be lost. The types of targeted sanctions imposed by the

---

[34] F. Giumelli, *Coercing, Constraining and Signalling. Explaining UN and EU Sanctions after the Cold War* (Colchester: ECPR Press, 2011), pp. 33–5.

Security Council also changed over time, from an arms embargo, to a commodity ban on diamond and timber exports, to individual asset freezes and travel bans.

To address this analytical challenge, we break down all UN targeted sanctions country regimes into discrete case episodes and consider these as our fundamental unit of analysis.[35] Each episode is defined as a period of time within a larger country sanctions regime in which the relationship between target and sender remains stable in terms of (1) the purposes of the sanctions, (2) its targets, (3) the combination of sanctions imposed, and (4) the broad political context in which the episode takes place (i.e. with no drastic changes 'on the ground').[36] We define a sanctions episode from the vantage point of the sender in terms of significant modifications of the sanctions regime. Operationally this would include a major expansion of designees or lists of proscribed items, the addition of new types of sanctions, a significant relaxation of existing measures, changes in the target designated, or changes in the stated objectives of the sanctions (e.g. from counterterrorism to non-proliferation). This determination of different episodes was made following extensive qualitative analyses of each country sanctions regime prepared by both country and sanctions specialists and by carefully reviewing successive UN Security Council resolutions to determine precisely when one episode ends and another begins. Detailed summaries of each episode, including the beginning and end dates and types of sanctions imposed, are contained in Appendix 1 of this book.

As already discussed in Chapter 1, we recognize the methodological challenges of using case episodes as a unit of analysis. For the purposes of statistical analysis, it is not always possible to assume the independence of the different case episodes. While there are sometimes major continuities within a single country case, including the same regional context, the same key targets, or the same key players internationally, there are often significant discontinuities within larger country sanctions regimes, especially those that remain in place for a long period of time. For example, the combination of different types of targeted sanctions being applied frequently changes, as the Security Council attempts to increase (or relieve) pressure on targets. The targets of sanctions also change, either because the sanctions have been in place for a long time (as in Somalia) or as sanctions become increasingly targeted over time (as in Angola). Sometimes the territory over which the sanctions apply is variable (as in

---

[35] As noted above, this builds upon but adapts the method proposed by Mikael Eriksson in his 2011 book, *Targeting Peace*.
[36] The episodes for each country case are listed in Appendix 1.

Angola and the DRC), and the Security Council even changes its core objectives (as it did in the current sanctions regimes in Libya and Somalia). There are instances in which nearly all of these components have changed from one episode to another (e.g. primary objectives, types of sanctions, and targets). Thus, we contend that there is sufficient variation across different case episodes to warrant their comparison as distinct units of analysis.[37] At the same time, we are mindful of the methodological challenges and refrain from making causal claims (as opposed to correlational observations) in this chapter.

Another way in which the analytical framework utilized here contributes to the 'sanctions effectiveness' debate discussed above is by expanding what is considered to be the potential purposes of sanctions regimes. Instead of focusing exclusively on the coercion of the targets to change behaviour as the sole purpose of sanctions, this research includes constraining and signalling/stigmatizing as additional purposes of sanctions.[38] We do not, however, assume that all sanctions regimes intend to coerce, constrain, and signal, although we have empirically found that, to different degrees, most do. We also recognize that there are complex interrelationships among these different purposes, as already discussed above, and that constraint can be used to coerce, just as coercion can be used to constrain.

The choice of multiple purposes was not only analytical, but at least in part a product of empirical observation. Because targeted sanctions are more flexible measures than comprehensive sanctions and can be calibrated to specific objectives,[39] the UN Security Council often does not seek only or primarily to change the behaviour of the target. For example, when sanctions are in place to support broader peacebuilding initiatives in post-conflict scenarios, they serve primarily to constrain spoilers from engaging in activities that could derail the peace process and start a new cycle of violence.[40] As mentioned in Chapter 1, it is also clear that counterterrorism sanctions against Al-Qaida, for example, do not seek to change behaviour directly, but rather to deny Al-Qaida the resources necessary to conduct its proscribed activities.[41] UN targeted sanctions are

---

[37] The focus on country cases as a unit of analysis in most large-N studies does not fully solve the problem of statistical independence, since different country sanctions regimes are embedded in highly interdependent regional settings (as illustrated by the West African conflict cases (Sierra Leone, Liberia, and Côte d'Ivoire), the DRC conflict, the conflicts in Eastern Africa, and the spillover from Libya to the Central African Republic.
[38] This builds upon but adapts the typology proposed by F. Giumelli in *Coercing, Constraining and Signalling*.
[39] See Chapter 1.
[40] See, for example, episodes 4 and 5 in Liberia and 5 in Sierra Leone and Côte d'Ivoire.
[41] See episodes 3 and 4 of Al-Qaida/Taliban regime.

also routinely crafted to convey a particular normative signal to a target and/or some larger audience, whether it is about non-proliferation, terrorism, or the use of armed violence to settle a dispute. When it sends a signal, the Council both names a target but implicitly also tries to shame or stigmatize the target in some way. Signalling involves not only communicating a sanction but also attempting to influence the social context within which the signal is received. Typically, but not in all instances, the Council pursues more than one of these three different purposes simultaneously.

Following the general approach introduced by Hufbauer, Schott, and Elliott,[42] for the purpose of sanctions evaluation, *effectiveness* is understood broadly as a function of two variables: the overall policy outcome for each purpose, and the distinct contribution of UN targeted sanctions measures to that outcome. For each episode, effectiveness is measured first along a continuum ranging, for example, in the case of coercion, from 'complete intransigence/no change' in behaviour by the target, to 'all principal objectives of sanctions being met'. A five-point scale, with a score of 1 representing least effective and 5 constituting most effective, is utilized.[43] For constraint, a score of 1 equates to 'no discernible constraints experienced by the target', and 5 indicates 'significant costs to the target resulting in a change of strategy or difficulties in engaging in proscribed activities.' In the case of signalling/stigmatizing, a score of 1 constitutes 'failure of international norms to be articulated and/or no stigmatization of the target', with 5 indicating 'clearly articulated norms and full stigmatization/isolation of the target.'[44]

Whether a particular goal of the Security Council is achieved is a necessary, but by no means sufficient, condition for the determination of whether UN sanctions are effective policy instruments. Following scoring of the policy outcome for each purpose in each episode, the specific contribution of UN targeted sanctions to that outcome is assessed for each episode – typically the most difficult analytical aspect of the exercise. Measurement of sanctions contribution considers all of the other instruments utilized by the international community at the same time (such as diplomatic pressure, threats of or the use of force, legal referrals, unilateral or regional sanctions, etc.), indications by the target of the impact and role of UN sanctions, and the relationship between the

---

[42] Hufbauer et al., *Economic Sanctions Reconsidered.*

[43] Note, however, that we have adapted Hufbauer, Schott, and Elliott's metric by creating a five-point scale, rather than the four-point scale they utilize (discussed in more detail below).

[44] The complete coding scheme and scales for each are elaborated in detail in the Codebook in Appendix 3.

specific measures imposed, their purposes, and the policy outcome. Also, an explicit counterfactual analysis is used to consider what might have been the outcome had UN targeted sanctions not been imposed. A six-point scale is used, in which a score of 1 means 'no discernible sanctions contribution', 5 indicates that UN sanctions are the 'single most important factor' to the policy outcome, and 0 signifies that the sanctions contribution is 'negative' (the target is either strengthened or increases its proscribed activity).

The overall effectiveness of UN sanctions is determined for each relevant purpose[45] by creating a new variable which combines minimal threshold scores for both policy outcome and sanctions contribution to that outcome. To be considered effective, a score of 4 or 5 must be attained for policy outcome and a score of 3 or above must be attained for the UN sanctions contribution to that outcome (meaning that in the very least, there should be evidence that sanctions reinforced other policy measures in place at the same time).

The five- and six-point scales and the two-component minimum threshold framework for evaluation are important adaptations of the method used by Hufbauer, Schott, and Elliot in their analysis. While they correctly identify two core components needed for analysis of sanctions effectiveness, their method of assessment is skewed towards overstating positive outcomes. Their scale of policy outcome contains four possible results: failed outcome, unclear, but possibly positive outcome, positive outcome, and successful outcome.[46] Three of their four possible outcomes could be considered positive, potentially biasing their results in the direction of overestimating a change in policy. By contrast, the five-point scale mentioned above contains an equal number of positive and negative possibilities, with a mid-point for ambiguous outcomes. With regard to assessment of sanctions contribution to outcomes, Hufbauer, Schott, and Elliott again utilize a four-point scale, ranging from a negative contribution to three possible types of contribution (little or no, substantial or decisive).[47] Again, in contrast to the six-point scale described above, their measure is skewed towards overestimating sanctions contribution.

To correct for this potential bias, Hufbauer, Schott, and Elliott multiply their two scales to produce a 'success score' ranging in value from 1 to 16 and consider a score of 9 or higher as a 'successful' outcome. Their minimum threshold is high enough to ensure that only positive outcomes to which sanctions made a substantial contribution are considered

---

[45] We say each *relevant* purpose, since all purposes are not present in each episode.
[46] Hufbauer et al., *Economic Sanctions Reconsidered*, pp. 49–50.   [47] *Ibid.*, p. 50.

successful. The problem of using their multiplication formula for the five- and six-point scales discussed above, however, is that a decisive contribution to a mediocre policy outcome would be evaluated the same as a sanction with little or no contribution to a successful policy outcome. Using minimum threshold levels for each dimension (a 4 or 5 for policy outcome and 3 or above for sanctions contribution) avoids this potential problem.

The following coding rules were applied to assess the effectiveness of each purpose within each episode of the UN targeted sanctions surveyed in the TSC research.[48] Coercion is defined in terms of a change of behaviour of the target. Effectiveness of coercion is measured on a continuum ranging from one to five, where (1) is a lack of significant change in behaviour, ignoring the UNSCR, or complete intransigence, (2) refers to agreeing to a process and/or engaging in negotiations that could result in settling or resolving the dispute or in obfuscation, delaying, or changing terms of debate, (3) accommodation or significant concessions to resolve the dispute, (4) meeting most of the objectives of the UNSCR and/or approximating the core purposes as originally articulated in the UNSCR (but not necessarily according to the explicit terms spelled out in the original UNSCR), and (5) is meeting all the principal objectives of the UNSCR.

UN sanctions contribution to coercion is measured on a continuum ranging from zero to five, where (0) is negative because the regime is strengthened and increases its proscribed activity, (1) is none, because there is no discernible sanctions contribution, (2) minor, because other measures taken appear most significant to outcome, (3) modest, because sanctions reinforced other measures, (4) major, because sanctions appear necessary, but not sufficient; or there is some acknowledgement by the target about their impact, and (5) is significant, because the single most important factor to the outcome is the presence of UNSC sanctions.

Constraint includes limiting access to essential resources (finance, goods/technology, arms, expertise, or political options), slowing target activities, buying time for negotiations, and raising costs for targets to continue proscribed activities. Effectiveness is measured on a continuum ranging from one to five, where (1) is no discernible constraints experienced by the target, (2) increases in costs can be managed by the target (sanctions are largely a nuisance factor) perhaps due to ease of evasion, (3) slight increases in costs to target (as evidenced by diversion of trade through third countries, and/or delay in engaging in proscribed activity and/or diminution in the frequency of engagement in proscribed activity),

---

[48] In each of the categories or purpose (coerce, constraint, and signal), there is a primary target or audience (parties to the conflict), which varies by episode.

(4) increases in costs, minor changes of strategy of the target, statement that target may be experiencing financial/material/logistical difficulties and/or constrained from engaging in proscribed activity, and (5) is significant increases in costs, changes of strategy of the target, and/or statement that target is experiencing financial/material/logistical difficulties and/or constrained from engaging in proscribed activity. UN sanctions contribution to constraint is measured in the same way it is measured for coercion.

Signalling/stigmatizing includes signalling targets, third parties, domestic constituencies, and the international community about the consequences of norm violation and stigmatizing or isolating targets and activities for violating international norms. It is measured on a five-point scale from 1 to 5, where (1) is norm (or norms) not articulated, no stigmatization, and/or clear evidence of legitimation, (2) norm (or norms) poorly articulated (e.g. too many, diffusely articulated), limited evidence of stigmatization, and/or possible legitimation, (3) norm (or norms) articulated, and some stigmatization of target, (4) norm (or norms) articulated and targets strongly stigmatized, and (5) norm (or norms) clearly articulated and target fully stigmatized and/or isolated.[49] UN sanctions contribution to signal/stigmatization is measured the same way as it is for coercion and constraint.

It should be noted that unlike many large databases, we have not relied on large numbers of research assistants to conduct the quantitative coding. Each critically important evaluation of UN targeted sanctions effectiveness has been made by the three editors of this volume on a deliberative, consensus (and/or exhaustion) basis. The detailed factual coding of information about each episode (considered for the evaluation of effectiveness in the episode) was made by at least two of the three authors of this chapter, and all of the coding decisions (along with copies of executive summaries of each of the cases) have been sent to the head of the original team of authors of the detailed qualitative case studies, to other country or sanctions experts, and in some cases to UN Panel of Experts members for their evaluation and corrections, as necessary. This significantly increases the reliability of the data by enhancing inter-coder reliability, checking facts, and ensuring a fairly strict process-oriented coding scheme. As a result of this process, the data provided are more sensitive to the history and politics involved in the implementation of targeted sanctions as policy tools.[50] Details about the rationale and

---

[49] This is focused on the international community as the principal audience for signalling. The evaluation of effectiveness of signalling would vary for other audiences.

[50] Kirshner, 'Economic Sanctions: The State of the Art', p. 169.

justification for the determination of effectiveness for each episode for every relevant purpose can be found in Appendix 2 of this book as well as in SanctionsApp, under the section 'Cases and Episodes'.

The effectiveness of UN targeted sanctions

Applying these coding rules and practices to sixty-three different episodes of targeted sanctions for the three different purposes of sanctions produced the following results. UN targeted sanctions were effective in only five out of fifty instances in which the Security Council attempted to coerce a change in target behaviour (or 10 per cent of the time). UN sanctions against Libya (and their strategic suspension at a crucial moment during the final episode of the regime) ultimately resulted in the suspects in the Lockerbie bombing being turned over for trial outside the country, trials conducted, victim compensation provided, and terrorism renounced. Secondary sanctions applied against Eritrea for its export of arms to Somalia resulted in a termination of Eritrea's direct support to Al Shabaab. UN sanctions played an important role in persuading warring factions temporarily to give up violence for participation in an electoral process in the DRC in 2005 and 2006. Diamond sanctions in Sierra Leone and secondary sanctions applied to Liberia contributed to the RUF's decision to sign an unconditional ceasefire agreement in November 2000, and UN targeted sanctions reinforced mediation efforts in the Côte d'Ivoire to persuade the Gbagbo government eventually to hold elections in 2010.

UN targeted sanctions were effective with greater frequency in constraining targets, in sixteen out of fifty-nine episodes (or slightly more than 27 per cent of the time). The sanctions applied against Liberia show evidence of constraint in multiple episodes. For example, in episode 4, following the departure of Charles Taylor and progress in the peace process in Sierra Leone, a peace enforcement sanctions regime was established in Liberia to ensure compliance with the comprehensive peace agreement and to support the transitional government of national unity. The Liberian ceasefire was maintained, DDR implemented, and elections were held during this episode. In late 2003, the Security Council lifted the previous sanctions and immediately reimposed them in support of a new objective: peace enforcement. The Council articulated specific criteria for lifting sanctions, and in March 2004 imposed financial sanctions on Charles Taylor, his family, and other close associates for misappropriating Liberian funds and property and using them to destabilize the transitional government during the early phase of the episode. The Liberia Sanctions Committee Panel of Experts concluded that sanctions helped to stabilize the situation in the country. There are similar examples of effective constraint in the latter stages of conflict and the transition to peacebuilding in other countries, including Angola and Sierra Leone in particular.

Effective signalling was found in a similar number of instances (seventeen) in a slightly larger sample of case episodes (sixty-three), or also about 27 per cent of the time. The fourth episode of the UN targeted sanctions against Angola provides a good illustration of effective signalling. The shooting down of the second of two UN aircraft over UNITA-controlled territory prompted a very strong reaction from the UN Security Council in early 1999. Canadian ambassador Robert Fowler assumed the chair of the Angola Sanctions Committee in the month of January, which set up two expert panels in May (one on financing of UNITA and another on arms) that were later merged. This resulted in a major strengthening of sanctions monitoring at the UN level. The Panel of Expert's 'Fowler Report' was released and created a storm of protest by naming and shaming of sitting African heads of state for their role in circumventing UN sanctions. The Security Council set up a mechanism for monitoring sanctions violations (and threatened secondary sanctions) in April 2000, but none were imposed. One of the purposes of the sanctions (and threatened sanctions) was to stigmatize UNITA and its supporters in other African countries.

The head of UNITA Jonas Savimbi was thoroughly isolated and stigmatized in a UN Security Council resolution in January 1999 (UNSCR 1221) that not only named him in the text of the resolution, but specifically blamed him for the resumption of the armed conflict. The naming of African heads of state in the so-called 'Fowler report' had the effect of publicly shaming them for violating a Chapter VII UN Security Council resolution. The messages were clear and the targets of the naming were either stigmatized or shamed. Sanctions on the territory controlled by UNITA were continued, and there was evidence that they had disrupted UNITA's supply lines. A December 2001 offensive against UNITA ended with Savimbi (and his vice president's) death in February 2002. A truce quickly followed in March, followed by negotiations in April, and UNITA dismantled its armed wing in August. The UN lifted sanctions in December 2002. There are sixteen other episodes during which UN targeted sanctions were effective in signalling and/or stigmatizing their targets, and Table 10.1 provides a list of effective UN targeted sanctions episodes (by purpose).

On average, our analysis of the entire universe of targeted sanctions imposed by the UN Security Council (sixty-three episodes in the last twenty-five years) indicates that sanctions are effective in coercing,

Table 10.1 *Effective UN targeted sanctions episodes*

Coerce	Constrain	Signal
Libya 1 EP3 (1999–2003)	Libya 1 EP1 (1992–1993)	Somalia EP4 (2009–2012)
Somalia EP4 (2009–2012)	Libya 1 EP2 (1993–1999)	Haiti EP1 (1993)
DRC EP2 (2005–2008)	Haiti EP1 (1993)	Haiti EP3 (1993–2004)
Sierra Leone EP4 (2000–2002)	Haiti EP3 (1993–1994)	Liberia EP2 (2001–2003)
Côte d'Ivoire EP3 (2005–2010)	Liberia EP2 (2001–2003)	Liberia EP3 (2003)
	Liberia EP3 (2003)	Liberia EP4 (2003–2006)
	Liberia EP4 (2003–2006)	Liberia EP5 (2006–)
	Liberia EP5 (2006–)	Angola EP3 (1998–1999)
	Angola EP3 (1998–1999)	Angola EP4 (1999–2002)
	Angola EP4 (1999–2002)	Sierra Leone EP1 (1997–1998)
	Sierra Leone EP4 (2000–2002)	Sierra Leone EP4 (2000–2002)
	Sierra Leone EP5 (2002–2010)	Sierra Leone EP5 (2002–2010)
	AQT EP3 (2001–2011)	AQT EP3 (2001–2011)
	AQT EP4 (2011–)	DRC EP2 (2005–2008)
	DRC EP3 (2008–2010)	Côte d'Ivoire EP4 (2010–2011)
	Libya 2 EP2 (2011)	Libya 2 EP1 (2011)
		Libya 2 EP3 (2011–2014)

constraining, or signalling a target about 22 per cent of the time.[51] This measure evaluates all three purposes as being of equal value, regardless of the priority assigned by the Council to each purpose or to the potential difficulty in achieving each of them. If one considers only the principal purpose of the UN Security Council in imposing sanctions during each episode (to coerce, to constrain, or to signal a target), the numbers decline slightly, and sanctions are effective overall about 19 per cent of the time. UN targeted sanctions are ineffective in all of their purposes in 37 per cent of the episodes, and ineffective in their principal purpose 68 per cent of the time.

The analysis becomes more interesting, however, if one disaggregates these numbers into the three distinct purposes of targeted sanctions: to

---

[51] This is calculated on the following basis: a total of thirty-eight case episodes have been evaluated as effective (five in coercing, sixteen in constraining, and seventeen in signalling) out of a total of 172 possible (sixty-three case episodes times three purposes minus seventeen cases of non-applicable objectives; thirteen in coercion and four in constraint): 38/172 = 22.09 per cent. This implies valuing the three distinct purposes of sanctions equally.

Table 10.2 *Sanctions effectiveness distribution*[1]

	Effective (%)	Mixed (%)	Ineffective (%)
Coerce	10	10	80
Constrain	27	17	56
Signal	27	29	44

[1] *Note:* For a detailed definition of these categories and illustrations of effective, ineffective, and mixed cases, see Appendix 2.

coerce, constrain, and to signal. It is immediately apparent that sanctions are far more effective in constraining and signalling (27 per cent) than in coercing a change of behaviour in the target (10 per cent) (Table 10.2).

These general results provide a potential explanation for the so-called sanctions effectiveness debate on the pages of the journal *International Security* during the 1990s. Much has been made of the differing estimates of sanctions effectiveness by Hufbauer, Schott, and Elliott and by Robert Pape from his reanalysis of their data. Pape focused on the coercive aspect of sanctions, and his estimate of effectiveness (6 per cent) is not very different from our estimate of 10 per cent for UN targeted sanctions. Hufbauer, Schott, and Elliott considered more than just the coercive purpose of sanctions, and our higher estimate for the effectiveness in constraining and signalling (27 per cent) is closer to their general estimate of 34 per cent. Figure 10.1 illustrates graphically in histogram form the distribution of effective, mixed, and ineffective case episodes by purpose of sanctions. More details on the basis for these assessments can be found in Appendix 2.

Given that UN targeted sanctions are used to tackle a variety of different challenges to international peace and security, it is useful to consider how effectiveness relates to the different objectives pursued by the Council. UN sanctions have not been effective in coercing, constraining, or signalling in *any* of the seven episodes in which non-proliferation was the principal objective of the Council. By contrast, there is evidence that they have been effective in two-thirds of the episodes when sanctions have been applied to constrain terrorism. They have been most effective in signalling when they are used to indicate concerns about non-constitutional changes of government and in support of peacebuilding efforts.[52] Given the large number of instances in which the Council imposes sanctions to settle

---

[52] While the percentage is high for responsibility to protect, the sample is very small (only two cases).

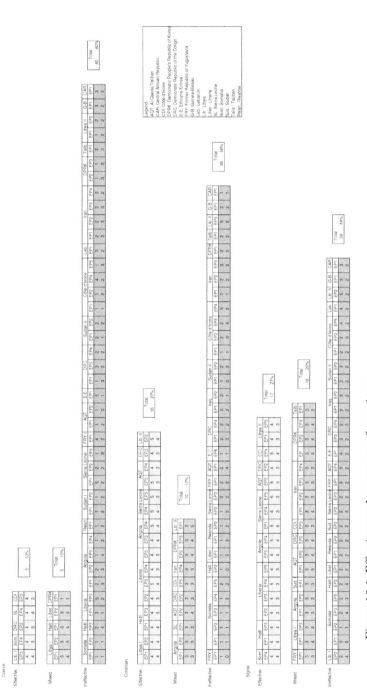

Figure 10.1 Effectiveness by purpose of sanctions

Table 10.3 *Effectiveness by primary objective*

Main objective	Coerce (%)		Constrain (%)		Signal (%)	
Non-proliferation	0/7	0	0/7	0	0/7	0
Counterterrorism	1/7	14	4/6	67	1/9	11
Armed conflict	4/28	14	8/37	22	10/37	27
Democracy support	0/5	0	2/6	33	4/6	67
Good governance	N/A	N/A	1/1	100	1/1	100
R2P	0/2	0	1/2	50	1/2	50
Support judicial process	0/1	0	0/0	N/A	0/1	0
TOTAL	5/50	10	16/59	27	17/63	27

armed conflict (achieve a ceasefire, negotiate a peace agreement, peace enforcement), it is not surprising that the distribution of effectiveness reflects the general distribution in the sample as a whole. Table 10.3 summarizes the results.

Building on the distinction between the different purposes of sanctions (to coerce, constrain, and/or signal), it is possible to discern elements of context, political will, design, relationship with other policy instruments, implementation, evasion, and unintended consequences correlated with effective and ineffective outcomes. It is important to emphasize that these are simply correlations; they are not causal inferences about which combinations of factors will produce particular outcomes. Some of them may be necessary, but they are not necessarily sufficient for effective (or ineffective) outcomes.

Coercion

The relatively small number of instances in which sanctions have been effective in coercing a change in target behaviour share some characteristics that distinguish them from the average patterns observed in the entire set of cases. For example, while they do not have to be based on a unanimous UN Security Council resolution, they are more likely to be effective if the goals are rather narrowly defined (such as to convene elections or turn over suspects in a criminal investigation). The presence of secondary sanctions on a neighbouring country (Liberia in the case of Sierra Leone and Eritrea with regard to Somalia) and efforts to target others in the region show strong evidence of correlation with effective coercion. Imposing financial sector sanctions (such as against the use of a diaspora tax) is strongly correlated with effective coercion, as is having a

Table 10.4 *Correlations with effective coercion*

Effective coercion	Variable	Relation†	Phi coefficient (correlation)	Statistical significance
Political will	United States among leading drafters of UNSCR	↘	−.391	.012
Target	Coerce regional constituencies	↗	.287	.042
	Secondary sanctions	↗↗	.477	.001
Sanction type	Financial sector (diaspora tax)	↗↗	.429	.002
	Kimberley process	↗	.333	.018
Impact	Direct political impact	↗	.297	.042
	Strengthening instruments of the security apparatus of senders	↗↗	.424	.007
Unintended consequences	Increases in corruption/ criminality	↘	−.340	.028

† ↗/↘ evidence of a relation ($p<0.05$*), ↗↗/↘↘ strong evidence of a relation ($p<0.01$**).

direct political impact on the target. The use of multi-stakeholder initiatives such as the Kimberley Process is also important. Among the unintended consequences strongly correlated with effective coercion are a strengthening of the security apparatus of the senders but not any notable increases in corruption and criminality (Table 10.4).

The instances in which attempts to coerce a change in behaviour are notably ineffective are far more numerous (thirty-one cases as opposed to five). They also share characteristics that distinguish them from the average pattern observed in the entire set of cases, often in the exact opposite direction as those just described: in instances of secondary sanctions, engagement of regional actors, financial sector measures, and the use of multi-stakeholder processes like Kimberley. There is good evidence of a correlation between ineffectiveness and attempts to coerce a group engaged in the commitment of acts of terrorism or a state that harbours them. The data suggest that the United States and the United Kingdom are important players in coercion, because if they are directly affected by or involved in the case episode, the episode is less likely to be associated with ineffectiveness. Arms embargoes imposed without other complementary measures (individual sanctions or commodity bans) and after protracted delays tend to be ineffective, as demonstrated in the cases of Somalia, Rwanda, and the Eritrea/Ethiopia war, as are sanctions that are authorized but never imposed, such as the aviation ban in the Sudan or the sanctions authorized, but never applied, in Lebanon (Table 10.5).

Table 10.5 *Correlations with ineffective coercion*

Ineffective coercion	Variable	Relation[†]	Phi coeffi- cient (correlation)	Statistical significance
Background	United States and United Kingdom affected or involved in episode	↘↘	−.505	.000
Sanctions regime details	Unilateral sanctions precede UN sanctions	↘	−.471	.031
Political will	P5 reservations	↘	−.330	.020
Norms signalled	Counterterrorism	↘	−.286	.043
Sanction type	Individual assets freeze on government	↘	−.327	.021
	Secondary sanctions	↘↘	−.505	.000
	Diplomatic: limiting number of diplomatic personnel	↘	−.333	.018
	Financial sector: (diaspora tax)	↘	−.286	.043
	Sectoral: oil services equipment ban	↘↘	−.408	.004
Other actors	Arab League involved	↘	−.327	.021
	Kimberley process	↘	−.333	.018
Other sanctions	OAS sanctions	↘	−.286	.043
Implementation	Cancelation of credits	↗↗	1.0	.008

[†] ↗/↘ evidence of a relation (*p*<0.05⋆), ↗↗/↘↘ strong evidence of a relation (*p*<0.01⋆⋆).

Constraint

There is evidence of a correlation between effective constraint when the primary objective of the sanction is to constrain a group engaged in acts of terrorism and if a terrorist group is the primary target of the sanction. Effective constraint is also strongly associated with support for a judicial process. Interestingly, support for human rights as an objective is inversely associated with effective constraint. With regard to targets, effective constraint is correlated with specific parties to the conflict being identified, rather than situations when 'all parties to the conflict' are identified as the target of the sanctions. There is strong evidence of a positive correlation if key regime supporters are meant to be constrained. With regard to the types of targeted sanctions associated with effective constraint, commodity sanctions (diamond embargoes, timber bans) and aviation bans are particularly effective. So too are government asset freezes and some diplomatic sanctions (such as a tightening of visas or the expulsion of categories of nationals).

Once again, the use of regional courts or special tribunals appears to be strongly correlated with effectiveness, as is the participation of some other actors, such as the Kimberley Process, where relevant (e.g. if diamonds are an important source of revenue for combatants). Although it is probably a reflection of the number of cases of effective constraint in the West African conflicts, there is evidence of correlation between the presence of regional (ECOWAS) sanctions and effective constraint facilitated by UN sanctions. With regard to implementation, there is strong evidence of correlation between travel ban implementation and effective constraint. Once again, evidence of a direct political impact on the target is strongly correlated with effectiveness, as are indications of a direct economic impact (Table 10.6).

When it comes to ineffective efforts to constrain a target, the comparative analysis of case episodes suggests that specific targets should be designated, including family members of the leadership. There is strong evidence of ineffectiveness when 'all parties to the conflict' are designated. There is also strong evidence of a correlation between the absence of commodity sanctions (where relevant), aviation bans, and diplomatic sanctions and ineffective efforts to constrain a target.

With regard to implementation, there is strong evidence of a correlation between ineffectiveness and the failure to specify enforcement authorities and the absence of evidence of direct political, economic, or social-psychological impact on the target. Not requesting Member State reports and the failure to freeze individual accounts are also associated with ineffective efforts to constrain.

Signalling

Effective signalling tends to be associated with UN Security Council attempts to support democracy (or restore unconstitutionally overthrown governments) and support for peace enforcement and peacebuilding activities. Signalling is likely to be effective if family members of the leadership and key regime supporters are targeted. The designation of specific individuals is a key part of effective signalling. In terms of types of sanctions, effective signalling is associated with commodity sanctions, individual sanctions, shipping and transportation restrictions, and secondary sanctions on a neighbouring country. The presence of a peacekeeping operation in a

Table 10.6 *Correlations with effective constraint*

Effective constraint	Variable	Relation†	Phi coefficient (correlation)	Statistical significance
Objectives	Support judicial process	↗↗	.379	.004
	Human rights	↘	−.313	.016
	Primarily counterterrorism	↗	.299	.022
Target	All parties to the conflict target of constraint	↘↘	−.339	.009
	Key regime supporters targets of constraint	↗↗	.377	.004
	Entire government primary target of constraint	↗	.290	.026
	All parties to the conflict primary target of constraint	↘	−.269	.039
	Primarily terrorist group	↗	.307	.018
	Leadership family members target of constraint	↗	.258	.047
Norm signalled	Authority of regional arrangements	↘	−.294	.024
	Primarily counterterrorism	↗	.299	.022
Sanction type	Assets freeze on political entities	↗	.258	.047
	Diplomatic: limit travel of diplomatic personnel	↗↗	.427	.001
	Diplomatic: revision of visa policy	↗↗	.362	.005
	Diplomatic: limit number of diplomatic personnel	↗	.307	.018
	Commodity sanctions	↗	.303	.020
	Sectoral: aviation ban	↗↗	.377	.004
	Commodity: diamonds export	↗↗	.491	.000
	Commodity: timber export	↗↗	.379	.004
	Diplomatic sanctions	↗↗	.436	.001
Other actors involved	Kimberley Process	↗↗	.427	.001
	World Food Programme	↘	−.333	.013
	UNDP	↘	−.293	.028
	IAEA	↘	−.259	.047
Other sanctions	ECOWAS sanctions	↗	.295	.023
Other policy instruments	Significant diplomatic pressure or multilateral negotiations	↘	−.307	.018
	Other international courts of tribunals	↗↗	.519	.000
	Force: naval blockade	↗	.307	.018
Implementation and enforcement	Evidence of travel ban implementation	↗↗	.520	.002

Table 10.6 (*cont.*)

Effective constraint	Variable	Relation[†]	Phi coefficient (correlation)	Statistical significance
Impact	Direct political impact	↗↗	.462	.001
	Direct economic impact	↗	.297	.031
Evasion/coping	Evasion: disguise vessels	↘	−.301	.032
	Evasion: disguise of identity/ use of forged documents	↗	.344	.017
	Coping: import substitutions or development of new technology	↘	−.277	.038
Unintended consequences	Reduction of local institutional capacity	↗	.287	.044
	Increase in international enforcement capacity in different issue domains	↗	.284	.044
	Widespread harmful economic consequences	↗	.392	.013

[†] ↗/↘ evidence of a relation (*p*<0.05*), ↗↗/↘↘ strong evidence of a relation (*p*<0.01**).

neighbouring country is also correlated with effective signalling, as are other processes (like commodity certification schemes), regional sanctions, and efforts to secure disarmament, demobilization, and reintegration of military forces.

With regard to implementation, effective signalling is correlated with enforcement authorities being clearly specified. Enforcement of a travel ban is also correlated with effective signalling. There is strong evidence of a correlation between effective signalling and indications of a direct political and social psychological impact. Effective signalling is strongly correlated with an increase in international enforcement capacity in different issue domains. Unfortunately, however, widespread economic harm and evidence of humanitarian consequences are also associated with effective signalling (Table 10.7).

There is strong evidence of a correlation between ineffective signalling and the absence of any direct political impact on the target. There is also evidence of an association between ineffective signalling and efforts to cease hostilities and negotiate a peace settlement when the facilitators of proscribed activity and the entire government are not targeted. The absence of commodity sanctions (where appropriate) is also associated with ineffective signalling.

Table 10.7 *Correlations with effective signalling*

Effective signalling	Variable	Relation[†]	Phi coefficient (correlation)	Statistical significance
General background	France is among states affected or involved by case	↘	−.256	.042
Objectives	Democracy support	↗↗	.355	.005
	Peace enforcement	↗	.260	.039
	Primarily democracy support	↗	.290	.021
Target	Leadership family members subject to signal	↗↗	.397	.002
	Key regime supporters subject to signal	↗↗	.350	.003
	Individual targets subject to signal	↗	.280	.026
Norm signalled	Support democracy/oppose non-constitutional changes of government	↗	.248	.049
	Primarily non-constitutional change in government	↗↗	.354	.005
Sanction type	Sanctions imposed for a specific time period	↗	.249	.048
	Individual sanctions	↗	.273	.031
	Arms imports embargo on government forces	↘	−.296	.028
	Shipping and transportation	↗↗	.368	.004
	Petroleum imports ban	↗	.305	.015
	Diamond exports	↗↗	.568	.000
	Timber exports	↗↗	.368	.004
	Commodity sanctions	↗↗	.507	.000
	Secondary sanctions	↗	.282	.025
Other actors	IAEA	↘	−.248	.049
	Kimberley Process	↗↗	.413	.001
	Peacekeeping mission in neighbouring country	↗	.282	.029
	ECOWAS	↗	.303	.016
Other sanctions	ECOWAS sanctions	↗↗	.380	.003
Other policy instruments	DDR/SSR	↗	.268	.033
Implementation and enforcement	Evidence of travel ban implementation	↗	.357	.028
	Enforcement authorities specified	↗	.288	.025
Impact	Direct political impact	↗↗	.448	.001
	Direct social or psychological impact	↗↗	.341	.009
	Direct economic impact	↗	.280	.035

Table 10.7 (*cont.*)

Effective signalling	Variable	Relation[†]	Phi coefficient (correlation)	Statistical significance
Unintended consequences	Increase in international enforcement capacity in different issue domains	↗↗	.377	.006
	Widespread harmful economic consequences	↗	.305	.045
	Humanitarian consequences	↗	.276	.042

[†] ↗/↘ evidence of a relation (*p*<0.05*), ↗↗/↘↘ strong evidence of a relation (*p*<0.01**).

Conclusion

The scholarly literature and public debate regarding the effectiveness of sanctions is still dominated by a preoccupation with their ability to coerce a change in behaviour of a target, and generally fail to differentiate between comprehensive and targeted measures. Since targeted sanctions are increasingly the instrument of choice (i.e. the only type of sanctions being imposed by the United Nations and the European Union, and the predominant form of sanctions being imposed by the United States), it is time that the scholarly and public analysis of sanctions effectiveness caught up with current practice. Targeted sanctions are imposed for multiple purposes, so it is also important that sanctions effectiveness be evaluated in terms of their differing purposes and that analysis take account of the variation over time in sanctions type, target, and scope.

This chapter reviewed the literature, proposed new concepts and ideas for the assessment of targeted sanctions, and applied those ideas to an analysis of the full universe of UN targeted sanctions imposed over the past twenty-five years. Breaking country regimes down into discrete case episodes as the unit of analysis allows a better understanding of transformations (of purpose, target, context, and sanctions measures) in the larger country regime that occur over time. The expansion of the potential purposes of targeted sanctions beyond coercing a change in the behaviour of targets to include constraining targets from engaging in proscribed activities and the signalling and stigmatizing of targets for violations of international norms permits deeper analysis of the multiple purposes pursued by the senders of sanctions.

There are, of course, limits to the preceding analysis, and further development and refinement of the framework for assessing the effectiveness of sanctions should be undertaken. First, the threat phase of sanctions was not included in the database or the preceding discussion. The formal model literature, in particular, argues that the threat of sanctions should be more effective on balance than the imposition of sanctions'.[53] This is an important insight, and in future developments of the two databases, we intend to add the threat phase to the initial episode of each country case.[54] Second, we do not systematically consider cases in which sanctions could have been imposed but were not. This counterfactual aspect would be necessary if we were to try to go beyond the consideration of correlation to suggest potential causation.

Two other factors merit consideration in future analyses of sanctions effectiveness. First, the unintended consequences of targeted sanctions should be factored explicitly into future analysis. There are instances in which the harmful unintended consequences of sanctions could overwhelm the significance of an effective policy outcome. This was certainly the case with comprehensive sanctions,[55] but the tendency to employ targeted sanctions with broader, less discriminating impacts (discussed in more detail in Chapter 12) suggests that it is important to include consideration of unintended consequences in the larger policy analysis of targeted sanctions as well. Second, while most of the cost–benefit analysis of sanctions policy concentrates on calculations made by the target, sanctions also have an impact on their senders. Although difficult to measure, the administrative costs for states implementing the measures should be included, not to mention the considerable costs of compliance borne by private sector institutions (particularly financial institutions, in the case of asset freezes).

Taking unintended consequences and costs to both targets and senders into consideration would provide a more accurate measurement of the utility of UN targeted sanctions as an instrument of global governance. They would also help us appreciate better the policy choices faced by decision-makers, as suggested by David Baldwin,[56] and to understand how sanctions actually work, as suggested by Jonathan Kirshner.[57]

---

[53] Hovi, Huseby, and Sprinz, 'When Do (Imposed) Economic Sanctions Work?'.
[54] It would be much more difficult, if not impossible, to discern the threat phase in subsequent episodes, since targeted sanctions are by their nature susceptible to constant adaptation and incremental adjustment and hence inherently contain an ongoing threat.
[55] J. Mueller and K. Mueller, 'Sanctions of Mass Destruction', *Foreign Affairs*, 78 (1999), pp. 43–51; T. G. Weiss et al.(eds.), *Political Gain and Civilian Pain: Humanitarian Impacts of Economic Sanctions* (Lanham: Rowman & Littlefield Publishers, 1997); J. Gordon, *Invisible War: The United States and the Iraq Sanctions* (Cambridge: Harvard University Press, 2010).
[56] Baldwin, 'The Sanctions Debate and the Logic of Choice'.
[57] Kirshner, 'Economic Sanctions: The State of the Art'.

Finally, the research approach described above could also be extended to include targeted sanctions imposed by other institutions, particularly at regional level.[58] Regional institutions like the African Union, the European Union, and the Economic Community of West African States frequently impose targeted sanctions and should be priorities for further research. Assembling data on their design and application of targeted sanctions would be useful not only for comparative analysis but also for a better understanding of their interaction with UN targeted sanctions.

[58] This could also be extended to the analysis of targeted sanctions measures imposed by individual states.

11 Institutional learning in targeting sanctions

Peter Wallensteen

Departing from the new TSC data on sanctions episodes, this chapter explores institutional learning in the use of UN targeted sanctions. Thus, lessons can be based on experiences accumulated since the early 1990s. Although there is an increase of sanctions regimes regionally, as well as by national governments, the UN remains the most legitimate international body for sanctions action universally, and hence it is the focus of the chapter.[1]

First, it is important to note how the sanctions debate has changed over the years, and how this results in new types of sanctions. The discussion has moved from the issue of automatic sanctions to counter aggression in the 1930s, to their use in the Cold War for furthering decolonization, to the hope of building a new post–Cold War order without civil wars, with fewer nuclear weapons states, and less terrorism, all to be achieved increasingly with targeted sanctions.[2]

Interestingly, there are now some typical differences in the aims of various sanctions senders. The contrast between the EU and the UN is particularly noteworthy, where the former focuses more on the conditions for democracy and human rights,[3] while the latter concentrates on peace and security. The African Union has also become an important

---

[1] K. A. Elliott, 'Trends in Economic Sanctions Policy: Challenges to Conventional Wisdom', in P. Wallensteen and C. Staibano (eds.), *International Sanctions: Between Words and Wars in the Global System* (New York, NY: Frank Cass, 2005), pp. 3–14.

[2] P. Wallensteen (ed.), 'A Century of Economic Sanctions: A Field Revisited', in *Peace Research: Theory and Practice* (London: Routledge, 2011), pp. 183–205.

[3] C. Portela, *European Union Sanctions and Foreign Policy: When and Why Do They Work?* (London: Routledge, 2010); M. Eriksson, *Targeting Peace, Understanding UN and EU Targeted Sanctions* (Farnham, UK: Ashgate, 2010); F. Giumelli, *Coercing, Constraining and Signalling: Explaining and Understanding International Sanctions After the End of the Cold War* (Colchester: ECPR Press, 2011); F. Giumelli, *The Success of Sanctions: Lessons Learned from the EU Experience* (Farnham, UK: Ashgate, 2013); P. Wallensteen, 'Sanctions in Africa: International Resolve and Prevention of Conflict Escalation', in T. Ohlson (ed.), *From Intra-State War to Durable Peace: Conflict and Its Resolution in Africa after the Cold War* (Dordrecht: Republic of Letters Publishing, 2012), pp. 121–43; also see Portela and Charron in Chapter 5 this volume.

international actor in sanctions, particularly for upholding constitutional rights in African countries and thus actively signalling that military and political coups (unconstitutional changes of government) are unacceptable.[4] (See Chapter 5 for a detailed discussion of variations in regional sanctions regimes.)

Thus, there is a proliferation of international actors using sanctions, which makes the question of sanctions effectiveness highly pertinent. There are, furthermore, several reasons to expect improvement in the sanctions record, as the sanctions debate has been vigorous, notably in relation to the Iraq sanctions and their observed humanitarian impact.[5] It is equally reasonable to anticipate an impact of the three major efforts at reforming sanctions: the Interlaken, Bonn-Berlin, and Stockholm processes.[6] There have been definite changes in the procedures of the UN Secretariat to improve sanctions implementation, in particular in administering more targeted sanctions measures.[7] Today there are no comprehensive UN sanctions. Other senders of sanctions may, however, have applied more general measures, notably the recent EU and US sanctions on Iran, that affect the entire economy of the target. The hope in targeting particular sectors, commodities, or individuals is, of course, that this would contribute to compliance, and at a lower cost in terms of human suffering.

With the database developed by the Targeted Sanctions Consortium, it is possible to measure more carefully what has actually happened in this regard. The contribution of TSC is at least twofold: developing the notion of sanctions episodes and making possible the independent evaluation of

---

[4] M. Eriksson, *Supporting Democracy in Africa: African Union's Use of Targeted Sanctions to Deal with Unconstitutional Changes of Government* (Stockholm: FOI Swedish Defence Research Agency, 2010).

[5] See D. Cortright and G. A. Lopez, *Smart Sanctions: Targeting Economic Statecraft* (Landham, MD: Rowman & Littlefield, 2002); A. Griffiths and C. Barnes (eds.), *Power of Persuasion: Incentives, Sanctions and Conditionality in Peacemaking* (London: Conciliation Resources, 2008); Wallensteen, 'A Century of Economic Sanctions: A Field Revisited', pp. 183–205.

[6] T. Biersteker, S. Eckert, A. Halegua, N. Reid, and P. Romaniuk, *Targeted Financial Sanctions: A Manual for Design and Implementation – Contributions from the Interlaken Process* (Brown University: Watson Institute for International Studies, 2001); M. Brzoska (ed.), *Design and Implementation of Arms Embargoes and Travel and Aviation Related Sanctions: Results of the 'Bonn-Berlin Process'* (Bonn: International Center for Conversion, 2001); P. Wallensteen, C. Staibano, and M. Eriksson, *Making Targeted Sanctions Effective: Guidelines for the Implementation of UN Policy Options* (Uppsala: Report from The Stockholm Process, 2003); Wallensteen and Staibano (eds.), *International Sanctions: Between Words and Wars in the Global System.*

[7] T. Biersteker, S. Eckert, A. Halegua, and P. Romaniuk, 'Consensus from the Bottom-Up? Assessing the Influence from the Sanctions Reform Process', in P. Wallensteen and C. Staibano (eds.), *International Sanctions. Between Words and Wars in the Global System* (New York: Frank Cass, 2005), pp. 15–30.

these episodes in a comparative, systematic way. The TSC has ventured into episodes of sanctions, which are defined as 'periods in which the sanctions regime remains stable in terms of purposes, types, targets, and context'.[8] This builds on previous research demonstrating the utility of such an approach,[9] and no project has pursued this as far as the TSC.

This approach means, in essence, capturing important turning points in the sanctions cases, notably the use of new sanctions or changes in the motive or targets of the sanctions. As explained more fully in Chapter 1, a new episode commences when there is a new and significant decision by the UN Security Council changing the sanctions operation qualitatively. Thus, the TSC database has sixty-three episodes of targeted sanctions, based on twenty-three country regimes of UN sanctions. All have been initiated since the end of the Cold War, that is, from 1991 onwards.[10]

An innovation in the TSC database is that cases of sanctions empirically vary between one and five different episodes, each of which is evaluated independently. Different researchers have been engaged for initial research on each of the country cases, following a clearly laid out template. This provides for a thorough assessment independent from various theoretical concerns. In particular, it makes considerable sense to expect sanctions to be more effective immediately after their imposition. The classical approach of evaluating sanctions as an entire case makes this more difficult. A traditional sanctions hypothesis has been that the measures will have more effect after a longer period of time. It is, however, more likely that, as sanctions continue, politics and economics will adjust to the new situation. Thus, each new sanctions decision, or sanctions episode, is likely to have a renewed impact on the targeted actors. At a minimum, it serves to remind the targeted actors of the

---

[8] T. Biersteker, S. Eckert, M. Tourinho, and Z. Hudáková, *The Effectiveness of United Nations Targeted Sanctions: Findings from the Targeted Sanctions Consortium (TSC)* (Geneva: the Graduate Institute, 2013), p. 12.

[9] M. Eriksson, *Targeting the Leadership of Zimbabwe: A Path to Democracy and Normalization?* (Uppsala: Uppsala University, SPITS, 2007), available at: http://pcr.uu .se/research/smartsanctions/spits_news_and_publications/; Eriksson, *Targeting Peace, Understanding UN and EU Targeted Sanctions*.

[10] This means that the comprehensive sanctions on Iraq, wisely, are omitted from the analysis. This still points to an interesting follow-up project of evaluating the Iraq sanctions in the same way as is done here for the other cases. There has been surprisingly little independent analysis of the Iraq case (one attempt was *The 2004 Workshop* on UN Sanctions against Iraq: Lessons Learned), even though many of the documents of the former Iraqi regime of Saddam Hussein have been obtained after the US-led invasion of 2003 and are available to scholars. Similarly, with the exception of the work by N. Crawford and A. Klotz, *How Sanctions Worked in South Africa* (Palgrave: Macmillan, 1999), there has been little interest in South Africa in evaluating the impact of the international sanctions on the fall of *apartheid*. Historically inclined sanctions researchers face interesting challenges!

international concern that their action has generated; at a maximum it may increase pressure and the likelihood of compliance. The basic methodological assumption is that each episode can be treated as independent from the previous ones in the same case. Chapters 1 and 10 of this volume have a more elaborate treatment of the methodological implications of this issue. This chapter discusses – based on the TSC data – lessons learned that are relevant for institutions using sanctions.

Sanctions effectiveness: a constant concern

The central policy question on sanctions has always been whether this particular tool is able to provide the outcome that the decision-makers desire.

The traditional way of dealing with the outcome has been to go country case by country case. If sanctions were instituted at time point T1, does the target comply with the demands at T2? When T2 becomes T3 or T4, it will mostly not correspond to the political timetable of decision-makers. There is an expectation of early results. Much of sanctions research has, however, been country case oriented, meaning that each case is followed to its logical conclusion. Thus, sanctions impact is often measured long after the imposition of sanctions. This makes it hard to assess the specific impact of sanctions on the outcome. As time goes by, there are also other events that affect the final outcome. Having a much broader definition of sanctions or a much larger number of sanctions (including also unilateral and regional sanctions) is one way to reach conclusions with a statistical method. However, there are not that many cases of UN sanctions for statistics to be as useful. The TSC identifies only twenty-three country cases or regimes in the entire universe of UN targeted sanctions initiated before 1 January 2014. Thus, the idea of studying different episodes within a country sanctions regime increases the number of cases and shortens the time between imposition and the evaluation of impact. In this way, the TSC database provides a basis for systematic inquiry that can respond to questions such as these: Do sanctions achieve the goals set by the sender (in a short time), and, if not, what can be done to improve sanctions effectiveness?

However, sanctions research demonstrates the complications with such simple questions. First of all, it is not always the case that the sender of sanctions actually expects an immediate result. If compliance takes place that is a bonus, but often there are more immediate goals that lead to a decision to impose sanctions. For instance, there is often a political need to manage a crisis situation, demonstrate resolve, and score points for action. It is not likely to be admitted by policymakers, but the pattern is visible when looking at sanctions in a more historical light.[11] From this point of view, it means that sanctions are not imposed under optimal conditions or when they are most likely to be effective. It may also mean that the 'political will' to pursue the sanctions is limited, which affects their effectiveness.

Second, the kind of compliance that is expected can be variously defined, ranging from a limited ambition of making the targeted actor willing to enter into negotiations to fundamental demands of regime change. It should be emphasized that the latter is really challenging: whatever means are used, it is likely to be difficult to bring down governments or achieve a basic revision of policies that leaders have been committed to for many years. It goes without saying that the more limited the goals of the sanctions, the more likely sanctions are to be effective. However, the decision to impose sanctions may not be limited to such achievable goals, and we can note that sanctions often tend to have more ambitious aims. This affects their credibility as a coercive, but non-military instrument for the international community.

In the TSC project there are three ways in which sanctions are seen to be effective. The first is through *coercing* an actor to do something (that it seems unwilling to do in the first place), notably to change its behaviour. Such change is measured on a five-point scale based on the level of compliance with the demands of the UN Security Council. What is unique is that the TSC assesses the UN sanctions contribution to such a change. This is measured, on a six-point scale. Similarly, the way an actor is *constrained* is evaluated, notably, through the observable costs to, or change in the strategy of, the target. This is also done for the third effectiveness variable where *signalling and/or stigmatization* of the target are evaluated.

This provides us with highly useful information, not the least since the episodes cover all UN sanctions from 1991 until the end of 2013 – that is, from the case of former Yugoslavia in 1991 to the one of CAR in 2013.[12] The variety of cases is large, and together the cases demonstrate that considerable international energy has often gone into making sanctions effective. One can always debate if the 'energy' devoted to the sanctions is sufficient, but that is another matter. The database provides for an independent evaluation of the outcome. This is of value for the practitioners of sanctions decision-making as well as for the scholarly analysts.

---

[11] A first work along this line was by Fredrik Hoffman in 1967. See F. Hoffman, 'The Functions of Economic Sanctions', *Journal of Peace Research*, 4 (1967), pp. 40–160.

[12] A new sanctions regime was imposed on Yemen in 2014, but is not included in the data presented here.

Table 11.1 *Effectiveness of UN targeted sanctions over time and by sanctions purpose, 1992–2013*

| | Effective targeted sanctions | | | | | | | |
| | Coerce | | Constrain | | Signal | | Total | |
Period	Frequency	%	Frequency	%	Frequency	%	Frequency	%
1992–2002	1/21	5	7/21	33	6/23	26	14/65	22
2003–2013	4/29	14	9/38	24	11/40	28	24/107	22
Entire period	5/50	10	16/59	27	17/63	27	38/172	22

Note: Percentages are calculated from valid cases only; non-applicable and missing data are excluded. Sanctions episodes are allocated into the two time periods based on the end date of each episode. The total number of sanctions episodes is sixty-three in twenty-three country sanctions regimes. The purposes vary for each episode, making a total of 172 in Table 11.1. Effectiveness is as assessed by the TSC team. For details see Appendix 2. I am grateful for Ms Zuzana Hudáková for compiling the data.

The most demanding of the three purposes of sanctions is coercing – that is, changing the target's behaviour to meet the demands of the UN. Although there are no examples of effective coercion before 2002, it is difficult to discern much of a trend over time. The percentage of case episodes coded as effective in coercing a change in target behaviour is generally low, as has also been reported from other sanctions studies. The TSC database yields only a 10 per cent effectiveness for all the episodes of UN targeted sanctions where there was an intention to coerce, that is, five of fifty (see also Biersteker et al.,[13] Chapter 10 in this volume, and Table 11.1 above).[14] Moreover, it is difficult to establish a noticeable rate of improved effectiveness during the period.

However, this cannot be considered as the full story. As mentioned, the TSC database includes two additional purposes against which to measure effectiveness: constraining and signalling. For the sanctions episodes, there is a reported constraining effect in more than one quarter of the cases and similarly for signalling. Considering all three purposes taken together, this means that there is effectiveness 22 per cent of the time.[15]

[13] Biersteker, Eckert, Tourinho, and Hudáková, *The effectiveness of United Nations Targeted Sanctions: Findings from the Targeted Sanctions Consortium (TSC)*.

[14] TSC coding considers UN Sanctions effective if signal outcome is 4 or 5 on an outcome scale and sanctions contribution to outcome is coded 3, 4, or 5.

[15] This is calculated on the following basis: a total of thirty-eight case episodes have been evaluated as effective (five in coercing, sixteen in constraining, and seventeen in signalling) out of a total of 172 possible (sixty-three case episodes times three purposes minus seventeen cases of non-applicable objectives; thirteen in coercion and four in constraint).

The yardstick for effectiveness can be debated, as few international instruments are evaluated in a comparable way – something we will come back to later in this chapter. Still, we can conclude that the less ambitious goals of constraining and signalling may be easier to achieve.

For leaders in targeted countries, sanctions may give them more problems than has previously been the case. In related research, signalling has been observed as important in EU sanctions.[16] It remains to be seen how it could eventually translate into the political compliance the UN is demanding.

Obviously, the three types of purposes are defined independently of each other, which makes it possible to see if there is a combined effect of sanctions that is more pronounced today than previously. There is, however, only one episode that can be defined as fully effective (i.e. scoring high on all three purposes of UN targeted sanctions): Sierra Leone, episode 4. In addition, two-fifths of case episodes have achieved at least one or two ratings as effective, which for four case episodes meant the sanctions were effective in both of their intended purposes.[17] The number of cases with no sanction purpose considered effective remains the largest category, with about three-fifths of all cases. The inevitable conclusion is that sanctions, in spite of attempts at improving their performance, continue to have difficulties in achieving stated goals. Certainly, many, not to say most, sanctions do make the life of a recalcitrant actor more uncomfortable than before. But the possibility for the target to sustain its preferred policy remains, as long as it is encountering sanctions as the only or primary vehicle for compliance. It remains true that sanctions provide the target with an incentive to adjust its position or initiate negotiations. For most actors, be they governments or non-state actors, it is preferable not to be exposed to such visible, external pressures. The targeted actor must carefully weigh the cost of compliance against the cost of non-compliance. Stigmatization could be even more costly in a day and age of social media where matters of 'good will' and 'bad will' are quickly communicated, thus affecting increasingly large audiences, including those inside the targeted country.

Still, a clear lesson is that sanctions, by themselves, have difficulties in achieving the change the sender may desire. For any sending institution, in other words, the use of sanctions has to be considered in a larger, more strategic perspective. This is an important lesson that also needs to be

---

38/172 = 22.09 per cent. This implies valuing the three distinct purposes of sanctions equally.

[16] See Giumelli, *Coercing, Constraining and Signalling: Explaining and Understanding International Sanctions after the End of the Cold War.*

[17] These are AQT episode 3, Sierra Leone episode 5, and Liberia episodes 4 and 5.

institutionalized in sanctions institutions. It remains challenging to determine how this can be done, as it has to do with the onset of sanctions. Which are the procedures involved in deciding on sanctions in a particular case? The strategic use of sanctions means that the targeting of sectors, as well as of individuals, has to be subjected to a careful analysis. Institutionally this may mean that a secretariat in an international body should also be entrusted with the task of developing contingency plans for particular crisis situations. In this way the ultimate decision-makers would have more options when deciding how to act in a particular crisis situation. If sanctions were used in cases where they are more likely to be effective in causing a change in the target, the rates of effectiveness would also be affected. The lesson that needs to be institutionalized, in other words, is this: 'Use sanctions only when there is a good chance of having a desired impact.'

Studying sequencing: a new possibility

There could also be an observable pattern where sanctions become increasingly effective as the case goes on. This is contrary to many theories that anticipate a decline in sanctions efficiency as targets adapt to the measures over time.[18] The episode approach makes it possible to study this proposition more carefully, which will be illustrated below.

From the data, we can observe that it is mostly during the first or second episode that sanctions do not have a discernible impact, while in subsequent episodes they are more likely to be assessed to be effective by the TSC data. We can observe this pattern when we consider the sequence of sanctions episodes within individual cases – within case analysis as suggested by George and Bennett[19] – with regard to coercing Libya in the 1990s, Sierra Leone, and the Côte d'Ivoire.[20] It suggests that the renewal and extension of sanctions are observed by the targets and thus are likely to have an observable impact. This comes closer to a type of sanctions policy where a first set of sanctions are followed by increasingly 'harsher' measures at other junctures, providing for a cumulative effect on the target. The third and fourth round of sanctions may demonstrate the international community's persistence, and thus, in particular, contribute

---

[18] J. Galtung, 'On the Effects of International Economic Sanctions: With Examples from the Case of Rhodesia', *World Politics*, 19 (1967), pp. 378–416.

[19] A. L. George and A. Bennett, *Case Studies and Theory Development in the Social Sciences* (Cambridge, MA: MIT Press, 2005).

[20] Somalia is an extreme case; the sanctions from 1992 were not followed up until 2002 and then again not until 2008. For three episodes, little impact is recorded in the TSC database, but the most recent case from 2012 is rated higher.

to the stigmatizing effect. This, of course, assumes that the international authority does not change its purpose vis-à-vis the sanctions. In that situation, the sanctions case, so to say, starts all over again.

The dynamics can be seen most clearly in the situations where the sanctions are aimed at ending an ongoing war.[21] The first rounds of sanctions on Yugoslavia, Liberia, Angola, Sierra Leone, Côte d'Ivoire, AQT, and DRC were not judged to be effective, but later rounds were. This is also true when examining the coding of the effectiveness of coercion, as found in the TSC database. It is, furthermore, interesting to note that the post-war sanctions also appear to have a constraining effect on the actors (notably in Liberia and Sierra Leone). The sanctions with the least constraining effect on civil war situations were those of Sudan and the Taliban.

In a similar way, the targeting of particular individuals could follow a sequence, increasingly involving more significant actors, notably the leadership. However, there is little evidence of this in many of the sanctions implemented between 2000 and 2009.[22] Interestingly, the 2011 sanctions on the Libyan leader Muammar Qadhafi followed a sequence that may be more effective: beginning at the top, rather than targeting the lower echelons that can influence little in reality. In the TSC data, the case of Libya in 2011 gets high marks in constraining and signalling, that is, two of the three dimensions of effectiveness. This case may yield more important lessons for sanctions than it is normally credited with. It may still be an exceptional case.

Such critical remarks, however, do not lead to the conclusion that sanctions should be abandoned. Nor do we see empirically that this is what happens. It is clear that the first sanctions episodes are followed by new sanctions in nearly all the country regimes, although the time lag is sometimes quite large, notably in the case of Somalia, for which it was ten years between the first episode and the second one. In the Libya case, however, there were three sanctions episodes in relatively quick succession.

Bringing this together with the previous section, we can conclude that targeted sanctions have, on the whole, been generally as effective as comprehensive sanctions. The expectations may have been higher, no doubt, but it is still a noteworthy outcome, particularly given their generally more limited scope. The dynamics of the situation have been shifted. It means that the costs to innocent populations have been lowered

[21] War is defined in line with the criteria of Uppsala Conflict Data Program, see www.ucdp .uu.se.
[22] P. Wallensteen and H. Grusell, 'Targeting the Right Targets? The UN Use of Individual Sanctions', *Global Governance*, 18 (2012), pp. 207–30.

for achieving the same result, which must be regarded as a definite gain. However, we are far from a situation where sanctions achieve the rapid and uncompromising compliance that is often expected of them.

As we have just seen, there are indications that those later sanctions in the same case country regime do have more impact than the earlier sanctions in the same case. This is important to build on for the future. There are definite lessons to be learned and that is something new that emerges from this data.

Still, the finding on the low rate of effectiveness is consistent with a host of studies. It should be recalled that this is not something exclusive to sanctions as a policy tool. Military actions also seem limited in achieving the stated objectives, where, for instance, the 'success-rate' of air campaigns is routinely low,[23] as is the general effectiveness of military might as such.[24] The failure of the US air campaign against North Vietnam is a classic example, as is the German Blitz against Great Britain during the Second World War. In fact, there are many lessons to be learned from such military campaigns for sanctions research and sanctions policy. Air campaigns are particularly interesting, not the least as they seem to solve similar policy dilemmas as sanctions: there is a need to act, but the need does not involve putting one's own ground forces at substantial risk. More recently, the use of no-fly zones has drawn attention, for instance. In the military literature, the conclusion is often that actions have to be part of a strategy where different military tools are coordinated into a coherent international strategy. This also seems to be true for international sanctions.

The closest thing to a peaceful use of force is peacekeeping. Peacekeeping operations could be expected to contribute to constraining civil war actors, in particular, and have not been employed in cases of non-proliferation or terrorism.[25] However, there are often inspection teams in the cases of non-proliferation, notably United Nations Special Commission (UNSCOM) for Iraq in the 1990s and the IAEA in the cases of Iran and North Korea today. To some degree these are the functional equivalents to peacekeeping, as they are also monitoring the implementation of accords. For terrorism there is no clear-cut correspondence, unless one could see the International Security Assistance Force (ISAF)

---

[23] R. A. Pape, *Bombing to Win: Air Power and Coercion in War* (Ithaca, NY: Cornell University Press, 1996); M. Clodfelter, *The Limits of Air Power: The American Bombing of North Vietnam*, 2nd edn (New York, NY: Free Press, 2006).

[24] D. Byman and M. Waxman, *The Dynamics of Coercion: American Foreign Policy and the Limits of Military Might* (New York, NY: Cambridge University Press, 2002).

[25] This raises an interesting question of whether some of the sanctions, for instance, on North Korea, would benefit from a maritime peace operation.

operations in Afghanistan and United Nations Multidimensional Integrated Stabilization Mission (MINUSMA) in Mali in this light. The contribution of such operations pursued to achieve a ceasefire or promote peace talks, in parallel to the sanctions effort, would be important to analyse. A first cut at exploring this relationship demonstrates that in those cases where sanctions are coded as effective in constraining actors, for instance, in Libya in 2011, there was no peacekeeping operation. However, this case and others saw some military action. It remains legitimate to ask if the combination of sanctions and peacekeeping or more intrusive operations would be a stronger way for the international community to influence actors to comply with UN decisions. Again, we observe that the coordination of sanctions efforts, diplomacy, and peacekeeping remains a challenge for UN sanctions policy. It is important to integrate this observation with the one in the previous section: there is a need to find an institutional way in which to embed the strategic use of sanctions as part of a package of instruments. The lesson is quite obvious: each individual tool in the UN peacemaking kit would benefit from a closer coordination with the others. The challenge is to translate this into an effective institutional arrangement.

Learning implementation

There is no doubt that the UN and the UN Member States have learned a lot about the implementation of sanctions, particularly if we compare the very early post–Cold War sanctions to the present situation. The Security Council Sanctions Committees take more responsibility, visit the conflict zones, and involve themselves in novel ways. The innovation of highly committed Panels of Experts is a most useful device in highlighting the implementation of sanctions. The targeting of particular individuals has become more precise and more consonant with human rights considerations, although there is still a reluctance to target top leaders in many cases. Charles Taylor and the Qadhafi family constitute exceptions. There is more reporting on sanctions implementation by Member States, following more systematic inquiries from sanctions committees. Thus, there is an increased understanding of the way sanctions function, and also in the way the targets can evade sanctions.

One way to read the effectiveness statistics is that the UN has actually been able to keep up with the times. International globalization provides for more ways in which targets can learn how to evade sanctions. Measures such as travel bans and the freezing of financial resources could become more difficult to enforce as the banking system diversifies and travel options increase. Thus, we should have expected the effectiveness to gradually go down. In short, evasion benefits from globalization. However, the statistics make clear that there is no such reduction in effectiveness. Sanctions remain useful throughout the period. In the TSC data, as indicated in Table 11.1, sanctions appear somewhat more effective in coercing the target over time.[26] Dividing this into two equally long periods (eleven years), the rate of effectiveness goes from 5 to 14 per cent. It suggests that the learning of would-be or actual evaders is countered by lessons drawn by the sanctions senders. However, constraining and signalling purposes record less significant change in effectiveness (it slightly increases for signalling and declines for constraining targets). Thus, even if the new measures for monitoring compliance have contributed to keeping sanctions a credible instrument, it may require further elaboration for a lasting effect.

The ambitions could be higher, of course, but we have to observe that the UN institutional structure remains weak. However, it could be made stronger without resorting to major changes in the UN Charter: one way would be to create a separate organ for sanctions, what one might term an ISAC, International Sanctions Administrations Capacity, building on the model of the International Atomic Energy Agency or the Organization for the Prohibition of Chemical Weapons. Interestingly, both these authorities have received the Nobel Peace Prize, testifying to the idea that specialist agencies are important for peace in the world. Also, since the implementation of sanctions requires such concerted action, placing this outside the immediate reach of the UN Secretariat and the Security Council may merit further consideration.

Connected to this is the need to revisit the experience of Sanctions Assistance Missions (SAMs), as part of such a sanctions enforcement body. SAMs were used in some of the earlier cases of sanctions, most notably in the former Yugoslavia in the 1990s. Such missions could at the same time help monitor sanctions implementation and give support to the countries that remain weak in implementation capacity. This would also be a way to strengthen government capacity, by providing revenue, improving border control, and strengthening state regulation of financial institutions.

Target's learning

One important conclusion on targeted sanctions is a fact that is notable for its absence: the lack of a significant counter-campaign against the UN

---

[26] The unit of analysis is a case episode within a country sanctions regime (total of sixty-three case episodes in twenty-three sanctions regimes). Effectiveness is assessed for the calendar year in which the case episode ends or, in the case of ongoing country sanctions regimes, at the end of the latest calendar year. The figures of Table 11.1 are based on 2013 estimates.

that initiated the sanctions. One particular effect of targeted sanctions is that it has become more difficult for the targeted actor to appeal to the sender's feelings of guilt. The humanitarian consequences of the sanctions on Iraq made the UN and the Security Council gradually shift its policy away from comprehensive sanctions towards targeted ones. One intermediate step was instituting the unusual oil-for-food programme operated out of the UN Secretariat. This was clearly something the UN was not equipped to do, and it had many administrative shortcomings. It is also notable how Iraq could successfully exploit the shortcomings of this programme for the regime's survival. This was even more remarkable, as this government was not one that paid any regard to humanitarian concerns in its own practice. As we know, it led to a change in UN sanctions policy, and in so doing it also ended the effect of this counter-argument. Thus, during the 2000s, this argument has not been as important or convincing. Actually, the targeted countries now find themselves in a contradictory position: they want at the same time to portray themselves as victims of unjust actions and as unharmed and unvanquished, as Iran did in episode 3 and the early phases of episode 4. Iran, in fact, comes closer to such an argumentation, but is then more generalized against the United States and European Union, that is, the West at large. The UN sanctions, however, have had the support of the entire Security Council. It may project a more 'unbiased' standing in this dispute.

Thus, we might expect some counteraction against the leading countries of the UN Security Council, but seldom do targeted governments withdraw from the UN.[27] On the contrary, taking the opportunity to visit international meetings, such as the UN, seems to be an important element in demonstrating resolve, both internationally and domestically. Even if there are travel sanctions, leaders are exempt from them when attending approved international meetings, giving them a way of easy evasion. The UN has been reluctant to move a step further and ban targeted leaders from participation. In this regard, the UN acts differ from those of the International Criminal Court. The warrants issued by the ICC may in fact more effectively stigmatize particular leaders than does UN sanctions action.

There is little evidence of sanctions routinely escalating into military confrontations or interventions. This may be something targeted actors have observed and may have an impact on their behaviour. In some respects, senders impose sanctions instead of military action, even though

---

[27] Interestingly, there are examples of forms of cooperation developing among disparate targeted states, as illustrated in the Panel of Expert reports on Iran, North Korea, and the DRC.

sanctions are applied along with some degree of force in over half of the episodes in the TSC data set.

There has been considerable domestic pressure, for instance, on the US government to take military action – whether unilateral or with international authorization – on Iran and, to a lesser extent, on North Korea. Instead, sanctions have been sharpened even though succeeding US administrations have emphasized that 'all options' remain on the table. However, military escalation with air campaigns requires bases nearby and opposition forces that act on the ground for the same purposes. Thus, we find that sanctions were combined with military action in two recent cases that meet these requirements. In Libya, there were air campaigns that benefited opposition forces, in addition to the sanctions. In Côte d'Ivoire, French forces destroyed the government's air force capacity early on and then supported the forces of the winner of the presidential elections. In both of these cases, sanctions were combined with other measures and led to change in the direction favoured by the international community. Although there are some similarities with the earlier cases of the former Yugoslavia and Serbia over Kosovo, the new situations took place in 2011 and may send novel signals to presently or potentially targeted actors.

There is one other area where targets may try to counter the effects of UN sanctions: the human rights of the individuals who are targeted. However, most of the countries on the targeted list are non-democracies with abysmal records of human rights. In fact, they would run into a contradiction if they would pursue such an issue. In democratic countries, the issue has been important, and the UN has, albeit somewhat late, increasingly come to grips with the issue. The reforms introduced by the Security Council in resolution 1904 of December 2009 responded to many of the procedural criticisms of the 1267 Al-Qaida Sanctions Committee delisting process. It created an Office of the Ombudsperson to receive appeals directly from individuals. The reforms have not proven to be sufficiently persuasive to the European Court of Justice, however, as indicated by its July 2013 decision in the Kadi case. It is reasonable to assume that targeted actors will continue to learn from the practice of sanctions, and thus sanctions have continuously to adapt to new situations. It means that UN sanction policies continuously have to evolve, in order to keep up with changing times.

Unlearning targeting

For many governments, targeted sanctions were compatible with their strategies to deal with money laundering and tax evasion measures, performed by particular individuals often with criminal records. Thus, throughout the first decade of the 2000s, financial sanctions became increasingly important, but also changed character: from targeting the assets of particular individuals, firms, or non-state actors, sanctions are now also targeting aspects of the financial sector as such. Broad financial sanctions were imposed on Libya in 2011, and the United States and European Union have imposed broad unilateral measures on Iran since 2011. The UN sanctions against Iran have remained relatively targeted, but the language that encourages states to exercise vigilance with regard to Iranian financial transactions (that could be linked to proliferation activities) and similar provisions that block financial credits to entities in the DPRK (which are suspected of facilitating its nuclear programme) are both indicative of a broadening of targeted measures. There were some elements of this in the case of Yugoslavia in the early 1990s. However, financial sector sanctions seem to go beyond the original idea of targeted sanctions.

The idea of targeting particular individuals had logic of its own. It meant that those actually responsible for the policies the international community objected to would be subject to sanctions and thus, hopefully, change their behaviour or become internally weakened or constrained. This was in line with globalization, ideas about the rule of law, and individual accountability and had a moral appeal. Freezing financial assets for such individuals and preventing them from international travel was seen as appropriate. Thus, the first lists of sanctions were extensive and included leaders, followers, administrators, and sometimes also the traders that helped to undermine the sanctions. However, gradually this has changed. Today the lists are generally shorter, and, most remarkably, leaders are no longer targeted.[28] This is particularly true for the sanctions on Iran and North Korea. It is not difficult to understand politically why this happens. There are members of the Security Council who resist adding leaders to the sanctions lists. Rather, lower echelons have been targeted, particularly with respect to Iran. It not only means a retreat from the original idea of targeting financial sanctions but it also rests on an unrealistic expectation of how change can be brought about. The ability of lower-level administrators to bring about change is severely limited, or in fact can even be the reverse: as they are targeted by the international community, they have to work harder to demonstrate their loyalty to the nation and the regime.

Financial sanctions were important already from the beginning in the movement to reform sanctions,[29] but this idea seems to be slipping. The UN has opened the door to a broadening of financial sector sanctions, and

[28] Wallensteen and Grusell, 'Targeting the Right Targets? The UN Use of Individual Sanctions', p. 218.
[29] Biersteker, Eckert, Halegua, and Romaniuk, *Targeted Financial Sanctions: A Manual for Design and Implementation – Contributions from the Interlaken Process.*

they are no longer restricted to particular individuals or commercial enterprises. Occasionally, national banks are targeted. Potentially, this may give sanctions a more comprehensive character as such financial operations affect all parts of the economy. In a subsistence economy it might only directly affect a smaller part of the population, notably those in urban areas, although trickle-down effects would affect the rest of the population. In a monetized economy, however, it will affect many types of activities, whether commercial or welfare services. Thus targeting financial sectors – even if limited to their role in financing proliferation sensitive goods – may be a way of making sanctions comprehensive, as they were before. The basic idea of targeted sanctions, after all, was to make sure the regime was affected more adversely than the general population. The lessons from comprehensive sanctions were what gave the world targeted sanctions. Does the same world two decades later face a retreat from targeted sanctions? If so, this challenges a fundamental aspect of targeted sanctions and requires a closer look at how sanctions are actually expected to have an impact. Comprehensive sanctions led to a rally-around-the-flag phenomenon that seemed to strengthen the incumbent regime. Targeted sanctions sought to separate the regime from the population. The lessons we have seen in this chapter speak in favour of the latter approach rather than the former.

Concluding lessons

The sanctions record may still be below the high expectations for this instrument as an effective UN measure. The use of sanctions suggests that the world is in need of a tool placed somewhere between words and war, or in some combination with selective use of force, as argued earlier in this chapter. Thus, the further improvement of sanctions effectiveness is an important challenge for the international research and policy communities. The work of the Targeted Sanctions Consortium is a real contribution to this.

At this moment it is possible to conclude, based on the TSC data, that targeted sanctions on the whole have improved
• by increasingly focusing on stigmatizing targeted actors,
• by gradually becoming sharper when new measures are added to earlier ones; that appropriate sequencing improves sanctions effectiveness,
• by having particularly significant effects on actors in civil wars, rather than on actors pursuing other interests,
• by having improved implementation practices, through a series of institutional innovations, including Panels of Experts,

- by working better in conjunction with other UN measures, notably diplomacy, preventive action, and possibly also supporting peacekeeping operations, notably in civil war situations,
- by minimizing the target's ability to exploit the international concern for humanitarian effects,
- by dealing upfront with the human rights concerns, and
- by understanding that the idea of targeting leaders is still valid, but has become less common in sanctions practice.

Thus, there are new lessons learned from the experience and analysis of sanctions episodes. Sanctions policy and practice have improved since the 1990s. Some of the lessons have been integrated into UN practice. At the same time expectations may have increased and also some lessons unlearned, particularly on the importance of targeting correctly and keeping to the agenda of targeted sanctions. In order to further the effectiveness of sanctions as a non-military instrument for the international community, there are reasons to consider strengthening the institutional capacity in sanctions policy. Thus, this chapter raises the idea of separate UN agency for sanctions implementation, tentatively called International Sanctions Administrations Capacity, and for revisiting the experience of Sanctions Assistance Missions. These would be ways in which learning can be institutionalized, institutional memory be maintained, and contingency thinking on sanctions be stimulated, thus increasing the options available to decisions-makers and ultimately improving effectiveness of targeted sanctions.

12   Conclusion

Thomas J. Biersteker, Marcos Tourinho,
and Sue E. Eckert

UN targeted sanctions, our subject of analysis, is a moving target. Throughout the five-year period of this research project, five new country case regimes and eleven new episodes were added to existing regimes, based on actions taken by the UN Security Council. Beyond the sheer number of cases, however, UN targeted sanctions as a policy tool and an instrument of global governance have changed in significant ways over the past quarter century. The instrument has been used for a growing variety of threats to international peace and security, beyond its initial focus on armed conflict and terrorism. The Security Council has subsequently added nuclear proliferation, non-constitutional changes of government, support for R2P, international criminal justice, and the maintenance of peacebuilding processes to its list of objectives in the use of sanctions.[1]

Through these twenty-five years, new types of targeted sanctions have been developed. Since the early 1990s, when the Council relied most heavily on arms embargoes, broad trade restrictions, and occasionally on comprehensive sanctions, it has now refined its use of sanctions to focus largely on the targeting of individuals and entities, as well as on the specific economic sectors that support proscribed activities (often minerals or commodities). Relatively non-discriminating measures such as aviation bans and oil embargoes on an entire country have not been imposed by the UN since 1998.[2] Arms embargoes continue to be utilized regularly and more frequently than any other type of targeted sanction, in spite of their overall ineffectiveness in constraining the use of violence by the targeted parties when used alone.[3]

---

[1] Although sporadic, UN targeted sanctions have been used to address non-constitutional changes of government throughout the entire period.

[2] Both aviation and oil sanctions have been used, but were territorially restricted to areas controlled by targets (e.g. UNITA in Angola, Taliban in Afghanistan).

[3] This is true of any type of targeted sanction imposed by the UN in isolation (i.e. alone, without any other type of targeted measure). See T. Biersteker with Z. Hudáková, *Types of UN Targeted Sanctions and Their Effectiveness: Research Note* (Geneva: the Graduate Institute). Note prepared for the Sanctions Unit of the UN Secretariat, New York, 23 July 2014.

In the last two decades, substantial institutional learning by the UN and Member States with regard to sanctions design and implementation has taken place. Sanctions resolutions now routinely require the creation of a sanctions committee, committee guidelines, clearly articulated designations criteria, Member State reporting, the formation of Panels of Experts to monitor implementation, and most recently, articulated enforcement authorities. The UN Security Council has become more precise in its resolution language,[4] with greater clarity in the resolution structure, more standardized use of terms, and greater detail in describing target groups and identifying information for individuals designated. Particularly in the non-proliferation cases, an enhanced focus on enforcement through the provisions authorizing inspection, seizure, and destruction of goods seized has been developed.

The use of targeted sanctions has become more tailored to the specific challenge faced by the UN Security Council. As the issues evolve, sanctions have been used in flexible ways, with incremental tightening to respond to perceived intransigence (e.g. DPRK, Iran) or loosening to address situational improvements on the ground (e.g. DRC, Somalia). Notably, we observe the emergence of peacebuilding sanctions designed to constrain potential spoilers of peace processes and challengers to the establishment of legitimate governmental authority throughout a territory. As Chapter 10 notes, targeted sanctions appear to be relatively effective in supporting other measures associated with the UN's international peacebuilding architecture.

Peter Wallensteen concludes in Chapter 11 that, according to TSC episode assessments, there have been improvements in the effectiveness of UN targeted sanctions over time in both coercing and signalling. Considering the broad range of challenges for which the tool has been applied, the complexity of implementation, and the limited resources employed in both its design and implementation, this is a significant outcome. The overall low rate of effectiveness of targeted sanctions for different purposes – between 10 per cent and 27 per cent of the episodes – indicates, however, that significant room for improvement remains. These challenges will be addressed in the remainder of this chapter.

What have we learned about how sanctions work?

Beyond a contribution to the debates on the effectiveness of UN targeted sanctions, the TSC project provides the opportunity to understand in

---

[4] This is generally true, except in those instances when UN Security Council resolutions run on with a seemingly endless list of current normative concerns.

greater detail *how* sanctions work. This was the subject of most of the chapters in this volume and one from which some important conclusions can be extracted.

First (and perhaps most importantly), UN targeted sanctions are not used exclusively to change the behaviour of targets, contrary to popular perception. As Chapters 1, 2 (by Francesco Giumelli), and 10 discuss extensively, this research considers *coercion, constraint, and signalling* as different purposes of targeted sanctions. Policy practitioners working in the realm of the UN Security Council have come to appreciate and understand that sanctions can achieve multiple purposes beyond coercion, to include constraining a target from engaging in a proscribed activity or signalling a target about the violation of an international norm. At the same time, the Security Council continues to focus disproportionally on the coercive purpose of sanctions as its principal goal (60 per cent of the time), a very difficult objective achieved in only 10 per cent of the cases. In contrast, UN targeted sanctions are more effective in constraining (27 per cent) or signalling a target (27 per cent) than in coercing a change of behaviour. If the UN Security Council clarifies at the outset and focuses its sanctioning efforts on the purposes for which the tool is more likely to work, the overall effectiveness of the policy instrument will likely increase.

Nonetheless, UN targeted sanctions do not operate in a vacuum. As Paul Bentall demonstrates in Chapter 4, sanctions are always used in combination with other policy instruments. Diplomatic initiatives (95 per cent of the time), peacekeeping operations (62 per cent), and some degree of military force (52 per cent) are the most common companion policies. Rather than being 'between words and war', UN targeted sanctions generally operate *with* diplomacy and, at times, with the use of military force, although not often with adequate coordination. In some cases, constraining sanctions served to 'buy time' for diplomatic negotiations to achieve their objectives (e.g. Libya in the 1990s, Iran) or were important in tipping the balance in a more traditional military conflict (e.g. Angola, Liberia, Libya after 2011). This means that any evaluation of targeted sanctions must be conceptualized more broadly than in terms of economic coercion alone and consider the general objectives of the Security Council and other actors involved. As discussed in Chapter 10, the specific contribution of UN targeted sanctions to a particular outcome is often difficult to discern, but still an indispensable dimension of the analysis.

The interaction of UN targeted sanctions with other sanctions regimes has also been an important subject of research and reflection throughout this project. Chapter 5 by Andrea Charron and Clara Portela highlights how in the last two decades a division of labour has emerged among different international institutions in their use of the tool. While the European Union uses targeted sanctions as an instrument of foreign policy and focuses largely on human rights issues, the African Union is more concerned with non-constitutional changes of government and routinely applies sanctions on its own members. More generally, the use of targeted sanctions by regional organizations has become widespread in Africa, with ECOWAS, in particular, having sanctioned more than half of its members. The United States continues to be a prolific (but not the only) unilateral imposer of targeted sanctions, seeking to extend its unilateral sanctions extraterritorially through secondary restrictive measures, particularly in the case of Iran.

Nonetheless, even if pursuing broadly similar objectives, the relationship between different sanctions regimes addressing the same target can be complex to manage. Because targeted sanctions are an adaptable tool, variations in design and targeting can be consequential. In stark contrast to comprehensive sanctions (which seek to inflict general pain with the aspiration of some future political gain), targeted sanctions are rarely adjusted simply in terms of 'volume'. Decisions about targeting (e.g. how narrow or broad, targeting which specific groups or sectors) send important messages about the path to a possible solution to an international crisis. Senders often disagree about the appropriate path, and targets may have difficulty in differentiating between senders, resulting in a dissonance in which multiple targeted sanctions regimes that appear to be similar are not necessarily aligned and mutually reinforcing. Unilateral and regional sanctions that 'go beyond' UN measures, therefore, can conflict and actually be counterproductive in achieving the objectives set out in UN resolutions (although they may be important for other national or regional objectives of the individual senders).

It is because of these differences that the Security Council at times includes ambiguous language (the deliberate use of 'constructive ambiguity') in its targeted sanctions resolutions. By using terms that allow differing interpretations, the Council provides legitimacy for some Member States to 'exercise vigilance' against targeted parties, while others (also legitimately) refuse to take discretionary action they consider inappropriate because it has not been required by the Security Council. However frustrating it is for those trying to interpret the UN Security Council resolution texts, this is an important part of the ongoing dynamics of a highly politicized body, as discussed in Chapter 3 by Michael Brzoska and George Lopez. While we and the authors in this volume often try to attribute rationality to the Council (when discussing senders of sanctions or attempting to attribute purposes), it is exceedingly difficult to analyse an essentially political body deliberating its decisions and negotiating among its different members in unitary, rationalist terms. Different goals and purposes are often papered over through language compromises or constructive ambiguity, building internal contradictions into Security Council resolutions.

That being said, there are times when the Council speaks with one voice, such as when it addresses the threat of transnational terrorism. The political priorities of the Security Council have important consequences for the development and implementation of targeted sanctions regimes. As Alix Boucher and Caty Clement illustrate in Chapter 6, significantly greater resources are invested in counterterrorism and non-proliferation regimes than in conflict-related cases. While this may help explain the relatively high rate of effectiveness of counterterrorism sanctions in constraining targets, the lack of adequate resources may limit the effectiveness of other sanctions, such as those supporting peacebuilding initiatives.

As addressed in Chapter 7 by Rico Carisch and Loraine Rickard-Martin, targeted sanctions are more complex to implement than comprehensive measures, and the expansion of actors, mandates, and instruments makes effective implementation of UN sanctions more difficult. Yet as compliance and enforcement challenges have become more difficult, Member States' capacity needs have grown, and the financial sector's essential role implementing financial sanctions has increased. There has been inadequate attention to how the effectiveness of UN sanctions is undermined by inadequate implementation.

Throughout the last twenty-five years, UN targeted sanctions regimes have been important forums for normative dialogue. Because all sanctions address the violation of an international norm, the imposition of sanctions often becomes a prime location for normative enforcement and contestation. In spite of the broad normative expansion observed in the work of the Security Council in the last two decades, targeted sanctions have remained largely focused on long-standing priorities of the Council: the prohibition of war, armed violence, and terrorism. More recently, concern about proliferation-related activities has been included on the Security Council's agenda. Support for human rights is a frequently cited norm in public discourse and often present in justifications for sanctions regimes, but it is never the *primary* purpose of sanctions. The responsibility to protect, still a highly contested norm in the international arena, was used as a justification for sanctions explicitly in Libya in 2011 but has not been utilized since.

As Mikael Eriksson notes in Chapter 9, the move from comprehensive to targeted sanctions occurred to a large extent in response to the widespread negative humanitarian consequences associated with comprehensive sanctions, but that unintended consequences remain an important feature of targeted sanctions as well. These include increases in corruption and criminality, the strengthening of authoritarian rule, burdens placed on neighbouring states, strengthening of political factions, resource diversion, and humanitarian impacts. While improved targeting can reduce the scale of unintended consequences of targeted sanctions, they are an inevitable element of sanctions that should be considered in the cost–benefit analysis that validates (or invalidates) sanctions as the policy instrument of choice in specific situations, as addressed in the conclusion of Chapter 10 on effectiveness.

Finally, sanctions are prohibitions that invariably create powerful incentives for the creation of corrupt networks to circumvent them. Evasion, even of relatively effective measures, always takes place. Common methods of evasion include the diversion of trade through third countries and front companies, use of private (black market) contractors, safe havens, and alternative value sources (e.g. diamonds), re-flagging or disguising vessels, diversification of funds and investment, and reliance on family members to facilitate transactions. Secondary sanctions can be applied to neighbouring states engaged in systematic and deliberate evasion of UN sanctions, and although they are rarely used (e.g. in only two instances, against Liberia and Eritrea in the Sierra Leone and Somalia sanctions regimes, respectively), they proved to be effective in both instances.

Contemporary challenges and policy recommendations

Several chapters in this volume raise the challenge of what increasingly appears to be a return to the use of broader or relatively more comprehensive sanctions. The reasons for this are several. First, the more distant the memory of the negative humanitarian effects of the comprehensive sanctions against Iraq become, the more likely policy practitioners and analysts are to forget one of the principal forces driving the move from comprehensive to targeted measures during the 1990s. Second, there are factors within the process of implementation of targeted sanctions that are likely to contribute to their broadening. It is not easy to keep targeted sanctions targeted.

For the most part, UN sanctions have remained relatively targeted in their design. As described in more detail in Chapter 1, targeted sanctions vary in their degree of discrimination, from individual sanctions at one end of the continuum to sanctions on sectors that affect the entire economy (such as financial and oil sector sanctions) at the other. With the exception of Libya in 2011,[5] the UN has not implemented broad sectoral sanctions on any country since it imposed oil import sanctions on Sierra Leone in 1998.

The broadened impact of UN sanctions is often unintentional, resulting from the efforts of Member States to translate UN measures into domestic law. National implementing agencies' interpretations of UN Security Council intent (to the extent there is collective intent during high-pressure negotiations or careful consideration given to national-level implementation) vary, and some governments may have more expansive goals for the measures. The same applies to private sector entities called upon to apply the measures directly. Financial institutions freezing assets or blocking transactions may find it simpler and less costly to forego transactions with a sanctioned country altogether, rather than go through the complex and costly process of identifying individual accounts and matching them to the list of names designated by UN sanctions committees. Sizeable penalties for violations and general warnings to financial institutions of the risks of any transactions with targeted countries (e.g. as employed by the United States related to Iran) have also contributed to the broadening of UN targeted sanctions, as described in more detail below.

The trend towards greater 'comprehensivization' of targeted sanctions has the potential to create longer-term problems of attenuated support for sanctions in general, particularly if greater civilian costs result. For this reason, the editors believe that UN targeted sanctions should remain targeted. Making sanctions more comprehensive in scope does not necessarily make them more effective. There are choices available. Sanctions can be deepened through careful and selective expansion of designations (adding names of targeted individuals or entities), as well as by imposing secondary sanctions on those facilitating the evasion of the measures, rather than widened with broad, relatively non-discriminating sanctions.

One of the principal factors contributing to the perception that UN targeted sanctions are becoming more comprehensive is the coexistence of multiple sanctions regimes and lack of clear coordination among them. The application of sanctions by regional organizations and by individual Member States, as discussed in Chapter 5, has extended sanctions beyond the relatively limited scope of UN sanctions in several instances. While for some, this might appear to be an important way of strengthening international sanctions, for others it creates an opportunity for forum

---

[5] Financial sector sanctions against Libya, though understandable given the context (both the urgency of the situation and the degree of the Qaddafi family's direct control over and access to central government finances), were relatively undiscriminating and very nearly had significant humanitarian consequences.

shopping that can weaken the legitimacy of UN multilateral sanctions. From the target's standpoint, there is often no differentiation between UN sanctions and the sometimes far more extensive sanctions applied by others. This creates legitimacy challenges for the UN.

The international sanctions against Iran over its nuclear programme provide a good illustration of the phenomenon. The initial UN targeted sanctions imposed in 2006 were introduced in the wake of pre-existing US measures. While the UN sanctions were more targeted in design and purpose, their potential scope of implementation was much broader, since they were to be applied by all Member States. Subsequent episodes expanded UN sanctions against Iran and added language encouraging Member States to 'exercise vigilance' for transactions that might contribute to the weaponization of Iran's nuclear programme. Some states, notably the United States and the leading members of the EU, used this as a basis for broadening their already more expansive measures on Iran. Others, notably Russia and China, argued that the UN sanctions constituted not the base (or floor) of legitimate international sanctions, but defined their legitimate limit (or ceiling) – described earlier in this volume as the 'floor-ceiling' debate.

This debate reflects fundamentally differing views among Member States, particularly permanent members of the UN Security Council, about the Council's use and scope of sanctions which likely foreshadows challenges to reaching agreement on difficult conflict situations in the future. The expansion of institutional players, each with their distinctive policy tools and differing mandates, also complicates the international coherence of sanctions, and further undermines UN sanctions' effectiveness.

Another challenge to the future of UN targeted sanctions is largely a product of its own making. The shift to targeting individuals, an innovation of the Security Council in the early 1990s, was introduced with little or no consideration of individual rights or how individuals might appeal their designations. The significant expansion of the lists, especially of individuals designated for being associated with Al-Qaida by the 1267 sanctions committee during late 2001 and early 2002 (resulting in hundreds of designations), was contested in courts worldwide, but particularly in Europe and to a lesser degree in the United States. While the Security Council has made consistent (albeit reluctant) improvements to due process procedures for designated individuals and entities over the past decade, important legal challenges persist. The longer-term repercussions of these challenges, such as Yassin Abdullah Kadi's success in the European Court of Justice in 2013, potentially have profound implications for the future use of individual designations. If countries or regions begin selectively to implement UN Security Council sanctions, it could lead to an unravelling of the instrument on a global level. Even if most current legal challenges relate to EU autonomous sanctions, the precedents established in Europe could affect individual targeting more generally. The attempt to minimize the risk of future litigation by targeting classes of activity, rather than individuals, may also result in broader sanctions, reinforcing the trend towards more comprehensive measures discussed above.

As we have argued elsewhere,[6] the due process procedures afforded by the Office of the Ombudsperson for the Al-Qaida designees should be extended to other UN country sanctions regimes. The denial of individual rights is fundamentally the same across different regimes. Given the sensitive nature of ongoing negotiations in many conflict situations and the Council's need for flexibility in de-listing individuals participating in peace processes, we recommend applying the model used in cases of Security Council referrals to the ICC, where it has the power to make periodic suspensions of the process, as necessary.

The UN Security Council was designed to deal with crises, most of which have a conceivable end point or resolution. The evolution of individual targeting and significant expansion by the Council in the Al-Qaida 1267 sanctions regime was understandable, particularly immediately following the attacks of 11 September 2001. The current Al-Qaida sanctions regime, however, has evolved into the realm of the permanent exception. Open-ended asset freezes, with no termination of the ongoing conflict in sight, have created a situation in which measures taken at a moment of exception have become *de facto* permanent confiscations, not temporary freezes of individual assets. The scope of the problem and the geographical reach of designations have expanded to include listings associated with Boko Harem in Nigeria, Al Shabaab in Somalia and Kenya, and the Islamic State of Iraq and the Levant (ISIL) operating in Iraq and Syria. Unlike other conflicts on the Security Council agenda, it is unlikely that terrorism, and therefore global counter terrorism efforts, will cease. This has led to ideas by some practitioners that the freezing of assets of individuals supporting acts of terrorism might be best managed by a separate body rather than a UN Security Council sanctions committee (which, after all, is not a policing body). A subsidiary body or a separate agency, perhaps modelled in part after the IAEA or OPCW, could address what, in effect, is an ongoing problem and more effectively handle due process concerns related to targeting, sensitive information,

---

[6] Sue Eckert and Thomas Biersteker, *Due Process and Targeted Sanctions: An Update of the Watson Report* (Providence: The Watson Institute, Brown University, 2012).

and assessments, while potentially being both more accessible and accountable for its decisions.

Another example of incremental, unintended extension of UN sanctions mandates is presented by the Council's practice of extending sanctions automatically without serious review and adjustment to reflect changes in a conflict over time. The sanctions against the Taliban or in Somalia have been extended repeatedly without substantial reconsideration to reflect current objectives/realities. The result is an ever-expanding list of demands on targets that address too many different concerns (often in excessively long resolutions) that weaken and diffuse the signals of the Council. It also makes it difficult for targeted parties to understand and address the demands, even if they were persuaded to do so. This 'pile-on' effect and lack of clarity ultimately undermines UN sanctions. A better alternative may be to terminate the regime and negotiate a new one based on current realities, in effect, hitting the reset button, as was done in episode 3 of the Liberia sanctions regime. The Security Council should avoid the temptation to include everything agreed in a previous resolution, tailoring new resolutions to the specific, changing circumstances of the conflict based upon a re-evaluation of UN objectives and the best ways to achieve them. This not only clarifies the purposes and criteria for the targets but also strengthens the sanctions through a recommitment and reassertion of political will by the Council.

In addition to the emerging political challenges already discussed – of gradual re-comprehensivization, the complexity and confusion from multiple, coexisting sanctions regimes, reduced legitimacy caused by due process concerns over individual designations, and the consequences of accumulated of demands over time – UN targeted sanctions face other more practical challenges. For example, papering over differences among members of the Security Council through ambiguous language invites uneven implementation and less effective sanctions. The Council should be as clear as possible in the resolution with regard to the purposes of the sanctions and in the design, language, measures to be employed, and procedures for implementation and enforcement.

Notwithstanding the important institutional learning that has taken place over the past two decades of UN targeted sanctions, significant challenges to effective implementation remain. Inattention, or the absence of political will among the P5 members, divisions within the UN Secretariat regarding perceived conflicting mandates, and lack of coordination, information sharing, and even awareness or understanding of sanctions within the Secretariat have hampered implementation at the UN level. Member States face even greater capacity needs in administering and enforcing sanctions and providing guidance to the private sector, in particular financial institutions, that ultimately are responsible for compliance with financial measures.

As noted by Alix Boucher and Caty Clement in Chapter 6, politicizing Panels of Experts by appointing 'national representatives' to non-proliferation sanctions regimes by permanent members of the Security Council has limited the scope of the panels' findings and raised questions about their credibility. Targeting is also important, and the list of targets should reflect the purposes of the sanctions. Too many, too few, or the wrong targets (or insufficiently identified) undermine the credibility of the measures. Finally, there should be more thought given to how to end sanctions. Most UN sanctions regimes are open-ended arrangements, and it is often difficult to terminate them. The failure to do so, however, creates problems for the capacity of the Secretariat staff to support sanctions committees, not to mention for 193 Member States responsible for their implementation. In the first decade of targeted sanctions, there were never more than eight regimes in place at the same time (and usually no more than six or seven). At the beginning of 2014 there were fourteen sanctions regimes and rumours of more to come. Failure to lift sanctions when the situation changes undermines the instrument and the Council's legitimacy.

Policymakers need to be realistic about what UN targeted sanctions can reasonably achieve. Based on analysis of the relative effectiveness of targeted sanctions (they are far more effective in constraining and signalling than in coercing a change in behaviour), expectations should be adjusted accordingly. The discursive treatment of UN sanctions also matters. Characterizations of sanctions as 'crippling', while perhaps useful politically with domestic audiences, reinforce misperceptions about the nature of UN targeted sanctions as punitive, rather than protective or preventative measures.

Future research

Based on the preceding review of contemporary challenges facing UN targeted sanctions, as well as reflections on the research presented in the chapters in this volume, a number of ideas for future research emerge. First, following the insights offered by Jonathan Kirshner more than a decade ago,[7] there should be a greater effort to try to understand precisely *how* sanctions work, not just whether they work. In particular, it is important to look at sanctions from the perspective of the target,

---

[7] J. Kirshner, 'Review Essay: Economic Sanctions: The State of the Art', *Security Studies*, 11 (2002), pp. 160–79.

something we originally intended to do in the case study research on which the TSC project was originally based.[8] Understanding how sanctions affected targets (if at all) is important not only for assessing the different dimensions of impact (as explored by Kimberly Elliott in Chapter 8) but also for exploring what might have been more effective (persuasive) measures. Given the considerable investment in the existing global sanctions regime, this kind of research could yield important insights for the future design of targeted sanctions.

Given the use and relative effectiveness of commodity sanctions, it is important to understand better how they actually work. Too much of the analysis is focused on the relationship between sender and target of sanctions, rather than on how their relationship is mediated by other factors, such as the local conflict economies in which the targets are embedded. Like gaining access to the targets, this is not easy research, but sanctions research would benefit from greater linkages to those studying the conflicts overall, and conflict economies in particular. A related project should be a systemic exploration of evasion strategies associated with different types of targeted sanctions. Not only would this research contribute to criminology and transnational crime literatures, but it would also be potentially useful information for Panels of Experts' investigations concerning evasion strategies.

Understanding the signalling aspects of targeted sanctions is an area ripe for inquiry. Too much of the literature and popular discussion reflects the attitude that signalling is little more than a symbolic measure, cheap talk, or a simple gesture. It always comes in third, after coercing and constraining, even in the analysis in this volume. Yet signalling by the UN Security Council is an important way to articulate, refine, contest, or enforce norms. Norms matter, and the counterfactual alternative of *not* signalling with sanctions at key moments could have consequences far beyond the immediate case concerned.[9] Both aspects of signalling – the articulation of the signal (the communications factor) and the social environment(s) in which the signal is received (the potential stigmatization factor) – deserve further scrutiny. The differences between stigmatization and shaming also merit further study, since a target cannot be shamed if it does not share the norm.

---

[8] Beyond the inherent difficulty in gaining access to targets of UN Security Council sanctions, we were unsuccessful in securing sufficient funding to support the field research that would have been necessary to conduct this kind of research. As a result, we had to rely on the previous research interviews conducted by members of the TSC, including ourselves, to gain insights into the experiences and perspectives of the targets.

[9] N. L. Miller, 'The Secret Success of Nonproliferation Sanctions', *International Organization*, 68, 4 (September 2014), pp. 913–44.

As suggested in Chapter 4 by Paul Bentall, research is needed regarding the complex relationships between targeted sanctions and other policy instruments. The increasing use of referrals to special courts and the ICC, whereby the same individuals could be subject to both court proceedings and UN sanctions, raises new issues and highlights the need for aware-ness-raising of respective mandates, as well as the need for cooperation and information exchange between the UN and international criminal justice actors. The research presented in Chapter 10 suggests strong correlation between legal referrals and effective sanctions in constraining a target, but how they interact has not been explored. Another important question warranting exploration is whether legal referrals with inflexible procedures might reduce the incentive for targeted parties to engage in negotiation and compromise or whether they drive targets into a corner from which there is no escape. Had Muammar Qadhafi fought his way into a stalemate in a divided Libya, would the ICC referral in the UNSC resolution have precluded a negotiated settlement of the conflict? Again, the sanctions community could benefit by greater engagement with the transitional justice community.

UN targeted sanctions are never imposed in isolation, but rather work in conjunction with other policy instruments, as discussed extensively in Chapter 4. Yet what are the relationships between targeted sanctions and mediation efforts, peacekeeping operations, or humanitarian support activities? They may complement and reinforce Security Council objec-tives, but they also can contradict one another (or exist in separate bureaucratic domains, with little awareness of their interactive effects), potentially undermining the coherence of the Council's actions. Additional research as to how the range of policy instruments can work together to optimize impact could be quite significant.

Another potentially fruitful area of investigation concerns the role and perspective of the private sector, particularly the financial sector, which implements targeted financial sanctions on individuals and firms. Since the costs of sanctions are not directly borne by Member States, it would be useful to understand better the compliance challenges and costs for firms and, as discussed at the end of Chapter 10, try to factor those costs into an analysis of the efficacy of targeted sanctions (to the extent possible). The extent to which the private sector amplifies the scope of sanctions through lack of understanding or excessively cautious imple-mentation, as suggested in the discussion of challenges above, would also be useful to know in determining the need to change our assessment of the extent to which we are still analysing *targeted* sanctions.

Given the infrequency of their use, but the high rate of effectiveness, greater analysis of how secondary sanctions affect countries actively evading

UN measures should be conducted. Given the re-comprehensivization of targeted sanctions recently, it is important to understand potential alternatives to broadening sanctions and how they might work. As noted above, while public discourse reflects the belief that widening sanctions is the most effective way to strengthen them, deepening them might be more efficacious (and certainly more normatively desirable, given the fact that they remain more targeted). Targeted sanctions can be strengthened both by extending them to neighbouring countries most involved in evasion or by applying them to those individuals and firms most active in facilitating evasion, particularly those located in the sender states themselves (where enforcement is likely to be more effective). Panels of Experts could be encouraged to enhance existing efforts to identify evading firms and individuals operating in third countries.

Finally, given the increased frequency with which regional organizations impose sanctions of their own, extending the analysis of UN sanctions to the dynamics and impacts of other targeted sanctions would be valuable. Not only would this provide an interesting basis for comparative research on the choice of sanctions and internal assessments of their impacts, but it would also provide insights into the complex interrelationships between the different sanctions regimes, described above as one of the contemporary challenges facing UN targeted sanctions.

Conclusion

Targeted sanctions are more complex to design and implement than comprehensive sanctions, and they require greater skill and capacity of the Security Council, UN officials, Member States, and private sector institutions. Given their multiple purposes, it is important to shift the focus from the primary use of sanctions for coercion to constraining and signalling, where they are more likely to be effective.

Targeted sanctions need to be conceptualized in strategic terms, in relationship with other measures, and should be designed with deliberative planning characteristic of military operations, that is, with clear advance consideration of purposes, objectives, consequences, impact assessments, evasion, contingency planning, and exit strategies. The decision to impose targeted sanctions by the Security Council should be made with as much consideration, preparation, and deliberation as the use of force.

In the final analysis, it is important to raise the quality of public understanding of and discourse about sanctions. As mentioned in the Introduction to this volume, concern about the public debate on UN sanctions was one of the principal motivations of the TSC project from the outset. Effective implementation of sanctions is made more difficult by the lack of accurate information and misperceptions about the impacts and effectiveness of UN targeted sanctions. Empirically based information such as contained in this volume can provide an informed basis to engage relevant communities (international, national, and regional organizations, NGOs, the private sector, scholars, and broader civil society) to improve the effectiveness of UN sanctions. It is our hope that this book is an important step in the direction of informing and reinvigorating the global public debate about this important instrument of contemporary global governance.

Appendix 1 List of cases and episodes

Sanction regime	Episode	Start date	End date	Duration	Main objective	Sanction type	Effectiveness*		
							Coerce	Constrain	Signal
Al-Qaida/ Taliban	Episode 1	15.10.1999	19.12.2000	1 year 2 months	Counterterrorism	**Aviation ban, asset freeze** (political entity – government)	Ineffective	Ineffective	Mixed
	Episode 2	19.12.2000	11.09.2001	9 months	Counterterrorism	Aviation ban, asset freeze (political entity – government, **individual/entity), arms imports embargo** (government forces, territorial delimitation), **diplomatic sanctions** (limit diplomatic representation), **chemical acetic anhydride imports ban** (heroin processing)	Ineffective	Mixed	Mixed
	Episode 3	11.09.2001	17.06.2011	9 years 9 months	Counterterrorism	Aviation ban **(lifted Jan 2002)**, asset freeze (political entity – **former regime and rebel faction**, individual/entity), arms imports embargo **(non-governmental entities)**, diplomatic sanctions (limit diplomatic representation – **expired** Dec 2001), chemical acetic anhydride imports ban **(expired** Dec 2001), **travel ban**	N/A	**Effective**	**Effective**
	Episode 4	17.06.2011	Ongoing	> 3 years	Counterterrorism	Asset freeze (political entity – rebel faction, individual/ entity), arms imports embargo (non-governmental entities), travel ban	N/A	**Effective**	Ineffective
Angola	Episode 1	15.09.1993	28.08.1997	3 years 11 months	Armed conflict	**Arms imports embargo** (non-governmental entity), **petroleum imports ban** (non-governmental entity)	Ineffective	Mixed	Mixed
	Episode 2	28.08.1997	12.06.1998	9 months	Armed conflict	Arms imports embargo (non-governmental entity), petroleum imports ban (non-governmental entity), **aviation ban, diplomatic sanctions** (limit diplomatic representation, limit travel, visa cancellation)	Ineffective	Mixed	Mixed
	Episode 3	12.06.1998	12.01.1999	7 months	Armed conflict	Arms imports embargo (non-governmental entity), petroleum imports ban (territorial delimitation), aviation ban, diplomatic sanctions (limit diplomatic representation, limit travel, visa cancellation), **asset freeze** (political entity – rebel faction), **diamond exports ban, mining services and equipment imports ban** (territorial delimitation), **ground and waterborne transportation services and equipment imports ban** (territorial delimitation)	Ineffective	**Effective**	**Effective**

(cont.)

Sanction regime	Episode	Start date	End date	Duration	Main objective	Sanction type	Effectiveness*		
							Coerce	Constrain	Signal
	Episode 4	12.01.1999	09.12.2002	3 years 11 months	Armed conflict	Arms imports embargo (non-governmental entity), petroleum imports ban, aviation ban, diplomatic sanctions (limit diplomatic representation; limit travel and visa cancellation – **suspended** May 2002, **lifted** Nov 2002), asset freeze (political entity – rebel faction), diamond exports ban, mining services equipment imports ban (territorial delimitation), ground and waterborne transportation services and equipment imports ban (territorial delimitation)	Ineffective	**Effective**	**Effective**
Central African Republic	Episode 1	05.12.2013	Ongoing	< 1 year	Armed conflict	**Arms imports embargo** (non-governmental entities), **travel ban, asset freeze** (individual/entity)	Ineffective	Ineffective	Ineffective
Côte d'Ivoire	Episode 1	15.11.2004	01.02.2005	3 months	Armed conflict	**Arms imports embargo** (all parties), **travel ban, asset freeze** (individual/entity),	Ineffective	Ineffective	Ineffective
	Episode 2	01.02.2005	15.12.2005	10 months	Armed conflict	Arms imports embargo (all parties), travel ban, asset freeze (individual/entity),	Ineffective	Ineffective	Ineffective
	Episode 3	15.12.2005	20.12.2010	5 years	Armed conflict	Arms imports embargo (all parties), travel ban, asset freeze (individual/entity), **diamond exports ban**	**Effective**	Ineffective	Mixed
	Episode 4	20.12.2010	28.04.2011	4 months	Democracy support	Arms imports embargo (all parties), travel ban, asset freeze (individual/entity), **diamond exports ban**	Ineffective	Ineffective	**Effective**
	Episode 5	28.04.2011	Ongoing	> 3 years	Armed conflict	Arms imports embargo (**non-governmental entities** – from Apr 2012), travel ban, asset freeze (individual/entity), diamond exports ban	Ineffective	Mixed	Ineffective
Democratic People's Republic of Korea	Episode 1	14.10.2006	13.04.2009	2 years 6 months	Non-proliferation	**Arms imports** (government forces – specific arms) **and exports embargo, proliferation sensitive goods and technology imports and exports ban, luxury goods ban, asset freeze** (individual/entity), **travel ban**	Mixed	Ineffective	Mixed

Country	Episode	Start	End	Duration	Type	Sanctions			
	Episode 2	13.04.2009	07.03.2013	3 years 11 months	Non-proliferation	Arms imports (government forces – **all arms**) and exports embargo, proliferation sensitive goods and technology imports and exports ban, luxury goods ban, asset freeze (individual/entity), travel ban, **bunkering ban**	Ineffective	Mixed	Mixed
	Episode 3	07.03.2013	Ongoing	> 1 year	Non-proliferation	Arms imports (government forces) and exports embargo, proliferation sensitive goods and technology imports and exports ban, luxury goods ban, asset freeze (individual/entity), travel ban, bunkering ban, **financial sector restrictions** (financial services, transfers, and public support, including bulk cash, export credits, guarantees and insurance)	Ineffective	Mixed	Mixed
Democratic Republic of the Congo	Episode 1	28.07.2003	18.04.2005	1 year 9 months	Armed conflict	**Arms imports embargo** (non-governmental entities, territorial delimitation)	Ineffective	Ineffective	Mixed
	Episode 2	18.04.2005	31.03.2008	2 years 11 months	Armed conflict	Arms imports embargo (non-governmental entities, **entire country**), **travel ban, asset freeze** (individual/entity)	Effective	Mixed	**Effective**
	Episode 3	31.03.2008	28.05.2010	2 years 2 months	Armed conflict	Arms imports embargo (non-governmental entities), travel ban, asset freeze (individual/entity)	Ineffective	**Effective**	Ineffective
	Episode 4	28.05.2010	Ongoing	> 4 years	Armed conflict	Arms imports embargo (non-governmental entities), travel ban, asset freeze (individual/entity)	Ineffective	Ineffective	Mixed
Eritrea/ Ethiopia	Episode 1	17.05.2000	16.05.2001	1 year	Armed conflict	**Arms imports embargo** (government forces)	Ineffective	Ineffective	Ineffective
Former Yugoslavia I	Episode 1	25.09.1991	30.05.1992	8 months	Armed conflict	**Arms imports embargo** (all parties)	N/A	Ineffective	Mixed
	Episode 2	30.05.1992	01.10.1996	4 years 4 months	Armed conflict	**Comprehensive sanctions**	-	-	-
Former Yugoslavia II	Episode 1	31.03.1998	10.09.2001	3 years 5 months	Armed conflict	**Arms imports embargo** (all parties)	Ineffective	Ineffective	Ineffective
Guinea-Bissau	Episode 1	18.05.2012	Ongoing	> 2 year	Democracy support	**Travel ban**	Ineffective	Ineffective	Ineffective
Haiti	Episode 1	16.06.1993	27.08.1993	2 months	Democracy support	**Petroleum imports ban, arms imports embargo** (all parties), **asset freeze** (political entity – government)	Mixed	**Effective**	**Effective**
	Episode 2	27.08.1993	13.10.1993	2 months	Democracy support	**Suspension of sanctions**	N/A	Ineffective	Ineffective

(cont.)

Sanction regime	Episode	Start date	End date	Duration	Main objective	Sanction type	Effectiveness*		
							Coerce	Constrain	Signal
	Episode 3	13.10.1993	06.05.1994	7 months	Democracy support	Petroleum imports ban, arms imports embargo (all parties), asset freeze (political entity – government), **asset transfer**	Ineffective	**Effective**	**Effective**
	Episode 4	06.05.1994	31.07.1994	3 months	Democracy support	**Comprehensive sanctions**	–	–	–
	Episode 5	31.07.1994	16.10.1994	3 months	Democracy support	Comprehensive sanctions	–	–	–
Iran	Episode 1	23.12.2006	24.03.2007	3 months	Non-proliferation	**Proliferation sensitive goods and technology imports and exports ban, asset freeze** (individual/entity)	Ineffective	Ineffective	Mixed
	Episode 2	24.03.2007	03.03.2008	11 months	Non-proliferation	Proliferation sensitive goods and technology imports and exports ban, asset freeze (individual/entity), **arms exports embargo**	Ineffective	Ineffective	Mixed
	Episode 3	03.03.2008	09.06.2010	2 years 3 months	Non-proliferation	Proliferation sensitive goods and technology imports and exports ban, asset freeze (individual/entity), arms exports embargo, **travel ban**	Ineffective	Ineffective	Mixed
	Episode 4	09.06.2010	Ongoing	> 4 years	Non-proliferation	Proliferation sensitive goods and technology imports and exports ban, asset freeze (individual/entity), arms exports embargo, travel ban, **financial sector restrictions** (investment ban), **arms imports embargo** (government forces – specific weapons), **bunkering ban**	Ineffective	Mixed	Mixed
Iraq	Episode 1	22.05.2003	08.06.2004	1 year 1 month	Armed conflict	**Iraqi cultural property trade or transfer ban, arms imports embargo** (all parties)**, asset freeze** (individual/entity, political entity – former regime)**, asset transfer**	N/A	Ineffective	Ineffective
	Episode 2	08.06.2004	Ongoing	>10 years	Armed conflict	Iraqi cultural property trade or transfer ban, arms imports embargo (**non-governmental entities**), asset freeze (individual/entity, political entity – former regime), asset transfer (**until Dec 2016**)	N/A	Ineffective	Ineffective

Country	Episode	Start	End	Duration	Objective	Measures			
Lebanon	Episode 1	31.10.2005	Ongoing	> 8 years	Judicial process	**Travel ban, asset freeze** (individual/entity) [No designations made to date]	Ineffective	N/A	Ineffective
Liberia	Episode 1	19.11.1992	07.03.2001	8 years 4 months	Armed conflict	**Arms imports embargo** (all parties)	Ineffective	Ineffective	Ineffective
	Episode 2	07.03.2001	06.05.2003	2 years 2 months	Armed conflict	Arms imports embargo (all parties), **diamond exports ban, travel ban, diplomatic sanctions** (limit travel)	Mixed	**Effective**	**Effective**
	Episode 3	06.05.2003	22.12.2003	8 months	Armed conflict	Arms imports embargo (all parties), diamond exports ban, travel ban, diplomatic sanctions (limit travel), **timber exports ban**	Ineffective	**Effective**	**Effective**
	Episode 4	22.12.2003	16.06.2006	2 years 6 months	Armed conflict	Arms imports embargo (**non-governmental entities**), diamond exports ban, travel ban, timber exports ban, **asset freeze** (individual/entity – from Mar 2004)	N/A	**Effective**	**Effective**
	Episode 5	16.06.2006	Ongoing	> 8 years	Good governance	Arms imports embargo (non-governmental entities), diamond exports ban (**lifted Apr 2007**), travel ban, timber exports ban (**lifted Jun 2006**), asset freeze (individual/entity)	N/A	**Effective**	**Effective**
Libya I	Episode 1	31.03.1992	11.11.1993	1 year 7 months	Counterterrorism	**Aviation ban, arms imports embargo** (government forces), **diplomatic sanctions** (limit travel and number of diplomatic personnel, limit visas)	Mixed	**Effective**	Mixed
	Episode 2	11.11.1993	05.04.1999	5 years 5 months	Counterterrorism	Aviation ban, arms imports embargo (government forces), diplomatic sanctions (limit travel and number of diplomatic personnel, limit visas), **asset freeze** (political entity – government), **oil services equipment ban**	Mixed	**Effective**	Ineffective
	Episode 3	05.04.1999	12.09.2003	4 years 5 months	Counterterrorism	**Sanctions suspension and termination**	**Effective**	N/A	Mixed
Libya II	Episode 1	26.02.2011	17.03.2011	1 month	R2P	**Arms imports (all parties) and exports embargo, travel ban, asset freeze** (individual/entity)	Ineffective	Mixed	**Effective**
	Episode 2	17.03.2011	16.09.2011	6 months	R2P	Arms imports (all parties) and exports embargo, travel ban, asset freeze (individual/entity, **political entity – government**), **financial sector restrictions** (sovereign wealth funds/Central Bank), **aviation ban**	Ineffective	**Effective**	Ineffective
	Episode 3	16.09.2011	Ongoing	> 2 years	Armed conflict	Arms imports (**non-governmental entities**) and exports embargo, travel ban, asset freeze (individual/entity, political entity – **former regime**), financial sector restrictions (sovereign wealth funds/Central Bank – **lifted Dec 2011**), **bunkering ban, illicit crude oil exports ban**	N/A	Ineffective	**Effective**

(cont.)

Sanction regime	Episode	Start date	End date	Duration	Main objective	Sanction type	Effectiveness*		
							Coerce	Constrain	Signal
Rwanda	Episode 1	17.05.1994	16.08.1995	1 year 3 months	Armed conflict	**Arms imports embargo** (all parties)	Ineffective	Ineffective	Ineffective
	Episode 2	16.08.1995	10.07.2008	12 years 11 months	Armed conflict	Arms imports embargo (**non-governmental entities**)	N/A	Ineffective	Ineffective
Sierra Leone	Episode 1	08.10.1997	16.03.1998	5 months	Democracy support	**Diplomatic sanctions** (limit travel), **petroleum imports ban, arms imports embargo** (all parties)	Ineffective	Mixed	**Effective**
	Episode 2	16.03.1998	22.10.1999	1 year 7 months	Armed conflict	**Travel ban**, arms imports embargo (**non-governmental entities**)	Ineffective	Ineffective	Ineffective
	Episode 3	22.10.1999	05.07.2000	8 months	Armed conflict	Travel ban, arms imports embargo (non-governmental entities)	Ineffective	Ineffective	Ineffective
	Episode 4	05.07.2000	16.01.2002	1 year 6 months	Armed conflict	Travel ban, arms imports embargo (non-governmental entities), **diamond exports ban**	**Effective**	**Effective**	**Effective**
	Episode 5	16.01.2002	29.09.2010	8 years 8 months	Armed conflict	Travel ban, arms imports embargo (non-governmental entities), diamond exports ban (**expired** June 2003)	N/A	**Effective**	**Effective**
Somalia	Episode 1	23.01.1992	03.05.2002	10 years 3 months	Armed conflict	**Arms imports embargo** (all parties)	Ineffective	Ineffective	Ineffective
	Episode 2	03.05.2002	20.11.2008	6 years 7 months	Armed conflict	Arms imports embargo (all parties)	Ineffective	Ineffective	Ineffective
	Episode 3	20.11.2008	23.12.2009	1 year 1 month	Armed conflict	Arms imports embargo (all parties), **travel ban, asset freeze** (individual/entity, political entity – rebel faction)	N/A	Ineffective	Ineffective
	Episode 4	23.12.2009	22.02.2012	2 years 2 months	Armed conflict	Arms imports embargo (all parties), travel ban, asset freeze (individual/entity, political entity – rebel faction) **Secondary sanctions on Eritrea – arms imports** (all parties, individual/entities) **and exports embargo, travel ban, asset freeze** (individual/entity, political entity – government), **diaspora tax ban** (from Dec 2011)	**Effective**	Ineffective	**Effective**

	Start	End	Duration	Type	Sanctions			
Episode 5	22.02.2012	Ongoing	> 2 years	Armed conflict	Arms imports embargo (**non-governmental entities** – since Mar 2013), travel ban, asset freeze (individual/ entity, political entity – rebel faction), **charcoal exports ban** Secondary sanctions on Eritrea – arms imports (all parties, individual/entities) and exports embargo, travel ban, asset freeze (individual/entity, political entity – government), diaspora tax ban	N/A	Ineffective	Ineffective
Sudan I								
Episode 1	26.04.1996	16.08.1996	4 months	Ccunterterrorism	**Diplomatic sanctions** (limit travel and number of diplomatic personnel)	Ineffective	N/A	Mixed
Episode 2	16.08.1996	28.09.2001	5 years 1 month	Ccunterterrorism	Diplomatic sanctions (limit travel and number of diplomatic personnel), aviation ban [never in effect]	Ineffective	N/A	Ineffective
Sudan II								
Episode 1	30.07.2004	29.03.2005	8 months	Armed conflict	**Arms imports embargo** (non-governmental entities, territorially delimited)	Ineffective	Ineffective	Ineffective
Episode 2	29.03.2005	Ongoing	> 9 years	Armed conflict	Arms imports embargo (**all parties**, territorially delimited), **travel ban, asset freeze** (individual, from Feb 2012 also entity)	Ineffective	Ineffective	Ineffective
Taliban								
Episode 1	17.06.2011	Ongoing	> 3 years	Armed conflict	**Arms imports embargo** (non-governmental entities), **asset freeze** (individual/entity, political entity – former regime and rebel faction), **travel ban**	Ineffective	Ineffective	Mixed

* For the general evaluation criteria of effectiveness and Episode specific coding decisions, see Appendix 2.

Appendix 2   Sanctions effectiveness

Evaluation criteria for effectiveness

Sanctions effectiveness during each episode is determined based on a combined evaluation of (a) the overall policy outcome for each of the three purposes (coerce, constrain, signal) and (b) the United Nations targeted sanctions contribution to this outcome.

The 'policy outcome' uses a five-point scale with indicators specific to each purpose of sanctions (see below). The 'UN sanctions contribution' variable uses a six-point scale ranging from negative contribution to being the most significant of all policy instruments employed.

Effective episodes have an overall policy outcome of at least 4 and sanctions contribution of at least 3 (sanctions reinforce other measures).

Mixed effectiveness cases have an overall policy outcome of 3 and sanctions contribution of 3, 4, or 5.

Ineffective cases have an overall policy outcome of 1 or 2 or an outcome of 3, 4, or 5 and sanctions contribution of 0, 1, or 2.

Evaluation Criteria for Sanction Effectiveness

Overall policy outcome (coerce)	United Nations sanctions contribution to the outcome (coerce)
(1) Lack of significant change in behaviour, ignoring the UNSCR, or complete intransigence.	(0) Negative (regime is strengthened and/or increases its proscribed activity).
(2) Agreeing to a process and/or engaging in negotiations that could result in settling or resolving the dispute or in obfuscation, delaying, or changing terms of debate.	(1) None (no discernible sanctions contribution).
	(2) Minor (other measures taken appear most significant to outcome).
(3) Accommodation or significant concessions to resolve the dispute.	(3) Modest (sanctions reinforced other measures).
(4) Meeting most of the objectives of the UNSCR and/or approximating the core purposes as originally articulated in the UNSCR (not necessarily according to the explicit terms spelled out in the original UNSCR).	(4) Major (sanctions appear necessary, but not sufficient; or some acknowledgement by the target).
	(5) Significant (the single most important factor is the presence of UNSC sanctions).
(5) Meeting all the principal objectives of the UNSCR.	

Overall policy outcome (constrain)	United Nations sanctions contribution to the outcome (constrain)
(1) No discernible constraints experienced by the target.	(0) Negative (regime is strengthened and/or increases its proscribed activity).
(2) Increases in costs can be managed by the target (sanctions are largely a nuisance factor) perhaps due to ease of evasion.	(1) None (no discernible sanctions contribution).
(3) Slight increases in costs to target (as evidenced by diversion of trade through third countries, and/or delay in engaging in proscribed activity and/or diminution in the frequency of engagement in proscribed activity).	(2) Minor (other measures taken appear most significant to outcome).
	(3) Modest (sanctions reinforced other measures).
(4) Increases in costs, minor changes of strategy of the target, statement that target may be experiencing financial/material/logistical difficulties and/or constrained from engaging in proscribed activity.	(4) Major (sanctions appear necessary but not sufficient; or some acknowledgement by target).
	(5) Significant (the single most important factor is the presence of UNSC sanctions).
(5) Significant increases in costs, changes of strategy of the target, statement that target is experiencing financial/material/logistical difficulties and/or constrained from engaging in proscribed activity.	

Overall policy outcome (signal)	United Nations sanctions contribution to the outcome (signal)
(1) Norm (or norms) not articulated, no stigmatization and/or clear evidence of legitimation.	(0) Negative (regime is strengthened and/or increases its proscribed activity).
(2) Norm (or norms) poorly articulated (e.g. too many, diffusely articulated), limited evidence of stigmatization, and/or possible legitimation.	(1) None (no discernible sanctions contribution).
(3) Norm (or norms) articulated, and some stigmatization of target.	(2) Minor (other measures taken appear most significant to outcome).
(4) Norm (or norms) articulated and targets strongly stigmatized.	(3) Modest (sanctions reinforced other measures).
(5) Norm (or norms) clearly articulated and target fully stigmatized and/or isolated (e.g. effective signalling to the international community and stigmatizing and/or isolation of the target).	(4) Major (sanctions appear necessary, but not sufficient; or some acknowledgement by the target).
	(5) Significant (the single most important factor is the presence of UNSC sanctions).

Effective, mixed, and ineffective cases

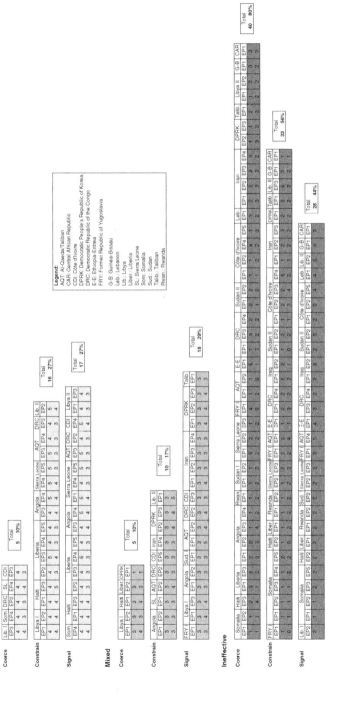

Episode-specific coding decisions

Al-Qaida/Taliban

EPISODE 1		
Coercion		
Policy outcome	Sanction contribution	Evaluation
1/5 Taliban refused to extradite bin Laden.	2/5 UN sanctions were not the primary tool for coercion; international diplomacy and US unilateral sanctions appeared more significant at the time (US legal proceedings were focused on bin Laden, not the Taliban).	Ineffective
Constraint		
Policy outcome	Sanction contribution	Evaluation
2/5 Restrictions on Ariana Airlines forced the Taliban to find new sources of supply (Viktor Bout).	4/5 UN sanctions multi-lateralized US unilateral measures (affecting the Gulf and western China).	Ineffective
Signalling		
Policy outcome	Sanction contribution	Evaluation
3/5 UNSCRs (1214 and 1267) clearly articulated violation of norm against terrorism under Chapter VII, but degree of stigmatization was limited (Taliban increased their proscribed activities and became increasingly intransigent).	5/5 The UNSCRs were the principal mechanism for communicating the international norm against terrorism, and Taliban was strongly stigmatized.	Mixed effectiveness

EPISODE 2		
Coercion		
Policy outcome	Sanction contribution	Evaluation
1/5 Taliban refused to extradite bin Laden and indeed became more closely aligned with him during this episode.	0/5 Additional sanctions pushed the Taliban closer to bin Laden.	Ineffective

Constraint		
Policy outcome	Sanction contribution	Evaluation
3/5 Ariana Airlines was fully grounded during this episode, but the other sanctions appeared to inconvenience, rather than constrain, the targets.	4/5 Sanctions appear critical to grounding of Ariana Airlines.	Mixed effectiveness

Signalling		
Policy outcome	Sanction contribution	Evaluation
3/5 Clear articulation of violation of norm against terrorism and further isolation of the Taliban, but degree of stigmatization felt by the targets was limited.	4/5 Expansion of sanctions against Taliban and extension to Al-Qaida was the principal mechanism for diffusing the international norm. However, Taliban behaviour also contributed to its stigmatization internationally.	Mixed effectiveness

EPISODE 3

Coercion		
Policy outcome	Sanction contribution	Evaluation
N/A (Individuals and supporters became the principal focus of coercion, but in order to constrain AQ/T. Individuals designated became unable to access their funds in some countries; others were deterred from providing continuing support.)	N/A	N/A

Constraint		
Policy outcome	Sanction contribution	Evaluation
5/5 AQ had very limited access to formal sector financial institutions; had limited funds to transfer; complained of limits on funds; moved to decentralized, locally sourced financing; change of strategy of Al-Qaida, both in its sources of financing (towards crime and local sources) and in the	3/5 Other factors, such as the NATO military intervention, clearly played a key role in the disruption of the organization and its change of strategy (at least at the outset); use of drones played a key role in the disruption of the organization; support of military operations in various parts of the world	Effective

Constraint		
Policy outcome	Sanction contribution	Evaluation
location of many of its attacks (increasingly in the developing world); at the beginning of the episode, AQ was still directing and financing attacks (Bali 1); by the middle, there was no evidence of direct command and control or financing from AQ central (Bali 2, Madrid, London); there was evidence of disruption of plots due to financial intelligence; AQ central virtually disappeared as a command and control centre during this episode.	increasingly important against affiliated entities (Somalia, Yemen).	

Signalling		
Policy outcome	Sanction contribution	Evaluation
5/5 AQ was strongly stigmatized and isolated, as were its principal financial supporters; strong reinforcement of norm against terrorism.	3/5 Creation of a global sanctions regime was critical for signalling AQ, its associates, and the global community about the norm against terrorism, but AQ actions and their repercussions played an increasingly important role in stigmatizing the group over the course of the episode (attacks on Muslims, attacks on soft targets in the developing world, diffuseness of attacks, i.e. not focused on the United States).	Effective

EPISODE 4

Coercion		
Policy outcome	Sanction contribution	Evaluation
N/A	N/A	N/A

Constraint		
Policy outcome	Sanction contribution	Evaluation
4/5 Al-Qaida core has been constrained in financial and operational terms. Its central leadership has been weakened and financial and operational cooperation between different affiliates globally remains difficult to pursue. This has led to changes of strategy in fundraising (towards criminal and local sources), operations (towards local and regional initiatives), and targets (local and regional targets in Asia and Africa) which have enabled them to commit acts of terrorism and take control of territory (Mali, Yemen, Somalia, Syria, and Iraq).	3/5 Other factors, such as regular drone attacks, multiple military interventions in regions where AQ affiliates operate, have clearly played a key role in the disruption of the core of the organization, and it setbacks for its affiliates in East Africa and the Sahel.	Effective

Signalling		
Policy outcome	Sanction contribution	Evaluation
5/5 AQ is strongly stigmatized and isolated globally, as well as locally, in most regions it operates. While AQ affiliates (through its 'franchise' system, such as AQ in the Islamic Maghreb, AQ in the Arabian Peninsula) constitute the majority of new designations, they are still able to mobilize local and regional rivalries on occasion to gain some support for their operations.	2/5 UN designations have begun to reflect changes within AQ, but AQ actions and their repercussions appear to play a more important role in stigmatizing the group (attacks on Muslims, criminal activities, theological differences, attacks on soft targets in the developing world, diffuseness of attacks, i.e. not retaining a focus on the United States).	Ineffective

Angola

EPISODE 1		
Coercion		
Policy outcome	Sanction contribution	Evaluation
2/5 UNITA agreed to a process, but there were frequent violations during the episode (particularly with regard to ceasefire and DDR).	3/5 The Angolan government captured UNITA's HQ 10 days before UNITA signed the Lusaka Protocol, but sanctions and the threat of further sanctions also played a role in unsettling UNITA commanders about maintaining access to weapons.	Ineffective
Constraint		
Policy outcome	Sanction contribution	Evaluation
3/5 Weapons remained available (from Zaire), but some diminution of the conflict at times during the episode.	3/5 Sanctions and the threat of further sanctions had, according to HRW, a psychological impact on UNITA leadership about maintaining access to weapons.	Mixed effectiveness
Signalling		
Policy outcome	Sanction contribution	Evaluation
3/5 Norms stated in UNSCR, but ambivalence from the United States and support from African allies ameliorated.	3/5 Sanctions and the threat of further sanctions coexisted with ongoing negotiations.	Mixed effectiveness
EPISODE 2		
Coercion		
Policy outcome	Sanction contribution	Evaluation
2/5 Some UNITA concessions, but not implemented in good faith during the episode, tactical ceasefire in March 1998, but UNITA maintained 30 to 50K forces during this period.	3/5 The Angolan government used the sanctions to its advantage militarily.	Ineffective

Constraint		
Policy outcome	Sanction contribution	Evaluation
3/5 Some demobilization, some increase in costs of target (diplomatic diversions, renaming of closed consulates).	3/5 The Angolan government used the sanctions to its advantage militarily.	Mixed effectiveness

Signalling		
Policy outcome	Sanction contribution	Evaluation
3/5 UNITA was increasingly isolated (UNSCR 1127 increasingly focused on UNITA), but initially benefits from a rally round the flag moment from its leadership.	3/5 The Angolan government used the sanctions to its advantage militarily.	Mixed effectiveness

EPISODE 3

Coercion		
Policy outcome	Sanction contribution	Evaluation
1/5 Asset freeze and especially diamond sanctions prompted Savimbi to break the agreement, a split emerged within UNITA.	4/5 Target acknowledged the significance of diamonds sanctions, but UNITA was also driven militarily from access to diamond areas.	Ineffective

Constraint		
Policy outcome	Sanction contribution	Evaluation
4/5 Revenues from diamonds were reduced, and split developed within UNITA (which was taken advantage of by the Angolan government).	4/5 Acknowledgement by the target about the significance of diamonds, but UNITA also driven militarily from access to diamond areas.	Effective

Signalling		
Policy outcome	Sanction contribution	Evaluation
4/5 Savimbi branch of UNITA became increasingly isolated (only UNITA referenced as principal party in UNSCR 1173).	4/5 Target acknowledged the significance of diamonds sanctions, but UNITA was also driven militarily from access to diamond areas.	Effective

EPISODE 4

Coercion

Policy outcome	Sanction contribution	Evaluation
1/5 Sanctions contributed to shifting the balance of forces, but Savimbi showed no sign of concessions before his death.	2/5 Ultimately, the use of force was decisive.	Ineffective

Constraint

Policy outcome	Sanction contribution	Evaluation
5/5 Diplomatic sanctions terminated much of UNITA's official presence abroad; diamond sanctions weakened the prospects of UNITA's raising of funds; squeezing the financial sources led to no salt, no beer, and demoralization of Savimbi's forces.	4/5 Acknowledgement by the target of the impact of sanctions.	Effective

Signalling

Policy outcome	Sanction contribution	Evaluation
5/5 Savimbi became the principal target and was thoroughly isolated by UNSCR 1221.	4/5 Diplomatic pressure was also significant.	Effective

Central African Republic

EPISODE 1

Coercion

Policy outcome	Sanction contribution	Evaluation
2/5 Despite political instability and violence, 20 January 2014 appointment of new president and government could result in future progress towards implementation of transitional arrangements.	1/5 Insufficient time for sanctions to have much effect, diplomatic negotiations, and presence of military forces on the ground (including the French) more significant to the outcome.	Ineffective

Constraint		
Policy outcome	Sanction contribution	Evaluation
1/5 Security and humanitarian situation continues to deteriorate with escalating violence and human rights abuses by Séléka and anti-Balaka groups.	1/5 Insufficient time for sanctions to have much effect; region is awash in arms; presence of military forces on the ground (including the French) more significant to the outcome.	Ineffective

Signalling		
Policy outcome	Sanction contribution	Evaluation
3/5 UN authorization of African-led Mission signalled support for regional (AU and ECCAS) peacekeeping operations, and reinforced transitional and peace agreements. Specific naming of Séléka and the anti-Balaka militias provided some stigmatization.	2/5 Other measures (peacekeeping mission) were more significant.	Ineffective

Côte d'Ivoire

EPISODE 1		

Coercion		
Policy outcome	Sanction contribution	Evaluation
1/5 No positive movement towards convening of elections.	1/5 Individual sanctions, but no names designated; no evidence of enforcement of arms embargo; presence of French and ECOWAS forces.	Ineffective

Constraint		
Policy outcome	Sanction contribution	Evaluation
1/5 No discernible constraints experienced by the target, given the limited enforcement of the arms embargo.	1/5 No designations, no enforcement.	Ineffective

Signalling		
Policy outcome	Sanction contribution	Evaluation
2/5 Individual sanctions were delayed 30 days and then not implemented by the Sanctions Committee, no evidence of target stigmatization.	2/5 Minor, due to the French use of force in response to attacks.	Ineffective

EPISODE 2

Coercion		
Policy outcome	Sanction contribution	Evaluation
1/5 No positive movement towards convening of elections, but following ECOWAS, UNSCR 1633 recognized the difficulty and legitimized Gbagbo's mandate for an additional year.	2/5 Regional initiatives by ECOWAS and other countries (Mbeki in April 2005) appeared more significant; no individuals targeted to date.	Ineffective

Constraint		
Policy outcome	Sanction contribution	Evaluation
2/5 Increase in costs could be managed by target because of the availability of weapons stock in the country.	3/5 Implementation was good according to PoE, but weapons were widely available and borders unregulated (reference to both Liberia and Sierra Leone in UNSCR 1584); sanctions reinforced DDR efforts.	Ineffective

Signalling		
Policy outcome	Sanction contribution	Evaluation
2/5 Norm poorly articulated (due to ambiguity of goals, absence of designations, and lack of focus in target selection); but signalled support for regional initiatives; UNSCR 1633 (following ECOWAS) legitimated Gbagbo's decision to postpone elections.	3/5 Mediation efforts by ECOWAS and other parties and presence of peacekeeping forces both significant.	Ineffective

EPISODE 3

Coercion		
Policy outcome	Sanction contribution	Evaluation
4/5 Elections were finally held in December of 2010, but they were delayed five times during the long episode and the post-election crisis reveals a lack of commitment to democratic processes.	3/5 Sanctions coexisted with, and reinforced, the mediation efforts (particularly the Ouagadougou power-sharing agreement).	Effective

Constraint		
Policy outcome	Sanction contribution	Evaluation
2/5 Neither the diamond embargo nor the arms inspections facilitated a significant reduction in access to weapons by the government or rebel group.	4/5 Sanctions were necessary for constraint and indirectly acknowledged by the target (given government evasion of inspections and diversion of trade in diamonds).	Ineffective

Signalling		
Policy outcome	Sanction contribution	Evaluation
3/5 Norm was articulated, but not well (because so many different norms were invoked in UNSCRs over the 5-year period of the episode), yet some stigmatization from delays in holding elections.	3/5 Due to mediation efforts underway (Ouagadougou).	Mixed effectiveness

EPISODE 4

Coercion		
Policy outcome	Sanction contribution	Evaluation
4/5 Outtara installed as president following ECOWAS closing of Central Bank and Gbagbo's arrest by French/UN/rebel forces.	2/5 Changes on the ground were decisive militarily; rescinding Gbagbo's authority to access funds from the Central Bank also appears to have been a critical factor in undermining the regime.	Ineffective

Constraint		
Policy outcome	Sanction contribution	Evaluation
5/5 Rescinding Gbagbo's authority to access funds from the Central Bank appears to have been a critical factor in constraining the Gbagbo regime; e.g. Gbagbo's reliance on extortion from prominent businesses for financial support in April and May.	2/5 UN sanctions followed measures taken by regional organizations in Africa and Europe.	Ineffective

Signalling		
Policy outcome	Sanction contribution	Evaluation
5/5 Norm clearly articulated and target (former president Gbagbo) fully stigmatized by being added to a UN sanctions list and referred to the ICC.	4/5 Designations of both Gbagbo and his wife were significant.	Effective

EPISODE 5

Coercion		
Policy outcome	Sanction contribution	Evaluation
1/5 Gbagbo supporters boycotted the parliamentary elections and some Gbagbo supporters continued to resist militarily and remained a threat to peace and reconciliation. The Outtara government, not the principal target of sanctions, held parliamentary elections, initiated a Truth and Reconciliation Commission, cooperated with DDR and SSR activities and generally abided by international human rights norms in pursuit of core peacebuilding goals, but there are questions about the slow pace of reconciliation, the lack of progress in both DDR and SSR, and despite progress on Kimberley Process certification, the government's failure to address diamond smuggling.	3/5 Sanctions appear to be supporting the activities of other agents and actors involved in peacebuilding, including UNOCI, ECOWAS.	Ineffective

Constraint		
Policy outcome	Sanction contribution	Evaluation
3/5 The boycott of parliamentary elections in December 2011 and military challenges on both the western and eastern borders suggest Gbagbo supporters were constrained, but still able to engage in military challenges to the government.	3/5 Sanctions reinforced the outcome of military action and the ICC referral.	Mixed effectiveness

Signalling		
Policy outcome	Sanction contribution	Evaluation
4/5 Gbagbo was strongly stigmatized with the ICC referral, but this may have prompted potential spoilers to try to destabilize the regime, and some armed resistance has continued on the border.	2/5 ICC referral sent a more powerful signal to other potential spoilers than sanctions.	Ineffective

Democratic People's Republic of Korea

EPISODE 1		
Coercion		
Policy outcome	Sanction contribution	Evaluation
3/5 DPRK returned to negotiations, destroyed a cooling tower, shut down a plant, turned over 18,000 pages of documents, and agreed to denuclearization plan and process to achieve 1718 conditions, but the talks ultimately broke down in December 2008 and DPRK subsequently resumed its missile and nuclear programmes.	3/5 Because sanctions were not rigorously implemented and enforced, it appears that the US unilateral sanctions and desire for US engagement/ removal from state sponsors of terrorism list may have been more significant than UN sanctions in returning DPRK to negotiations.	Mixed effectiveness

Constraint		
Policy outcome	Sanction contribution	Evaluation
2/5 Little evidence of constraining effect on North Korea, other than luxury goods being stopped from some countries.	2/5 UN sanctions were poorly implemented; US unilateral financial sanctions are most significant.	Ineffective

Signalling		
Policy outcome	Sanction contribution	Evaluation
3/5 Non-proliferation norm clearly articulated by unanimous UNSC resolution; unprecedented support from China to sanction North Korea; but unclear degree of stigmatization experienced by DPRK.	4/5 Ban on luxury goods aimed at leadership and supporters represents important signal; diplomatic pressure, Six-Party Talks also underway.	Mixed effectiveness

EPISODE 2

Coercion		
Policy outcome	Sanction contribution	Evaluation
1/5 Despite occasional (and short-lived) diplomatic engagements throughout the episode, the DPRK has, according to the Panel of Experts, 'continued to reject and to violate Security Council Resolutions.' In spite of the UN resolutions and widespread international protest, the DPRK has repeatedly tested ballistic missile technology and detonated another nuclear device in February 2013.	3/5 While UN sanctions have been an important tool to coerce the target, other sanctions, international pressure and diplomatic efforts (particularly from China) have also been significant to the outcome.	Ineffective

Constraint		
Policy outcome	Sanction contribution	Evaluation
3/5 According to the Panel of Experts, international efforts appear to make it more difficult and expensive for	4/5 UN sanctions were primary instruments of constraint; other sanctions have also played an important role in	Mixed effectiveness

Constraint		
Policy outcome	Sanction contribution	Evaluation
the DPRK to continue its nuclear and missile programmes. However, they also indicate adaptation by DPRK in sanctions evasion techniques, and that arms exports continue (though partly constrained by the sanctions). November 2010 revelations (the Hecker report) regarding ability of DPRK to construct uranium facility in face of sanctions and continued progress of ballistic missiles programme indicated limited constraining impact.	constraining DPRK's nuclear programme.	

Signalling		
Policy outcome	Sanction contribution	Evaluation
3/5 Non-proliferation norm was continuously articulated by consistent and unanimous responses by the Council against tests conducted by the DPRK, but the strength of the signal remained limited, since measures have not gone beyond improved enforcement, repeated condemnations and moderate increases in the targets designated.	4/5 Sanctions are a primary means for signalling the non-proliferation norm, but diplomatic pressure has also played an important role.	Mixed effectiveness

EPISODE 3

Coercion

Policy outcome	Sanction contribution	Evaluation
1/5 Despite occasional (and short-lived) diplomatic engagements, there has been no breakthrough, or return to the Six Party Talks or evidence that the DPRK has scaled back its proscribed activity. Reports that it has resumed its Yongbon facility suggest the opposite.	3/5 While UN sanctions have been an important tool to coerce the target, other unilateral sanctions (including from China), international pressure and diplomatic efforts (particularly from China) have also been significant to the outcome.	Ineffective

Constraint

Policy outcome	Sanction contribution	Evaluation
3/5 According to the June 2013 Panel of Experts report, while sanctions have not stopped DPRK's nuclear and ballistic missile programmes, they have 'in all likelihood considerably delayed (North Korea's) timetable and, through the imposition of financial sanctions and the bans on the trade in weapons, has choked off significant funding which would have been channeled into its prohibited activities.'	4/5 UN sanctions were primary instruments of constraint, other sanctions, particularly from China, have also played an important role in constraining DPRK's nuclear programme.	Mixed effectiveness

Signalling

Policy outcome	Sanction contribution	Evaluation
3/5 Non-proliferation norm was continuously articulated by consistent and unanimous responses by the Council against tests conducted by the DPRK, but the strength of the signal remained limited, since measures have not gone beyond repeated condemnations and moderate increases in the targets designated.	4/5 Sanctions are a primary means for signalling the non-proliferation norm, but diplomatic pressure has also played an important role.	Mixed effectiveness

Democratic Republic of Congo

EPISODE 1		
Coercion		
Policy outcome	Sanction contribution	Evaluation
1/5 No evidence of any belligerents agreeing to sign the GPA.	3/5 Sanctions coexisted with MONUC (UN PKO) and GPA (diplomatic efforts).	Ineffective
Constraint		
Policy outcome	Sanction contribution	Evaluation
2/5 Some mid-level combatants deserted the rebel groups and there was a general reduction in levels of armed violence (although the war had ended, the region was already awash in arms and armed violence continued in many local areas).	3/5 Given statements from combatants who felt threatened by the embargo and joined government forces, but the existence of the peace agreement and end of the war also played important roles (even though local armed violence continued).	Ineffective
Signalling		
Policy outcome	Sanction contribution	Evaluation
3/5 Peace enforcement and cessation of hostilities were clearly signaled and some stigmatization of the target through PoE reports; also increased awareness of sanctions regime by regional actors.	4/5 Sanctions appeared necessary, but not sufficient, and there was some acknowledgement by the target.	Mixed effectiveness
EPISODE 2		
Coercion		
Policy outcome	Sanction contribution	Evaluation
4/5 Major warring factions concluded that elections were preferable to violence, while some others interested in future political careers in the DRC changed their behaviour and joined the process.	3/5 Sanctions contributed to a larger effort during this episode, including increased international attention, DDR, SSR, EU efforts, and elections that signalled the potential for peace; changes in Ituri region were due to numerous small peace agreements with different armed groups.	Effective

Constraint		
Policy outcome	Sanction contribution	Evaluation
3/5 There is limited evidence that total levels of arms were reduced, but there was some evidence of a disruption of the gold trade through Ugandan traders used to finance arms purchases.	3/5 Given the presence of arms in the region, the porosity of borders, and the problems associated with MONUC forces (low capacity and unwillingness to carry out its mandate) and evidence of the selling of arms to belligerents in the Ituri region during this episode; sanctions disrupted the gold trade.	Mixed effectiveness

Signalling		
Policy outcome	Sanction contribution	Evaluation
4/5 Transition government was signalled as legitimate to domestic, regional, and international actors and targets were identified and stigmatized.	3/5 Sanctions contributed to a larger diplomatic effort during this episode, including increased international attention, DDR, SSR, EU efforts, and elections that signaled the potential for peace.	Effective

EPISODE 3

Coercion		
Policy outcome	Sanction contribution	Evaluation
3/5 Some combatants began to negotiate a ceasefire and sign agreements (following joint DRC/Rwanda military operations against them), but others who were integrated became renegade DRC army forces within the region; some of the relevant neighbouring countries (Rwanda) began cooperating with the DRC government.	2/5 ICC prosecutions, diplomatic pressure on Rwanda, arrests of belligerents from the FDLR in Germany and France, and use of force appeared more important than sanctions.	Ineffective

Constraint		
Policy outcome	Sanction contribution	Evaluation
4/5 Integration and renaming indicated a change of strategy for some groups, and some pushed out of resource rich areas (the Governor of North Kivu did not allow planes to leave with resources or to land with weapons); Rwandan joint operations with DRC resulted in arrest of Nkunda and weakening of rebel forces.	3/5 Sanctions triggered a political process through donors who put pressure on Rwanda (naming and shaming were critical during this episode), but the final outcome cannot be attributed to the sanctions alone, but to other factors, particularly given the military offensives.	Effective

Signalling		
Policy outcome	Sanction contribution	Evaluation
3/5 Many combatants appeared to respond to the DDR process by abandoning militia groups, but poor integration of rebel forces into the armed forces of the DRC (which legitimates them) limited the overall effect.	2/5 Military offensive and arrest or capture of key rebel leaders appeared more significant than sanctions.	Ineffective

EPISODE 4

Coercion		
Policy outcome	Sanction contribution	Evaluation
2/5 Although the M23 has been militarily defeated in 2013, other rebel groups (the FDLR, LRA, ADF-NALU, etc.) have continued to engage in violence, systematic human rights violations and remained a major threat to DRC territorial integrity.	2/5 Due to weak implementation by neighboring states, sanctions have had a minor role in determining this outcome. Military engagement, diplomatic initiatives and ICC prosecution (the first ICC conviction and sentence was of a DRC combatant) were more significant policy instruments used by the Council. In 2013, MONUSCO's intervention brigade is widely considered to have been significant in the military advances of the FARDC.	Ineffective

Constraint		
Policy outcome	Sanction contribution	Evaluation
2/5 The re-emergence of foreign-backed rebel groups and their continued activity have indicated the continued availability of arms and access to resources.	2/5 Territorial control by rebel groups, particularly when supported by neighboring countries, has been most significant to grant access to the resources that fuel the conflict.	Ineffective

Signalling		
Policy outcome	Sanction contribution	Evaluation
3/5 UNSCRs supported the DRC and the peace process, but there is little indication that foreign backers of rebel groups have been stigmatized within the region or internationally (Rwandan denials of involvement and elected to UNSC in 2012). However, the establishment of the intervention brigade signalled strong intent to resolve the issue.	3/5 Sanctions reinforced regional diplomatic initiatives and UN PKO.	Mixed effectiveness

Ethiopia-Eritrea

EPISODE 1		
Coercion		
Policy outcome	Sanction contribution	Evaluation
5/5 A ceasefire and peace agreement were agreed to by the end of 2000.	1/5 UN arms embargo was imposed only 8 days before Ethiopia declared military victory; changes on the ground were most significant to the outcome.	Ineffective

	Constraint	
Policy outcome	Sanction contribution	Evaluation
1/5 No discernible constraints were experienced by the targets before the cessation of the conflict.	1/5 Given the limited amount of time to implement the arms embargo.	Ineffective

	Signalling	
Policy outcome	Sanction contribution	Evaluation
4/5 Support for OAU mediation clearly signalled, and both countries clearly encouraged to engage in OAU-mediated talks.	2/5 Military changes on the ground were most significant to the outcome (agreement to OAU mediation).	Ineffective

Former Yugoslavia I

	EPISODE 1	

	Coercion	
Policy outcome	Sanction contribution	Evaluation
N/A No coercive demands made in either UNSCR 713 or 724.	N/A	N/A

	Constraint	
Policy outcome	Sanction contribution	Evaluation
1/5 The arms embargo worked to the advantage of Serbia, given its own production capabilities and given that the embargo was imposed equally on the other parties.	0/5 The Serbian regime was strengthened militarily and there was an escalation of violence throughout the region.	Ineffective

	Signalling	
Policy outcome	Sanction contribution	Evaluation
3/5 Cutting off arms to cease hostilities, some stigmatization of Serbia.	3/5 The arms embargo reinforced diplomatic pressure, the presence of a peacekeeping force (UNPROFOR), and threat of the use of force.	Mixed effectiveness

Former Yugoslavia II

EPISODE 1		
Coercion		
Policy outcome	Sanction contribution	Evaluation
4/5 UNSCR 1367 terminating the sanctions noted with satisfaction that a substantive dialogue had begun, special police units were withdrawn, and access was provided to humanitarian organizations.	2/5 UN arms embargo was in place a year before NATO bombing campaign began but NATO airstrikes were most significant to the outcome.	Ineffective
Constraint		
Policy outcome	Sanction contribution	Evaluation
2/5 Increases in costs were managed by both parties; Serbia had access to domestic arms production and the KLA had support from Albania.	2/5 NATO airstrikes and KVM monitoring most significant to the outcome.	Ineffective
Signalling		
Policy outcome	Sanction contribution	Evaluation
3/5 Opposition to escalation of force was signalled, and both parties were clearly encouraged to engage in Contact Group and OSCE-mediated talks.	2/5 Contact Group diplomacy and legal referrals to the ICC and ICTY were the most important signals.	Ineffective

Guinea-Bissau

	EPISODE 1	
	Coercion	
Policy outcome	Sanction contribution	Evaluation
3/5 A more inclusive transitional government and roadmap plan was established in May 2013. Concerns about the country's stability and the influence of the military in civilian affairs remain significant as the elections were delayed twice.	2/5 UNSC sanctions indicated the lack of legitimacy of the coup but have been only marginal in the conduct of political negotiations. The SRSG, the PBC and UN Integrated Office in Guinea-Bissau (UNIOGBIS), as well as ECOWAS, have played the most important roles.	Ineffective
	Constraint	
Policy outcome	Sanction contribution	Evaluation
2/5 Minor constraint experienced by the military leadership in their continuous interference in political affairs, as evidenced by the changes in the 'transitional government' and the acceptance of preparation of new elections.	2/5 UN sanctions played a minor role as compared diplomatic initiatives by the UN and regional actors (AU, CPLP, ECOWAS), including the presence of 600 ECOWAS peacekeepers and UNIOGBIS.	Ineffective
	Signalling	
Policy outcome	Sanction contribution	Evaluation
3/5 Even though the initial resolution signalled the Security Council's concern with the situation and support for regional arrangements, narrow sanctions measures indicated limited conviction at the outset. There has been some stigmatization of the targets, as indicated by international efforts in support of political transition.	2/5 While targeted sanctions were the main mechanism through which the UNSC sought to delegitimize the coup, other international actors (CPLP, EU, UN PBC, SRSG) have since been more prominent in signalling international norms and stigmatizing unconstitutional changes of government in the country.	Ineffective

Haiti

	EPISODE 1	
Coercion		
Policy outcome	Sanction contribution	Evaluation
3/5 Cédras agreed to a process of negotiation 5 days after the sanctions were imposed (resulting in the Governor's Island Agreement or GIA) and appointed a new prime minister, selected by Aristide.	4/5 Sanctions appear to have been necessary to force move to negotiations, based on target response rate (5 days). It was not the impact of the sanctions, but the decision to initiate them.	Mixed effectiveness
Constraint		
Policy outcome	Sanction contribution	Evaluation
4/5 No material constraints experienced by the target (given the limited amount of time between sanctions initiation and target response), but the regime had less political room for manoeuver following the imposition of sanctions and changed its strategy.	4/5 Sanctions were the most significant new element in the continuing negotiation process between the OAS, the UN, and the regime.	Effective
Signalling		
Policy outcome	Sanction contribution	Evaluation
4/5 Norm clearly articulated in UNSCR 841, with repeated references to the legitimate Aristide government, specific demands to reinstate the ousted regime, and unanimous support of UNSC and OAS; targets strongly stigmatized as 'de facto authorities'.	4/5 The norm would not have been broadly articulated without the backing of the UNSC, but they followed OAS action, unilateral measures, and diplomatic processes.	Effective

EPISODE 2

Coercion		
Policy outcome	Sanction contribution	Evaluation
N/A No demands were made of any party in UNSCR 861.	N/A	N/A

Constraint		
Policy outcome	Sanction contribution	Evaluation
1/5 Neither party lived up to the terms: Cédras used the period to stockpile weapons; Aristide was slow to submit an amnesty decree to Parliament.	0/5 Sanctions were suspended because of the terms of the GIA. Some evidence of strengthening of the regime during the period.	Ineffective

Signalling		
Policy outcome	Sanction contribution	Evaluation
2/5 Norm clearly articulated, but due to vagueness of GIA, on which the sanctions suspension was based, the application of the norm resulted in the partial legitimation of the Cédras regime (by implying both parties potentially equally at fault).	4/5 Lifting of sanctions was the main instrument for the international community to signal support for the negotiated return to democracy in Haiti.	Ineffective

EPISODE 3

Coercion		
Policy outcome	Sanction contribution	Evaluation
2/5 Cédras agreed to parliamentary proposal for resolving the impasse between the de factos and the Aristide government on February 19, but his motives were suspect.	4/5 Reimposition of sanctions is important but not the only major initiative during the period (Friends of the SG on Haiti, SG involvement, and unilateral measures from the United States).	Ineffective

Constraint		
Policy outcome	Sanction contribution	Evaluation
4/5 The de factos were not prevented from committing violence against their opponents in Haiti, but the increasing costs of sanctions overall affected the ability of the Cédras regime to constitute a viable government; the regime was able to use sanctions to insulate themselves and pass costs on to the population.	5/5 Sanctions appear to have been the principal source of constraint on the ability to govern.	Effective

Signalling		
Policy outcome	Sanction contribution	Evaluation
4/5 Norm was articulated about the return of Aristide and strong stigmatization due to reimposition of sanctions.	4/5 Diplomatic initiatives underway at this time also conveyed a strong signal to the regime.	Effective

Iran

EPISODE 1		
Coercion		
Policy outcome	Sanction contribution	Evaluation
2/5 Iran participated in talks with the IAEA, but did not have any apparent change of behaviour or notable cooperation with IAEA within the relatively short time period to comply.	3/5 The threat and imposition of sanctions reinforced the IAEA process, as did diplomatic pressure (E3+3); unilateral measures were also in place.	Ineffective

Constraint		
Policy outcome	Sanction contribution	Evaluation
1/5 Iran continued to make progress on nuclear processing during this episode.	1/5 Too short a period for sanctions to be effective (EU didn't implement until April 2007, after the conclusion of the episode) and no focus on enforcement.	Ineffective

Signalling		
Policy outcome	Sanction contribution	Evaluation
3/5 Support for non-proliferation norm and reinforcing IAEA authority clear, as well as signal that violations of norm will result in price; first time UNSC threatened and applied sanctions in support of non-proliferation norm; but unclear that target felt much stigmatization (due to the widespread support within Iran for its right to develop nuclear energy and the fact that the IAEA cannot confirm Iranian programme is not for peaceful purposes).	4/5 Precedent established regarding use of UN sanctions to enforce non-proliferation norm (and promote IAEA role in negotiations).	Mixed effectiveness

EPISODE 2

Coercion		
Policy outcome	Sanction contribution	Evaluation
2/5 IAEA noted progress by Iran on addressing some outstanding issues in February 2008, but no clear progress or concessions on the major issue (clarity on the purposes of the programme).	3/5 Sanctions and diplomatic pressure reinforced IAEA negotiations with Iran.	Ineffective

Constraint		
Policy outcome	Sanction contribution	Evaluation
2/5 Iranian exports of arms appeared to decline, but the data were spotty; Russian sales of arms also declined in the episode.	2/5 Primary effect from non-UN sanctions and informal US pressure on financial sector to limit Iranian business; little UN attention to implementation.	Ineffective

Signalling		
Policy outcome	Sanction contribution	Evaluation
3/5 Support for non-proliferation norm and reinforcing IAEA authority clear.	3/5 Sanctions reinforced other measures (diplomatic pressure).	Mixed effectiveness

EPISODE 3

Coercion		
Policy outcome	Sanction contribution	Evaluation
2/5 Iran remained engaged with the IAEA, but no substantial concessions were made.	3/5 Sanctions and diplomatic pressure reinforced IAEA negotiations with Iran.	Ineffective

Constraint		
Policy outcome	Sanction contribution	Evaluation
3/5 Indications of increasing difficulties by Iranian traders in obtaining financing.	2/5 US unilateral measures and strong pressure on other countries to adopt financial sanctions, as well as EU pressure, appeared most significant.	Ineffective

Signalling		
Policy outcome	Sanction contribution	Evaluation
3/5 Norm against proliferation was articulated in the UNSCR, but the signal was weakened slightly by the reservations over the imposition of additional sanctions after progress in the negotiations.	3/5 Because initial progress in negotiations was followed by a 'rush to sanctions', the legitimacy of the UNSC role in reinforcing the norm (by imposing sanctions) was weakened; IAEA negotiations also underway.	Mixed effectiveness

EPISODE 4

Coercion		
Policy outcome	Sanction contribution	Evaluation
3/5 After several years of negotiations with little progress, recently elected president Rouhani significantly changed the dynamics of negotiation. In November 2013 a preliminary agreement was reached with the E3+3 to settle all outstanding nuclear-related issues.	2/5 Concessions were largely a product of diplomatic initiatives and, later, of the change of government in Iran. While the overall link between increasingly comprehensive sanctions and change of behaviour in return to negotiations is unclear, UN sanctions were secondary to non-UN sanctions on the Central Bank and petroleum sector and not the primary source of escalating pressure on the Iranian economy.	Ineffective

Constraint		
Policy outcome	Sanction contribution	Evaluation
3/5 PoE reports (June 2012) argued that sanctions were slowing Iranian procurement of some critical items required for its nuclear programme, but that further development in the programme has continued (June 2012, 2013); enhanced sanctions enforcement (inspections,	3/5 The creation of PoE has enhanced enforcement capability and PoE's June 2012 report noted the interdiction of critical items needed for the Iranian nuclear capability, slowing its development; other instruments (cyber sabotage, targeted assassinations, general economic sanctions	Mixed effectiveness

Constraint		
Policy outcome	Sanction contribution	Evaluation
seizures, export controls, etc.) appear to have forced changes of Iranian procurement strategies and design choices, the effect of which is to increase costs and delay nuclear activities.	from US/EU also contributed to constraint.	

Signalling		
Policy outcome	Sanction contribution	Evaluation
3/5 P-5 agreement to put in place a stronger monitoring and enforcement capability sent strong signal to Iran and underscored the importance of the non-proliferation norm at the beginning of the episode. But the non-unanimous vote, with opposition from Brazil and Turkey, and lack of support for further measures since then have somewhat diluted the degree of stigmatization at the outset, and illustrated the contested nature of norms about enrichment and reprocessing. The broader economic measures imposed by the US/EU since 2011 have confused the clarity of the UN signal (as illustrated by MS concerns about implementation of UN sanctions in the June 2012 PoE report).	3/5 Greater monitoring, implementation, and enforcement of UN sanctions have signalled to Iran a willingness to reinforce the non-proliferation norm. Reduced clarity of the signal has resulted primarily from confusion between UN measures and more stringent non-UN sanctions on Central Bank and oil.	Mixed effectiveness

Iraq

EPISODE 1		
Coercion		
Policy outcome	Sanction contribution	Evaluation
N/A	N/A	N/A
Constraint		
Policy outcome	Sanction contribution	Evaluation
5/5 Baathist government forces never mounted a significant counter campaign during the episode, and most of its key officials were arrested, killed, or captured after the 2003 invasion. Saddam Hussein's sons were killed in a firefight with the occupying coalition forces in July, and Saddam Hussein was captured in December of 2003.	2/5 The military occupation forces played a far more significant role in constraining remnants of the Baathist regime.	Ineffective
Signalling		
Policy outcome	Sanction contribution	Evaluation
2/5 Norms were not clearly articulated in the targeted financial measures against former members of the Baathist regime (more concern about the private appropriation of government funds); UNSCR was focused on end of the 661 regime, oil for food, and recognition of the authority of the occupying regime, re-engaging the UN with a request for an SRSG.	2/5 Targeted sanctions stigmatized more sharply than comprehensive sanctions (which these replaced), but the overthrow of the Baathist regime was more important in stigmatizing individuals associated with the former government.	Ineffective
EPISODE 2		
Coercion		
Policy outcome	Sanction contribution	Evaluation
N/A	N/A	N/A

Constraint		
Policy outcome	Sanction contribution	Evaluation
2/5 Baathist government forces never became a serious threat to the regime, but multiple insurgencies (in Basra, Fallujah, and later from Al-Qaida in Iraq) continued to challenge the regime.	1/5 Only 9 additional individuals and entities were added to the list during this long episode and foreign military engagement (including a surge in American forces) continued until 2010.	Ineffective

Signalling		
Policy outcome	Sanction contribution	Evaluation
3/5 UNSCR 1546 focused primarily on the legitimacy and the transfer of authority to the new Iraqi-led government, but occupying forces remained to provide core security until 2010, qualifying the terms of the regime's authority.	2/5 Lifting the arms embargo on the regime and maintaining targeted measures on remnants of the Baathist regime contributed to reinforcing the signal, but targeted sanctions did not focus on the main threats to the regime during this episode (no designations were made of individuals associated with the multiple insurgencies), and diplomatic recognition and state building efforts were more significant to the outcome.	Ineffective

Lebanon

EPISODE 1		
Coercion		
Policy outcome	Sanction contribution	Evaluation
3/5 Syria cooperated with the Commission regarding access to individuals, sites, and information, but although Syria withdrew its military forces, it did not cease to interfere in Lebanese political life.	2/5 No individual designations made; UNIIIC investigation and reports, diplomatic pressure, and Syria/Lebanon bilateral relations most significant to outcome.	Ineffective

Constraint		
Policy outcome	Sanction contribution	Evaluation
N/A Neither the Commission (whose mandate ended in 2009) nor the Government of Lebanon has ever notified the UNSC to apply the sanctions.	N/A	N/A

Signalling		
Policy outcome	Sanction contribution	Evaluation
4/5 Creation of a special Commission and Court has sent a strong signal in support of an international judicial process, internationalizing the case.	2/5 Although sanctions have been threatened, the lack of use has weakened the signal; judicial processes under UNIIIC and STL are most significant source of signalling.	Ineffective

Liberia

EPISODE 1		

Coercion		
Policy outcome	Sanction contribution	Evaluation
3/5 The implementation of a ceasefire was not achieved until 1996, a transitional government was established and elections were held in 1997, but the armed conflict (both by domestic opponents against Taylor after the election, and by Taylor in support of the RUF in Sierra Leone) continued thereafter.	1/5 Changes on the ground were more important than sanctions (Taylor was winning militarily and consolidated his authority with the election); ECOWAS took the lead in managing the conflict (peace process and peacekeeping).	Ineffective

Constraint		
Policy outcome	Sanction contribution	Evaluation
1/5 The ability of different Liberian parties to the conflict to	2/5 ECOMOG was a major presence within Liberia, other countries (Guinea) intervened in the	Ineffective

Constraint		
Policy outcome	Sanction contribution	Evaluation
continue fighting was not significantly constrained.	conflict, and weapons were widely available throughout the region.	

Signalling		
Policy outcome	Sanction contribution	Evaluation
2/5 Support for peace enforcement (the various Accords and the role of ECOMOG) was clearly articulated in the initial UNSCRs (for the first half of the episode), but stigmatization was diffused to all parties, Taylor was partially legitimated by the elections, and the silence after 1997 election sent an unclear signal in the second half of the episode.	2/5 The presence of the arms embargo was less important than UNSC support for ECOMOG and the peace accords (and its silence following their implementation).	Ineffective

EPISODE 2

Coercion		
Policy outcome	Sanction contribution	Evaluation
3/5 Liberia began to distance itself from the RUF, but much of this was apparently window dressing; Monrovia's grip on the RUF was gradually loosened and sanctions on Liberia contributed to the RUF's decision to reaffirm its ceasefire agreement in May 2001 (British forces were also present in Sierra Leone from September 2000); the conflict in Sierra Leone effectively came to an end in January 2002; however, Liberia intervened in the affairs of Cote d'Ivoire during this episode.	3/5 Sanctions on their own did not achieve the RUF ceasefire; use of military force and diplomatic pressure were also significant.	Mixed effectiveness

Constraint		
Policy outcome	Sanction contribution	Evaluation
4/5 UN sanctions stopped some deliveries of ammunition and heavy equipment, but significant amounts of arms and ammunition continued to be delivered to Liberia during the episode; there is insufficient information in Panel of Expert reports to indicate whether Liberia was constrained from supporting the RUF during this episode, though there is strong evidence of severe economic and budgetary crisis in Liberia (high levels of unemployment, increased taxes to pay for military operations).	3/5 Sanctions contributed to the disappearance of Liberia-labelled rough diamonds from official markets; at the same time, the regime was also under military challenge on two fronts and the government had difficulty in accessing some diamond producing areas.	Effective

Signalling		
Policy outcome	Sanction contribution	Evaluation
4/5 Secondary sanctions were very clearly articulated in UNSCR 1343; Liberia and individual targets in the government were strongly stigmatized.	3/5 The principal target's own actions (destabilizing the entire region) also contributed to his stigmatization.	Effective

EPISODE 3

Coercion		
Policy outcome	Sanction contribution	Evaluation
5/5 Taylor and the LURD agreed to a ceasefire on 17 June and subsequently participated in and agreed to a comprehensive Liberian peace settlement (including a ceasefire, transitional government, DDR, SSR, TRC) on 18 August 2003.	2/5 Loss of territory to LURD and MODEL forces, Nigerian mediation, and indictment by the Sierra Leone Tribunal played a significant role.	Ineffective

Constraint		
Policy outcome	Sanction contribution	Evaluation
5/5 Taylor acknowledged that he was constrained by the timber sanctions, arguing that the international community had denied Liberians the right to defend themselves by imposing an arms embargo and that timber sanctions starved Liberia of revenue: 'Something as simple as a toothpick cannot be exported from Liberia', according to Taylor.	4/5 Acknowledgement by the target; but changes on the ground, diplomatic pressure (Nigeria), and limited use of force (LT 100 US marines) also played a role in constraining (and eventually toppling) the regime.	Effective

Signalling		
Policy outcome	Sanction contribution	Evaluation
4/5 Taylor and the Government of Liberia were strongly stigmatized in UNSCR 1478.	3/5 Special Court indictment and Nigerian mediation (offering Taylor asylum) also contributed to stigmatization.	Effective

EPISODE 4

Coercion		
Policy outcome	Sanction contribution	Evaluation
N/A	N/A	N/A

Constraint		
Policy outcome	Sanction contribution	Evaluation
4/5 Panel of Experts concludes that sanctions helped to stabilize the situation in Liberia; elections were held, DDR took place, though Taylor tried to destabilize the process at the outset.	3/5 Sanctions against the remnants of Taylor's regime reinforced the peacebuilding efforts of the Government of Liberia, but international tribunals (the Sierra Leone Special Court and ICC) played a major role in constraining Charles Taylor.	Effective

Signalling		
Policy outcome	Sanction contribution	Evaluation
5/5 Potential spoilers were deterred from destabilizing the regime.	3/5 Sanctions reinforced the peacebuilding efforts of the Government of Liberia and international tribunals played a major role in constraining the remnants of Charles Taylor's regime.	Effective

EPISODE 5

Coercion		
Policy outcome	Sanction contribution	Evaluation
N/A	N/A	N/A

Constraint		
Policy outcome	Sanction contribution	Evaluation
4/5 No major challenges to the Johnson Sirleaf government from remnants of Taylor's forces or other potential spoilers; peaceful elections held and government enters Kimberley Process.	3/5 Sanctions reinforced the peacebuilding efforts of the Government of Liberia but international tribunal played a major role in constraining the remnants of Charles Taylor's regime.	Effective

Signalling		
Policy outcome	Sanction contribution	Evaluation
4/5 International tribunal's first conviction of a former head of state since World War II sends powerful signal-deterring spoilers from destabilizing the government; signal in support of more effective resource management less clear and effectiveness of signal diminishes over time without action to reinforce.	3/5 Sanctions reinforce the peacebuilding efforts of the Liberian government, but the lifting of sanctions on diamonds and timber and move to delist without adding new measures focused on resources weakens the signal.	Effective

Libya I

EPISODE 1		
Coercion		
Policy outcome	Sanction contribution	Evaluation
3/5 Libya initially offered to turn over suspects to a court monitored by the Arab League or the UN in June 1992, a move rejected by the United States and the United Kingdom; later, in late September early October 1993, the Government of Libya stated its intent to encourage those charged in the Lockerbie bombing to appear for trial in Scotland and expressed willingness to cooperate with French authorities.	4/5 US and UK sanctions were also present, but UN Targeted Sanctions appear to have been necessary for Libya counter-proposals.	Mixed effectiveness
Constraint		
Policy outcome	Sanction contribution	Evaluation
4/5 Statements of Libyan official regarding costs of sanctions and decision to offer suspects indicated a change of strategy away from previous non-response.	4/5 Sanctions were probably necessary for the outcome, but coexisted with unilateral sanctions.	Effective
Signalling		
Policy outcome	Sanction contribution	Evaluation
3/5 Norm was well articulated, but target's ability to mobilize external support (from Morocco and Zimbabwe, both UNSC members at the time) limited its degree of stigmatization.	4/5 UN sanctions were the primary mechanism through which the norm is being enforced.	Mixed effectiveness

EPISODE 2

Coercion		
Policy outcome	**Sanction contribution**	**Evaluation**
3/5 Given the similarity to a Libyan proposal offered years before (trial before a Scottish court), the central change in behaviour came from accommodation on the part of the United States and United Kingdom, concerned about the decline in support for sanction against Libya.	3/5 Sanctions reinforced other measures. They constrained Qadhafi and prompted him to an extensive effort to counter their effects. Growing sanctions fatigue also played a major role.	Mixed effectiveness

Constraint		
Policy outcome	**Sanction contribution**	**Evaluation**
4/5 Clear evidence of economic impact and some evidence of reduction in proscribed activity (state support for terrorism).	4/5 UN Aviation ban and cumulative effect of petroleum services sector sanctions appear to have played a major role.	Effective

Signalling		
Policy outcome	**Sanction contribution**	**Evaluation**
2/5 Stigmatization of the regime declined over time. Signal to Libya that by delivering two individuals for trial the sanctions would be suspended; also a signal to Libya's many supporters in the AU and AL that their requests had been taken into consideration.	4/5 UN sanctions clearly specified the terms of an agreement, but Qadhafi's diplomatic counter-offensive reduced his stigmatization.	Ineffective

EPISODE 3

Coercion		
Policy outcome	**Sanction contribution**	**Evaluation**
4/5 Suspects were turned over, trials conducted, compensation provided, and terrorism renounced, but not on the precise terms of the original UNSCRs.	4/5 Suspension of sanctions was significant to reinforce legal procedures underway in domestic and international courts regarding compensation.	Effective

Constraint		
Policy outcome	Sanction contribution	Evaluation
N/A	N/A	N/A

Signalling		
Policy outcome	Sanction contribution	Evaluation
3/5 Norms against state-sponsored terrorism were consistently articulated in relevant UNSCRs (1192 and 1506), but Qadhafi was able to mobilize support from the AU. Arab League, Non-Aligned Movement and Organization of the Islamic Conference to limit the extent of his stigmatization.	4/5 Sanctions suspension created an incentive to accept norms against state-sponsored terrorism in order for Libya to be relegitimized and reintegrated into the international community.	Mixed effectiveness

Libya II

EPISODE 1		
Coercion		
Policy outcome	Sanction contribution	Evaluation
1/5 Qadhafi regime was intransigent and increased threats to, and attacks on, its population.	2/5 In addition to sanctions, the ICC referral reduced Qadhafi's room for manoeuver; regime was precarious and was losing control on the ground to rebel forces.	Ineffective

Constraint		
Policy outcome	Sanction contribution	Evaluation
3/5 Immediate drying up of liquidity made it more difficult for the Qadhafi regime to support its mercenary forces.	5/5 Financial sanctions were the single most important factor in constraining the regime during this episode.	Mixed effectiveness

Signalling		
Policy outcome	Sanction contribution	Evaluation
4/5 Some key regime members defected and invocation of R2P was widely noted in the region and globally.	3/5 UN sanctions were the primary mechanism through which the norm is being enforced.	Effective

EPISODE 2

Coercion		
Policy outcome	Sanction contribution	Evaluation
2/5 Qadhafi attacked Benghazi, but was driven back by NTC forces and French fighter planes enforcing the no-fly zone; Qadhafi agreed to AU peace process, but it was rejected by the NTC.	2/5 No-fly zone more important than sanctions in repelling attack on Benghazi.	Ineffective

Constraint		
Policy outcome	Sanction contribution	Evaluation
5/5 Evidence of significant financial constraint, as sanctions were expanded (ATM cash withdrawals were capped in the country, interest rates were doubled to try to attract capital) cash disbursements were critical to the payment of mercenary forces.	4/5 Financial sanctions were necessary, but many other constraints on the regime were created by the imposition of the no-fly zone.	Effective

Signalling		
Policy outcome	Sanction contribution	Evaluation
5/5 Defections continued, and even Qadhafi's supporters outside the country were more concerned with how to manage his exit than to maintain his rule.	2/5 No-fly zone, ICC referral, and diplomatic pressure were major factors.	Ineffective

EPISODE 3

Coercion		
Policy outcome	Sanction contribution	Evaluation
N/A No specific demands for change of behaviour were articulated in the relevant UNSCRs (2009, 2016, 2017, 2022, 2040, or 2095).	N/A	N/A

Constraint		
Policy outcome	Sanction contribution	Evaluation
5/5 Sanctions were lifted on most activities of Libyan government financial institutions, but were retained on those believed to retain linkages to key family members and Qadhafi regime supporters; pro-Qadhafi regime efforts to counter the NTC are absent.	2/5 The exile, arrest, or killing of key regime members and supporters, combined with military defeat have been most significant in constraining targets.	Ineffective

Signalling		
Policy outcome	Sanction contribution	Evaluation
3/5 The legitimacy of the NTC as a transitional Government of Libya was established at the outset, but its successor, the GNC, faced serious ongoing challenges from local militias.	3/5 Relatively quick release of most funds and successive UNSCRs during the first half of this episode signalled recognition of NTC as the legitimate government, but degree of consolidation of regime away from its predecessor is due also to the death of Qadhafi, diplomatic recognition by many states, public opinion within Libya, and the ICC pursuit of prosecution of cases.	Mixed effectiveness

Rwanda

EPISODE 1		
Coercion		
Policy outcome	Sanction contribution	Evaluation
1/5 RPF won militarily and Hutu elements used refugee camps in Zaire to mobilize continued opposition to the interim government of national unity.	2/5 Lack of deployment of UN peacekeeping force and victory of one party of the conflict were most significant to the negative outcome.	Ineffective
Constraint		
Policy outcome	Sanction contribution	Evaluation
1/5 While the genocide ended in July 1994, the armed conflict continued.	2/5 The arms embargo only went into effect 3 months before the RPF military victory.	Ineffective
Signalling		
Policy outcome	Sanction contribution	Evaluation
2/5 References to genocide were implied, not explicitly stated in UNSCR 918 and perpetrators are not mentioned.	2/5 The withdrawal and slow deployment of UN peacekeeping forces also contributed to a weak signal.	Ineffective

EPISODE 2		
Coercion		
Policy outcome	Sanction contribution	Evaluation
N/A No demands were made in any of the relevant UNSCRs.	N/A	N/A
Constraint		
Policy outcome	Sanction contribution	Evaluation
1/5 The conflict continued even after the lifting of the arms embargo in 2008 (although it has largely been displaced into the DRC).	2/5 Weapons remain freely available in neighbouring countries (DRC) and the borders are largely unenforced; regional war underway in the Great Lakes region throughout the long episode.	Ineffective

Signalling		
Policy outcome	Sanction contribution	Evaluation
2/5 Weakly articulated in the UNSCRs; continues to be challenged by rebel forces.	2/5 Diplomatic recognition of the government and increase in aid flows to the government were most significant to the outcome.	Ineffective

Sierra Leone

EPISODE 1		
Coercion		
Policy outcome	Sanction contribution	Evaluation
5/5 Regional ceasefire and agreement to restore constitutional rule (the Conakry Communiqué) was negotiated on 23 October 1997; Kabbah was restored to office on 10 March 1998 after ECOMOG forces recaptured Freetown.	2/5 ECOMOG forces intervened in the country and there were active ECOWAS diplomatic activities.	Ineffective
Constraint		
Policy outcome	Sanction contribution	Evaluation
3/5 AFRC was constrained, while fighting between RUF and ECOMOG forces continued throughout the episode.	3/5 Reinforced ECOWAS sanctions and ECOMOG activity.	Mixed effectiveness
Signalling		
Policy outcome	Sanction contribution	Evaluation
5/5 Goals (democracy support) clearly articulated in the UNSCR, as well as reinforcement of regional initiatives (ECOWAS).	4/5 No country recognized the regime during this episode.	Effective

EPISODE 2

Coercion

Policy outcome	Sanction contribution	Evaluation
2/5 Lomé Agreement was reached on 7 July 1999, but the agreement was flawed because it legitimized the RUF and gave it access to and control over diamond resources.	2/5 ECOMOG and Togolese diplomatic intervention appear to have been more salient.	Ineffective

Constraint

Policy outcome	Sanction contribution	Evaluation
1/5 RUF controlled most of the territory of the country during this period and challenged the Kabbah government.	2/5 Lomé Agreement legitimized RUF and access to diamond resources, arms amply available, and mobility was not constrained due to porosity of borders.	Ineffective

Signalling

Policy outcome	Sanction contribution	Evaluation
2/5 Diffuse norms, rebels were told to cease hostilities, no mention of RUF, and Lomé peace agreement legitimized them.	3/5 Legitimation came from the Lomé peace agreement.	Ineffective

EPISODE 3

Coercion

Policy outcome	Sanction contribution	Evaluation
1/5 Significant increase in armed violence by RUF during this episode, abduction of UN troops, war between UNAMIL and RUF intensified, RUF closed in on Freetown (May 2000), British intervened (8–10 May 2000).	2/5 Sanctions remained unchanged and major increase in external military intervention by UNAMSIL (February 2000) and later by the United Kingdom (May 2000).	Ineffective

Constraint		
Policy outcome	Sanction contribution	Evaluation
2/5 RUF was not significantly constrained until major UN and UK forces arrive in 2000.	2/5 Sanctions remained unchanged and major increase in external military intervention.	Ineffective

Signalling		
Policy outcome	Sanction contribution	Evaluation
2/5 Diffuse norms (protection of civilians, human rights, HIV/ AIDS, attacks on UN personnel), still trying to reinforce Lomé agreement, while doubling the number of UNAMSIL forces.	2/5 Sanctions remained unchanged and major increase in external military intervention.	Ineffective

EPISODE 4

Coercion		
Policy outcome	Sanction contribution	Evaluation
4/5 Ceasefire agreement (Abuja) was signed on 10 November 2000, UN troops arrived in November/December 2000 to enforce ceasefire, UN began to deploy in rebel held territory (March 2001), and disarmament of rebels began (May 2001).	4/5 Diamond sanctions were applied to reinforce PKOs and tip the balance against the RUF; secondary sanctions (UNSCR 1343) applied to Liberia during this period 'probably contributed to the RUF's decision to sign an unconditional ceasefire in November 2000 and reaffirm the agreement in May 2001' (UN Expert Meeting on Natural Resources and Conflict in Africa, Cairo, 2006). Sanctions, however, reinforced other measures including the deployment of UK troops in May 2000 and military operations launched from Guinea against the RUF.	Effective

Constraint		
Policy outcome	Sanction contribution	Evaluation
5/5 While there is evidence of evasion, the diamond embargo was credited with 'an almost complete halt to the traffic in illicit diamonds from Sierra Leone to Liberia'.	4/5 Diamond sanctions were applied to reinforce PKOs and tip the balance against the RUF; secondary sanctions applied to Liberia (UNSCR 1343) during this period.	Effective

Signalling		
Policy outcome	Sanction contribution	Evaluation
4/5 Primary signal was to RUF. Created the basis for a Special Court (SCSL), and signalling support of the Kimberly Process for Certification of Origin of rough diamonds.	3/5 Other measures (negotiations, Abuja accord, and basis for special court) were also major factors in signalling.	Effective

EPISODE 5

Coercion		
Policy outcome	Sanction contribution	Evaluation
N/A	N/A	N/A

Constraint		
Policy outcome	Sanction contribution	Evaluation
5/5 Potential spoilers were constrained; substantial DDR as early as February 2004, local elections took place, war crimes trials began, peacekeepers departed, and peaceful transition from Kabbah regime to opposition party.	3/5 Sanctions supported complementary peacebuilding activities.	Effective

Signalling		
Policy outcome	Sanction contribution	Evaluation
5/5 Potential spoilers were deterred from destabilizing the regime; PBC credited with some success.	3/5 Sanctions combined with rulings of the special court to stigmatize former RUF leaders.	Effective

Somalia

EPISODE 1

Coercion

Policy outcome	Sanction contribution	Evaluation
1/5 Due to intransigence of the principal parties to the conflict, continued hostilities, failure of more than 35 attempts to negotiate a peace settlement, and the withdrawal of UN peacekeeping forces during the episode.	1/5 UN peacekeeping forces (and UNITAF) were more significant than sanctions, the country was already awash in arms, and neighbouring states were major violators of the arms embargo.	Ineffective

Constraint

Policy outcome	Sanction contribution	Evaluation
1/5 Principal parties continued to engage in violence throughout the episode.	1/5 UNITAF and UNOSOM II were the principal sources of constraining interference with humanitarian operations.	Ineffective

Signalling

Policy outcome	Sanction contribution	Evaluation
1/5 Although the signal in support of humanitarianism was initially strong, the UN withdrawal from the country 2 years later, followed by 7 years of virtual inaction, actually weakened the norm.	0/5 Non-implementation of the arms embargo weakened the signal (in addition to UN withdrawal and later inaction).	Ineffective

EPISODE 2

Coercion

Policy outcome	Sanction contribution	Evaluation
1/5 The UIC was not coerced by sanctions, but defeated militarily.	1/5 Although the UNSC had re-engaged with Somalia, the Ethiopian invasion was the single most important factor.	Ineffective

Constraint		
Policy outcome	Sanction contribution	Evaluation
1/5 No reduction in the level of arms in the conflict during the episode, but evidence that the flow of weapons into Somalia increased during the episode.	1/5 The proxy war increased the flow of arms into the region, AMISOM given no authorization to enforce the arms embargo.	Ineffective

Signalling		
Policy outcome	Sanction contribution	Evaluation
1/5 Degree of external interference increased during the episode; Somalia was invaded by one neighbour, and proxy war broke out within the region.	1/5 Re-engagement of the UNSC initially supported the signal, but sanctions remained essentially unchanged; other measures (US backing for Ethiopia) and the lack of UNSC response following the invasion weakened the signal.	Ineffective

EPISODE 3

Coercion		
Policy outcome	Sanction contribution	Evaluation
N/A N/A	N/A N/A	N/A

Constraint		
Policy outcome	Sanction contribution	Evaluation
1/5 No one was designated during this episode; arms continued to be freely available in the country.	1/5 Since there were no designations during the episode, their contribution to constraint was not discernible.	Ineffective

Signalling		
Policy outcome	Sanction contribution	Evaluation
2/5 The lack of focus in articulation of purposes in the UNSCRs during the episode – challengers to the Djibouti Agreement, Al Shabaab, piracy, support for the transitional government, condemnation of external	3/5 Poor design of the sanctions (and the absence of designations) rendered their effectiveness in signalling limited.	Ineffective

Signalling		
Policy outcome	Sanction contribution	Evaluation
intervention – combined with the absence of designations, contributed to a poorly articulated signal.		

EPISODE 4

Coercion		
Policy outcome	Sanction contribution	Evaluation
4/5 The Monitoring Group reported that Eritrea has responded to international pressure to curb its involvement in Somalia and found no evidence of direct support to Al Shabaab from Eritrea between July 2011 and the end of the episode; but Eritrea continued to violate UNSCRs by deploying troops in part of the country.	3/5 There is evidence that a portion of the Eritrean air force was grounded due to the sanctions, but there was also strong diplomatic pressure from IGAD; Eritrea fall-out with a faction of the leadership of Al Shabaab.	Effective

Constraint		
Policy outcome	Sanction contribution	Evaluation
1/5 Arms continued to be available in the region and Al Shabaab gained both territory and popular support in the territory it controlled in Somalia during the first half of the episode (even after individual designations were made in 2010).	2/5 Territorial gains early in the episode enabled Al Shabaab to find alternative financial sources of support, particularly from charcoal exports; AMISOM was present but given no authorization to enforce the arms embargo; but military reversals from the October 2011 Kenyan invasion were significant towards the end of the episode.	Ineffective

Signalling		
Policy outcome	Sanction contribution	Evaluation
4/5 Secondary sanctions are unusual and sent a strong signal; Eritrea denied that it was interfering in	4/5 Secondary sanctions sent a strong stigmatizing signal, and the UNSCR was unusually explicit	Effective

Signalling		
Policy outcome	Sanction contribution	Evaluation
the conflict, but it was widely recognized as heavily involved in the conflict.	in its condemnation of Eritrea's role; there was also diplomatic pressure on Eritrea from IGAD.	

EPISODE 5

Coercion		
Policy outcome	Sanction contribution	Evaluation
N/A	N/A	N/A

Constraint		
Policy outcome	Sanction contribution	Evaluation
2/5 The Monitoring Group argues that although Al Shabaab has suffered conventional military setbacks since 2012, its military strength remained 'arguably intact' in terms of operational readiness in 2013. There is limited evidence of impact of the charcoal ban, and the Monitoring Group reported flagrant violation of the ban on exports by Kenyan forces and their local allies, particularly operating out of Kismayo. Although the Monitoring Group reported improvement in implementation of the revised arms embargo by Member States, arms continue to be freely available in the country, and at least early in the current episode, one of the major sources was from diversion of weapons from regular Somali transitional government forces.	2/5 Military intervention by Kenya appears to have been the most significant source of setback to Al Shabaab forces.	Ineffective

Signalling		
Policy outcome	Sanction contribution	Evaluation
2/5 There continue to be diffuse purposes contained in UNSCRs (five in 2013 alone) – Al Shabaab, piracy, support to transitional government, condemnation of external intervention, secondary sanctions on Eritrea, humanitarian relief operations, human rights violations, treatment of women and children.	3/5 Diplomatic pressure on Eritrea from IGAD; UN SRSG negotiated peace settlement.	Ineffective

Sudan I

EPISODE 1		
Coercion		
Policy outcome	Sanction contribution	Evaluation
1/5 Sudan apparently made some efforts to locate suspects and to investigate immigration records in response to OAU investigation prior to the imposition of UNSCR 1044 (January 1996), but did not cooperate thereafter (indicating that it could not fulfil an impossible request), hence UNSCR 1054 (April 1996) imposing diplomatic sanctions; suspects never handed over and some evidence that one fled with Bin Laden to Afghanistan in May 1996.	2/5 OAU mediation efforts appear to have been more significant; diplomatic sanctions were largely a nuisance for Sudan.	Ineffective
Constraint		
Policy outcome	Sanction contribution	Evaluation
N/A	N/A	N/A

Signalling		
Policy outcome	Sanction contribution	Evaluation
3/5 Norms against state-sponsored terrorism and in support of initiatives taken by regional organizations articulated, but only modest stigmatization (due to Egyptian toning down of sanctions content of UNSCR 1054, which was criticized by the United States).	3/5 UNSCRs were not the only source of stigmatization, but the ongoing OAU efforts.	Mixed effectiveness

EPISODE 2

Coercion		
Policy outcome	Sanction contribution	Evaluation
1/5 Suspects were never handed over (Sudan possibly assisted the flight of one of them before the authorization of the aviation ban), but it is unclear whether the suspects remained in Sudan; there was no evident increase in state sponsorship of terrorism; indeed, some evidence that Sudan was reducing its involvement in state-sponsored terrorism during this period.	2/5 OAU and bilateral negotiations also continued during the episode; US unilateral measures against harbouring of bin Laden (who left in May 1996) and its cruise missile attacks on pharmaceutical complex in August 1998 also probably played an important role.	Ineffective

Constraint		
Policy outcome	Sanction contribution	Evaluation
N/A	N/A	N/A

Signalling		
Policy outcome	Sanction contribution	Evaluation
2/5 Authorizing and then not imposing a sanction is not a strong signal; reduction in evidence of stigmatization by OAU and non-aligned members of the UNSC over the course of the episode.	2/5 The key instrument of signalling (a potential aviation ban) was never imposed. Lack of follow-up on what triggered the initial concern (the assassination attempt) suggests that growing apathy (or possibly a view that this was a largely bilateral or regional matter) explained the weakness of the signal.	Ineffective

Sudan II

EPISODE 1		
Coercion		
Policy outcome	Sanction contribution	Evaluation
2/5 The Government of Sudan outlined steps to disarm the Janjaweed (June 2004), but did not carry them out during the episode.	1/5 The agreement for disarmament took place before the sanctions were imposed.	Ineffective
Constraint		
Policy outcome	Sanction contribution	Evaluation
1/5 No discernible constraints observed (particularly on the Janjaweed militias), and local production of arms increased.	0/5 Janjaweed militias were strengthened by being incorporated into the police, and therefore legitimated by being brought into the state (which is not a targeted party).	Ineffective

Signalling		
Policy outcome	Sanction contribution	Evaluation
2/5 The norm was poorly articulated (due to the complexity of the negotiations underway in the southern Sudan, the North/ South conflict, and to clear divisions on UNSC), but there is some evidence of stigmatization.	2/5 Other measures (negotiations, ongoing diplomacy, and intensifying NGO pressure) appear to have been more significant than sanctions.	Ineffective

EPISODE 2

Coercion		
Policy outcome	Sanction contribution	Evaluation
2/5 The Government of Sudan agreed to a process and signed the agreements in May 2006, and again in 2011; the terms of the agreements have not, however, been fulfilled (and the most recent agreement did not include two of the major parties to the conflict).	2/5 Little evidence of significant sanctions contribution to the signing of the May 2006 or July 2011 agreements; AU and regional member state mediation and AMIS/ UNAMID peace keeping missions have played major roles.	Ineffective

Constraint		
Policy outcome	Sanction contribution	Evaluation
2/5 Evidence of slight decline in small arms imports, but constraints appear to have been easily managed by the target (Government of Sudan).	2/5 Limited evidence of significant sanctions contribution; presence of AMIS/UNAMID peacekeeping missions with mandate for enforcement.	Ineffective

Signalling		
Policy outcome	Sanction contribution	Evaluation
3/5 While the Government of Sudan is still under some stigmatization, al-Bashir is increasingly able to travel. In June 2012 an AU summit was moved from Malawi to Ethiopia to ensure his participation, following the Government of Malawi's refusal to accept his attendance to the meeting in light of its obligations with the ICC.	2/5 ICC actions have been more significant than the listing of only four individuals in 2006.	Ineffective

Taliban

	EPISODE 1	
Coercion		
Policy outcome	Sanction contribution	Evaluation
2/5 While some Taliban have sporadically joined reconciliation talks, for the most part, there is no clear process and violence has continued, with no substantial concessions by the Taliban.	3/5 Some targeted individuals have demanded delisting as a prerequisite to engagement in talks; emphasis by the government on the need for flexibility to remove listed individuals and increasing importance of travel for reconciliation talks indicates that sanctions have been important for some individuals, yet most of the Taliban have remained outside the process, NATO military engagement with Afghan and ISAF forces remains significant to the outcome, and other diplomatic efforts are also underway.	Ineffective
Constraint		
Policy outcome	Sanction contribution	Evaluation
2/5 Taliban continues to control significant territory, has increased levels of violence, and has access to resources (primarily through forms of taxation/extortion).	2/5 Listings remain relevant; frozen assets are reported, but the Taliban nonetheless are able to substitute outside contributions with revenue derived from the territory they control.	Ineffective

Signalling		
Policy outcome	Sanction contribution	Evaluation
3/5 The creation of the new sanctions committee (the 1988 Committee) revived the sanctions against the Taliban at the beginning of the episode (which had been secondary given the emphasis on Al-Qaida in the 1267 regime since 2001). The addition of names and of flexibility for travel exemptions differentiating among the Taliban legitimates some, but strongly stigmatizes others (particularly the Haqqani Network).	3/5 Sanctions playing important role in reconciliation process, with listing and delisting reinforcing bilateral and multilateral negotiations with the Taliban.	Mixed effectiveness

Appendix 3   TSC database codebook

Coding key

Variable number	Variable name	Standard coding			
	Variable description	Yes: 1	No: 0	N/A: −99	Missing:.

General background

		Time in months			
v1	**United Nations Security Council (UNSC)** *responsiveness* The time between the UNSC first taking note of a conflict or situation (presidential note, official conversation/discussion, item on the agenda, etc.) and the imposition of sanctions. Only relevant for the first episode. NOTE: Adjustments in the middle of existing sanction regimes (i.e. Taliban and Iraq) are coded as N/A (−99).				
v2	**Is a permanent member of the Security Council (P5)** *directly affected or involved?* Direct involvement refers to the degree of engagement between a P5 member and the targeted country or region. A high degree of engagement will generally exist between bordering territories, former colonial powers and subjects, Cold War and contemporary allies, patron states and their clients, as well as between states with a history of close interaction (due to large diaspora constituencies residing in a P5 country, for example).	Yes: 1	No: 0		
v3	**Identity of P5 member affected or involved?** More than one P5 member may be affected or involved (as indicated in extra columns v3a and v3b). NOTE: N/A refers to cases where no P5 member was affected or involved.	US: 1 France: 5	China: 2	UK: 3	Russia: 4
v4	**Is an elected Security Council (SC) member directly** *affected or involved?* See v2.	Yes: 1	No: 0		
v5	**Is a regional organization involved?** Involvement of regional organizations includes, among others, mediation, peacekeeping, sanctions, or humanitarian assistance. NOTE: For regional organizations involved, see v168–v176.	Yes: 1	No: 0		

(*cont.*)

v6	**Is the conflict part of another conflict within the region?** Conflict has well-acknowledged/established links to a preceding conflict in another country/countries in the region. Only relevant for the first episode.	Yes: 1	No: 0
v7	**What is the target's degree of global interdependence?** Measured as trade as a percentage of GDP. NOTE: This variable has not yet been coded.	Open field	
v8	**Distinctively unique aspects of this case** This variable covers a broad variety of distinctive elements that can be contained within the design of the sanctions themselves or within the environment they aim to address. Anything novel associated with the relevant sanctions regime.	Open field	
v9	**Cases involve regime change?** Refers to regime change as an outcome at some point throughout the duration of UN targeted sanctions. Causality is not implied. Information for the whole sanctions regime is provided in the first episode. NOTE: In cases where sanctions regimes are split (e.g. AQT), regime change is coded only for the first episode of the original regime.	Yes: 1	No: 0

Objectives

Refers to objectives articulated in the UNSC resolutions that trigger new episodes. More than one objective may apply.

v10	*Objective: Nuclear non-proliferation*	Yes: 1	No: 0
v11	*Objective: Counterterrorism*	Yes: 1	No: 0
v12	*Objective: Armed conflict – Cease hostilities*	Yes: 1	No: 0
v13	*Objective: Armed conflict – Negotiate peace agreement*	Yes: 1	No: 0
v14	*Objective: Armed conflict – Peace enforcement*	Yes: 1	No: 0
v15	*Objective: Armed conflict – Peacebuilding* Support initiatives such as disarmament, demobilization, and reintegration (DDR), security sector reform (SSR), or United Nations Peacebuilding Support Office (UNPBSO) support.	Yes: 1	No: 0
v16	*Objective: Democracy support* Such as restoring constitutionally elected governments or supporting transitional governments and dissuading spoilers.	Yes: 1	No: 0
v17	*Objective: Good governance* Such as rule of law, transparency and accountability mechanisms (i.e. Extractive Industries Transparency Initiative or Kimberley Process).	Yes: 1	No: 0
v18	*Objective: Human rights*	Yes: 1	No: 0
v19	*Objective: Protect population under the Responsibility to Protect (R2P)*	Yes: 1	No: 0
v20	*Objective: Support humanitarian efforts*	Yes: 1	No: 0
v21	*Objective: Support judicial process*	Yes: 1	No: 0
v22	*Primary objective* Acknowledging the complexity of the situation, the primary objective in each episode was based on the text of the principal UNSC resolution that triggered the episode.	Nuclear non-proliferation: 1 Counterterrorism: 2 Armed conflict (cease hostilities, negotiate peace agreement, peace enforcement, and/or peace building): 3 Democracy support: 4 Good governance: 5 Human rights: 6 Protect population under R2P: 7 Support humanitarian efforts: 8 Support judicial process: 9	

Sanctions regime details

v23	**Number of episodes** Episodes are defined principally by change in the nature of the targeted sanction (type of sanctions, target of sanctions, purpose of sanctions, or significant change in enforcement). Dramatic changes on the ground may also trigger a new episode, but variable generally remains dependent on a new UNSCR to start each episode. Information for the whole sanctions regime is provided in the first episode. NOTE: In some cases, targeted sanctions regimes transformed into comprehensive ones. Episodes of comprehensive sanctions are excluded from the database and not considered in this variable.	Number of episodes	
v24	**Sanctions terminated?** Refers to sanctions terminated explicitly in UNSC resolution. Only relevant for the last episode. NOTE: Sanctions regimes that changed from targeted to comprehensive sanctions (i.e. Former Yugoslavia I and Haiti) are considered terminated.	Yes: 1	No: 0
v25	**UN sanctions preceded by other sanctions?** Autonomous unilateral or regional sanctions put in place with similar objectives prior to UN sanction imposition. Only relevant for the first episode.	Yes: 1	No: 0
v26	**Unilateral sanctions preceded UN sanctions?** Autonomous sanctions imposed by single countries with similar objectives prior to UN sanction imposition. Only relevant for the first episode.	Yes: 1	No: 0
v27	**Regional sanctions preceded UN sanctions?** Autonomous sanctions imposed by regional organizations (such as European Union or African Union) with similar objectives prior to UN sanction imposition. Only relevant for the first episode.	Yes: 1	No: 0
v28	**Did a threat of sanctions precede its imposition?** A threat must be contained within a formal UN pronouncement or articulated by a public official in a position to bring the proposal of sanctions forward to the UN. Only relevant for the first episode.	Yes: 1	No: 0
v29	**Episode start date** For definition of an episode, see v23.	dd/mm/yyyy	
v30	**Episode end date** For definition of an episode, see v23.	dd/mm/yyyy	
v31	**Duration of episode** Rounded to the nearest half month. For definition of an episode, see v23. NOTE: N/A refers to sanctions regimes that are ongoing.	Time in months	

Political will

v32	**What prompted UNSC action** Typically based on opening paragraphs of the principal UNSC resolution that triggered the episode.	Open field			
v33	**Is NGO pressure significant to UN deliberation?** Evidence of strong lobbying on behalf of an affected party or NGO activists.	Yes: 1	No: 0		
v34	**Which country leads drafting UNSC resolution?**	US: 1	China: 2	UK: 3	Russia: 4
	Information generally found through the Security Council Report and UN press releases. More than one country can lead resolution drafting (as indicated in extra columns v34a and v34b).	France: 5	Other: 6		
v35	**Number of votes in favour**	Number of votes			
v36	**Number of votes opposed**	Number of votes			
v37	**Number of abstentions**	Number of votes			
v38	**Was the vote unanimous?**	Yes: 1		No: 0	
v39	**Number of abstentions from P5 members**	Number of abstentions			
v40	**Stated reasons for opposition or abstention**	Open field			
	Information available in UN press releases, case studies, and credible media reporting.				
v41	**Were there P5 reservations to the sanctions?**	Yes: 1		No: 0	
	Information available in UN press releases, case studies, and credible media reporting.				
v42	**Identity of P5 member with reservations to the sanctions**	US: 1	China: 2	UK: 3	Russia: 4
	Refers to a P5 member statement of reservation at the time of resolution passage. May be more than one country (as indicated in the extra column v42a). NOTE: N/A refers to cases with no P5 member reservations.	France: 5			
v43	**Was Sanctions Committee formed at the beginning of the episode?**	Yes: 1		No: 0	
	Sanctions Committee formed at the passage of the first UNSCR in the episode. Coded as 1 for subsequent episodes if the Committee was already in place at the beginning of the episode. NOTE: Episodes where Sanctions Committee is formed later in the episode (FRY 1 EP1, Somalia EP1, Liberia EP1, and DRC EP1) are coded as 0.				
v44	**Is there a Panel of Experts/Monitoring Team?**	Yes: 1		No: 0	

(cont.)

Established or in place at any point during the episode.		

v45 **If individual sanctions are authorized, are individual targets designated?**   Yes: 1   No: 0

Refers to whether any designations of individuals and/or corporate entities were made during the episode.
NOTE: N/A refers to cases where no individual sanctions were authorized.

v46 **Time between UNSCR authorization of individual sanctions and designation of targets**   Time in months

Applies only to episodes where targets of individual sanctions (v106) have been designated (v45). Continuing designations from previous episodes are coded as 0 months (i.e. immediate designation) and 'ongoing' if no one was designated and the episode has not yet ended. If the first designations took place in later episodes, the time reported includes also the length of the previous episodes where individual sanctions were authorized but no designations were made.

v47 **Member state reporting**   No reporting: 0   Called for/Urged: 1

Based on UNSC resolution text. Refers to whether member states reporting is requested, required, or conditional – that is, if it is requested or required (a) upon completion of a certain action (such as cargo inspection) or (b) only by a specific category of member states (such as those in the region or those participating in a peacekeeping operation).   Conditional: 2   Requested: 3   Required: 4

NOTE: When more than one reporting requirement is present in the same episode, priority goes to the one considered more strongly worded (i.e. reverse order of the coding rule: required, requested, conditional, called upon/ urged). Coded N/A (-99) when sanctions suspended.

Purpose and target

Articulated by UNSC resolutions and inferred from the specific design of the sanctions and the targets to whom sanctions apply. More than one purpose is possible.

v48	**Purpose: Coerce a change of behaviour** Specific demands to a target in the form of 'desist from . . . ' or 'join the talks', etc. found in the text of the UNSC resolutions. For evaluation of effectiveness in coercing, see v282–286.	Yes: 1	No: 0	
v49	**Purpose: Constrain a target's behaviour** Drawn from the text of the relevant resolution and the design of respective measures. The pattern of individual and sectoral targeting in each case can provide a clear indication of the purpose. For evaluation of effectiveness in constraining, see v287–291.	Yes: 1	No: 0	
v50	**Purpose: Signal and/or stigmatize a target** Drawn from UNSC resolution text, sanction targets, and regime design. This variable looks at how sanctions interact with norms (contestations and reinforcement). It also looks at how targets feel stigmatized. There are, consequently, two dimensions or components to the variable: the clarity of the signal communicated and the degree of stigmatization experienced (social psychological aspect). For evaluation of effectiveness in signalling, see v292–296.	Yes: 1	No: 0	
v51	**Principal purpose of sanctions in the episode** Acknowledging the complexity of the situation and the multiple purposes often associated with sanctions, the principal purpose in each episode was based on the text of the principal UNSC resolution that triggered the episode and the design of the sanctions regime.	Coerce: 1	Constrain: 2	Signal: 3
v52	**Who is meant to be coerced: Entire government** NOTE: Applies only to episodes where coercion is a purpose.	Yes: 1	No: 0	
v53	**Who is meant to be coerced: Government leadership** NOTE: Applies only to episodes where coercion is a purpose.	Yes: 1	No: 0	
v54	**Who is meant to be coerced: Rebel faction** NOTE: Applies only to episodes where coercion is a purpose.	Yes: 1	No: 0	
v55	**Who is meant to be coerced: All parties to the conflict** NOTE: Applies only to episodes where coercion is a purpose.	Yes: 1	No: 0	

(cont.)

v56	***Who is meant to be coerced: Terrorist group*** NOTE: Applies only to episodes where coercion is a purpose.	Yes: 1	No: 0
v57	***Who is meant to be coerced: Leadership family members*** NOTE: Applies only to episodes where coercion is a purpose.	Yes: 1	No: 0
v58	***Who is meant to be coerced: Facilitators of proscribed activity*** NOTE: Applies only to episodes where coercion is a purpose.	Yes: 1	No: 0
v59	***Who is meant to be coerced: Individual targets*** Includes both individual and corporate/political entities. NOTE: Applies only to episodes where coercion is a purpose.	Yes: 1	No: 0
v60	***Who is meant to be coerced: Key regime supporters*** Refers to domestic regime supporters. Regional supporters (such as neighbouring countries) are captured by v62. NOTE: Applies only to episodes where coercion is a purpose.	Yes: 1	No: 0
v61	***Who is meant to be coerced: Domestic constituencies in target country*** NOTE: Applies only to episodes where coercion is a purpose.	Yes: 1	No: 0
v62	***Who is meant to be coerced: Regional constituencies*** Such as regional organizations or neighbouring states. NOTE: Applies only to episodes where coercion is a purpose.	Yes: 1	No: 0
v63	***Who is meant to be coerced: Global constituencies*** Such as global human rights organizations. NOTE: Applies only to episodes where coercion is a purpose.	Yes: 1	No: 0
v64	***Primary target of coercion*** Drawn from UNSC resolution text, sanctions regime design, and implementation/enforcement during the episode. NOTE: Applies only to episodes where coercion is a purpose.	Entire government: 1 Government leadership: 2 Rebel faction: 3 All parties to the conflict: 4 Terrorist group: 5 Leadership family members: 6 Facilitators of proscribed activity: 7 Individual targets: 8 Key regime supporters: 9 Domestic constituencies in target: 10 Regional constituencies: 11 Global constituencies: 12	

(*cont.*)

v65	**Who is meant to be constrained: Entire government** NOTE: Applies only to episodes where constraint is a purpose.	Yes: 1	No: 0
v66	**Who is meant to be constrained: Government leadership** NOTE: Applies only to episodes where constraint is a purpose.	Yes: 1	No: 0
v67	**Who is meant to be constrained: Rebel faction** NOTE: Applies only to episodes where constraint is a purpose.	Yes: 1	No: 0
v68	**Who is meant to be constrained: All parties to the conflict** NOTE: Applies only to episodes where constraint is a purpose.	Yes: 1	No: 0
v69	**Who is meant to be constrained: Terrorist group** NOTE: Applies only to episodes where constraint is a purpose.	Yes: 1	No: 0
v70	**Who is meant to be constrained: Leadership family members** NOTE: Applies only to episodes where constraint is a purpose.	Yes: 1	No: 0
v71	**Who is meant to be constrained: Facilitators of proscribed activity** NOTE: Applies only to episodes where constraint is a purpose.	Yes: 1	No: 0
v72	**Who is meant to be constrained: Individual targets** Includes both individual and corporate/political entities. NOTE: Applies only to episodes where constraint is a purpose.	Yes: 1	No: 0
v73	**Who is meant to be constrained: Key regime supporters** Refers to domestic regime supporters. Regional supporters (such as neighbouring countries) are captured by v75. NOTE: Applies only to episodes where constraint is a purpose.	Yes: 1	No: 0
v74	**Who is meant to be constrained: Domestic constituencies in target countries** NOTE: Applies only to episodes where constraint is a purpose.	Yes: 1	No: 0
v75	**Who is meant to be constrained: Regional constituencies** Such as regional organizations or neighbouring states. NOTE: Applies only to episodes where constraint is a purpose.	Yes: 1	No: 0

(cont.)

v76	***Who is meant to be constrained: Global constituencies*** Such as global human rights organizations. NOTE: Applies only to episodes where constraint is a purpose.	Yes: 1	No: 0

v77	***Primary target of constraint***
	Drawn from UNSC resolution text, sanctions regime design, and implementation/enforcement during the episode.
	NOTE: Applies only to episodes where constraint is a purpose.
		Entire government: 1
		Government leadership: 2
		Rebel faction: 3
		All parties to the conflict: 4
		Terrorist group: 5
		Leadership family members: 6
		Facilitators of proscribed
		  activity: 7
		Individual targets: 8
		Key regime supporters: 9
		Domestic constituencies in
		  target: 10
		Regional constituencies: 11
		Global constituencies: 12	

v78	***Who is meant to be signalled: Entire government*** NOTE: Applies only to episodes where signalling is a purpose.	Yes: 1	No: 0
v79	***Who is meant to be signalled: Government leadership*** NOTE: Applies only to episodes where signalling is a purpose.	Yes: 1	No: 0
v80	***Who is meant to be signalled: Rebel faction*** NOTE: Applies only to episodes where signalling is a purpose.	Yes: 1	No: 0
v81	***Who is meant to be signalled: All parties to the conflict*** NOTE: Applies only to episodes where signalling is a purpose.	Yes: 1	No: 0
v82	***Who is meant to be signalled: Terrorist group*** NOTE: Applies only to episodes where signalling is a purpose.	Yes: 1	No: 0
v83	***Who is meant to be signalled: Leadership family members*** NOTE: Applies only to episodes where signalling is a purpose.	Yes: 1	No: 0
v84	***Who is meant to be signalled: Facilitators of proscribed activity*** NOTE: Applies only to episodes where signalling is a purpose.	Yes: 1	No: 0
v85	***Who is meant to be signalled: Individual targets*** Includes both individual and corporate/political entities. NOTE: Applies only to episodes where signalling is a purpose.	Yes: 1	No: 0

(*cont.*)

v86	***Who is meant to be signalled: Key regime supporters*** Refers to domestic regime supporters. Regional supporters (such as neighbouring countries) are captured by v88. NOTE: Applies only to episodes where signalling is a purpose.	Yes: 1	No: 0
v87	***Who is meant to be signalled: Domestic constituencies in sending countries*** NOTE: Applies only to episodes where signalling is a purpose.	Yes: 1	No: 0
v88	***Who is meant to be signalled: Regional constituencies*** Refers to signals being sent to regional organizations or neighbouring states; often the AU or ECOWAS are already on the ground and looking for a signal that their pursuits are internationally acknowledged and supported. NOTE: Applies only to episodes where signalling is a purpose.	Yes: 1	No: 0
v89	***Who is meant to be signalled: Global constituencies*** Refers to signals being sent to all global constituencies, often about a universal international norm. NOTE: Applies only to episodes where signalling is a purpose.	Yes: 1	No: 0
v90	***Primary target of the signal*** Drawn from UNSC resolution text and sanctions regime design during the episode. NOTE: Applies only to episodes where signalling is a purpose.	Entire government: 1 Government leadership: 2 Rebel faction: 3 All parties to the conflict: 4 Terrorist group: 5 Leadership family members: 6 Facilitators of proscribed activity: 7 Individual targets: 8 Key regime supporters: 9 Domestic constituencies: 10 Regional constituencies: 11 Global constituencies: 12	

Norm signalling

Norms are generally explicitly articulated in the text of UNSC resolutions or implied by the specific design of each sanctions regime. More than one norm can be signalled.

v91	*Norm signalled: Nuclear non-proliferation*	Yes: 1	No: 0
v92	*Norm signalled: Counterterrorism*	Yes: 1	No: 0
v93	*Norm signalled: Prohibition of war/ armed conflict*	Yes: 1	No: 0
v94	*Norm signalled: Support democracy/ oppose non-constitutional change in government*	Yes: 1	No: 0
v95	*Norm signalled: Improve governance* In particular with regard to the governance of natural resources and/or the security sector.	Yes: 1	No: 0
v96	*Norm signalled: Human rights* Human rights violations (such as the use of child soldiers, treatment of minorities, gender-based violence, and ethnic cleansing) articulated in text of UNSC resolution.	Yes: 1	No: 0
v97	*Norm signalled: Protect population under R2P*	Yes: 1	No: 0
v98	*Norm signalled: Authority of the UN Security Council*	Yes: 1	No: 0
v99	*Norm signalled: Authority of regional arrangements* Includes, for example, regional organizations, peace negotiation initiatives, and peacekeeping forces.	Yes: 1	No: 0
v100	*Norm signalled: Support judicial process* Including legal referrals to the ICC, creation of specialized courts, and/or support for national legal prosecutions.	Yes: 1	No: 0
v101	*Principal norm signalled* Acknowledging the complexity of the situation, the principal norm signalled in each episode was based on the text of the principal UNSC resolution that triggered the episode.	Non-proliferation: 1 Counterterrorism: 2 Prohibition of war/armed conflict: 3 Non-constitutional change in government: 4 Improved governance: 5 Human rights: 6 Protect population under R2P: 7 Authority of UN Security Council: 8 Authority of regional arrangements: 9 Support judicial process: 10	

Type of sanctions

NOTE: The specific type of sanction is coded as 'yes' (1) if it was in place at one point during the episode. In the case of sanctions suspensions (Libya 1 EP3 and Haiti EP2), suspended sanctions are coded as 'yes' (1).

V102	**Was sanctions implementation deliberately delayed?**	Yes: 1	No: 0
	Refers to UNSC resolutions passed with delayed implementation date for at least one of the sanctions imposed, at least one time during the episode, with explicit delay (of 30 days, for example) before sanctions come into force.		
V103	**Were sanctions imposed for a specific time period?**	Yes: 1	No: 0
	Refers to sanctions imposed for a limited time period (e.g. 1 year).		
v104	**Were sanctions regionally limited within a country?**	Yes: 1	No: 0
	Includes delimitations by demarcated provinces and areas controlled by targeted group.		
v105	**Did this episode involve secondary sanctions?**	Yes: 1	No: 0
	Imposed on another country for sanctions violations or other actions taken in support of the target(s).		
v106	**Were individual sanctions imposed?**	Yes: 1	No: 0
	For designations, see v45.		
v107	**Individual sanction: Travel ban**	Yes: 1	No: 0
	Refers to individual travel bans. For travel bans on classes of government officials or diplomats, see v118.		
v108	**Number of travel ban designees**	Number of designees	
	Coded according to the highest cumulative number of designees during each episode.		
v109	**Individual sanction: Individual/corporate entity asset freeze**	Yes: 1	No: 0
	Refers to individual and/or corporate entities (companies, non-governmental organizations, or political entities) asset freeze. NOTE: For the subcategory of this variable referring to political entities (government, former regime, or rebel faction) specified directly in the sanctions resolution text, see v110-3.		
v110	**Were assets of political entities frozen?**	Yes: 1	No: 0
	Refers to the subcategory of individual asset freeze, explicitly targeting political entities (government, former regime, or rebel faction) in the resolution text. NOTE: For the broader category of individual/corporate entity asset freeze, see v109.		

(*cont.*)

v111	*Target of political entities asset freeze: Government* Refers to a subcategory of political entities asset freeze (v110).	Yes: 1	No: 0
v112	*Target of political entities asset freeze: Former regime* Refers to a subcategory of political entities asset freeze (v110).	Yes: 1	No: 0
v113	*Target of political entities asset freeze: Rebel faction* Refers to a subcategory of political entities asset freeze (v110).	Yes: 1	No: 0
v114	*Number of asset freeze designees* Coded according to the highest cumulative number of designees during each episode. NOTE: Applies only to individual/corporate entity asset freeze (v109), including all of its subcategories.	Number of designees	
v115	*Individual sanction: Asset freeze and transfer* Refers to the specific cases in which in addition to an asset freeze (v109) the resolution demands the transfer of assets to a particular source.	Yes: 1	No: 0
v116	*Number of asset freeze and transfer designees* Coded according to the highest cumulative number of designees (both individuals and corporate entities or political entities) for asset freeze and transfer during each episode.	Number of designees	
v117	*Were diplomatic sanctions imposed?*	Yes: 1	No: 0
v118	*Diplomatic sanction: Limiting travel of diplomatic or government personnel* Refers to travel limitations on classes of government officials or diplomats (such as government, armed forces, or military junta). For individual travel bans, see v107.	Yes: 1	No: 0
v119	*Diplomatic sanction: Limiting diplomatic representation* Including offices of official representation.	Yes: 1	No: 0
v120	*Diplomatic sanction: Revision of visa policy* Refers to limiting, suspending, or cancelling entry visas and/or expulsion of categories of nationals.	Yes: 1	No: 0
v121	*Diplomatic sanction: Limiting number of diplomatic personnel*	Yes: 1	No: 0
v122	*Were sectoral sanctions imposed?*	Yes: 1	No: 0
v123	*Sectoral sanction: Aviation ban*	Yes: 1	No: 0
v124	*Sectoral sanction: Arms imports embargo* For arms exports embargo, see v128.	Yes: 1	No: 0

(cont.)

v125	**Arms imports embargo: Non-governmental entities** Refers to a subcategory of arms imports embargo (v124).	Yes: 1	No: 0
v126	**Arms imports embargo: Government forces** Refers to a subcategory of arms imports embargo (v124).	Yes: 1	No: 0
v127	**Arms imports embargo: All parties to the conflict** Refers to a subcategory of arms imports embargo (v124).	Yes: 1	No: 0
v128	**Sectoral sanction: Arms exports ban** For arms imports embargo, see v124.	Yes: 1	No: 0
v129	**Sectoral sanction: Proliferation-sensitive material** Including both imports and exports ban on proliferation-sensitive material.	Yes: 1	No: 0
v130	**Sectoral sanction: Oil services equipment imports ban**	Yes: 1	No: 0
v131	**Sectoral sanction: Shipping and transportation** Includes bunkering bans and ground or waterborne transportation services and equipment bans.	Yes: 1	No: 0
v132	**Were commodity sanctions imposed?**	Yes: 1	No: 0
v133	**Commodity sanction: Petroleum imports ban**	Yes: 1	No: 0
v134	**Commodity sanction: Diamond exports ban**	Yes: 1	No: 0
v135	**Relevance of diamonds to total exports** Sources may vary but will be indicated and held constant across commodity type where possible.	Percentage	
v136	**Commodity sanction: Timber exports ban**	Yes: 1	No: 0
v137	**Relevance of timber to total exports** Sources may vary but will be indicated and held constant across commodity type where possible.	Percentage	
v138	**Commodity sanction: Charcoal exports ban**	Yes: 1	No: 0
v139	**Relevance of charcoal to total exports** Sources may vary but will be indicated and held constant across commodity type where possible.	Percentage	
v140	**Commodity sanction: Luxury goods imports ban**	Yes: 1	No: 0
v141	**Relevance of luxury goods to total imports** Sources may vary but will be indicated and held constant across commodity type where possible.	Percentage	
v142	**Commodity sanction: Other** Including both commodity imports and exports bans. Other commodities include heroin-processing chemicals, cultural property, or illegal crude oil exports.	Yes: 1	No: 0

(cont.)

v143	**Relevance of other commodity to total exports** Sources may vary but will be indicated and held constant across commodity type where possible.	Percentage	
v144	**Were financial sector sanctions imposed?** Refers to broader financial sector sanctions. For individual/corporate asset freeze, see v109.	Yes: 1	No: 0
v145	**Financial sector sanction: Central Bank asset** **freeze**	Yes: 1	No: 0
v146	**Financial sector sanction: Investment ban**	Yes: 1	No: 0
v147	**Financial sector sanction: Financial services** Such as transfers or public support, including provisions of bulk cash, export credits, loans, guarantees, or insurance.	Yes: 1	No: 0
v148	**Financial sector sanction: Sovereign wealth** **funds**	Yes: 1	No: 0
v149	**Estimated size of frozen sovereign wealth** **funds**	Size in US dollars	
v150	**Financial sector sanction: Diaspora tax**	Yes: 1	No: 0

Other actors involved

Significant players or contributors to policy outcomes on the ground by virtue of a coordination/directing role (regardless of whether they directly interact with the sanctions regime) mentioned in UN reports (Panels of Experts or Monitoring Groups, for example) or documented well by media or academic observers. Information of involvement may also be drawn from specific actors' websites. The objective of these variables is to gain insight into the nature of the environment on the ground. This information is used to asses UN sanctions contribution to policy outcomes (v283, v288, v293). Actor is coded as 'yes' (1) if it was involved at one point during the episode.

v151	**Conflict-related actor: Peacekeeping forces**	Yes: 1	No: 0
	Includes both UN and regional peacekeeping operations (PKOs). Does not consider exclusively civilian or political missions.		
	NOTE: Excludes PKOs that do not address the same issue as the UN sanctions (i.e. Lebanon and Sudan I are coded as 0).		
v152	**Conflict-related actor: Peacekeeping mission in neighbouring country**	Yes: 1	No: 0
	Includes both UN and regional peacekeeping operations.		
v153	**Conflict-related actor: Office for the Coordination of Humanitarian Affairs (OCHA)**	Yes: 1	No: 0
	Pre-OCHA institutions (i.e. Department of Humanitarian Affairs) included.		
v154	**Conflict-related actor: Office of the United Nations High Commissioner for Refugees (UNHCR)**	Yes: 1	No: 0
v155	**Conflict-related actor: World Food Programme (WFP)**	Yes: 1	No: 0
v156	**Conflict-related actor: United Nations Development Programme (UNDP)**	Yes: 1	No: 0
v157	**Conflict-related actor: Kimberley Process**	Yes: 1	No: 0
v158	**Conflict-related actor: Human Rights Council/ Commission**	Yes: 1	No: 0
v159	**Conflict-related actor: Other**	Yes: 1	No: 0
	Includes the full spectrum of established actors active in conflict zones (e.g. International Committee of the Red Cross, UN Peacebuilding Commission).		
	NOTE: The name of the actor(s) is indicated in the extra column (open field).		
v160	**Proliferation-related actor: International Atomic Energy Agency (IAEA)**	Yes: 1	No: 0

(cont.)

v161	*Proliferation-related actor: Other* For example, the Nuclear Suppliers Group or US-led proliferation security initiative. NOTE: The name of the actor(s) is indicated in the extra column (open field).	Yes: 1	No: 0
v162	*Terrorism-related actor: Counter-Terrorism Implementation Task Force (CTITF)*	Yes: 1	No: 0
v163	*Terrorism-related actor: Financial Action Task Force (FATF)*	Yes: 1	No: 0
v164	*Terrorism-related actor: International Bank for Reconstruction and Development (IBRD)/International Monetary Fund (IMF)*	Yes: 1	No: 0
v165	*Terrorism-related actor: Counter-Terrorism Committee Executive Directorate (CTED)*	Yes: 1	No: 0
v166	*Terrorism-related actor: United Nations Office on Drugs and Crime (UNODC)*	Yes: 1	No: 0
v167	*Terrorism-related actor: Other* For example, United Nations Counterterrorism Committee (UNCTC) or Global Community Engagement and Resilience Fund (GCERF). NOTE: The name of the actor(s) is indicated in the extra column (open field).	Yes: 1	No: 0
v168	*Regional actor: Economic Community of West African States (ECOWAS)*	Yes: 1	No: 0
v169	*Regional actor: African Union (AU)*	Yes: 1	No: 0
v170	*Regional actor: Organization of American States (OAS)*	Yes: 1	No: 0
v171	*Regional actor: European Union (EU)*	Yes: 1	No: 0
v172	*Regional actor: North Atlantic Treaty Organization (NATO)*	Yes: 1	No: 0
v173	*Regional actor: Arab League*	Yes: 1	No: 0
v174	*Regional actor: Organization of Islamic Conference*	Yes: 1	No: 0
v175	*Regional actor: Organization for Security and Co-operation in Europe (OSCE)*	Yes: 1	No: 0
v176	*Regional actor: Other* Such as Intergovernmental Authority on Development (IGAD) or Economic Community of Central African States (ECCAS). NOTE: The name of the actor(s) is indicated in the extra column (open field).	Yes: 1	No: 0
v177	*Is there a special representative for the Secretary-General?*	Yes: 1	No: 0
v178	*Is there any functionally specific special representative?* For example, a special representative for the UN High Commissioner for Human Rights.	Yes: 1	No: 0

(cont.)

v179	*Are the Panels of Experts interacting with other actors?* For presence of Panel of Experts/Monitoring Teams, see v44.	Yes: 1 No: 0
v180	*On balance, did UN sanctions complement or conflict with the activities of other UN actors?* NOTE: This variable has not yet been coded.	Complement: 1 Conflict: 2 Unable to determine: 3
v181	*On balance, did UN sanctions complement or conflict with the activities of other multilateral actors?* NOTE: This variable has not yet been coded.	Complement: 1 Conflict: 2 Unable to determine: 3
v182	*With which other multilateral actors did UN sanctions conflict or cooperate?*	Open field

Other sanctions

Refers to autonomous sanctions in place that differ from UN sanctions during the episode.

v183	*Are sanctions by regional organizations in place?* Refers to autonomous sanctions by regional organizations that were in place at one point during the episode. Autonomous sanctions refer to measures imposed in addition to those authorized by UNSC (including additional designations). NOTE: For autonomous sanctions imposed by regional organizations prior to UN sanction imposition, see v27.	Yes: 1	No: 0	
v184	*Regional sanctions: Are European Union (EU) sanctions in place?* Refers to autonomous EU sanctions that were in place at one point during the episode. Autonomous sanctions refer to measures imposed in addition to those authorized by UNSC (including additional designations).	No: 0	Targeted: 1	Comprehensive: 2
v185	*Regional sanctions: Are African Union (AU) sanctions in place?* Refers to autonomous AU sanctions that were in place at one point during the episode. Autonomous sanctions refer to measures imposed in addition to those authorized by UNSC (including additional designations).	No: 0	Targeted: 1	Comprehensive: 2
v186	*Regional sanctions: Are Organization of American States sanctions in place?* Refers to autonomous OAS sanctions that were in place at one point during the episode. Autonomous sanctions refer to measures imposed in addition to those authorized by UNSC (including additional designations).	No: 0	Targeted: 1	Comprehensive: 2
v187	*Regional sanctions: Are Association of Southeast Asian Nations (ASEAN) sanctions in place?* Refers to autonomous ASEAN sanctions that were in place at one point during the episode. Autonomous sanctions refer to measures imposed in addition to those	No: 0	Targeted: 1	Comprehensive: 2

(*cont.*)

	authorized by UNSC (including additional designations).			
v188	***Regional sanctions: Are Economic Community Of West African States (ECOWAS) sanctions in place?***	No: 0	Targeted: 1	Comprehensive: 2
	Refers to autonomous ECOWAS sanctions that were in place at one point during the episode. Autonomous sanctions refer to measures imposed in addition to those authorized by UNSC (including additional designations).			
v189	***Are unilateral sanctions in place?***	Yes: 1	No: 0	
	Refers to unilateral sanctions that were in place at one point during the episode. Unilateral sanctions refer specifically to measures imposed in addition to those authorized by UNSC (including additional designations). NOTE: For autonomous sanctions imposed by single countries prior to UN sanction imposition, see v26.			
v190	***Unilateral sanctions: Are United States (US) unilateral sanctions in place?***	No: 0	Targeted: 1	Comprehensive: 2
	Refers to unilateral US sanctions that were in place at one point during the episode. Unilateral sanctions refer specifically to measures imposed in addition to those authorized by UNSC (including additional designations).			
v191	***Unilateral sanctions: Are United Kingdom (UK) unilateral sanctions in place?***	No: 0	Targeted: 1	Comprehensive: 2
	Refers to unilateral UK sanctions that were in place at one point during the episode. Unilateral sanctions refer specifically to measures imposed in addition to those authorized by UNSC (including additional designations).			
v192	***Unilateral sanctions: Are other unilateral sanctions in place?***	No: 0	Targeted: 1	Comprehensive: 2
	Refers to unilateral sanctions by other countries that were in place at one point during the episode. Unilateral sanctions refer specifically to measures imposed in addition to those authorized by UNSC (including additional designations).			
v193	***Are there sanctions regimes in neighbouring countries?***	Yes: 1	No: 0	
	Refers to UN sanctions imposed on immediate neighbours (i.e. sharing contiguous borders) in place at one point during the episode.			

Other policy instruments

Other policy instruments include significant measures taken by the United Nations, individual Member States, or regional organizations.

v194	***Other policy instruments: Threat of use of force*** Refers to a credible threat by or on behalf of a public official in a position to affect the circumstances.	Yes: 1	No: 0
v195	***Other policy instruments: Force, limited strikes and operations***	Yes: 1	No: 0
v196	***Other policy instruments: Force, robust military force***	Yes: 1	No: 0
v197	***Other policy instruments: Force, no-fly zone***	Yes: 1	No: 0
v198	***Other policy instruments: Force, naval blockade***	Yes: 1	No: 0
v199	***Other policy instruments: Peacekeeping operations***	Yes: 1	No: 0
V200	***Other policy instruments: Disarmament, demobilization and reintegration (DDR)***	Yes: 1	No: 0
V201	***Other policy instruments: Covert, cyber-sabotage***	Yes: 1	No: 0
v202	***Other policy instruments: Covert, targeted assassinations***	Yes: 1	No: 0
v203	***Other policy instruments: International Criminal Court (ICC)/International Court of Justice (ICJ)***	Yes: 1	No: 0
v204	***Other policy instruments: Other international courts and tribunals*** For example, International Criminal Tribunal for the former Yugoslavia (ICTY) or Special Court on Sierra Leone.	Yes: 1	No: 0
v205	***Other policy instruments: Significant diplomatic pressure and/or multilateral negotiation*** Refers to efforts to influence on the part of regional groups or other multilateral coalitions such as the Six Party Talks on DPRK or the E3+3 (China, Russia, United States, France, United Kingdom, and Germany) on Iran.	Yes: 1	No: 0

Implementation and enforcement

v206	**Were substantive member state reports received?** Refers to reports that address more than a simple acknowledgement of compliance or translation into domestic law. Demonstrates that member is actively engaging with the sanctions. NOTE: Coded N/A (-99) when sanctions suspended. For member state reporting requirements, see v47.	Yes: 1	No: 0
v207	**Are Sanctions Committee guidelines in place?** Refers to the procedural guidelines for the operation of the Sanctions Committee. NOTE: For presence of Sanctions Committee at the beginning of each episode, see v43.	Yes: 1	No: 0
v208	**Are designation criteria specified?** NOTE: Applies only to individual sanctions (v106).	Yes: 1	No: 0
v209	**Are enforcement authorities specified?** Refers to enforcement authorities specified in UNSC resolution text. NOTE: Coded N/A (-99) when sanctions suspended.	Yes: 1	No: 0
v210	**Are there clear instances of enforcement?** Refers to examples of enforcement that go beyond implementation articulated by policy or law. NOTE: Coded N/A (-99) when sanctions suspended.	Yes: 1	No: 0
v211	**Specific instances of enforcement** Instances must refer to documented examples that demonstrate enforcement, not simply implementation as articulated by policy or law.	Open field	
v212	**Does a Peacekeeping Operation have an enforcement role?** Information derived from UNSCRs and UNDPKO site lists the mandates. NOTE: Applies only for episodes where peacekeeping operations are present (v151). Coded N/A (-99) when sanctions suspended.	Yes: 1	No: 0
v213	**Are there indications of national-level implementation?** Primarily refers to implementation by sending countries but could be applied to targets (in the case of certification schemes, for example). NOTE: Coded N/A (-99) when sanctions suspended.	Yes: 1	No: 0
v214	**Specific indications of national level implementation** Instances must refer to documented examples that demonstrate enforcement, not simply implementation as articulated by policy or law.	Open field	

(cont.)

v215	*Is there evidence of travel ban implementation?* Refers to both individual (v107) and governmental (v118) travel bans. NOTE: Coded N/A (-99) when sanctions suspended.	Yes: 1	No: 0
v216	*Specific evidence of travel ban implementation* Instances must refer to documented examples that demonstrate enforcement, not simply implementation as articulated by policy or law.	Open field	
v217	*Were assets frozen?* Refers to individual/corporate entity asset freeze (v109), including all of its subcategories. NOTE: Coded N/A (-99) when sanctions suspended.	Yes: 1	No: 0
v218	*Total volume of assets frozen* NOTE: Only applies to episodes in which assets were frozen (v217). NOTE: Coded N/A (-99) when sanctions suspended.	Volume in USD	
v219	*Were accounts frozen?* Refers to individual/corporate entity asset freeze (v109), including all of its subcategories. NOTE: Coded N/A (-99) when sanctions suspended.	Yes: 1	No: 0
v220	*Total number of accounts frozen* NOTE: Only applies to episodes in which accounts were frozen (v219). NOTE: Coded N/A (-99) when sanctions suspended.	Number of accounts frozen	
v221	*Were diplomatic sanctions enforced?* NOTE: Applies only to diplomatic sanctions (v117). For the different types of diplomatic sanctions, see v118–21. NOTE: Coded N/A (-99) when sanctions suspended.	Yes: 1	No: 0
v222	*Instances of diplomatic sanctions enforcement* Instances must refer to documented examples that demonstrate enforcement, not simply implementation as articulated by policy or law.	Open field	
v223	*Were landing rights denied?* Related to aviation ban (v123). NOTE: Coded N/A (-99) when sanctions suspended.	Yes: 1	No: 0
v224	*Specific instances of landing rights being denied* Instances must refer to documented examples that demonstrate enforcement, not simply implementation as articulated by policy or law.	Open field	

(cont.)

v225	**Was servicing denied?**	Yes: 1	No: 0
	Servicing restrictions are primarily related to the implementation of aviation bans (v123), but may extend to other sanctions (such as shipping v131 and specific prohibitions on arms, proliferation, or Internet hosting related servicing) if relevant. NOTE: Coded N/A (-99) when sanctions suspended or relevant sanctions never entered in force. Coded as 1 for cases where servicing was denied based on recommended actions by the UNSC.		
v226	**Specific instances of denial of service**	Open field	
	Instances must refer to documented examples that demonstrate enforcement, not simply implementation as articulated by policy or law.		
v227	**Is there any evidence of interdiction?**	Yes: 1	No: 0
	Refers to boarding a vessel, inspection of a vessel or other means of transport, or otherwise arresting the movement of embargoed goods. Where relevant. NOTE: Coded N/A (-99) when sanctions suspended.		
v228	**Specific evidence of interdiction**	Open field	
	Instances must refer to documented examples that demonstrate enforcement, not simply implementation as articulated by policy or law.		
v229	**Is there any evidence of detention of vessels?**	Yes: 1	No: 0
	Where relevant. NOTE: Coded N/A (-99) when sanctions suspended.		
v230	**Evidence of vessels detention**	Open field	
	Instances must refer to documented examples that demonstrate enforcement, not simply implementation as articulated by policy or law.		
v231	**Is there any evidence of the cancellation of credits?**	Yes: 1	No: 0
	Where relevant. NOTE: Coded N/A (-99) when sanctions suspended.		
v232	**Evidence of credits cancelled**	Open field	
	Instances must refer to documented examples that demonstrate enforcement, not simply implementation as articulated by policy or law.		

Impact assessment

The following variables indicate direct and indirect impacts of targeted sanctions. Impacts of targeted sanctions are direct when they affect principal parties to the conflict or situation that prompted sanctions. Direct impacts include assessments of the economic disadvantages to the target of sanctions and on the target's ability to continue proscribed activities. Variables representing direct political, social, and psychological (stigmatizing or isolating) effects on the targeted parties are also important, including assessments of reputational costs to legitimate actors engaged with targeted parties. Indirect impacts refer to the extent to which the measures had impacts on non-targeted, but inter-related economic, political, and social dynamics, processes, or groups (such as creating incentives for import substitution, as an economic example, or the sociological implications of targeted measures that have indirect implications for gender or ethnicity).

v233	***Indications of direct economic impact*** Assets frozen, change in arms supplies, measure of resource exports, and other measures of diminished trade and/or access to financing.	Yes: 1	No: 0
v234	***Specific indications of direct economic impact*** Instances must refer to documented examples that demonstrate direct impact.	Open field	
v235	***Indications of direct political impact*** Refers to a change in the political dynamics associated with the targeted regime or faction. For example, if a commodities embargo directly contributes to the fracturing of a rebel group or to a regime's decision to call a ceasefire.	Yes: 1	No: 0
v236	***Specific indications of direct political impact*** Instances must refer to documented examples that demonstrate direct impact.	Open field	
v237	***Indications of direct social or psychological impact*** Stigmatizing or isolating effects on the targeted party or legitimate actors engaged with the targeted party.	Yes: 1	No: 0
v238	***Specific indications of direct social or psychological impact*** Instances must refer to documented examples that demonstrate direct impact.	Open field	
v239	***Indications of indirect economic impact*** For example, creating incentives for import substitution, the development of new technologies, or the diversion of foreign investment and credit.	Yes: 1	No: 0

(cont.)

v240	**Specific indications of indirect economic impact** Instances must refer to documented examples that demonstrate indirect impact.	Open field	
v241	**Indications of indirect political impact** For example, divisions within political leadership, introduction of rationing schemes, undermining state infrastructure, or weakening state institutional capacity.	Yes: 1	No: 0
v242	**Specific indications of indirect political impact** Instances must refer to documented examples that demonstrate indirect impact.	Open field	
v243	**Indications of indirect social or psychological impact** Refers to implications of measures that go beyond the targeted parties and affect social or psychological dynamics (associated with gender or ethnicity, for example).	Yes: 1	No: 0
v244	**Specific indications of indirect social or psychological impact** Instances must refer to documented examples that demonstrate indirect impact.	Open field	

Evasion/coping strategies

v245	**Are there indications of sanctions evasion/** **coping strategies?**	Yes: 1	No: 0
v246	**Evasion: Disguise of identity or use of forged** **documents** NOTE: Coded N/A (-99) when sanctions suspended.	Yes: 1	No: 0
v247	**Evasion: Use of front companies** NOTE: Coded N/A (-99) when sanctions suspended.	Yes: 1	No: 0
v248	**Evasion: Reliance on family members** Utilizing a relative's bank account to move money when assets are frozen, for example. NOTE: Coded N/A (-99) when sanctions suspended.	Yes: 1	No: 0
v249	**Evasion: Use of informal value transfer** **systems** Refers to an informal yet defined mechanism for transferring funds or financing evasion, such as the Hawala system. NOTE: Coded N/A (-99) when sanctions suspended.	Yes: 1	No: 0
v250	**Evasion: Use of safe havens** Refers broadly to any place of refuge safeguarded by sympathizers, whether a specific location, region, or foreign country. NOTE: Coded N/A (-99) when sanctions suspended.	Yes: 1	No: 0
v251	**Evasion: Disguise vessels** Refer to seaborne vessels and other means of transport (for example, switching the tail numbers of aircraft). NOTE: Coded N/A (-99) when sanctions suspended.	Yes: 1	No: 0
v252	**Evasion: Use of black market contractors** NOTE: Coded N/A (-99) when sanctions suspended.	Yes: 1	No: 0
v253	**Evasion: Denial of inspection** NOTE: Coded N/A (-99) when sanctions suspended.	Yes: 1	No: 0
v254	**Coping: Use of alternative value source** Refers to a substitute commodity or industry.	Yes: 1	No: 0
v255	**Coping: Shifting terms of debate or change** **subject (diplomatically)** For example, mobilization of AU and Arab League against UN sanctions implementation during Libya 1.	Yes: 1	No: 0

(*cont.*)

v256	*Coping: Stockpiling supplies*	Yes: 1	No: 0
v257	*Coping: Diversion of trade through third countries*	Yes: 1	No: 0
v258	*Coping: Coerce or put pressure on major trade partners not to enforce sanctions*	Yes: 1	No: 0
v259	*Coping: Import substitution, development of new technology.*	Yes: 1	No: 0
v260	*Coping: Diversify sources of funds and investment*	Yes: 1	No: 0
v261	*Evasion/Coping: Others* Efforts to complicate litigation, for example. NOTE: The specific type of other evasion/coping strategies is indicated in the extra column (open field).	Yes: 1	No: 0

Unintended consequences

The following variables identify the principal unintended consequences (both positive and negative) of the sanctions imposed in each episode. Among the possible negative externalities of targeted sanctions are the legacies of corruption and criminality often left by sanctions, the strengthening of instruments of authoritarian rule, a 'rally around the flag' effect, an increase in human rights violations, and harmful effects on neighbouring states. Positive externalities might include increased capacity to regulate internationally in different issue domains (such as financial controls) or opportunities for capacity building training for financial controls, immigration, or customs.

v262	*Are there indications of unintended consequences?* As indicated in PoE reports or other authoritative sources.	Yes: 1	No: 0
v263	*Unintended consequences: Increase in corruption and/or criminality* Refers to the tendency for sanctions to contribute to a proliferation of illicit means and networks that function in place of previously legitimate channels.	Yes: 1	No: 0
v264	*Unintended consequences: Strengthening of authoritarian rule* Refers to increased repressive capacity by the state and/or the deterioration of civil liberties under targeted regimes.	Yes: 1	No: 0
v265	*Unintended consequences: Strengthening instruments of the security apparatus of senders* Typically considered a negative externality because it provides justification for a state to build its surveillance and intelligence capacities and puts civil liberties at risk. However, it may also have positive externalities such as strengthening a sending state's capacity for border security.	Yes: 1	No: 0
v266	*Unintended consequences: Rally round the flag effect* Sanctions are used to justify diversionary policy, resulting in an Increase of short-run popular support for a regime.	Yes: 1	No: 0
v267	*Unintended consequences: Increase in human rights violations* Under targeted regime or by targeted parties.	Yes: 1	No: 0
v268	*Unintended consequences: Harmful effects on neighbouring states* Article 50 concerns and spillover effects of the sanctions regime on other states.	Yes: 1	No: 0
v269	*Unintended consequences: Strengthening of political factions* Sanctions contribute to a disproportional strengthening of a political faction, either within the government structure or outside of it.	Yes: 1	No: 0

(*cont.*)

v270	**Unintended consequences: Enhancing stature of targeted individuals** The imposition of sanctions generates sympathy or support for a designated target, possibly encouraging others to emulate the targeted individual. NOTE: Applies only to episodes in which individuals designated (v45).	Yes: 1	No: 0
v271	**Unintended consequences: Increase in international regulatory capacity in different issue domains** Creation of new international institutions, laws, or norms in response to proscribed activity, though not designed to establish autonomous regulatory regimes. For example, the Kimberley Process (in diamond cases) or improved anti-money laundering provisions established under the 1267 (AQ/T) regime.	Yes: 1	No: 0
v272	**Unintended consequences: Increase in international enforcement capacity in different issue domains** Refers to an empirically observed increase in enforcement and the capacity to enforce as a result of the imposition of a sanctions regime.	Yes: 1	No: 0
v273	**Unintended consequences: Resource diversion** Refers to the diversion of resources from one sector to another as a result of sanctions constraints (for example, health-care allocations being cut to supplement the military budget).	Yes: 1	No: 0
v274	**Unintended consequences: Increase in the growth of the state role in the economy** Refers broadly to a variety of ways a state may intervene in the economy as a response to UN sanctions (e.g. allocation, direct ownership, regulation, or subsuming activity previously conducted by private enterprise).	Yes: 1	No: 0
v275	**Unintended consequences: Significant burden on implementing states** The implementation burden is not confined to the public sector; private sector costs are included as well.	Yes: 1	No: 0
v276	**Unintended consequences: Humanitarian consequences** Situations in which sanctions are directly linked to the disruption of basic services and the realization of basic needs (for example, undelivered	Yes: 1	No: 0

(cont.)

	pharmaceutical materials or medical equipment or food access blocked due to the sanctions regime).		
v277	**Unintended consequences: Human rights implications for sending states** Negative impact on human rights in sending states as a result of imposing and implementing sanctions (for example, increased surveillance due to expansion of the global counterterrorism regime).	Yes: 1	No: 0
v278	**Unintended consequences: Decline in the credibility and/or legitimacy of UN Security Council** Situations in which a popular loss of faith in the UNSC occurs, whether in sending states or under targeted regimes, due, for example, to a failure to implement sanctions that have been imposed in a UNSC resolution. May also refer to a situation in which UN sanctions are mismanaged (by targeting or designating the wrong individuals) or flawed more generally.	Yes: 1	No: 0
v279	**Unintended consequences: Reduction of local institutional capacity** Situation in which sanctions unintentionally disrupt or prevent local institutions from functioning properly.	Yes: 1	No: 0
v280	**Unintended consequences: Widespread harmful economic consequences** Circumstances in which sanctions injure the productive capacity of the country or prevent segments of the population from engaging in the economy (national, regional, or sectoral).	Yes: 1	No: 0
v281	**Unintended consequences: Other** NOTE: The specific type of other unintended consequences is indicated in the extra column (open field).	Yes: 1	No: 0

Effectiveness

---

v282 ***Policy outcome: Coercion***
Evaluates the extent to which the target
changed its behaviour and the demands
of the Security Council have been met.
NOTE: For indicators of coercion as a
purpose of sanctions, see v48. For
overall sanction effectiveness in
coercing, see v284–286.

1: Lack of significant change in
behaviour, ignoring the UNSCR, or
complete intransigence.
2: Agreeing to a process and/or engaging
in negotiations that could result in
settling or resolving the dispute or in
obfuscation, delaying, or changing
terms of debate.
3: Accommodation or significant
concessions to resolve the dispute.
4: Meeting most of the objectives of the
UNSCR and/or approximating the
core purposes as originally articulated
in the UNSCR (but not necessarily
according to the explicit terms spelled
out in the original UNSCR).
5: Meeting all the principal objectives of
the UNSCR.

v283 ***UN Sanctions contribution: Coercion***
Measurement of sanctions contribution
considers all other instruments utilized
by the international community at the
time (such as diplomatic pressure, use
of force, other sanctions, etc.) and
indications by the target of the impact
and role of UN sanctions.
NOTE: For indicators of coercion as a
purpose of sanctions, see v48. For
overall sanction effectiveness in
coercing, see v284–286.

0: Negative (regime is strengthened
and/or increases its proscribed
activity)
1: None (no discernible sanctions
contribution)
2: Minor (other measures taken appear
most significant to outcome)
3: Modest (sanctions reinforced other
measures)
4: Major (sanctions appear necessary,
but not sufficient; or some
acknowledgement by the target)
5: Significant (the single most
important factor is the presence of
UNSC sanctions)

v284 ***UN sanctions effectiveness:***
Coercion – Effective
Sanctions effectiveness is determined
based on a combined evaluation of (1)
Policy outcome and (2) UN sanctions
contribution to this outcome. UN
sanctions are considered *effective* if:
(a) Policy outcome is 4 or 5, and
(b) UN sanctions contribution to the
outcome is modest (3), major (4) or
significant (5).

NOTE: For criteria used for evaluating
Policy outcome in coercing, see v282;
for UN sanctions contribution to
coercion, see v283.

Yes: 1   No: 0

(cont.)

v285	***UN sanctions effectiveness:*** Yes: 1	No: 0

v285 ***UN sanctions effectiveness:***   Yes: 1   No: 0
Coercion – Mixed
Sanctions effectiveness is determined
based on a combined evaluation of (1)
Policy outcome and (2) UN sanctions
contribution to this outcome. UN
sanctions are considered *mixed* if:
(c) Policy outcome is 3, and
(d) UN sanctions contribution to the
     outcome is modest (3), major (4) or
     significant (5).

NOTE: For criteria used for evaluating
Policy outcome in coercing, see v282;
for UN sanctions contribution to
coercion, see v283.

v286 ***UN sanctions effectiveness:***   Yes: 1   No: 0
Coercion – Ineffective
Sanctions effectiveness is determined
based on a combined evaluation of (1)
Policy outcome and (2) UN sanctions
contribution to this outcome. UN
sanctions are considered *ineffective* if:
(e) Policy outcome is 1 or 2, or
(f) Policy outcome is 3, 4, or 5 but UN
     sanctions contribution to the
     outcome is negative (0), absent (1) or
     minor (2).

NOTE: For criteria used for evaluating
Policy outcome in coercing, see v282;
for UN sanctions contribution to
coercion, see v283.

v287 ***Policy outcome: Constraint***
Evaluates the extent to which the target
has been constrained in proscribed
activities (raising costs/changing
strategies).
NOTE: For indicators of constraint as a
purpose of sanctions, see v49. For
overall sanction effectiveness in
constraining, see v289–291.

1: No discernible constraints
experienced by the target.
2: Increases in costs can be managed by
the target (sanctions are largely a
nuisance factor) perhaps due to ease of
evasion.
3: Slight increases in costs to target (as
evidenced by diversion of trade
through third countries, and/or delay
in engaging in proscribed activity and/
or diminution in the frequency of
engagement in proscribed activity).
4: Increases in costs, minor changes of
strategy of the target, statement that
target may be experiencing financial/
material/logistical difficulties and/or
constrained from engaging in
proscribed activity.

(cont.)

5: Significant increases in costs, changes of strategy of the target, statement that target is experiencing financial/material/logistical difficulties and/or constrained from engaging in proscribed activity.

v288 **UN Sanctions contribution: Constraint**
Measurement of sanctions contribution considers all other instruments utilized by the international community at the time (such as diplomatic pressure, use of force, other sanctions, etc.) and indications by the target of the impact and role of UN sanctions.
NOTE: For indicators of constraint as a purpose of sanctions, see v49. For overall sanction effectiveness in constraining, see v289–291.

0: **Negative** (regime is strengthened and/or increases its proscribed activity)
1: **None** (no discernible sanctions contribution)
2: **Minor** (other measures taken appear most significant to outcome)
3: **Modest** (sanctions reinforced other measures)
4: **Major** (sanctions appear necessary, but not sufficient; or some acknowledgement by the target)
5: **Significant** (the single most important factor is the presence of UNSC sanctions)

v289 **UN sanctions effectiveness: Constraint – Effective**
Sanctions effectiveness is determined based on a combined evaluation of (1) Policy outcome and (2) UN sanctions contribution to this outcome. UN sanctions are considered *effective* if:
(g) Policy outcome is 4 or 5, and
(h) UN sanctions contribution to the outcome is modest (3), major (4), or significant (5).
NOTE: For criteria used for evaluating Policy outcome in constraining, see v287; for UN sanctions contribution to constraint, see v288.

Yes: 1   No: 0

v290 **UN sanctions effectiveness: Constraint – Mixed**
Sanctions effectiveness is determined based on a combined evaluation of (1) Policy outcome and (2) UN sanctions contribution to this outcome. UN sanctions are considered *mixed* if:
(i) Policy outcome is 3, and
(j) UN sanctions contribution to the outcome is modest (3), major (4), or significant (5).
NOTE: For criteria used for evaluating Policy outcome in constraining, see v287; for UN sanctions contribution to constraint, see v288.

Yes: 1   No: 0

(cont.)

v291	***UN sanctions effectiveness:*** Yes: 1	No: 0

v291 *UN sanctions effectiveness: Constraint – Ineffective* — Yes: 1   No: 0

Sanctions effectiveness is determined based on a combined evaluation of (1) Policy outcome and (2) UN sanctions contribution to this outcome. UN sanctions are considered *ineffective* if:
(k) Policy outcome is 1 or 2, or
(l) Policy outcome is 3, 4, or 5 but UN sanctions contribution to the outcome is negative (0), absent (1) or minor (2).

NOTE: For criteria used for evaluating Policy outcome in constraining, see v287; for UN sanctions contribution to constraint, see v288.

v292 *Policy outcome: Signalling*
Evaluates the extent to which a norm has been articulated and the target stigmatised.
NOTE: For indicators of signalling as a purpose of sanctions, see v50. For overall sanction effectiveness in signalling, see v294–296.

1: Norm (or norms) not articulated, no stigmatization and/or clear evidence of legitimation.
2: Norm (or norms) poorly articulated (e.g. too many, diffusely articulated), limited evidence of stigmatization and/or possible legitimation.
3: Norm (or norms) articulated, and some stigmatization of target.
4: Norm (or norms) articulated and targets strongly stigmatized.
5: Norm (or norms) clearly articulated and target fully stigmatized and/or isolated
(e.g. effective signalling to the international community and stigmatizing and/or isolation of the target).

v293 *UN Sanctions contribution: Signalling*
Measurement of sanctions contribution considers all other instruments utilized by the international community at the time (such as diplomatic pressure, use of force, other sanctions, etc.) and indications by the target of the impact and role of UN sanctions.
NOTE: For indicators of signalling as a purpose of sanctions, see v50. For overall sanction effectiveness in signalling, see v294–296.

0: **Negative** (regime is strengthened and/or increases its proscribed activity)
1: **None** (no discernible sanctions contribution)
2: **Minor** (other measures taken appear most significant to outcome)
3: **Modest** (sanctions reinforced other measures)
4: **Major** (sanctions appear necessary, but not sufficient; or some acknowledgement by the target)
5: **Significant** (the single most important factor is the presence of UNSC sanctions)

(cont.)

v294	***UN sanctions effectiveness:*** *Signalling – Effective*	Yes: 1	No: 0

Sanctions effectiveness is determined based on a combined evaluation of (1) Policy outcome and (2) UN sanctions contribution to this outcome. UN sanctions are considered *effective* if:
• Policy outcome is 4 or 5, and
• UN sanctions contribution to the outcome is modest (3), major (4), or significant (5).

NOTE: For criteria used for evaluating Policy outcome in signalling, see v292; for UN sanctions contribution to signalling, see v293.

v295	***UN sanctions effectiveness:*** *Signalling – Mixed*	Yes: 1	No: 0

Sanctions effectiveness is determined based on a combined evaluation of (1) Policy outcome and (2) UN sanctions contribution to this outcome. UN sanctions are considered *mixed* if:
(a) Policy outcome is 3, and
(b) UN sanctions contribution to the outcome is modest (3), major (4), or significant (5).

NOTE: For criteria used for evaluating Policy outcome in signalling, see v292; for UN sanctions contribution to signalling, see v293.

v296	***UN sanctions effectiveness:*** *Signalling – Ineffective*	Yes: 1	No: 0

Sanctions effectiveness is determined based on a combined evaluation of (1) Policy outcome and (2) UN sanctions contribution to this outcome. UN sanctions are considered *ineffective* if:
(c) Policy outcome is 1 or 2, or
(d) Policy outcome is 3, 4, or 5 but UN sanctions contribution to the outcome is negative (0), absent (1) or minor (2).

NOTE: For criteria used for evaluating Policy outcome in signalling, see v292; for UN sanctions contribution to signalling, see v293.

Appendix 4 Targeted Sanctions Consortium (TSC) participants

The project has been co-directed by Professor Thomas J. Biersteker, Gasteyger Professor of International Security and Director of the Programme for the Study of International Governance at the Graduate Institute, Geneva (thomas.biersteker@graduateinstitute. ch), and the Honorable Sue E. Eckert, Senior Fellow, Watson Institute for International and Public Affairs, Brown University (sue_eckert@brown.edu).

Academic researchers, sanctions experts, and practitioners with direct participation in one of the TSC events (conferences, workshops, planning meetings) include the following:

Scholars
John Agbonifo, Osun State University, Nigeria
Andrea Bianchi, The Graduate Institute, Geneva, Switzerland
Alix Boucher, Center for Global Counterterrorism Cooperation, New York, USA
Jane Boulden, Royal Military College, Canada
Michael Brzoska, Hamburg University, Germany
Thomas Cargill, Chatham House, London, UK
Andrea Charron, University of Manitoba, Canada
Caty Clement, Geneva Centre for Security Policy, Geneva, Switzerland
Neta Crawford, Boston University, USA
Margaret Doxey, University of Trent, Canada
Chioma Ebeniro, University of Port Harcourt, Nigeria
Kimberly Elliott, Center for Global Development, Washington, DC, USA
Mikael Eriksson, Swedish Defense Research Institute, Sweden
Elena Gadjanova, The Graduate Institute, Geneva, Switzerland
Francesco Giumelli, Groningen University, Netherlands
Vera Gowlland-Debbas, The Graduate Institute, Geneva, Switzerland

Zuzana Hudáková, The Graduate Institute, Geneva, Switzerland
George Lopez, University of Notre Dame, USA
Shawna Meister, Carleton University, Ottawa, Canada
Clara Portela, Singapore Management University, Singapore
Detlof Sprinz, Potsdam University, Germany
David Sylvan, The Graduate Institute, Geneva, Switzerland
Masataka Tamai, Ritsumeikan University, Japan
Marcos Tourinho, Fundação Getulio Vargas, Brazil
Mineko Usui, Komazawa Women's University, Japan
Alex Vines, Chatham House, UK
Peter Wallensteen, Uppsala University, Sweden
Takehiko Yamamoto, Waseda University, Japan

Policy practitioners
Richard Barrett, former Al-Qaida Monitoring Team, New York, UK
Paul Bentall, Foreign and Commonwealth Office, London, UK
David Biggs, UN Secretariat Sanctions Unit, New York, USA
Joshua Black, US Mission to the UN, New York, USA
Rico Carisch, former member, UN Panels of Experts, New York, Switzerland
Kiho Cha, UN Secretariat Sanctions Unit, New York, USA
Riccarda Chanda-Trippel, Federal Department of Foreign Affairs, Switzerland
Jasmin Cheung-Gertler, Department of Foreign Affairs and International Trade, Ottawa, Canada
Peter Grk, Foreign Ministry, Slovenia
Ralf Heckner, Federal Department of Foreign Affairs, Switzerland
Benno Laggner, Foreign Ministry, Bern, Switzerland
Christine Lee, former Al-Qaida Monitoring Team, Singapore
Loraine Rickard-Martin, former UN Secretariat, New York, Jamaica
Jennifer McNaughton, UK Mission to the UN, New York, UK
Eric Rosand, US Department of State, Washington, DC, USA
Daniela Schneider, Federal Department of Foreign Affairs, Switzerland
Joseph Stephanides, former UN Secretariat, New York, Cyprus
Jay Sutterlin, UN Secretariat, New York, USA
Maria Telalian, Foreign Ministry of Greece, Athens, Greece

Gerhard Thallinger, Austrian Mission to the United Nations, Austria

Caterina Ventura, Canadian Mission to the United Nations, New York, Canada

Dawn Wood-Memic, Department of Foreign Affairs and International Trade, Ottawa, Canada

Christopher Yvon, Foreign and Commonwealth Office, London, UK

For more information about TSC, please visit the websites at: gradua teinstitute.ch/internationalgovernance/UN_Targeted_Sanctions.html and www.watsoninstitute.org/project_detail.cfm?id=4.

For access to the Web version of SanctionsApp, please visit: sanctionsapp.com.

Bibliography

Althaus, Catherine, Peter Bridgman, and Glyn Davis, *The Australian Policy Handbook*, 5th edn, Sydney: Allen & Unwin, 2013.

Andreas, Peter, *Blue Helmets and Black Markets: The Business of Survival in the Siege of Sarajevo*, Ithaca: Cornell University Press, 2008.

Andreas, Peter, Unintended Criminalizing Consequences of Sanctions: Lessons from the Balkans', in Christopher Daase and Cornelius Friesendorf (eds.), *Rethinking Security Governance: The Problem of Unintended Consequences*, Abingdon, Oxon: Routledge, 2010, pp. 102–26.

Annan, Kofi, *In Larger Freedom: Towards Development, Security and Human Rights for All*, New York: United Nations, 2005, para 109.

Anthony, Iain, 'Sanctions Applied by the European Union and the United Nations', in *SIPRI Yearbook 2002 Armaments, Disarmament and International Security*, Oxford: Oxford University Press, 2002.

Baert, Patrick, 'Unintended Consequences: A Typology and Examples', in *International Sociology*, 6, 2 (1991), pp. 201–10.

Baldwin, David A., *Economic Statecraft*, Princeton: Princeton University Press, 1985.

Baldwin, David A., 'The Sanctions Debate and the Logic of Choice', *International Security* 24, 3 (1999/2000), pp. 80–107.

Baldwin, David A., 'Power and International Relations', in Walter Carlnaes, Thomas Risse, and Beth A. Simmons (eds.), *Handbook of International Relations*, 2nd edn, Thousand Oaks, CA: SAGE Publications, 2013, pp. 273–97.

Bapat, Navin A. and T. Clifton Morgan, 'Multilateral versus Unilateral Sanctions Reconsidered: A Test Using New Data', *International Studies Quarterly* 53 (2009), p. 1082.

Barber, James, 'Economic Sanctions as a Policy Instrument', *International Affairs* 55, 3 (1979), pp. 367–84.

Barka, H. Ben and M. Ncube, 'Political Fragility in Africa: Are Military Coups d'états a Never-ending Phenomenon?' *African Development Bank* (September), (2012), pp. 1–16.

Barnett, Michael and Raymond Duvall (eds.), *Power in Global Governance* (Cambridge Studies in International Relations), Cambridge: Cambridge University Press, 2005.

Berenskoetter, Felix and Michael Williams (eds.), *Power in World Politics*, London, New York: Routledge, 2007, pp. 1–22.

Bessler, Manuel, Richard Garfield, and Gerard McHugh, *Sanctions Assessment Handbook: Assessing the Humanitarian Implications of Sanctions*. United Nations Inter-Agency Standing Committee, New York: United Nations Office for the Coordination of Humanitarian Affairs, OCHA and the Policy Development Studies Branch, 2004.

Bianchi, Andrea, 'Assessing the Effectiveness of the UN Security Council's Anti-Terrorism Measures: The Quest for Legitimacy and Cohesion', *European Journal of International Law* 17 (2007), p. 881.

Biersteker, Thomas J., Sue Eckert, Aaron Halegua, N. Reid, and Peter Romaniuk, *Targeted Financial Sanctions: A Manual for Design and Implementation – Contributions from the Interlaken Process*, Brown University: Watson Institute for International Studies, 2001.

Biersteker, Thomas J. and Sue Eckert, *Strengthening Targeted Sanctions through Fair and Clear Procedures*. Report commissioned by the governments of Germany, Switzerland and Sweden, Providence, RI: Watson Institute for International Studies, Brown University, 2006.

Biersteker, Thomas J. and Sue Eckert, *Countering the Financing of Terrorism*, New York and London: Routledge Publishers, 2008.

Biersteker, Thomas J., 'Targeted Sanctions and Individual Human Rights', *International Journal*, 65, 1 (Winter 2009–2010), pp. 85–103.

Biersteker, Thomas J. and Sue E. Eckert, *Addressing Challenges to Targeted Sanctions: An Update to the 'Watson Report'*, Geneva: The Graduate Institute, 2009.

Biersteker, Thomas J., 'Unintended Consequences of Measures to Counter the Financing of Terrorism', in Daase and Friesendorf (eds.), *Rethinking Security Governance: The Problem of Unintended Consequences*, Abingdon, Oxon: Routledge, 2010, pp. 127–36.

Biersteker, Thomas J., Sue E. Eckert, and Marcos Tourinho, *Designing United Nations Targeted Sanctions. Evaluating Impacts and Effectiveness of UN Targeted Sanctions*, Geneva: Targeted Sanctions Consortium, 2012.

Biersteker, Thomas, Sue E. Eckert, Marcos Tourinho, and Zuzana Hudáková, *The Effectiveness of United Nations Targeted Sanctions: Findings from the Targeted Sanctions Consortium (TSC)*, Geneva: Graduate Institute, 2013.

Biersteker, Thomas, Sue Eckert, Zuzana Hudakova, and Marcos Tourinho, *SanctionsApp*, Computer software, *Apple App Store*, 21 June 2013.

Biersteker, Thomas J. and Sue E. Eckert. 'Targeted Sanctions Consortium (TSC)'. Graduate Institute in Geneva and Watson Institute for International Studies, graduateinstitute.ch/internationalgovernance/UN_Targeted_Sanctions.html.

Biersteker, Thomas J., Sue E. Eckert, Aaron Halegua, and Peter Romaniuk, 'Consensus from the Bottom-Up? Assessing the Influence from the Sanctions Reform Process', in Peter Wallensteen and Carina Staibano (eds.), *International Sanctions. Between Words and Wars in the Global System*, New York: Frank Cass, 2005.

Blanchard, Jean-Marc F. and Norrin M. Ripsman, 'Asking the Right Question: When Do Economic Sanctions Work Best?' *Security Studies* 9, 1–2 (1999), pp. 219–53.

Boisseau du Rocher, S., 'The European Union, Burma/Myanmar and ASEAN', *Asia Europe Journal* 10 (2012), pp. 165–80.

Bosco, David L., *Five to Rule Them All: The UN Security Council and the Making of the Modern World*, Oxford: Oxford University Press, 2009.

Boucher, Alix J., William Durch, Sarah Rose, and Jason Terry, *Mapping and Fighting Corruption in War-torn States*, Washington, DC: Stimson Center, 2007, pp. 53–5.

Boucher, Alix J. and Victoria K. Holt, *Targeting Spoilers: The Role of United Nations Panels of Experts*, Washington, DC: Stimson Center, 2009.

Boucher, Alix J., *UN Panels of Experts and UN Peace Operations: Exploiting Synergies for Peacebuilding*, Washington, DC: Stimson Center, 2010.

Brady, Lawrence J., 'The Utility of Economic Sanctions as a policy instrument', in Layton-Brown, D. (ed.), *The Utility of International Economic Sanctions*, New York: St. Martin's Press, 1987, pp. 297–302.

Brooks, Risa, 'Sanctions and Regime Type: What Works, When?' *Security Studies* 11, 4 (2002), p. 2.

Brzoska, Michael (ed.). *Design and Implementation of Arms Embargoes and Travel and Aviation Related Sanctions: Results of the 'Bonn-Berlin Process'*: Bonn: Bonn International Center for Conversion, 2001.

Brzoska, Michael, 'Sanktionen als instrument der europäischen Außen- und sicherheitspolitik', *Friedensgutachten* (2006), pp. 247–55.

Byman, Daniel and Matthew Waxman, *The Dynamics of Coercion: American Foreign Policy and the Limits of Military Might*, New York: Cambridge University Press, 2002.

Cameron, Iain (ed.), *EU Sanctions: Law and Policy Issues Concerning Restrictive Measures*, Cambridge: Intersentia, 2013.

Cantwell, Douglas, *Sanctioning Justice: The Security Council and the International Criminal Court among Words and Wars*, MA Thesis, The Graduate Institute, Geneva, 2012, chapter IV.

Carisch, Enrico and Loraine Rickard-Martin, *Global Threats and the Role of United Nations Sanctions Report*, International Policy Analysis, *Friedrich Ebert Stiftung*, 2011.

Carisch, Enrico and Loraine Rickard-Martin, 'Sanctions and the Effort to Globalize Natural Resources Governance', *Friedrich Ebert Stiftung*, January 2013.

Charron, Andrea, *UN Sanctions and Conflict: Responding to Peace and Security Threats*, London: Routledge, 2011.

Chesterman, Simon and Pouligny, Beatrice, 'Are Sanctions Meant to Work? The Politics of Creating and Implementing Sanctions Through the United Nations', *Global Governance* 9 (2003), pp. 503–18.

Chivers, C. J., 'A Trail of Bullets Casings Leads from Africa's Wars Back to Iran', *The New York Times*, 11 January 2013.

Clodfelter, Mark, *The Limits of Air Power: The American Bombing of North Vietnam*, 2nd edn, New York: Free Press, 2006.

Cortright, David and George A. Lopez, *Economic Sanctions: Panacea or Peacebuilding in a Post-Cold War World?*, Boulder: Westview Press, 1995.

Cortright, David and George A. Lopez, 'Are Sanctions Just? The Problematic Case of Iraq', *Journal of International Affairs* 52, 2 (1999), pp. 735–55.

Cortright, David and George A. Lopez, *The Sanctions Decade: Assessing UN Strategies in the 1990s*, Boulder: Lynne Rienner Publishers, 2000.

Cortright, David and George A. Lopez, *Sanctions and the Search for Security: Challenges to UN Action*, Boulder, CO: Lynne Rienner Publishers, 2002.

Cortright, David and George A. Lopez, *Smart Sanctions: Targeting Economic Statecraft*, Lanham, MD: Rowman & Littlefield Publishers, 2002.

Cortright, David, *Patterns of Implementation. Do Listing Practices Impede Compliance with UN Sanctions? A Critical Assessment*. Policy Brief. Sanctions and Security Research Program, Fourth Freedom Foundation and Kroc Institute of International Peace Studies, University of Notre Dame, 2009.

Cortright, David, George A. Lopez, Linda Gerber, Eliot Fackler, and Joshua Weaver, *Integrating UN sanctions for Peace and Security*, Goshen Indiana: Fourth Freedom Forum and Kroc Center, University of Notre Dame, 2010. Available at: sanctionsandsecurity.nd.edu/.

Cosgrove, Erica, 'Examining Targeted Sanctions: Are Travel Bans Effective?' in Peter Wallensteen and Carina Staibano (eds.), *International Sanctions: Between Words and Wars in the Global System*, New York: Frank Cass, 2005, pp. 207–28.

Crawford, Neta and Audie Klotz (eds.), *How Sanctions Worked in South Africa*, London: Palgrave Macmillan, 1999.

Daase, Christopher and Cornelius Friesendorf (eds.), 'Introduction: Security Governance and the Problem of Unintended Consequences', in *Rethinking Security Governance: The Problem of Unintended Consequences*, Abingdon, Oxon: Routledge, 2010.

Dahl, Robert A., *Who Governs? Democracy and Power in an American City*, New Haven: Yale University Press, 1961.

Daoudi, Mohammed S. and M. S. Dajani, *Economic Sanctions: Ideas and Experience*, London: Routledge and Kegan Paul, 1983.

Deen, Thalif, "Politics: U.N Faulted for Toothless Sanctions in Civil Wars," in *Inter Press Service News Agency*, located at www.ipsnews.net/2010/01/politics-un-faulted-for-toothless-sanctions-in-civil-wars/.

Deutsche Welle, "UN Security Council Unanimously Passes Sanctions against Gadhafi", *Deutsche Welle*, 26 February 2011, Bonn: Germany.

dos Reis Stefanopoulos, Alexandra and George A. Lopez, 'Sanctions and the Responsibility to Protect', in Monica Serrano and Thomas G. Weiss (eds.), *Rallying to the R2P Cause? The International Politics of Human Rights*, Oxford: Oxford University Press, 2013.

Doxey, Margaret P., 'International Sanctions: A Framework for Analysis with Special Reference to the UN and Southern Africa', *International Organization* 26, 3 (1972) p. 535.

Doxey, Margaret P., *International Sanctions in Contemporary Perspective*, Basingstoke: Macmillan, 1987.

Doxey, Margaret P., *International Sanctions in Contemporary Perspective*, New York: St. Martin's Press, 1996.

Drezner, Daniel W., *The Sanctions Paradox: Economic Statecraft and International Relations*, Cambridge: Cambridge University Press, 1999.

Drezner, Daniel W., 'Bargaining, Enforcement, and Multilateral Sanctions: When Is Cooperation Counterproductive?' *International Organization* 54 (2000), pp. 73–102.

Drezner, Daniel W. 'The Hidden Hand of Economic Coercion', *International Organization* 57 (2003), pp. 643–59.

Drezner, Daniel W., 'Sanctions Sometimes Smart: Targeted Sanctions in Theory and Practice', *International Studies Review* 13 (2011), pp. 96–108.

Drieskens, E. and C. Boucher, 'Researching the European Union at the United Nations in New York: Current Trends and Future Agendas' in K. E. Jorgensen and K. Laatikainen (eds.), *Handbook on Europe and Multilateral Institutions*, London: Routledge, 2012.

Eckert, Sue E. and Thomas J. Biersteker, *Due Process and Targeted Sanctions: An Update to the Watson Report*, Providence, RI: Watson Institute for International Studies, Brown University, 2012.

Elliott, Kimberly Ann, 'The Sanctions Glass: Half Full or Completely Empty?' *International Security* 23, 1 (1998), pp. 50–65.

Elliott, Kimberly Ann, 'Trends in Economic Sanctions Policy: Challenges to Conventional Wisdom', in Wallensteen and Staibano (eds.), *International Sanctions. Between Words and Wars in the Global System*, New York, London: Routledge/Frank Cass, 2005.

Eriksson, Mikael, *Results from the Stockholm Process on the Implementation of Targeted Sanctions*, Uppsala: Department of Peace and Conflict Research, Uppsala University, 2003.

Eriksson, Mikael, *Targeting the Leadership of Zimbabwe: A Path to Democracy and Normalization?*, Uppsala: Uppsala University: SPITS, 2007. Available at pcr.uu.se/research/smartsanctions/spits_news_and_publications/.

Eriksson, Mikael, *In Search of a Due Process: Listing and Delisting Practices of the European Union*, Uppsala: Department of Peace and Conflict Research, Uppsala University, 2009.

Eriksson, Mikael, *Supporting Democracy in Africa: African Union's Use of Targeted Sanctions to Deal with Unconstitutional Changes of Government*, Stockholm, Sweden: FOI, Swedish Defence Research Agency, 2010.

Eriksson, Mikael, *Targeting Peace, Understanding UN and EU Targeted Sanctions*, Farnham, UK: Ashgate, 2010.

Eriksson, Mikael, 'Unintended Consequences of Targeted Sanctions', in Christopher Daase and Cornelius Friesendorf (eds.), *Rethinking Security Governance: The Problem of Unintended Consequences*, Abingdon, Oxon: Routledge, 2010, pp. 157–75.

Eriksson, Mikael, *Targeting Peace: Understanding UN and EU Targeted Sanctions*, Farnham, UK; Burlington, VT: Ashgate, 2011.

Fearon, James, 'Signaling Foreign Policy Interests: Tying Hands versus Sinking Costs', *The Journal of Conflict Resolution* 41, 1 (1997), pp. 68–90.

Flynn, E. J., 'The Security Council's Counter-Terrorism Committee and Human Rights', *Human Rights Law Review* 7, 2 (2007), pp. 371–84.

Foong Khong, Yuen, *Analogies at War: Korea, Munich, Dien Bien Phu, and the Vietnam Decisions of 1965*, Princeton, NJ: Princeton University Press, 1992.

Galtung, Johan, 'On the Effects of International Economic Sanctions: With Examples from the Case of Rhodesia', *World Politics* 19, 3 (1967), pp. 378–416.

Geoffrey-Leslie, Simons, *Imposing Economic Sanctions: Legal Remedy or Genocidal Tool?*, London; Sterling, VA: Pluto Press, 1999.

George, Alexander L., David K. Hall, and William E. Simons, *The Limits of Coercive Diplomacy; Laos, Cuba, Vietnam*, Boston, MA: Little, 1971.

George, Alexander L. and Andrew Bennett, *Case Studies and Theory Development in the Social Sciences*, Cambridge, MA: MIT Press, 2005.

Gibbons, Elizabeth D., *Sanctions in Haiti: Human Rights and Democracy under Assault*, Westport, CT: Praeger, 1999.

Giumelli, Francesco, 'The Restrictive Measures of the European Union: Developing Analytical Categories to Understand Functions and Utility of EU Sanctions', *The International Spectator* 45, 3 (2010), pp. 131–44.

Giumelli, Francesco, *Coercing, Constraining and Signalling: Explaining UN and EU Sanctions after the Cold War*, Colchester: ECPR Press, 2011.

Giumelli, Francesco, 'How EU Sanctions Work: A New Narrative', in *Chaillot Paper*, Paris: EU Institute for Security Studies (EUISS), 2013.

Giumelli, Francesco, *The Success of Sanctions Lessons Learned from the EU Experience*, Farnham, UK: Ashgate, 2013.

Gordon, Joy, *Invisible War: The United States and the Iraq Sanctions*, Cambridge: Harvard University Press, 2010.

Gordon, Joy, 'Smart Sanctions Revisited', *Ethics & International Affairs* 25, 3 (2011), pp. 315–35.

Griffiths, Aaron and Barnes, Catherine (eds.), *Power of Persuasion: Incentives, Sanctions and Conditionality in Peacemaking*, London: Conciliation Resources, 2008.

Haass, Richard *Economic Sanctions and American Diplomacy*, New York: Council on Foreign Relations, 1998.

Hellquist, E., 'Regional Organisations and Sanctions against Members: Explaining the Different Trajectories of the African Union, the League of Arab States, and the Association of Southeast Asian Nations', Berlin: *KFG The Transformative Power of Europe Working Paper* 59 (2014), pp. 1–46.

Heupel, Monika, 'Multilateral Sanctions against Terror Suspects and the Violation of Due Process Standards', in *International Affairs* 85, 2 (2009), pp. 307–21.

Hoffman, Fredrik, 'The Functions of Economic Sanctions', *Journal of Peace Research* 4 (1967), pp. 140–160.

Hovi, Jon, Robert Huseby, and Detlef F. Sprinz. 'When Do (Imposed) Economic Sanctions Work?' *World Politics* 57, 4 (2005): 479–499.

Hufbauer, Gary C., Jeffrey J. Schott, and Kimberly A. Elliott, *Economic Sanctions Reconsidered*, 2nd edn, 2 vols., Washington, DC: Peterson Institute for International Economics, 1990.

Hufbauer, Gary C., Jeffrey J. Schott, Kimberly A. Elliott, and Barbara Oegg, *Economic Sanctions Reconsidered*, 3rd edn, Washington, DC: Peterson Institute for International Economics, 2007.

Hulton, Susan C., 'Council Working Methods and Procedures', in Malone (ed.), *The Security Council in the 21st Century*, Boulder: Lynne Rienner, 2004.

Hurd, Ian, *After Anarchy: Legitimacy & Power in the United Nations Security Council*, Princeton: Princeton University Press, 2007, chapter 6.

Jentlesson, Bruce W., 'Economic Sanctions and Post-Cold-War Conflict: Challenges for Theory and Practice', in Paul C. Stern and Daniel Druckman (eds.), *International Conflict Resolution after the Cold War*, Washington, DC: National Academies Press, 2000, pp. 123–77

Jones, Seth, *European Security Co-operation*, Cambridge: Cambridge University Press, 2007.

Kaempfer, William H. and Anton David, Lowenberg, *International Economic Sanctions: A Public Choice Perspective*, Boulder: Westview, 1992.

Kerr, Rachel, *The International Criminal Tribunal for the Former Yugoslavia: An Exercise in Law, Politics, and Diplomacy*, Oxford: Oxford University Press, 2004.

Kirshner, Jonathan, 'Economic Sanctions: The State of the Art', *Security Studies* 11, 4 (2002), p. 169.

Krisch, Nico, 'The Security Council and the Great Powers', in Vaughan Lowe et al. (eds.), *The United Nations Security Council and War*, Oxford: Oxford University Press, 2008, pp. 133–53.

Lasswell, Harold D. and Abraham Kaplan, *Power and Society: A Framework for Political Inquiry*, New Haven: Yale University Press, 1950.

Lee, Christine, 'United Nations Sanctions: Background and Analysis of the Kadi Court Cases', November 2013, available at www.comcapint.com/pdfs/kadi-court-cases-christine-lee.pdf.

Lindsay, James, 'Trade Sanctions as Policy Instruments: A Re-Examination', *International Studies Quarterly* 30, 2 (1986), pp. 153–73.

Lopez, George A. and David Cortright, 'Containing Iraq: Sanctions Worked', *Foreign Affairs* 83, 4 (2004), pp. 90–103.

Lopez, George A. and David Cortright, 'Sanctions as Alternatives to War', in Christopher J. Coyne and Rachel L. Mathers (eds.), *The Handbook on the Political Economy of War*, Northampton, MA: Edward Elgar Publishing, 2011, pp. 534–70.

Lopez, George A., 'Enforcing Human Rights Through Economic and Other Sanctions', in Dinah Shelton (ed.), *The Handbook of International Human Rights Law*, Oxford: Oxford University Press, 2013.

Malone, David M. (ed.), *The Security Council in the 21ˢᵗ Century*, Boulder: Lynne Rienner, 2004.

Manson, Katrina (in Nairobi), James Shotter (in Zurich), and Jack Farchy, 'Swiss Investigate Congo Gold Bought by Biggest Refiner', *Financial Times*, 4 November 2013.

Mollander, Anders, *UN Angola Sanctions: A Committee Success Revisited*, Uppsala: Department of Peace and Conflict Research, Uppsala University, 2009.

Morgan, Clifton, Navin Bapat, and Valentina Krustev, 'The Threat and Imposition of Economic Sanctions, 1971–2000', *Conflict Management and Peace Science* 28, 1 (2008), pp. 92–110.

Morgan, T. Clifton and Valerie L. Schwebach, 'Fools Suffer Gladly: The Use of Economic Sanctions in International Crises', *International Studies Quarterly* 41, 1 (1997), pp. 27–50.

Morgan, T. Clifton, Valentin Krustev, and Navin A. Bapat, 'Threat and Implementation of Sanctions (TIES) Codebook' (2006), available at www.personal.psu.edu/nab12/sanctionspage.htm.

Mueller, John and Karl Mueller, 'Sanctions of Mass Destruction', *Foreign Affairs* 78, 3 (1999), pp. 43–53.

Nossal, Kim Richard, 'International Sanctions as International Punishment', *International Organization*, 43, 2 (1989), pp. 301–22.

Notaras, Mark and Vesselin Popovski, *The Responsibility to Protect*, Tokyo: United Nations University, 2011.

Pape, Robert A., *Bombing to Win: Air Power and Coercion in War*, Ithaca, NY: Cornell University Press, 1996.

Pape, Robert A. 'Why Economic Sanctions Do Not Work', *International Security*, 22, 2 (1997), pp. 90–136.

Pape, Robert A., 'Why Economic Sanctions Still Do Not Work', *International Security* 23 (1998), pp. 66–77.

Pedersen, Morten B., *Promoting Human Rights in Burma. A Critique of Western Sanctions Policy*, Plymouth: Rowman & Littlefield Publishers, 2008.

Porretto, Gabriele, 'The European Union, Counter-terrorism Sanctions against Individuals and Human Rights', in M. Gani and P. Matthew (eds.), *Fresh Perspectives on the 'War on Terror'*, Canberra: ANU E Press, 2008.

Portela, Clara, 'Where and Why Does the EU Impose Sanctions?' *Politique Européenne* 17, 4 (2005), pp. 83–111.

Portela, Clara, *European Union Sanctions and Foreign Policy*, London: Routledge, 2010.

Portela, Clara, 'European Union Sanctions as a Foreign Policy Tool: Do They Work?' in S. B. Gareis, G. Hauser, and F. Kernic (eds.), *Europe as a Global Actor*, Leverkusen: Budrich, 2012.

Prantl, Jochen, 'Informal Groups of States and the UN Security Council' *International Organization* 59 (2005), pp. 559–92.

Preeg, E. H., *Feeling Good or Doing Good with Sanctions: Unilateral Economic Sanctions and the U.S. National Interest*, Washington, DC: Center for Strategic & International Studies, 1999.

Rogers, Elizabeth S., 'Using Economic Sanctions to Control Regional Conflicts', *Security Studies* 5, 4 (1996), pp. 43–72.

Schwebach, Valerie L., 'Sanctions as Signals: A Line in the Sand or a Lack of Resolve?' in Steve Chan and Cooper A. Drury (eds.), *Sanctions as Economic Statecraft: Theory and Practice*, Basingstoke: McMillan Press, 2000.

Shambaugh, David, Eberhard Sandschneider, and Zhou Hong (eds.), *China-Europe Relations. Perceptions, Policies and Prospects*, London; New York: Routledge, 2007.

Sikkink, Kathryn, 'From Pariah State to Global Protagonist: Argentina and the Struggle for International Human Rights', *Latin American Politics and Society*, 50, 1 (2008), pp. 1–29.

Taylor, Brendan, *Sanctions as Grand Strategy*, London: IISS/Routledge, 2010.

Tostensen, Arne and Beate Bull, 'Are Smart Sanctions Feasible?' *World Politics* 54, 3 (2002), pp. 373–403.

Uppsala Conflict Data Program, UCDP, website www.ucdp.uu.se.

Vines, Alex, 'The Effectiveness of UN and EU Sanctions: Lessons for the Twenty-First Century', *International Affairs* 88, 4 (2012), pp. 867–77.

von Soest, Christian and Michael Wahman, *Sanctions and Democratization in the post-Cold War Era*, Hamburg: *GIGA Working Paper*, Number 212, 2013.

Wallensteen, Peter, 'Characteristics of Economic Sanctions', *Journal of Peace Research* 5, 3 (1968), pp. 248–67.

Wallensteen, Peter, Carina Staibano, and Mikael Eriksson, *Making Targeted Sanctions Effective. Guidelines for the Implementation of UN Policy Options*, Uppsala: Department of Peace and Conflict Research, Uppsala University, 2003.

Wallensteen, Peter and Carina, Staibano (eds.), *International Sanctions. Between Words and Wars in the Global System*, New York; London: Routledge/Frank Cass, 2005.

Wallensteen, Peter, Carina Staibano, and Mikael Eriksson, *Roundtable on UN Sanctions against Iraq: Lessons Learned. Executive Summary*, Uppsala: Department of Peace and Conflict Research, 2005. Available at pcr.uu. se/research/smartsanctions/spits_news_and_publications/.

Wallensteen, Peter, Mikael Eriksson, and Daniel Strandow, *Sanctions for Conflict Prevention and Peace Building: Lessons Learned from Côte d'Ivoire and Liberia*, Uppsala: Department of Peace and Conflict Research, Uppsala University, 2006.

Wallensteen, Peter (ed.), 'A Century of Economic Sanctions: A Field Revisited', in *Peace Research: Theory and Practice*, London: Routledge, 2011.

Wallensteen, Peter, 'Sanctions in Africa: International Resolve and Prevention of Conflict Escalation', in Thomas Ohlson (ed.), *From Intra-State War to Durable Peace: Conflict and Its Resolution in Africa after the Cold War*, Dordrecht: Republic of Letters Publishing, 2012.

Wallensteen, Peter and Helena Grusell 'Targeting the Right Targets? The UN Use of Individual Sanctions', *Global Governance*, 18 (2012), pp. 207–30.

Weiss, Thomas G., David Cortright, George A. Lopez, and Larry Minear (eds.), *Political Gain and Civilian Pain: Humanitarian Impacts of Economic Sanctions*, Lanham: Rowman & Littlefield Publishers, 1997.

Weschler, Joanna, 'The Evolution of Security Council Innovations on Sanctions', *International Journal*, 10 (2009), pp. 31–43.

Whitfield, Teresa, 'Groups of Friends', in David Malone (ed.), *The Security Council in the 21st Century*, Boulder: Lynne Rienner, 2004.

Index

Printed in Great Britain
by Amazon